Music as Theology

Princeton Theological Monograph Series

K. C. Hanson, Charles M. Collier, D. Christopher Spinks,
and Robin Parry, Series Editors

Recent volumes in the series:

James L. Papandrea
Novatian of Rome and the Culmination of Pre-Nicene Orthodoxy

Aliou Cissé Niang
*Text, Image, and Christians in the Graeco-Roman World:
A Festschrift in Honor of David Lee Balch*

Sara M. Koenig
Isn't This Bathsheba?: A Study in Characterization

Gale Heide
*Timeless Truth in the Hands of History:
A Short History of System in Theology*

Koo Dong Yun
*The Holy Spirit and Ch'i (Qi):
A Chiological Approach to Pneumatology*

Stanley S. MacLean
*Resurrection, Apocalypse, and the Kingdom of Christ:
The Eschatology of Thomas F. Torrance*

Brian Neil Peterson
*Ezekiel in Context: Ezekiel's Message Understood
in Its Historical Setting of Covenant Curses
and Ancient Near Eastern Mythological Motifs*

Susan Marie Smith
*Christian Ritualizing and the Baptismal Process:
Liturgical Explorations toward a Realized Baptismal Ecclesiology*

Music as Theology
What Music Has to Say about the Word

MAEVE LOUISE HEANEY VDMF

◆PICKWICK *Publications* • Eugene, Oregon

MUSIC AS THEOLOGY
What Music Has to Say about the Word

Princeton Theological Monograph Series 184

Copyright © 2012 Maeve Louise Heaney. All rights reserved. Except for brief quotations in critical publications or reviews, no part of this book may be reproduced in any manner without prior written permission from the publisher. Write: Permissions, Wipf and Stock Publishers, 199 W. 8th Ave., Suite 3, Eugene, OR 97401.

Pickwick Publications
An Imprint of Wipf and Stock Publishers
199 W. 8th Ave., Suite 3
Eugene, OR 97401

www.wipfandstock.com

ISBN 13: 978-1-61097-450-9

Cataloging-in-Publication data:

Heaney, Maeve Louise.

    Music as theology : what music has to say about the Word / Maeve Louise Heaney.

    xiv + 346 pp. ; 23 cm. — Includes bibliographical references and index.

    Princeton Theological Monograph Series 184

    ISBN 13: 978-1-61097-450-9

    1. Music—Religious aspects. 2. Theology. I. Title. II. Series.

ML3921 H44 2012

Manufactured in the U.S.A.

For J. C. and Kathleen

Out of time, out of tune with the rhythm that
passes us by, as we hide
in the thoughts of old times:
Dancing in our minds . . .
Out of place, in this space there's no moving around
what you've found: it is now!
that you give or you take:
Dancing in our minds . . .
And the Word became human . . .
and Eternity entered time
tasting the sound of your voice in mine . . .

—Maeve L. Heaney VDMF, "Dancing in Our Minds"[1]

---

1. The first verse of a song recently composed, which gathers something of the theological and spiritual backdrop I propose for the comprehension of music in theology. See http://www.fmverbumdei.com/main/maeveheaney/index.html.

Contents

Foreword / ix
Acknowledgments / xi
Figures / xiii

Introduction / 1

1. Meaning in Music / 27
2. Towards a Hermeneutical Understanding of Music / 69
3. An Approach to Musical Semiotics / 103
4. Towards a Theological Epistemology of Music / 135
5. Theological Aesthetics in Contemporary Theology / 183
6. Theology of the Body of Christ and Contemporary Music / 254

Conclusion / 306

Appendix / 315
Bibliography / 321
Index of Authors / 343

Foreword

THE CONVERSATION BETWEEN MUSIC AND THEOLOGY, DORMANT FOR too long in recent years, is at last gathering pace. And rightly so. There will always be theologians who will regard music as a somewhat peripheral concern, too trivial to trouble the serious scholar, and in any case almost impossible to engage because of its notorious resistance to words and concepts. But an increasing number are discovering again what many of our forbears realized centuries ago, that the kinship between this pervasive feature of human life and the search for a Christian "intelligence of faith" is intimate and ineradicable.

Maeve Heaney's ambitious, wide-ranging, and energetic book pushes the conversation further forward still. Her approach is unapologetically theological, grounded in the passions and concerns of mainstream doctrinal theology. And yet she is insisting, rightly in my view, that music must be given its due place in the ecology of theology. Although convinced that music should not be set up as a rival to linguistic or conceptual articulation, let alone swallow up "traditional" modes of theological language and thought, she is equally convinced that music is an irreducible means of coming to terms with the world, a unique vehicle of world-disclosure, and as such, can generate a particular form of "understanding": "there are things which God may only be saying through music." If this is so, it is incumbent on the theologian to listen.

Several features of this book are worth highlighting. The first is that Heaney's primary sources of wisdom come from Roman Catholic sources. In other regions of the theology and arts interface today, Catholic accents are pervasive and prominent. Indeed, it is common in many quarters to find it assumed without question that the most enriching resources for engaging the arts will be Catholic. But when it comes to theology and music, for some reason the assumption is less common. Heaney is immersed in the theological world of Roman Catholicism (though certainly not exclusively or narrowly—she listens to those far beyond her tradition). The reader will be introduced to many theologians who for one reason or another have not yet been prominent voices in the musical sphere—among them Bernard Lonergan, Rosemary Haughton, Pierangelo Sequeri, and the (predominantly Catholic) movement known as "transformation theology" (based at King's College, London). Another noticeable feature is Heaney's exploration of semiotic theory in relation to music (chapter 3). This is notoriously complex territory, and much discussed in music theory circles, but has not received much attention from theologians to date—something Heaney is determined to set right.

Finally, the driving motor behind Heaney's enterprise is clearly practical and cultural. The fact that she heads up her introduction and conclusion with words from her own songs is no accident—she is an accomplished songwriter and performer. She is convinced that music's prevalence in contemporary society, not least among the young, is of immense cultural significance—music is acting as a form of "faith transmission" in ways we ignore at our peril. "What is music 'saying' to us in this moment of history, and why is it emerging as a symbolic form of faith transmission?" This is her guiding question. And her book will make us ponder it deeply.

Jeremy Begbie

Acknowledgments

Thank You, Thank You

> We are not alone in our loneliness,
> Others have been here and known
> Griefs we thought our special own
>
> —Patrick Kavanagh[1]

ALTHOUGH THE FINAL WRITING OF A BOOK CAN BE SOLITARY WORK, this one is ultimately the fruit of many years of work and a multitude of rich encounters, shared experiences and difficulties, insightful conversations, and interweaved lives. I wish to thank those I can name and those I cannot:

Michael Paul Gallagher, SJ—for helping find and express my own voice, at the same time as accompanying me in the quest for solid and appropriated theological thinking. *Go mbeannaí Dia thú.*

The professors and students of the Pontifical Gregorian University. Theological thought, although personal, is never individual. The thoughts expressed here are the fruit of many shared concerns, joys and griefs. It has been through you that Rome has graced me.

I cannot thank all the scholars who have marked my journey, but I must thank those who have marked the rhythm of this book, offering time, encouragement, wisdom, and even "as yet unpublished" work to further my quest for clarity. In particular I want to mention Willem Marie Speelman, Oliver Davies, Jim Corkery, Paul Janz, Alejandro García-Rivera, Frank Burch Brown, Pierangelo Sequeri, Fintan Vallely, Xavier Morlans, and José-Carlos Coupeau.

My community: those who have given me the time and space for this research, in the recognition of its importance both for our shared

---

1. From "Thank You, Thank You," in Kavanagh, *Collected Poems*, 247.

mission and for my own calling. I pray God may walk with us opening new paths in this world.

Peter Hatlie and the staff at Due Santi, the Rome base of the Catholic University of Dallas, for both the beautiful setting in which the final draft of this book was written, and the friendship that accompanied it.

The people of the parish of San Bernardo di Chiaravalle: *per pregare di cuore la musica che vi insegnavo.*

The people with whom I make music, without whom my life would be so much less than it is. That amazing presence we enter into from the moment the first beat of music marks the rhythm of our encounters, is the one this book seeks to honour, understand and open to others.

My friends: you know who you are.

My family, who have been and always will be the ground I am rooted in and grow from, for your unfailing, unconditional support and love.

And my God, in Jesus, who gave me life, and faith, the gift of music, and a calling to be His. "Hold my hand in your side . . ."

Thank you. Thank you.

Figures

Figure 2.1: The Sign according to Ferdinand de Saussure / 80

Figure 2.2: The Sign according to Charles S. Pierce / 82

Figure 2.3: Conventional Understanding of Communication / 85

Figure 2.4: A Semiological Understanding of the Symbol in Human Understanding / 85

Figure 2.5: Musical Analysis according to the Tripartitional Method / 95

Figure 3.1: Music and Noise in Triparitional Analysis / 106

Figure 3.2: Musical and Verbal Semiotics according to W. M. Speelman / 117

Figure 3.3: The Semiotic Square / 121

Figure 3:4: The Semiotic Square Applied / 121

Figure 3.5: From Oppositions to Curves—the Semiotic Square as Applied to Music / 123

Figure 3.6: First bars of the song "Meanwhile," by Maeve Louise Heaney, 2007 / 124

Figure 4.1: Music as Theology within Lonergan's Theological Method / 170

Figure 7.1: Points of Tension between the Christian and the Artistic Calling / 317

Introduction

"Music as theology" is, I admit, a rather pretentious title. Music *and* theology would sound more realistic, but that understated, humble word "and" spares us the effort of thinking through exactly what the relationship between the terms it links means. At the present moment of Christian theological thought on the arts, this is no longer enough. Music *in* theology would feel safer, as no one questions the use of the arts in our reflection on God and faith, but is music, or should music be, an "extra" one adds (in)to theology, to make it more presentable or tasty? Do the two remain self-contained and distinct, or at best with an extrinsic, complementary but in the last analysis, dispensable relationship between them? Given the importance of the arts and music in the history of Christian faith, this seems superficial and therefore unsatisfactory. If theology is "faith seeking understanding,"[1] could music not also be theological? Does it not offer us, at the very least, a form of understanding of our faith, and perhaps even an aid in attaining and entering into that faith?

The conviction underlying this book is that it can—that music offers a form of approach to or comprehension of faith that is different to our linguistic and conceptual understanding of the same, and for that very reason is complementary to it, in theological discourse. It is not a question of setting music against linguistic expressions of our faith, but I propose that there are aspects of the Logos, our God revealed in the Word made flesh, which are better expressed through music, and that theology would do well to integrate this symbolic form of expression. Hence the title: *Music as Theology: What Music Has to Say about the Word*. In fact, I would paraphrase the intuition of a profoundly insightful and beautifully written book by poet and biblical scholar Jean-Pierre Sonnet, called *Membra Jesu Nostri: Ce Que Dieu Ne Dit Que par le Corps*[2] and suggest that as there are things

---

1. St. Anselm's simple but undisputed definition of theology.
2. Translation: "The Limbs of Our Jesus: What God Only Says through the Body."

which God may *only* be saying through music, it would be advisable to listen. Of course, this implies accepting the challenge (and the gift) of trying to understand precisely how music "speaks" and the quest of how to interpret it. This book is one small attempt to *begin* to do just that.

Therefore, within our aim, and reflected in the book's title, there are two distinguishable but inseparable dimensions we will have to address: music's capacity of "saying" or revealing something of the Word to us, opening us to apprehend and perhaps even welcome God's presence, and its role in and as theology. One justifies and grounds the other. Since music has something to say to us about the Word, and can perhaps even be a means of mediating Christian faith, therefore music can and should be part of Christianity's quest to comprehend itself, which is the task of theological thought and praxis.

There are, however, two considerable challenges involved in addressing these two dimensions. The first is common to all interdisciplinary thought, that of trying to weave together two areas of thought that need to be placed in dialogue with one another—in this case, the study of music (musicology, ethnomusicology, semiotics of music, etc.), and theology. Finding the balance between entering into each area sufficiently to do it justice, at the same time as avoiding unnecessary or unhelpful detail or complication, is somehow like trying to assemble a jigsaw puzzle without the original picture, or navigate through a jungle (of information) without a compass. I can only hope I have either done the chosen authors justice, or left enough traces and clues for further development or follow-up research for whoever may be interested. The second challenge is that of addressing adequately the various people or publics I know to be interested in this area of study: colleagues working in the field of theological aesthetics and fundamental theology, composers and musicians active in outreach through music, as well as those collaborating in liturgical ministry, pastors and ministers interested in discerning and accompanying the potential role of music in their pastoral activities, not to mention the many Christians who simply love music and for whom music is a graced place of prayer and God's presence.

This introduction presents itself as a possible "visual map" or navigational compass for those who may open this book, drawn by the title. At the beginning of *The Passionate God*, Rosemary Haughton asks her readers, especially the habitual "introduction skippers," to make an exception for hers, as she considers it important for the understanding the book. Rather than asking the same, I will advance that the introduction will explain the underlying concerns as well as the structure and themes addressed in each of the chapters, so that each reader may find their point of interest. There is an autobiographical touch at the beginning of the introduction. In the "navigational" challenge of interdisciplinary thought, one of the tools I have used is the compass of my own life, concerns, sensibility and experience. It may help to understand the authors and themes I have chosen, and those I have left out. The book itself becomes quite technical at points, since the area of semiotics and the issue of meaning in music as dealt with by musicologists and philosophers can be detailed and dense. This first section explains why I believe they are necessary. The rest of this introduction presents the particular approach and focus of the book, looking at its key terms or notions: contemporary music, as the time frame of music we are focusing on; the Logos of God—Jesus Christ Incarnated, as the focus of our faith and therefore also of a theology of music that helps mediate us to faith; and theology understood as mediation as the underlying "harmony" of the rest of the book with the world of theological discourse.

As a premise I will state that the central theme of the book is not music, but the theological understanding of music. Musicologists and musicians are aware of the challenge involved in even attempting to "talk" or "reason" about music, such is the difference between verbal and musical communication. In the words of George Steiner: "where we try to speak of music, to speak music, language has us, resentfully, by the throat."[3] Theological discourse has been so verbal and conceptual in the Western tradition[4] that this challenge is clear, but unavoidable. As we shall see, it begins and ends with our faith in the incarnation: the Word made flesh, made human, made expressiveness of God and irrepressible source of life in our created world.

---

3. Steiner, *Real Presences*, 197.

4. Marco Rupnik, SJ, in a conversation on this thesis, pointed out to me that in Eastern theology art is considered a theological act. Not so in Latin theology! Rupnik and Tomàš Špidlík develop the theological value of art in relation to a theology of the symbol in a recent book on integral knowledge, or knowing: *Una conoscenza integrale: La via del simbolo*.

Prelude: Theological Praxis

It is the theologian who does theology. The thought of any writer or theologian is born of his or her biography, experience of faith or spirituality and its comprehension easier when made explicit. Hence, in this prelude, I wish to clarify my own theological approach: the sources from which it is born and the concerns that color its tone or mark its rhythm. My self-understanding includes that of being an Irish woman, called to dedicate my life to evangelization, to reflect on and teach theology, to compose and make music, and to understand and ground this whole endeavor in a coherent and solid Catholic framework.[5] I have been graced with the gift of a personal encounter with God, in and through Jesus of Nazareth, experienced, in the words of Lieven Boeve, as an "interruption" that marked the call to make of my life an expression of that Love beyond human imagination and calculations. In the quest to reach out and into the minds and hearts of the people entrusted to me, mainly young people in and of Western European culture, I have found music to be a powerful and mysterious means of touching and communicating God's love, before and after any words I could speak. As a theologian, seeking the "intelligence of faith,"[6] my attempts at loving God with my *mind*[7] are situated within the field of fundamental theology, seeking to answer questions born of pastoral concerns, specifically in relation to the *locus theologicus*[8] that is music. I have become convinced of the revelatory and spiritual potential music has for this particular moment in history, within God's ongoing plan of salvation. As a musician, I experience that few things awaken my senses, hold me in the present moment, and facilitate an

---

5. I had started this phrase with the following nouns, rather than verbs: "called to be a missionary, a theologian, a musician and a composer," only to feel that expressing the same in verbal form allows for a much more dynamic and ongoing way of perceiving my own life and the world around.

6. Cf. prologue of Sequeri, *Qualità spirituale*, 6. Unless otherwise stated, all translations are mine.

7. Cf. Luke 10:25.

8. Melchor Cano, after talking about Sacred Scripture, tradition, and other main sources or "places" of theology, adds those of natural reason, the work of philosophers, and the teaching or lessons drawn from history. The inclusion of human activity and history as a necessary part of and source for theological reflection is an underlying premise of the thesis, understood in a similar same way as some contemporary theologians talks about the signs of the times.

inner connection with God in prayer in the way music does. I therefore intuit that the acts of listening to and making music have something to teach us about who God is and who we are, and therefore, something to offer theology, both in its understanding of our triune God and our own anthropology. As a composer, I experience that music is born of a different place than my conceptual understanding of life and faith, and that, even so, it *is* the expression of an "understanding." I have found that it is not easy to hold together the Christian and musical callings, and I observe in other musicians and composers similar experiences. And yet music is simply one more beautiful gift of God to the world. For this reason, I reflect on the interaction between prayer, faith and the birth of musical expression, and seek to bring this experience and creative process to theological thought, with the growing conviction that both music and theology (and spirituality) will leave the encounter enriched.

As a woman, I have become aware of the importance being female has in my theological thought process.[9] There is, says Haughton, one of the authors I draw from, "a typically feminine approach to truth." Talking about the resurrection and the different reactions Jesus' female and male disciples have to the appearances of Jesus, she underlines this point:

> The masculine reaction is: "It can't be so, therefore it is not true." The women, turning logic upside-down, say, "It is so, therefore it must be true."[10]

Reality speaks. We need to welcome, receive and seek to understand it. Perhaps the church would get further and quicker in its evangelizing mission if this were our approach to faith, rather than trying to get reality to adapt to what our minds can imagine as possible, when, for God, everything is! Without denying that there are always exceptions, I wonder if this way of approaching life and thought is not more accessible to female imagination, and how valuable it would

---

9. Sandra Schneiders writes about how her feminist awareness emerged during her years of study in Rome. Cf. Schneiders, *Revelatory Text*, 3. Although I have never fully identified with feminist theology as I have encountered it, studying theology in Rome, where the number of women is minimal in comparison to men, has opened my eyes and mind to the different ways we have of approaching life, faith, and thought. I believe that difference has something positive to offer theology and the church in general, perhaps especially in our relationship to truth.

10. Haughton, *Passionate God*, 274.

be to allow that sensitivity mark and color theological reflection and pastoral work in general.

Contemporary Music

> *My heart is ready, God, my heart is ready;*
> *I will sing, and make music for you.*
>
> —Ps 57: 7–9

The Psalms were the songs of the people of Israel, that nation singled out and chosen by God to initiate his story of salvation with humanity.[11] Indeed, the verb "to sing" is one of the most commonly used in the Bible: 309 instances in the Old Testament and 36 in the New Testament.[12] This fact may not overly surprise us, but living as we do in a culture in which, in general, our nations' songs are not prayers, it can be helpful to stand back and contemplate the difference. The psalms we recite in the Eucharist and the Prayer of the Church were, in their origins, the cry of the heart of a people whose understanding of their existence and their faith were one and the same. Now, at least in the Western world, we are taken by surprise (albeit pleasantly) when an explicitly religious song reaches the public domain, especially if it is Christian. The cry of Western culture's heart does not spontaneously manifest itself in that way.[13]

And yet, the power of music in our culture is obvious, and on the increase. "Music has long been, and continues to be, the unwritten theology of those who lack or reject any formal creed."[14] But what is happening there? How are we to understand it when people find refuge in Coldplay's "Fix You" in a way they have long since ceased to in their local church?[15] How do we listen to and receive the obvious

---

11. There are various interesting studies on this theme in biblical studies. For example: Weitzman, *Song and Story*; Christensen, *Song of Power*.

12. Ratzinger, "Spirit of the Liturgy," 185.

13. The appearance, from time to time, of some such music, such as Sinéad O'Connor's recent CD, *Theology*, I would perceive as yet to highlight the distance, rather than herald the end, of this separation.

14. Steiner, *Real Presences*, 218.

15. Coldplay, *X&Y*. The song, while never explicitly religious, begins with the organ, includes polyphonic harmony and has lyrics that touch on themes of human weakness, suffering, and the need for healing.

prayer of desperation expressed in Damien Rice's "Cold Water"[16] or read the deep openness to search for God in "Never Went to Church" by The Streets,[17] and the unabashed link between the desire for justice and the metaphor of God as Father as professed in "Where Is the Love?" by the Black Eyed Peas?[18] And how do we relate or transfer this mega-phenomenon that is contemporary music to the world of Christian faith and practice? To what extent should we? There is something unreasonable about the (spoken or unspoken) expectation that young people upon coming to Christian faith should leave aside their love and passion for music as a form of expression and, it would seem, a means of self-understanding, relegating it to the outskirts of their life as believers, or instantly switching their musical allegiance. And yet with Christian and Catholic music, we are witnessing contrasts and tensions.

On the one hand, it is an undeniable fact that music plays a major role in the faith of young people in Europe and the States. From Taize to Charismatic renewal, from evangelical Praise and Worship music to Christian rock, rap and beyond, faith is sung. The Christian music market in the United States is an important one, and although in Europe the same cannot be said, no church effectively addresses pastoral work with young people without a serious consideration of music. There is a tremendous amount of music coming from evangelical churches, and a small but significant group of Catholic composers and musicians offering a steadily growing repertoire of Christian music for young people. However, as yet it feels like an ocean of different shaped waves: creative, exuberant and overwhelming, provoking the normal reactions of like and dislike, positions in favor and against, that all strong phenomena provoke.

On the other hand, we have the ongoing (and increasing) debate about music in our liturgies. Aware that the issue of music in and for the Eucharist is too complex to be blithe in our assessment of it, let me simply state that the difference in quality between the music that young people hear in everyday life and that which they find in our churches is surely too big to be healthy.[19] Meanwhile, in the

---

16. Damien Rice, "Cold Water," O.
17. The Streets, *The Hardest Way to Make an Easy Living*.
18. Black Eyed Peas, *Elephunk*.
19. Even the acoustics of many of our churches (especially the newer structures) are not taken into account, for any type of music, including contemporary, which is

pews among those who practice their faith, there are often musicians and composers for whom music is a major part of their life, and faith another, each running along parallel tracks that overlap without ever joining forces in an explicit and public way. This panorama is an unhealthy one, both for music and for the lived faith of those gifted with musical talents, and it stands in contrast with the history of Catholic faith, in which there have been times in which the church produced or sponsored great music. It constitutes a call for theology to reflect on the situation, in order to find ways forward. In the words of Cardinal Mauro Piacenza, former president of the Pontifical Commission for the Cultural Heritage of the Church, in a plenary assembly of the same in 2006:

> [T]he theoretical reformulation of Christian Art, which can only be lead by academic institutions, and to which we send out a request for help, cannot be postponed any longer.[20]

He talks of "the theoretical work of philosophical and theological reflection on the particularity of a theological aesthetics," in order that art could take its place among the *loci theologici* of our reflection on faith at the level of institutional courses of theology. And, most importantly, he does not limit that call to appreciating past artistic efforts, but also to opening paths to the future:

> If every period of the life of the Church has known how to produce masterpieces, as well as more ordinary works, which have interpreted its faith and singular religious sensitivity, so our era as well should consign to history expressions of *contemporary* Christian art.[21]

It is not enough to appreciate and integrate past music or art in the living out of our faith: lived Christianity can and should create for its time music that expresses and transmits the experience it is born of. Hence one of the keywords of this book: "*contemporary*" music, where the understanding of the term is etymological: *contemporarius*, from the Latin *con-* ("with") + *temporarius* ("of time," from *tempus*,

---

surprising, given the careful acoustic resonance of older churches and cathedrals.

20. From a speech on the artistic heritage of the church as a means of evangelization, catechesis, and dialogue. Piacenza, "Il patrimonio artistico della Chiesa." Translation mine.

21. Ibid. Emphasis mine.

"time")²²; that is to say, music born in the present tense of lived faith. I have resisted the temptation of focusing on any particular genre of music: the issue at stake is broader and needs to be addressed in an unbiased way. I am aware that this may make the book seem abstract or lacking in practical application, for some purposes, but one book cannot answer all the questions, and this one has as its aim to give clear, foundational thoughts on how to understand music. My own cultural background and the limits of my pastoral and theological experience remain within the realm of Western culture, but the intention is to seek theological keys that would aid and advance theological reflection in its general comprehension of music, in a way that could later be applied to different cultures and fields of pastoral work.

To better lay the basis for this aim, there are various layers of research underlying the book. Apart from the written material and theological authors on the theme and with the aim of provoking true interaction between the disciplines of music, research on music (musicology and ethnomusicology) and theology, I have sought to speak with people currently involved in Christian music ministry: musicians, liturgists, composers, and producers who feel called to and have effectively dedicated themselves to serving in this area of evangelization, as well as self-confessed music lovers, both believers and nonbelievers. My conversations with composers known and valued in this field have guided all the stages of this book. I am indebted to their generosity in sharing time, hopes and concerns about their work.²³ Those conversations, together with my own intuitions and reflection in the light of ten years of pastoral work with music, have lead me to conclude that we are lacking a foundational reflection on the role of music in revelation and faith transmission. Most Catholic reflection on music has been done within the area of liturgical theology, and

---

22. Cf. Hoad, *Concise Oxford Dictionary of English Etymology*.

23. In particular, Joshua Blakesley, Cyprian Consiglio, Don Crean, Cristobal Fones, Rob Grant, Bob Halligan, Sarah Hart, Bob Hurd, Steve Janco, Liam Lawton, Noirin ni Riain, Chris Padgett, Patricia Plude, Br. Ruffino, Dan Schutte, Curtis Stephen, Charlotte Kroecker, Edward Foley. Special thanks go to Robert Feduccia, director of Spirit and Song, the youth branch of Catholic Editorial OCP (http://www.ocp.org), for his insights on the aims and challenges facing this ministry, and for facilitating my contact with some of these composers. The conversation confirmed my intuition that we are lacking theological grounding for the understanding of the role of music in faith transmission that would form the basis for ulterior specialization and application.

many of the debates revolve around the aptness or appropriateness of different styles and genres for the liturgical setting. Yet, the liturgy is only one area of Catholic faith, albeit a central one, in which many aims and concerns converge. My conversations with producers and those involved in backing and promoting work with Christian music beyond the liturgical field identified as a major difficulty that of getting people to understand (and therefore back and invest in) their aims, since the Catholic mind-frame tends to cater for liturgical music, and lacks awareness of how important music is in evangelization, and indeed in other ways for our faith journey. For this reason, I clearly situate my research in the area of fundamental theology. Without doubt, there is need of clarity in the liturgical field, but a reflection on the nature of music in Catholic theology and spirituality and its revelatory capacity is a first step towards addressing that very need. Unless we understand the dynamics and potential of music, we can hardly discern its role in more ample and complex settings. What is music "saying" to us in this moment of history, and why is it emerging as a form of faith transmission?[24]

The entire book aims to answer that question, but three traits of music can help us begin to approach our theme: it is free, it is embodied, and it is truthful. Freedom is a trait of all art. "The primary text—the poem, picture, piece of music—is a phenomenon of freedom. It can be or it cannot be."[25] It is like Mary of Bethany's outpouring of perfume before Jesus' death (John 12:1–8)—unnecessary and extravagant, criticized even, in a pragmatic and technologically minded world, and yet so essential to human life that the origins of art and the emergence of human consciousness are practically simultaneous.[26] Precisely *because* it is free, the all-pervasive "scent" of music filling the world is somehow very appropriate to express the love of a God that is also extravagant and freely given and poured out. Music is embodied:

> Music does not transform the world. But in the meantime it makes it more habitable. Precisely suggesting that there is an incorruptibility of the corporeal, a spirituality of matter, an intelligence of the senses.[27]

---

24. I ask the question aware that answering it implies addressing whether and in what sense one can talk of music as a language.

25. Steiner, *Real Presences*, 151.

26. Cf. García-Rivera, *Wounded Innocence*, ch. 1.

27. Sequeri, *Anti-prometeo*, 128.

More than any other symbolic expression, music holds together matter and spirit. Nothing so strongly affects our bodies and spirits, our embodied spirits, as music does. The ancient Christian teaching of the spiritual senses finds in music one of its strongest witnesses. And music is truthful, not in the sense of conceptual content, which art, and especially music, does not express, but rather in the way it evokes experience. This is related to the creative space from which music emerges: born not solely of conceptual understanding, I am convinced that music transmits something of the place its composer inhabited while composing it; not, perhaps, the explicit message or intention, but rather the experience that was at its origin. Hence, music born of joy transmits joy, music born of pain can help you grieve, music born of inner dispersion can distract you, and music born of prayer can help you enter into and be held in God's presence.

Before we describe the process followed in the book, let me turn to two other notions that mark its rhythm:

The Logos of God—Jesus Christ Incarnated

> *In fact, God considers immoral a faith that lacks intimate persuasion.*
>
> —Pierangelo Sequeri[28]

"Although the end be last in the order of execution, yet it is first in the order of the agent's intention. And it is this way that it is a cause."[29] The end, or intention, of this book is a greater understanding of music's role in Christian faith and theology—"faith seeking understanding." Therefore, although the theme in focus will be the theological comprehension of *music* in relation to faith, some clarification on our end is necessary. If music does, indeed, offer us a form of understanding of faith, what is the *faith* we are speaking of? What do we understand by Christian *faith*? The question is basic, but the basics are important, and depending on how we understand what, indeed, faith is, we will

---

28. Sequeri, *Il timore di Dio*, 75.

29. *Ad primum ergo dicendum quod finis, etsi sit postremus in executione, est tamen primus in intentione agentis. Et hoc modo habet rationem causæ.* Aquinas, *Summa Theologiæ I-II*, 1, 1.

be able to comprehend as well if and how we can be helped towards living it. Vatican II, reiterating the teaching of the Councils of Orange and Vatican I,[30] describes faith in the following way:

> The obedience of faith (Rom 13:26; cf. Rom 1:5; 2 Cor 10:5–6) is to be given to God who reveals, an obedience by which [the human person] commits his [or her] whole self freely to God, offering the full submission of intellect and will to God who reveals, and freely assenting to the truth revealed by Him.[31]

The most significant phrase of this quotation, to my mind, is that our faith is a response "given to the God who reveals," because this is our key to understanding what faith actually is. This number on faith, in fact, follows immediately after *Dei Verbum*'s teaching on divine revelation, underlining the point that it is the revealing God who invites or calls us to faith. Could we not also understand that it is the faith of our revealing God that reveals (or "causes," to return to St. Thomas's premise above) what faith is? And the plenitude and perfection of Christian revelation is Jesus of Nazareth: his incarnation, life, words, deeds, death, resurrection, and ongoing presence in the church and in the world.

Much has been written on faith in recent years, producing interesting theological reflections,[32] but, given the richness of development of the reality of revelation in *Dei Verbum*, the description of faith seems somehow underdeveloped in comparison with the Christ-centered and eloquent description of Revelation that precedes it. The passionate love underlying and expressed in the words describing a God who "out of the abundance of His love speaks to [human beings] as friends (Exod 33:11; John 15:14–15) and lives among them (Bar 3:38), so that He may invite and take them into fellowship with Himself" (*Dei Verbum* 2), is somehow inadequately corresponded to in the answering "full submission of intellect and will" and free "assent to truth." This is important for our theme, because according to one's understanding of faith will follow that of what can help to lead

---

30. Cf. First Vatican Council, Dogmatic Constitution on the Catholic Faith, ch. 3, "On Faith": Denzinger 1789 (3008), and 1791 (3010); Second Council of Orange, Canon 7: Denzinger 180 (377).

31. Second Vatican Council, *Dei Verbum* 5.

32. I refer to the excellent article on "Faith" by Ardusso in the dictionary edited by Barbaglio et al., *Teologia*.

people to the same, and I intuit that some of the expressed preferences and opinions on "appropriate" or "good" music within Christian spirituality have some relation to the understanding of faith of those who express them, as well as its underlying anthropology and epistemology. How one understands faith has a clear correspondence with one's comprehension of the process of our knowing, *and* that of our embodied selves. What is faith and what is knowledge? How do they relate to one another? What kind of knowledge is faith? How do we come to know? What is the role of our bodily senses in knowledge? St. Thomas taught that all knowledge comes through the senses.[33] That includes our "knowledge" and experience of music. How do we understand this compound of matter and spirit that we are, as well as its interaction with the world outside us?

Answers will be offered as the book progresses, but as a premise, I will say that the truth of the Incarnation, and God's continued "corporal" presence among us, is at the core of this book, because it is there we witness God touching and entering fully into our human, created, embodied lives.

> We need to follow up some of the implications of the sheer fleshliness of the flesh-taking and think about the human body under the impact of that event: Christ's body, in all senses.[34]

Music—*all* music—is powerful because of how it affects our embodied spirits. Hence the attraction and the fear it provokes in us! We need to rethink our understanding of faith in the light of God's immersion in our human lives. Our faith is embodied. It is not solely a mental act, or an act of the heart. Faith involves mind, heart, soul, strength, body, senses . . . our whole being. And music is a very real way of being in touch with our embodied presence.

The history of Catholic apologetics and theology of faith is a complex one, caught up in and weaved by the cultural shifts of modernity and postmodernity, but there is no doubt that the lack of reference to the historical Jesus in the history of Apologetics and Catholic theology of faith impoverished the outcome. It has influenced our understanding both of God and of the human person, because in the life of the historical Jesus, we not only contemplate the God we are called to

33. Cf. *Sed intellectus nihil cognoscit nisi accipiendo a sensu*, Aquinas, *Summa Theologica* I, 78, 4, referring to Aristotle, *De Anima* IV, 1.

34. Haughton, *Passionate God*, 129.

believe in, but also the faith we are called to have and the very faith in which and by which we are saved.[35] One of its consequences lies in that we have inherited an understanding of faith, an "anthropology of the faculties" that accentuates intellect over feelings and will. In addition, this emphasis on the intellect contrasts with contemporary cultural experience, in which feelings and emotions are usually given priority, if not even free reign. It is not hard to intuit that such an understanding will not be overly predisposed or prepared to comprehend music as it works on the human psyche.

This is the repeated motif of this book. There are different authors who inspire these thoughts on faith, not least the biblical authors, but three complementary approaches merit presentation: Rosemary Haughton, Pierangelo Sequeri, and the School of Transformation Theology of King's College, London. Haughton takes Jesus of Nazareth's body: incarnation, resurrection, and continuation in the church, as well as our own embodied existence, very seriously. Two words describe her theology: embodied and dynamic. She presents being itself as dynamic, introducing three key words or images (as they are drawn from poetry and literature, more metaphorical than conceptual) to talk about the dynamic as opposed to static nature of reality: spheres, exchange, and breakthrough—being as love, as gift donating itself. She offers them in place of the static image of being we have interiorized over the centuries. Music relates naturally to these dynamic descriptions of reality.

Sequeri, musician and theologian, renowned for his theology of faith, rethinks faith in the light and awareness of the goodness of God, reflected among other places in the kenosis of the Incarnation (Phil 2:3–8), and of our own capacity to recognize it. Jesus, and his witness of God as *Abbá*, form the backbone of his thought.[36] He also talks

---

35. In this regard, I believe theology needs to take on more fully the importance of the *fides Iesu*, the faith of Jesus of Nazareth. Cf. Balthasar, "Fides Christi," 43–79. Antonio Gonzalez presents a well founded and convincing case for understanding the faith in which we are saved, referred to in Gal 2:20 as Jesus' faith, rather than our own. Cf. Gonzalez, *Teología de la praxis evangélica*, 329–40.

36. I take as background music to his theological thinking and structure, the "image" of God presented in *Il timore di Dio*, a small and eloquent essay of narrative theology, whose vision of God overflows into his other writings, directly in some (e.g., *L'estro di Dio*), or indirectly in others (e.g., *Il Dio affidabile*, and *L'idea della fede*) leading him to invite us to talk of God in terms of trustworthiness, rather than credibility.

about the symbolic nature of music as being operational (*operatività*) as opposed to semantic. Music is relational and dynamic. Could it not therefore be not only an aid to understanding and transmitting our faith, but perhaps more? An appropriate or privileged medium for living and understanding a faith such as ours that takes so seriously all aspects of our human living? That seems to be the case in the experience of many young people today. The challenge is to understand why and how that happens.

Finally, alongside the thought of Sequeri and Haughton, one of the theological approaches I find particularly helpful is a new strand of foundational theology coming to expression in King's College, London, called "Transformation Theology."[37] In their philosophical and theological outlooks, they also reflect on the embodiment of Jesus, focusing on the truth of faith of the ascension of Jesus, and the body of Christ as lived in the now of the church. The epistemology by which they contrast a logical or conceptual understanding of reasoning with a causal one could prove to be very helpful in explaining the symbolism at work in music. I would suggest that their theology offers a valid base on which to re-integrate the ancient Christian "sapiential" teaching on the spiritual senses, which emerges once again in current spirituality writings, but has not, as yet, been grounded on and in a coherent theological foundation that takes into account our thought processes since and as a result of modernity. All of these thinkers offer elements in the task of understanding music from the perspective of Christian faith, a faith professed in the incarnated Logos of God, since they bring into centre-stage of theological thought on faith the dimensions of embodiment, interaction and affectivity.

Finally, let us look at larger picture that organizes and gives form to my theological reasoning: theology understood as mediation between lived religion and culture.

---

37. This emerging area of theological thought is central to the book, as will be clear in the measure we progress. At the moment, its most complete presentation is to be found in the book: Davies et al., *Transformation Theology*. Coauthored by its three first representatives, the book presents the principles of their theological paradigm. Oliver Davies presents the more doctrinal backdrop and content, Paul Janz addresses the epistemological and philosophical infrastructure they work within, and Clemens Sedmak its application to the field of ethics and moral theology. It is, I believe, a significant witness to the fruitfulness of collaboration in theology, across and between different areas of theological reflection.

In Harmony with the Bigger Picture: Theology as Mediation

> *An essential pre-requisite for the salvaging of the truly real*
> *from among its surrounding confusion*
> *is that the individual existence should know about*
> *both the reality and the confusion.*
> *Accordingly, poetic activity can only occur in a frontier position.*
>
> —Ladislaus Boros[38]

If music needs to be grounded on and understood within a theological framework that helps us "make sense of it" so as to allow it (and the faith it seeks to mediate) to flourish, our theological research on music will be better understood if it is situated within a larger framework of theological thought. Although each reader will receive and understand these pages according to their own theological paradigm, my own understanding of what I am doing is grounded in Bernard Lonergan's framework of theology, as proposed in the second of his two major works, *Method in Theology*.[39] In this work, Lonergan presents the fruit of his quest to find a way of bringing together the immensely fragmented world of theological disciplines, so as to respond to what he perceived to be the crumbling structure of Catholic theology. He proposes a subdivision of tasks in eight "Functional Specialities" in which he distinguishes two phases, mediating and mediated: Research, Interpretation, History, and Dialectics (mediating); and Foundations, Doctrines, Systems, and Communications (mediated). I would describe this book as an exercise of communications in

---

38. Quoted in Haughton, *Passionate God*, 85.

39. Bernard Lonergan (1904–84), a Canadian Jesuit with a lifelong interest in mathematics and science that comes through in his writing, both for its systematic thoroughness and the grounded overcoming of the division between knowledge and belief, aware as he was that the sciences also are grounded on probability and faith. He was always passionate about finding the roots of problems, and taught dogmatic theology in Montreal and Rome (Gregorian University). He is best known for his work on understanding or epistemology, *Insight*, in which we see his passion for how we come to know truth that will mark his whole life, and his master work, *Method in Theology*. He has been well described by F. E. Crowe as a theologian of the future, rather than of the present, as most of his effort went towards constructing tools for the re-restructuring of the theology of the future, than to particular theological themes.

the area of contemporary Christian music, with a particular focus on music that has the intention of transmitting Christian faith, or preparing the way for a more explicit evangelization.

Why this framework and what do I mean by "an exercise in communications"? Lonergan's definition of the role of theology is well known: "A theology mediates between a cultural matrix and the significance and role of a religion in that matrix."[40] This is a relatively simple statement with enormous consequences: communication between the church and culture, past, present, and future, or to say it in other words: the transmission of meaning. When talking about this eighth and final functional specialty of theology, Lonergan says that here "theological reflection bears fruit," and that without it "the first seven are in vain, for they fail to mature."[41] In his own words:

> The Christian message is to be communicated to all nations. Such communication presupposes that preachers and teachers enlarge their horizons to include an accurate and intimate understanding of the culture and the language of the people they address. They must grasp the virtual resources of that culture and that language, and they must use those virtual resources creatively so that the Christian message becomes, not disruptive of culture, not an alien patch superimposed on it, but a line of development within the culture.[42]

So we are talking about the moment of interaction and interrelation of theology with its surrounding cultural contexts and societies, in which it hears and receives the questions put to it by the wider world and seeks answers for the same from the deposit of our faith, with the aim of feeding them back into the church, the world, and society. Robert Doran, disciple and interpreter of Lonergan emphasizes the need to perceive the two-way movement inherent in what Lonergan called "communications," the transmission of theological knowledge. He talks of the "situation" as a source for theology, alongside the data of Tradition:

---

40. Lonergan, *Method in Theology*, xi.
41. Ibid., 355.
42. Ibid., 362.

> In fact, I think, that such work on the situation is an essential prerequisite if one is to be able even to hand on and develop what one believes to be authentic in Tradition.[43]

So the very questions and issues thrown up by contemporary cultural situations are not just the end point but also the starting place in theological thought: two-way communication.[44] This places the church on a path of constant renewal at the service of the needs of our time, and theology where it belongs: in the heart of a three way dialogue in which it is called to be actively involved with the church, culture and the academy.

> [Communications] will remove from its action the widespread impression of complacent irrelevance and futility. It will bring theologians into close contact with experts in very many different fields. It will bring scientists and scholars into close contact with policy makers and planners and, through them, with clerical and lay workers engaged in applying solutions to the problems and finding ways to meet the needs both of Christian and of all mankind.[45]

The present book seeks to do this in the area of contemporary music, which in turn is situated in the wider theological field of theological aesthetics. Cardinal Weakland, ten years ago, made what reads as a passionate call for theology not to stay in abstract thought, but to help "create" a Catholic culture, in order to transmit our faith to the next generation. He did so precisely in the context of talking about the role of aesthetics in evangelization: "My plea is that we do not leave all of this thinking in the realm of the abstract but see the aesthetic as a powerful and evangelistic tool."[46] He called it "giving form to our belief,"[47] and the whole argument focused on the area of

---

43. Doran, *Theology and the Dialectics of History*, 8.

44. I make the point of two-way communication only to challenge our conception of theology "telling" culture what to believe and do, without the faith-inspired attempt to listen to how the Spirit is already at work in the world. In fact Lonergan does not function simply with a paradigm of two-way communication. His starting point is that of a primordial ontological unity of the human race, with a basic presupposition of the solidarity of the human race, which overflows in how he describes "intersubjectivity."

45. Lonergan, *Method in Theology*, 367.

46. Weakland, "Aesthetic and Religious Experience," 329.

47. Ibid., 319.

aesthetic and religious experience, and the need to allow the advances of recent times in theological aesthetics to filter down into Catholic culture. There have been important advances in integrating the concept of beauty and aesthetics into the heart of theology, pioneered by Balthasar and followed by others. It has been one of the areas at the forefront of theological thought in recent years.[48] However, the momentum needs be maintained, and although Balthasar it mentioned frequently, appreciation of his thought sometimes feels more like a "reverential nod" in his direction than a committed effort to follow the project through. Theological aesthetics has still to be integrated into the syllabi of many theology departments, and there is still much work to be done to influence and change the way in which theology interacts with the arts. Development is needed in creating and maintaining dialogue (i.e., two-way enrichment) with contemporary culture, both at ground level and in the academy, with experts in the different fields that overlap with theology's fields of interest.[49]

My conviction is that music is not only an apt but a privileged mode of communication of Christian faith in the contemporary cultural situation. It is true that transmission of the gospel is not a purely contemporary concern. Tradition, the passing on of our faith from one generation to the next, is an intrinsic part of Christian faith and doctrine, and has been from its birth—the difference is that today, the challenge is that of communicating the gospel to a generation that is in such a rapid process of change that gathering up the heritage of centuries of lived faith and tradition and passing it on seems ever more difficult.[50] However little one has sought to work in the area of faith

---

48. If one notes, for example, the theological conferences in Europe in the last few years on the themes of beauty, aesthetics, and the relationship between theology, spirituality and the arts: *Belleza y Teología Fundamental*, XIII Jornadas de Teología Fundamental (y Disciplinas Afines) de España y Portugal (Barcelona, June 7–9, 2007); *The Arts and Spirituality* (Manresa House, Dublin, August 24–26, 2007); *The Offence of Beauty* (St. Andrews, September 2–5, 2007); the recently organized conference by the Italian conference of bishops called *Dio Oggi* (Rome, December 10–12, 2009) in which the arts had a central role. The shift or development in recent months seems to be the accent on Drama and Theatre.

49. Within the field of theological reflection on art and music, I think it is indispensable that theology integrate the active involvement of artists, musicians and composers in the very genesis of its reflection, and that work at academic level is developed between theology and music departments.

50. I cannot overemphasize the importance of this problem. It is perhaps not the moment to expand further, but I remit to the following articles of Lonergan: "Belief:

transmission, one experiences the daily and double dilemma of feeling you have something to say that is not understood, and of hearing realities new to your ears, a way of seeing and perceiving things alien to your perception. I believe the following words of George Steiner give expression to that change:

> It is my belief that the contract is broken for the first time, in any thorough and consequent sense, in European, Central European and Russian culture and speculative consciousness during the decades from the 1870s to the 1930s. *It is this break of the covenant between the word and the world that constitutes one of the very few genuine revolutions of spirit in Western history and which defines modernity itself.* . . . My question is: what is the status of meaning after meaning, of communicative form, in the time of the "after-word"?[51]

Steiner basically makes the point that up to now our ways of self-perception and understanding have implied a continuous bond of trust between reality and its "sayability," its understanding from the beginning of history as we know it up to the present moment. However, that bond is no longer. In this time, which he calls the time of the "Epilogue," words no longer "say" in the way they used to. The consequences of this in a faith such as ours, in which the verbal word has so much importance, are not hard to imagine and are already being felt.

Furthermore, the issue is not only an external one, of communication from one generation to the next. The difficulty in contemporary western culture is not just that people don't understand God, the Word of God; they don't seem to understand themselves or the world either. The following quotation from Sequeri in some way explains or completes Steiner's definition of our time as "*Epi-logos*":

> Many no longer know either how to decipher their own feelings: they don't know if they love well or not, they don't know what they are scared of, they don't know what makes them euphoric at one moment and depressed at the next, they don't even know if they believe or not. They "try out" [*provono*] all these feelings ("experiences" they say, but more than anything

---

Today's Issue"; "Future of Christianity"; and "Theology in Its New Context"; and the book by Frederick E. Crowe, *Method in Theology*.

51. Steiner, *Real Presences*, 93–94.

they are "experiments" they do with themselves) and they are not capable of deciphering them.[52]

Irish singer-songwriter Damian Rice gives eloquent expression to this reality in this prayer-song, "Cold Water," in which the cry, in the midst of life experienced as cold water surrounding us, is:

> Lord can you hear me now?
> or am I lost?[53]

As Louth describes at the beginning of his book on theology today, we experience "the consciousness of a division, a yawning gulf, that penetrates into our very heart and mind, a failure, an inability to relate."[54]

> It's not a question of condemning this time as worse than ever: The scandalized denouncing of the universe of the young as one forged by hedonism, lack of values, superficiality of life, care of the external without commitment, seems to me to be quite pathetic (to not say something else).[55]

Such a negative attitude, more perhaps than the superficiality of postmodern culture, denounces our own superficiality in reading its strengths and its needs. But there is no doubt that it is changing. And the change is a profound one, which theology and pastoral work must seek to understand. Music here seems to be one way postmodern sensitivity "finds" or "understands" itself. Why? Because of how the musical form of symbolism "works." Lonergan talks about the role of the symbol in aiding internal communication:

> The need is for internal communication. . . . It is through symbols that mind and body, mind and heart, heart and body communicate. In that communication symbols have their proper meaning.[56]

Music is a very powerful form of symbolic communication, whose nature and theological relevance we will explore in this book. Rosemary Haughton talks extensively about the importance of language in life

52. Sequeri, *L'oro e la paglia*, 110.

53. Damien Rice, "Cold Water," *O*. Rice is an Irish songwriter, and this song is a beautiful contemporary "song-prayer" that paints the painful situation of not knowing either how to believe and how not to, and not really understanding where one is.

54. Louth, *Discerning the Mystery*, 1.

55. Sequeri, *L'oro e la paglia*, 114.

56. Lonergan, *Method in Theology*, 66–67.

and theology. Although the following quotation is a long one, I think it is worthwhile reproducing fully:

> "No one ever exposes the nerves and fibres of his being in order to make up a language." Maybe not, but nobody could make up a language without exposing the nerves and fibres of his being, however unintentionally. Conversely, it is only when the right language becomes available that certain "fibres" can be revealed at all. The need to uncover and communicate "pushes" the existing language towards change and, as change begins to be felt "under the surface," attention concentrates at that point, it is "rubbed thin" by experiment and desire. In the end something breaks through . . . and a new dimension of spiritual awareness becomes possible.[57]

Could music be a new "language" that certain fibers of our being, no longer containable in the philosophical and theological frameworks we have understood and expressed them in for centuries, are pushing to the surface in the quest for expression and recognition? Could this not be one way in which the Spirit of God seeks to "breakthrough" in postmodern culture, which Steiner so eloquently describes as the time of the "after-word," when words are just not enough? If this is the case, and I believe it is, then we need to understand how music works, the semantic "rules" it follows, and how they relate to our conceptual understanding. We need to find a way to inhabit the frontiers, as the words above from Boros suggest, both the external ones of faith and culture, and the internal ones of our own experience and understanding, certainty and doubt. This is the birthplace of what Haughton calls the poetry of good theology, and which we believe music can help lead us into and through:

> In other words, the poetry of good theology must grow from deep within the actual and concrete experience of people, so deep that when they hear that poetry they recognize in it both the accurate expression of their problems and hopes and loves and the evocation of deeper layers which they cannot touch but of which they are mutually aware, afraid and desirous.[58]

---

57. Haughton, *Passionate God*, 40–41.
58. Ibid., 279.

Outline of the Book

Given the broad readership I intuit may be drawn to the book's title, and the diversity of their interests and theological background, I will explain clearly the focus and remit of each chapter, in the hope that those reading may find and read that which is of more relevance to them. To a certain degree and for that reason, I have tried to make each chapter understandable in itself, though explaining the steps I am taking within the book.

Chapter 1 on meaning in music looks at the background of research on music in the area of musicology and ethnomusicology, presenting the thought of some of its main forerunners, such as Susanne K. Langer, Leonard B. Meyer, Charles Seeger, Bruno Nettl, Alan P. Merriam, and John A. R. Blacking. Some of the questions and recurring themes that the chapter highlights, which theology needs to take on board when reflecting on music, are the following:

- What is music? Can we call it a "language"? Is "universal language" a helpful or misleading approach to musical understanding?
- What does music "mean"? Does it signify anything outside itself, or is its meaning only and always internal to the piece of music?
- Is apprehending and understanding music more intellectual or emotional?
- Is music a specifically human phenomenon, or does the natural world 'make music'?
- Is music a universal activity? If so, what is there in music that is or common to all cultures?
- Is creativity best understood as discovery or as a process of composition and creation of something new?

The combination of insights drawn from musicology, (born and developed initially in Europe and the United States of America) and ethnomusicology, which has covered a wider range of musical expressions, underlines the importance of culture in musical practice, and the value of a hermeneutical approach to research into the same, in order to give proper attention to methodology in discourse on music. In this chapter the aim is to learn to recognize our explicit and implicit expectations, when we seek to listen to and "understand," or "find meaning in" music. Opinions on music, from the taste judgment of someone without musical formation to the "expert" critique of those who dedicate their lives to assessing and evaluating music, are always situated within a horizon of comprehension which affects their criteria. This chapter aims to help theological discourse on music grow in awareness of its own criteria of assessment, towards more fruitful discernment.

Chapter 2 takes a step forward in addressing this plurality and the complexity involved by introducing a particular hermeneutical approach to musical meaning, in the form of the musical analysis offered by musicologist Jean-Jacques Nattiez. Nattiez applies the model of tripartition found in the semiology studies of Jean Molino to music, differentiating between the threefold process of the intention and dynamic of music in its composition, the finished product in itself, and its reception. The parallel with hermeneutical studies in general is clear. Meaning in music will always involve a combination of these three perspectives. The aim of the chapter is that we learn to recognize our explicit and implicit expectations when we listen to and seek to "understand," or "find meaning in" music. Opinions on music, from the taste judgment of someone without musical formation to the "expert" critique of those who dedicate their lives to assessing and evaluating music, are *always* situated within a horizon of comprehension which affects their criteria. This chapter rests on my own conviction about the overall importance of hermeneutics in theology, and aims to help theological discourse on music grow in awareness of its own criteria of assessment, towards more fruitful discernment.

Chapter 3 focuses the lens further, asking the specific question of what music is. Conscious of the need to prepare the non-musically educated reader for some of the points made, this chapter begins with a brief presentation of the basics of music (rhythm, melody, harmony, tone color and timbre). Understanding music, however, implies going further, and asking about how music actually "works," and this leads us to the field of semiotics and semiology. I forewarn the reader that semiotics is a complex field of research, but that there is no other way, I believe, to understand the specific way in which music "speaks" the Word than understanding its own particular dynamic in comparison and contrast with linguistic semiotics. To that end, based on the work of Dutch theologian, semiotician, and musicologist Willem Marie

Speelman, we bring together semiotics and musicology by comparing musical and verbal discourse. The comprehension of that difference enables theology to better receive and welcome what music has to offer faith, evangelization and theology. Therefore, this chapter, although dense, is at the centre of what the book proposes, and provides fascinating insights which help understanding music's particular strengths at the service of the expression and communication of Christian faith. It bridges the musicological reflections of chapters 1 and 2 with the theological paradigm and understanding we wish to offer, underlining the elements of Speelman's analysis that are important to our chosen theological paradigm, such as the embodied symbolism of music, and the form of the relationship with the world that music creates.

Chapter 4 lays the foundations for a theological aesthetics of music with a reflection on what we would call a "theological epistemology." Epistemology is the discipline that studies how we know, and addressing it in this book is based on the conviction that understanding music and its role in Christian spirituality and theology implies a greater appreciation of how we inhabit and relate to the world around us, as well as *how* we come to faith in Christ. We analyze the need for an apologetics of Christian faith drawn from the specific ground of revelation. This chapter brings together three authors with converging epistemological stances, albeit with different accents: the intentional analysis of Bernard Lonergan and his understanding of the role of art and music in human life; the epistemology of Paul Janz,[59] who works on epistemology within and at the service of Christian revelation; and the theological-spiritual writings of Rosemary Haughton, who links epistemological considerations on how we approach and understand reality with the doctrines of incarnation, resurrection and the mystical body of Christ. Her emphasis on the centrality of our affectivity and embodied existence in Christian faith finds points of convergence both with Lonergan's notion of conversion and Speelman's understanding of musical symbolism.

In reality, chapters 4 and 6 belong together, but inserting a chapter on the return to theological aesthetics helps to understand the importance of the theme in contemporary thought, as well as to situate the position I take in the book alongside other approaches to

---

59. Janz is one of the team of theologians and philosophers that belong to Transformation Theology, our main theological paradigm for understanding music.

the theme. To this end, chapter 5 presents an introduction to the wider field of theological aesthetics and the reasons for its emergence now. It explains why aesthetics is an important theme for fundamental theology today, since the theme of beauty presents itself as a plausible and fruitful entry point to Christian faith for contemporary sensibility. Therefore it touches directly on the apologetic role of this area of theology. It then presents briefly the thought of some of the more important forerunners and contemporary authors on the subject, situating them in relation to my own theological paradigm. The chosen authors are Hans Urs von Balthasar, Pierangelo Sequeri, Richard Viladesau, Alejandro García-Rivera, Frank Burch Brown, Jeremy Begbie, and Don Saliers.

Finally, chapter 6 completes the theological paradigm presented in the book, integrating the theological epistemology of chapter 4 within a wider doctrinal framework, based on the authors mentioned earlier in this introduction. It brings together our findings on musical symbolism with a theology focused on the Incarnation, life, death, resurrection, ascension and continued embodied presence of Christ in the church and the world. The rediscovery of the ascension as a core truth of Christian faith is one I consider important for several areas of Christian spirituality and theology. In the light of this doctrine and theological paradigm, the book integrates musical analysis with Transformation Theology under three aspects: music as a means of access to faith, music as a source for the enrichment of theological praxis, and the vocation of the artist and musician as commissioning in the Body of Christ.

I include a brief appendix on one dimension of music-making that emerges often as the book advances, but would need more attention: that of the points of convergence and difference between the Christian calling and the musical one. There is very little written as yet on this subject. Its inclusion in the appendix wishes to provoke reflection, especially for those of us active in composing and performing, and to prepare the way for some more extensive thought and writing.

1

Meaning in Music

*Where we learn another language for the first time,
we discover more about the world.*

—Jeremy Begbie[1]

THIS CHAPTER ASKS THE QUESTION ABOUT WHAT MUSIC MEANS, AND how it does so. The issue of "meaning"—how we apprehend it and how it is passed on—is one of the main areas of reflection of the theologian whose paradigm and definition of theology we presented in the introduction, Bernard Lonergan.[2] It is in the context of that debate that we situate the question of if and how music has meaning. That music "means a lot" to people in contemporary culture, as the introduction tried to express, is obvious, but for theology to answer the question of how it is significant, it needs to listen to those who have researched specifically into the nature of music, and where its significance lies: so we turn to the fields of musicology and ethnomusicology. As we advance, the particular remit of these two areas of study will become clearer, but in broad terms, musicology was born in the context of Western culture and applied to European classical music, although it later extended to American music of European classical influence, and ethnomusicology emerged as a result of growing awareness of the music of other cultures beyond that sphere, and the desire to understand them. However, they are young sciences and, to a certain degree, are still evolving in their aims, methodology and areas of application. As we shall see, even the division between is no longer clear-cut.

1. Begbie, *Beholding the Glory*, xi.
2. Cf. by way of example, Lonergan, "Dimensions of Meaning," "Belief: Today's Issue," and "Future of Christianity."

Knowledge of the background of a given area of study is, I believe, indispensable to mature thought. This chapter, therefore, is somewhat dense and technical in nature, as the authors bring together and apply notions drawn from the areas of music, philosophy and cultural studies. Having said that, many of the issues they address underlie those which surface today in our dilemmas around music in faith ministry, albeit with a somewhat more complex language. For example, the ongoing debate on if, and how, we can understand music as a language.[3] This is not a new discussion: it touches on the core of musicological thought since it emerged. And yet, the description of music as a "universal language" is one of the first that emerges in conversations on music's importance and eloquence even now. Therefore, an effort to understand some of the history of thought in this area may give us tools to express and answer our own doubts.

The chapter is divided in two parts: firstly, a brief introduction to the history and main thinkers of this area of reflection as well as the key themes they address which are relevant to our theme; secondly, a summary of the issues that have surfaced and that remain actual. It is important to underline that the attempt at a systematic reflection of the meaning of music was born and developed in Western culture. The underlying presuppositions are influenced by Western philosophical frameworks, and frequently include an implicit and quite possibly unconscious assumption of the superiority of European classical music and/or the universal nature of the Western tonal system. Ethnomusicological studies are a development of recent years. Theological investigation on the meaning of music often overlooks their findings. My own cultural experience is limited to Western culture, and yet this book hopes to lay some basis for a broader reflection on the theme. For this reason, we will look at research into music drawn from both the field of musicology and ethnomusicology. I have chosen a handful of key writers on the subject, in order to introduce the reader to the landscape of issues underlying this field of research. It is in no way comprehensive, hoping only to help situate us and to understand the main conclusions or consensus points of this important, albeit young, area of research. I will briefly present six au-

---

3. There are those who would deny it carries any "meaning" in itself: cf. Foley, *Music in Ritual*. Other thinkers defend its capacity for carrying meaning, but *where* its meaning lies and what we "mean" by "musical meaning" is still a complex theme without apparent consensus.

thors: Susanne K. Langer, Leonard B. Meyer, Alan P. Merriam, Charles Seeger, Bruno Nettl, and John Blacking. This chapter has little explicit theological discourse in it, but is rather an indispensable introduction to the themes of philosophical research into music, as a first step in theology's quest to understand it.

Main Thinkers or Forerunners in Musicology and Ethnomusicology

Susanne K. Langer

> *If we would have new knowledge,*
> *we must get a whole world of new questions.*
> *Music can reveal the nature of feelings*
> *with a detail and truth that language cannot approach.*
>
> —S. Langer[4]

We shall start with Susanne K. Langer, for two reasons. The first is chronological, as she is a forerunner in thought on art and the symbolic nature of human apprehension and knowledge. The second is that her influence on our area of study is undeniable. In some it is explicit: Lonergan, one of the theologians who is important for this book, recognizes her explicit influence on his thought regarding art, and despite the fact that the definition of art he attributes to Langer in *Method in Theology* is actually not found in precisely that way in any of her works,[5] her influence on his thought is patent. We will come back to her epistemological influence on him in chapter 4. Her place at this point of our reflection is because although she is not a musicologist and some aspects of her thought on music are considered to be outdated, there is no doubt as to the originality and groundbreaking nature of her philosophical aesthetics, as well as her clear influence both on the musical theorists following her and on thought about art in general.

---

4. Langer, *Philosophy in a New Key*, 191.

5. Cf. Lonergan, *Method in Theology*, 61: "Here I borrow from Suzanne Langer's *Feeling and Form* where art is defined as the objectification of a purely experiential pattern and each term in this definition is carefully explained."

Susanne Langer (1895–1985)[6] was an American philosopher of German origin who was a pioneer in the area of symbolic logic and the philosophy of art. She also played the cello and had studied some music theory and composition. She is best known for her book *Philosophy in a New Key: A Study in the Symbolism of Reason, Rite, and Art*, in which she challenges traditional philosophical thinking by presenting symbolism as the "new key" in which the human mind grasps and seeks to express itself, and develops a general study of symbolic forms—language, scientific knowledge, ritual, myth and the arts, including a chapter on music.[7] In this book she refers to music as an "unconsummated symbol," due to the lack of a conventional reference point, which is to be found in language and visual art.[8] She develops this chapter into a comprehensive philosophy of art in the book *Feeling and Form: A Theory of Art*, in 1953, becoming known principally as a philosopher of art.[9]

A person's background and intellectual formation colors their use of language, and are therefore helpful to know, towards a greater comprehension of their thought. Langer's background is in the philosophy of logic, her first book being on symbolic logic, with mentors such as Alfred North Whitehead. This explains why, in *Philosophy in a New Key*, she uses an expression that we may find alien to the realm of aesthetics, calling art the "logical expression" of feelings and describing music as offering "a 'logical picture' of sentient, responsive life." Her understanding of logic, however, is wider than our current use of the term, and embraces a broad understanding of form: "anything may be said to have form that follows a pattern of any sort, exhibits order, internal connection."[10] In this sense, it is not only representational art and music that have symbolic expressivity. Her thought on art and music is embedded in her overall perception of the symbol and our apprehension of it. She talks about language as the most sophisticated means of symbolic representation that we have, propos-

---

6. Cf. Dryden, "Susanne K. Langer.

7. Langer, *Philosophy in a New Key*, 204–45.

8. Ibid., 240. We will explain shortly what is meant by "reference point."

9. She later wrote a book which she herself considered her most important work, a three-volume work called *Mind: An Essay on Human Feeling* (1967–1982).

10. Cf. Langer, *Introduction to Symbolic Logic*, 23, quoted by Dryden, "Susanne K. Langer," 192. Langer touches briefly on the theme of the musical form in *Introduction to Symbolic Logic*, 28.

ing that precise language is the generalization of metaphor and that everyday language is a series of "faded metaphors"; indeed it is our capacity for images, symbols, metaphors to apprehend reality that feeds our language.[11] It is not the place to develop this intuition, but contemporary interest in the areas of narrative, literature, and poetry and their potential for conveying truth points in the same direction. It leads to questions about how we apprehend reality, and seek to express it. In talking about the significance of music, Langer touches on the art of poetry, broadening the theme of how an aspect of reality is offered in this symbolic form that cannot be given in literal expression. Her reflection in *Philosophy in a New Key* is described by herself as a study of "symbolic transformation" and lays a foundation for her treatment of the arts and music. She identifies the human person as being, above all, a symbol-using animal:

> Under Cassirer's influence, and in response to her own literary and artistic sensibilities, Langer expands the definitions of knowledge and reason in *Philosophy in a New Key* to encompass nondiscursive formulations of experience embodied in the spontaneous activity of dreaming and in the cultural productions of myth, ritual, and the arts.[12]

This helps us to understand the perhaps most widely known aspect of her thought: the non-discursive and non-denotative nature of symbolic thought, of which the arts are the best exponents. Varying but similar definitions can be found in her writings: "Art is the creation of forms symbolic of human feeling," or "Art is the creation of forms expressive of human feeling."[13] She distinguishes in this way between the open "presentational" symbols of art and "discursive" symbols of language, which cannot reflect directly the subjective aspect of experience:

> [According to Langer], art works were nondiscursive, presentational symbols that expressed an artist's "life of feeling," by

---

11. Cf. Langer, *Philosophy in a New Key*, 141–47. The primacy and priority of poetry was underlined before her, most notably in the late seventeenth and early eighteenth century by Giambattista Vico, and more recently, Karl Rahner speaks eloquently of what he calls primordial words, in a piece called "Priest and Poet."
12. Dryden, "Susanne K. Langer," 194.
13. Cf. Langer, *Feeling and Form*, 40, 60; *Problems of Art*, 63.

> which observers, through a process of immediate apprehension (or intuition) came to acquire knowledge.[14]

She emphasizes the epistemological significance of the arts and in a chapter on the importance of artistic genius, she calls for a philosophy of art, saying that:

> the limits of language are not the last limits of experience, and things inaccessible to language may have their own forms of conception, that is to say, their own symbolic devices.[15]

In this way she is one of the first philosophers of art to shift the discussion on art from the meaning of the works of art in themselves to their import or significance for the receiver, with the capacity or quality of intuition as the epistemological "link" between the work of art perceived as symbol and its perceiver. She considered art to offer a privileged entry point to human subjectivity, in a way verbal discourse could not:

> People who are responsive to the arts live "through the eye, the musical hearing, the bodily senses," and "see more meaning in artistic wholes, i.e. in things, situations, feelings, etc., than they can ever find in propositions." There is no reason, Langer argues, to suppose that the apprehension of artistic significance is any more "irrational" or "alogical" than the process of understanding propositional knowledge, provided that reason and logical insight are defined in the broadest possible sense as the appreciation of patterns.[16]

Once again we find in Langer a broad understanding of human knowing, which colors her understanding of human feelings and how art influences them. In Langer's theory a work of art is what she calls a "significant form."[17] It *formulates an idea of feeling*, which Langer defines quite broadly as "inner life," "subjective reality," or "consciousness." What a work of art expresses, or formulates for one's conception, is not actual feeling, but ideas of any given feeling, in the same way as language does not express actual things and events but ideas about

---

14. Brand, "Susanne Katherina Knauth Langer."
15. Langer, *Philosophy in a New Key*, 265.
16. Dryden, "Susanne K. Langer," 194.
17. Langer, *Feeling and Form*, 24.

them.[18] In the words of Simon Frith, according to Langer and her followers, "music thus offers us the cognition of feelings rather than the feelings themselves."[19] This is coherent with her understanding of how symbols in general work:

> Symbols are not proxy for their objects but are *vehicles for the conception of objects*. . . . In talking *about* things we have conceptions of them, not the things themselves; and *it is the conceptions, not the things, that symbols directly mean*. . . . She adds that "If I say 'Napoleon,' you do not bow to the conqueror of Europe as though I had introduced him, but merely think of him."[20]

At first sight, these reflections may seem complex and abstract for the theme of this book, but in actual fact it is precisely our lack of understanding of how language and symbols work which causes confusion when we try to "talk about" music and what it means. Music is a symbolic, or indeed, semiotic form, as we shall develop in chapter 3. That music has a powerful effect on human feeling is, perhaps, not a surprise, but Langer attempts to describe just how the relationship between the two can be articulated.

Her understanding of music as a symbolic form is complex. First and foremost, she denies that music "provokes" or stimulates feelings, saying rather that its "meaning is symbolic: if it has an emotional content, it 'has' it in the same sense that language 'has' its conceptual content—symbolically."[21] Although she says that music can "only loosely and inexactly" be called a language,[22] she rejects theories that deny music any symbolic capacity, talking of the particular strength of musical expressiveness: "that music articulates forms which language cannot set forth."[23] These forms, above all, are those of human feelings:

---

18. Cf. Dryden, "Susanne K. Langer," 196.

19. Frith, *Performing Rights*, 238 n. 25. The book is a well-known and valuable first approach to these themes, as a resource for further research.

20. Langer, *Philosophy in a New Key*, 61. Although she does not refer to Ferdinand de Saussure, there is a parallel between how she perceives symbolic perception and how de Saussure understands the working of verbal language in the brain, as we shall see later on in the book.

21. Langer, *Philosophy in a New Key*, 218.

22. Langer, *Feeling and Form*, 31.

23. Langer, *Philosophy in a New Key*, 233. Emphasis original.

> Because the forms of human feeling are much more congruent with musical forms than with the forms of language, music can reveal the nature of feelings with a detail and a truth that language cannot approach.[24]

However, music is something more than an expression human feeling. "Music is not self-expression, but formulation and representation of emotions, mood, mental tensions and resolutions—a 'logical picture' of sentient, responsive life,"[25] and therefore, like all symbolic presentations, a source of insight and understanding, albeit by means other than language.[26] Langer argues that musical forms bear a close logical resemblance to the forms of human feelings. Music is a "presentational symbol" of psychic process and its tonal structures bear a close logical similarity to the forms of feeling, "forms of growth and of attenuation, flowing and stowing, conflict and resolution, speed, arrest, terrific excitement, calm, or subtle activation and dreamy lapses."[27] This dynamic of conflict and resolution, tension and release as mirroring human forms of feeling is very frequent in musicology. According to Anthony Storr, Langer thinks that music can put us in touch with emotions we have not yet experienced.[28]

In *Feeling and Form: A Theory of Art*, her later book on the comprehension of art, she takes her analysis of music as a symbolic form and uses it as a base for a comprehension of the arts in general. In a separate chapter she specifically relates the musical form to rhythm and the marking of time.[29] I believe this aspect of her understanding of how music works also influenced Lonergan's description of art and the artistic process. We will talk about its underlying consequences later, when we discuss the creative process involved. In the description of how music and human feeling are related, her thought is original and thought-provoking, although the direct link between them is highly

---

24. Ibid., 235.
25. Ibid., 222.
26. Dryden, "Susanne K. Langer," 195.
27. Langer, *Feeling and Form*, 27.
28. Cf. Storr, *Music and the Mind*, 76; 118. Storr was a doctor and psychiatrist with various writings on themes related with psychiatry and literature. This book is his only one on music, and is an invaluable, well researched and lucid gathering of current issues and debates, illumined by his own area of expertise.
29. Langer, *Feeling and Form*, 120–32.

contested.[30] Despite this fact, her thought continues to draw interest, both in the areas of her general theory of the mind and feeling, and that of music.[31]

Leonard B. Meyer

> [T]o whom is this book addressed?
> Frankly, I am not sure.
> Sometimes in those moments of doubt and depression
> that come when one is near to finishing,
> I have felt that it is addressed mostly to its author—
> though I hope not.
>
> —Leonard B. Meyer[32]

Leonard B. Meyer (1918–2007) was undoubtedly one of the most influential writers on music. He was an American composer, author, and philosopher with writings on the aesthetic theory of music and compositional analysis. His most influential work, *Emotion and Meaning in Music*, perhaps the first general treatise written on music, is a study of the problem of meaning in music and the manner of musical communication. He describes his quest as that of seeking "a detailed examination of the meanings of music and the processes by which they are communicated."[33] He takes this approach, differentiating it from one which investigates the "value" of music, although in later years he recognizes the inseparable nature of these two aspects of musical meaning (and indeed aesthetic meaning in general).[34] In *Emotion and*

---

30. One critique of her work comes from one of the authors we touch on in chapter 4, Richard Liddy, who completed his doctorate work on Langer's thought on art, with a thesis called *Art and Feeling: An Analysis and Critique of the Philosophy of Art of Susanne K. Langer*, and continued to write extensively on Lonergan's understanding of intellectual conversion. He criticizes her overall understanding of human consciousness as false and incompatible with a right apprehension of reality. Cf. Liddy, *Transforming Light*, iv–xv; 204–9.

31. Of particular interest in the context of this thesis is the use of Langer's theory in the book by Sbatella, *La mente orchestra*, 125–39. This book is a scientific reflection on the work and findings of Esagramma, the music therapy initiative lead by theologian and musician Pierangelo Sequeri, and directed by the author herself.

32. Meyer, *Explaining Music*, x.

33. Meyer, *Emotion and Meaning*, viii.

34. Cf. Meyer, *Music, the Arts, and Ideas*, 23.

Meaning, Meyer presents a psychological approach to emotion and meaning in music, combining Gestalt Theory and theories by pragmatists Charles Peirce and John Dewey to try to explain the existence of emotion in music and its relationship with meaning.[35]

As a starting point, he describes two contrasting dichotomies in philosophical aesthetics that inform thought on music: the absolutist position versus the referentialist one, and the formalist position versus the expressionist one. As these are viewpoints that resurface in other authors and continue to influence our evaluation of musical meaning, a brief explanation of their meaning in reference to music is called for:

- Absolutist–Referentialist: The absolutist position situates musical meaning exclusively within the work of music itself, whereas the referentialist one points to the extra-musical world of concepts, actions, and emotional states for the meaning of a given piece of music. "Absolute" music refers to music without words or explicit reference to the world outside music. For example, most music of the Baroque and Classical periods is absolute music, and it is therefore significant that the titles are often not names but numbers (Bach's concerto I in D minor, concerto II in E major, and so on), which could be understood as the explicit non-reference to anything beyond the music itself. A theorist taking an absolutist position would say that music never "means" anything outside itself. A referentialist position, on the contrary, seeks the meaning of music outside the musical structure, 'in reference to' something other than the music. Program music, such as opera and ballet music, for example, is a clear example of music *specifically* written to evoke or imitate something beyond itself, but referentialists will seek the extra-musical meaning of absolute music as well.

- Formalist–Expressionist: A formalist stance situates the meaning of a work of music in the structure of and relationships within the piece of music itself, and its form of cognition is under-

---

35. In his 1967 book, *Music, the Arts, and Ideas*, he deals with issues such as the value and greatness of music and the convergence of music theory and information theory; in *Style and Music: Theory, History and Ideology*, published in 1989, he develops his thought on style in music in relation to history. He also coedited a book with G. Cooper called *The Rhythmic Structure of Music*. His thought was dynamic and evolved over time, but he remains most well known for his first work on emotion and meaning in music.

stood as mainly intellectual. An expressionist one highlights the capacity of music to excite feelings or emotions, or sometimes even the emotional meaning to be found in the music itself.[36] These positions have become more nuanced as musicological research has advanced, and it is now rare to find them defended in pure form, but it useful to understand the differences in this way, as they still inform many of the on-going debates within musicology and cultural studies on music.

Meyer's stance with regard to the former position is a conciliatory one, which recognizes the existence of both types of meaning in music. "[A]bsolute meanings and referential meanings are not mutually exclusive . . . they can and do coexist in one and the same piece of music."[37] Although Meyer proposes a compromise or middle ground between both these dichotomies, his own stance could be described as leaning towards absolutist expressionist, in the sense that, although he does not deny that music can refer to something beyond itself, he explicitly focuses his attention on its internal meaning:

> The present study is concerned with an examination and analysis of those aspects of meaning which result from the understanding of and response to relationships inherent in the musical progress rather than with any relationships between the musical organization and the extramusical world of concepts, actions, characters, and situations.[38]

The reason for this focus is because he believed that no analysis had been offered as to what and how music "means," and how it could be related to other forms of human meaning or signifying, even by those who would defend the particular meaning music has as intrinsic to its structure. In his quest to comprehend the meaning of music, under the influence of Charles S. Pierce's understanding of the sign, Meyer refers to what he calls the "triadic" relationship involved in all making of meaning, involving an object or stimulus, an event or consequence to which the stimulus points, and the conscious observer.[39]

36. Cf. Meyer, *Emotion and Meaning*, 3.
37. Ibid., 1.
38. Ibid., 3.
39. Cf. ibid., 34. As we shall observe in chapters 2 and 3, Pierce's triadic notion of the semiotic structure of the sign provides a helpful framework in which to approach musical understanding.

It is in this context that one can comprehend his attempt to reconcile referentialists and absolutists (those who ascribe external "content" to music and those who do not) in recognizing the particular nature of musical meaning, which is not linguistic:

> Not only does music use no linguistic signs but, on one level at least, it operates as a closed system, that is, it employs no signs or symbols referring to the non-musical world of objects, concepts, and human desires.[40]

He seeks to overcome this impasse in understanding musical meaning by differentiating meaning into two classes, according to the nature of the event or consequence to which the stimulus points. In the words of musicologist Willem Speelman:

> Meyer differentiates meaning into two classes: designative and embodied meaning. Designative meaning is a function between two entities of a different nature.... Embodied meaning is a function between two entities of a similar nature.... According to Meyer music does not have designative meanings but embodies them. And music does not refer to emotions, but produces them (by inhibiting a tendency to respond).[41]

Since most of the meanings used in human communication are designative, the danger or tendency is to overlook or ignore embodied meaning. Yet musical meaning is "embodied," in the sense that "a musical stimulus or a series of stimuli indicate and point to . . . not extramusical concepts and objects but other musical events which are about to happen."[42] In chapter 3 of this book we will underline the importance of the embodied nature of music, although the explicit content of the word here in Meyer does not fully correspond to our own understanding of the term. (He later refers to embodied meaning in relation to music also as "syntactical meaning.") However, the similarity in the direction of his reflections remains, as does his significant challenge to our division in thinking about both reason in relation to emotion, and mind in relation to body, when talking about embodied meaning:

---

40. Meyer, *Emotion and Meaning*, vii.

41. Speelman, *Generation of Meaning*, 56–57. Meyer does not recognize it explicitly, but the influence of Langer in regard to the non-designative quality of music is present. His stance on music and emotions, however, diverges.

42. Meyer, *Emotion and Meaning*, 35.

> But this is a dilemma only so long as the traditional dichotomy between reason and emotion and the parent polarity between mind and body are adopted. Once it is recognized that affective experience is just as dependent upon intelligent cognition as conscious intellection . . . then thinking and feeling need not be viewed as polar opposites but as different manifestations of a single psychological process. There is no diametric opposition, no inseparable gulf, between the affective and the intellectual responses made to music.

This text presents one of the strengths of Meyer's work, that of seeking to bridge between theorists of music (usually absolutist and formalist) and music lovers (who tend to be expressionist and referentialist). His own underlying tendency is towards an absolutist position, in that he seems to think that the relationships evident in the work itself can account for feelings and emotions in the listener. Although some authors think he leaves space for referential meaning, it is clear that he considers music's internal meaning, its "embodied" meaning, as more important than any external reference. In keeping with this tendency, he will later value the internal "syntactical" analysis and value of music over the sensuous-associative responses provoked in its listeners.[43]

Underlying Meyer's analysis is the psychological theory of emotions as presented, amongst others, by John Dewey and J. T. MacCurdy, which relates emotions to the dynamics of expectation, suspense, inhibition, and resolution.[44] The last phrase of the above quotation from Speelman (music does not refer to emotions, but produces them, by inhibiting a tendency to respond) summarizes both his expressionist view and its theoretical grounding: Dewey's understanding of emotions as being aroused when a tendency to respond is inhibited or prevented. "Meyer claims that great composers arouse our emotions because they are expert at heightening expectation and postponing resolution."[45] As this postponing is what provokes emotion, therein would lie the emotional power of music: "musical meaning arises when the listener's expectation of that which follows what he has al-

---

43. Cf. Meyer, *Music, the Arts*, 35–36.

44. For an interesting analysis of his theory of expectation in musical meaning, see, Huron, *Sweet Anticipation*.

45. Cf. Storr, *Music and the Mind*, 84–85.

ready heard is contradicted,"[46] that is to say, when the path a musical phrase takes surprises us due to its unpredictability.

> Affect or emotion-felt is aroused when an expectation—a tendency to respond—activated by the musical stimulus situation, is temporarily inhibited or permanently blocked.[47]

This aspect of his thought is perhaps the weakest one, as it based on a link between expectation, emotion and meaning drawn from information theorists who later revised the link between expectation and information. It is a slightly narrow view to present delayed or "surprised" fulfillment as the sole cause of emotional response to music. The theory also implies both a skilful composer and an experienced and well-formed listener, which may be ideal but does not exhaust the range of musical experience and meaning. As a consequence, the issues involved in listening to music from another culture, with the changes in expectation and fulfillment this would cause, are only summarily addressed, in the alleged "meaningless" of music taken from a style that is unfamiliar to the listener, and therefore incapable of provoking emotional expectation or resolved suspense.[48]

However, despite these limitations, Meyer's merit is undisputed, having sought directly to face the issue of meaning and affect in music. If Meyer's aim was to "establish and explain the general causes and conditions for the affective aesthetic response to music,"[49] his answer is expressed in terms of both music and the mind: there is "a direct interaction between a series of musical stimuli and an individual who understands the style of the work being heard."[50]

> [According to Meyer] the ability of music to evoke meaning is facilitated through a conformity between the structures of music and the structures of the human mind.[51]

---

46. Ibid., 85.
47. Meyer, *Emotion and Meaning*, 31.
48. Cf. ibid., 35.
49. Ibid., 197.
50. Ibid., 256.

51. Shepherd and Wicke, *Music and Cultural Theory*, 12. This book constitutes a lucid attempt to bring together musicology and cultural studies, feeding the results of the first into the second.

In this aspect, Meyer's position points in the same direction as Langer, when she talks about how "the 'inner life' has formal properties similar to those of music,"[52] although Langer's perspective is philosophical whereas Meyer's is musicological. Both accentuate an intrinsic affinity between human apprehension or thought processes and musical symbolism.

Alan P. Merriam

An interesting and complementary theory can be found in ethnomusicologist Alan P. Merriam (1923–80), who presents what could be called an anthropological approach to musical meaning, involving three analytical levels: conceptualization about music, behavior in relation to music, and the sound of music. He began referring to his research as "music in culture,"[53] later amending it to "music *as* culture,"[54] in recognition of how musical meaning works and interacts in a complex way with how we make sense of our lives: "Music is an element in a culture."[55] Just as human life is cultural (formed in a culture and formative of culture), so music cannot be understood without attention to the context in which it is born and heard, as well as how it interacts with our apprehension of meaning at other levels. Merriam, therefore, accentuates the functions and uses of music as one semiotic within other semiotic and cultural discourses. He proposes ten major functions overall, including liturgical, emotional expression, communication and physical response.[56]

This recognition of the difference and complementary nature of music as a semiotic system, whose meaning interacts in a complex way with the world around us, comes close to areas of reflection this book will present more fully in chapter 3. Music, in the moment of its being put to use, enters into relationship with the domain in which it is used, at many levels. For example, we often relate the meaning of a given piece of music with the situation we were living when we heard

52. Langer, *Philosophy in a New Key*, 227–28.
53. Merriam, *Anthropology of Music*, 247.
54. The parallel with our own understanding of music *as* theology is clear.
55. Cf. Merriam, "Definitions of 'Comparative Musicology' and 'Ethnomusicology.'" Quotations from 202 and 204.
56. Merriam, *Anthropology of Music*, 219–27, quoted in Speelman, *Generation of Meaning*, 57.

it for the same time, which may have nothing to do with what the composer intended the music to mean, or with the nature of the music itself. The very freedom of music from referential meaning intrinsic to linguistic communication allows this happen. And yet, from the moment one recognizes that music forms part of a cultural semiotic system and that it contracts relations with other extra-musical semiotics, the meaning emerging is a form of referential or designative meaning, as it points beyond itself to something else.[57]

Placed alongside the work of an ethnomusicologist who deals with the area of music in culture, it is not hard to perceive the shortcomings of the previous line of research in limiting itself to the psychological implications and effects of music. Can we really isolate a piece of music from its surrounding context and understand its meaning, without taking into account both how and why it came into being as well as how it is received? Music is born in and of a specific culture and therefore that culture conditions its reception. Meyer's explanation does not take into account *why* musical processes and subjective processes interact meaningfully—to do so implies taking into account the social mediations in which they are imbedded. The omission is significant and has the consequence of allowing the analysis and mode of evaluation of a specific style music to be offered as comprehensive and applicable to all (leading once again in this case, to the evaluation of "classical" music, which was the main object of this form of analysis, as superior). This is the concern of musicologists such as John Shepherd and Peter Wicke, who bring together the analysis of culture and music. Although they value the persuasive analyses offered by Meyer, who has certainly advanced the structural analysis of music, they criticize him for not taking into account context (social ecology) in the meaning of music: individual appreciation of music is not autonomous.[58] Our musical "ears" are formed in a certain musical sensibility, be it through explicit musical formation, or mere social exposure. For this reason, "understanding" music outside one's own cultural environment cannot be taken for granted. It is this awareness that forms the basis for dedicating chapter 2 of this book to the hermeneutical dimensions of musical meaning.

---

57. Cf. Speelman, *Generation of Meaning*, 57–58.
58. Cf. Shepherd and Wicke, *Music and Cultural Theory*, 12–16.

Charles Seeger

> *How do you look at music from the inside?*
> *You know! That is what the musician does-in making music.*
> *Strictly speaking, you don't look; you just make music.*
>
> —Charles Seeger[59]

Charles Seeger (1886–1979) was a musicologist, composer, and teacher born in Mexico City who lived and taught in various parts of the United States. He was a pioneer in musicology, being the first professor to teach the subject in the States, in Berkeley,[60] and played a unique and central role in the beginnings of ethnomusicology, tying musicology to other disciplines and domains of culture. One of his main concerns was that of building the foundations of musicology, as he was worried by the lack of explicit reflection on its aims and methods. The amplitude of vision in his approach is eye-opening:

> They [articles on musicology] don't inquire into or speak of the need to inquire into the foundations of the study—that is, its necessary assumptions—nor do they treat or speak of the need to treat of its aims and methods beyond service to the routine pursuit of a profession. . . . Musicology is presented, therefore, as a relatively isolated study . . . an ongoing professional activity the vast majority of whose adepts are strongly disinclined to stop and ask what their initial assumptions are, on what ground they are travelling, where they are going, and why they are cultivating it.[61]

Are there not echoes in this quotation of similar concerns in the areas of theology and philosophy? Certainly Lonergan was convinced that unawareness of the underlying philosophical positions lead to conflicting stances in areas of theological truth, and that the need to re-think method in theological research was an indispensable means

---

59. C. Seeger, "Toward a Unitary Field Theory," 119.

60. The two books that gather his thought and research over the years are: C. Seeger, *Studies in Musicology, 1935–1975*, and *Studies in Musicology II, 1929–1979*. An interesting and in depth presentation of his work can be found in Greer, *Question of Balance*, in particular chapter 4, on "Seeger's Theory of Music Criticism," and chapter 7, on "Seeger's Vision of Musicology."

61. Seeger, "Toward a Unitary Field Theory," 110–11. This article presents Seeger's ideal vision of musicology, or what he called "unified field theory."

of coming to any clarity with regard to content. One of my own growing convictions (re-enforced by the process of research of this study) is that any serious attempt at intellectual reflection and collaboration implies both that the researcher be very aware of their own foundations, context, aims, and methodology, and that they clarify them for their reader or interlocutor. In my understanding, this forms part of what Lonergan calls self-appropriation and intellectual conversion.[62]

The introduction of this book underlined the tendency within theological discourse on music to underestimate or even overlook completely the complications involved in using verbal language to "describe" non-verbal communication, such as music. With the challenging aim of laying foundations for musicology, Seeger focuses on musicology as speech about music, and constantly averts musicologists of the need to be aware of the fact that speech about music is at the core of musicology, and it is dangerous not to be aware of the complexity involved in moving between these two essentially different forms of human communication. In line with this, he creates an explicit theory around the notion that different musics of the world should be treated somewhat like language systems, rather than as a universal language.[63] His work is exceptional, for the breadth and foundational nature of his thought, and for that reason I shall briefly present an overview of the areas he covers and the issues he seeks to address, amongst which three are of particular importance:

i. He differentiates speech discourse from musical discourse, affirming that musicology is speech about music, and that this is the case due to what he calls the "lingocentric" predicament of human existence, which is "a universal predicament of the use of speech."[64] There are different ways of making and transmitting meaning. "Music 'meaning'" is in the sound and the actual arrangement of it presented by the music makers, whereas speech meaning is in what the sound stands for, represents and symbolizes."[65] Although he does not affirm that one is superior to the other, he does, however, criticize an over-trusting of

---

62. It is an aspect that Jean-Jacques Nattiez gives much importance to, as we shall see in chapter 2.

63. Cf. Nettl, *Ethnomusicology*, 44–45.

64. Seeger, "Toward a Unitary Field Theory," 103.

65. Ibid.," 112.

speech communication above other forms. He also gives great importance to the musician's implicit "understanding" of that which is music, which he refers to as knowing music "from within":

> [T]he speech account of music value is not to be confused with the music value as the musician may know it—we must not confuse the word with what it stands for.[66]

ii. He identifies in music and musicology the possibility of a critique or a corrective of speech. In the history of communication, logical discourse, with its quest for distinction and problem solving, has been overdeveloped, and other forms of human communication neglected. Music, which, according to Seeger, can affirm but cannot deny, "is presentational, embodied, semiotic, but not symbolic. Music does not "mean" what is not music; it identifies with it . . . it does not say so; it does so."[67] Music, in that sense, complements and corrects verbal speech. This echoes my own intuition on calling the book music "as" and not simply "in" theological discourse. Theology is so imbedded in verbal discourse that it becomes difficult to imagine it "being" in any other form, and yet would it not be a question of recognizing the horizon we are working within and pushing its frontiers further?

iii. He goes a step further, situating musicology within a broad theory of reality, philosophy and knowledge. He identifies six overlapping "worldviews" or "universes"; that is to say, six universes of perception that intertwine in our apprehension:

- the physical universe;
- the speech universe (that which our language gives us access to), which he describes as representational, symbolic, semantic;
- the musical universe, which is presentational, embodied, semiotic but not symbolic;[68]

---

66. Ibid., 119.
67. Ibid., 109.
68. In this sense, with regard to the debated question of whether music is a symbolic system, Seeger considers instead that it is semiotic one. We will clarify our own understanding of this term in chapters 2 and 3.

- the universe of each individual: experiential, solipsistic, aesthetic;
- the cultural world we are shaped in, which is axiological, consensual and valual; and
- the world of our values and priorities.

In this way he seeks to situate musicology within the wider "unitary field" of knowledge, postulating that its place would be within a larger philosophical understanding—one that recognizes and leaves room for an open and integral form of human knowing that integrates feeling and corporeality, rather than just the head, or mind. Perceived in this light, Seeger would have hoped in the capacity of music to correct the current scientific crisis by integrating value and fact, rather than opposing them. An ambitious project indeed, for the musicological endeavor!

One other aspect of his thought that is worth mentioning here and that we will revisit later in this chapter concerns the dynamics involved in writing music down, or notation. The context of this point is that of research into and analysis of musics from cultures which do not use the European method of notation.[69] One of the first steps in ethnomusicological studies in their attempt to analyze and comprehend the diversity of the music they came across was to attempt to notate music which had not been written before and that did not follow the same rules as Western music. Seeger identifies two modes or forms of notation, which he differentiates according to their intention, calling them "prescriptive" and "descriptive," respectively. The former is intended for the performer, to provide a sort of blueprint or guide as to how the music "should" be played, the latter is "intended" for the music itself, to record or describe that which in sound has occurred, in order to be able to analyze it. Despite thinking that the distinction is not quite that clear-cut, Bruno Nettl explains these terms saying that they could also be described as notation for performance and notation for analysis, in that the former "prescribes," at least to a certain extent, how the music should be played, in accordance perhaps with its composition or the expectation of its listeners, and the latter limits itself to describing

---

69. It is also worthwhile remembering that in Europe, music only began to be written down in the ninth century, with Gregorian chant, and that the beginnings of our current form of musical notation is attributed to Guido d'Arezzo, an Italian Benedictine monk of the eleventh century, and its generalized use was gradual.

what is taking place in sound in the music played. He refers to them as the *emic* versus the *etic* approach, relating them to the linguistics areas of phonemics and phonetics. The former is accomplished from the "insider's" position, the latter from that of the "outsider." The former seeks the systems apparent in language, whereas the latter is a detailed analysis of the sounds, without the interpretation implied in phonemics.[70] Awareness of these differences helps those of us active in making and playing music to understand *how* we receive and pass on the music we receive and/ or compose.

These reflections bring to the fore two important issues with regard to our theme, which we will deal with later. The first is to note the importance of oral versus written music. In the quest to understand music, we are faced with two steps: that of dealing with "speech discourse about music" to use Seeger's terminology, and that of writing music down, albeit in musical notation: what importance does it have? What are its limitations and consequences? This becomes especially relevant if we recognize that there seems to be a sort of return to a form of oral transmission in musical composition and expression in contemporary music. Although the heritage of musical history undoubtedly underlies their music, many contemporary musicians and bands never attempt to notate the music they write, and arrange it based on musical improvisation or 'jamming sessions." The second issue opens the door to the problem of interpretation and hermeneutics. Prescriptive and descriptive notation are implicitly understood to be done by the "insider" and the "outsider," respectively, of a given musical culture. The former offers the performer what he or she needs to know in order to play, presuming (inside) knowledge of style, and the latter offers a detailed description for someone who does not. The assumption is that only someone who knows the expectations of a certain piece or style of music can write down how it could or should be played. And yet, what about later versions of a given piece of music that become more popular or well known than the original? What about the changes in style over time? Are they automatically wrong? And could it be said that only someone from "outside" a given culture can hear or describe given aspects of a piece of music? What about the implicit understanding and description of that music by its composer? These questions are at the heart of the research of Jean Jacques Nattiez,

---

70. Cf. Nettl, *Ethnomusicology*, 69.

whose thought we look at in the following chapter. Far from being theoretical, they are at the core of many discussions on hearing and assessing music in church circles, and I would hope that our becoming conscious of the standpoint we take could facilitate clarity and understanding in our discussions.

With regard to the area of ethnomusicology, Seeger highlighted the limitations and misunderstandings inherent in its title, lamenting the lack of an ethnomusicological approach to European music, as one whole. He linked this failing with the obsession or over-emphasis of American musicological research on "the fine art of European music," claiming that maturity in the study of music would imply overcoming these two failings. He also predicted that the borderline between fine art composition and popular music would be broken down in time, seeing as he did the growing strength of the latter and its trend in borrowing from elite concert repertoires. It would appear that he was right.

Bruno Nettl

Let us enter more deeply into the world of ethnomusicology, with one of its most well-known representatives. Bruno Nettl is an active musicologist and ethnomusicologist, born in Czechoslovakia, who lived and taught for many years in the United States, in Illinois. He is most known for his work in ethnomusicology, having specialized in fieldwork and research on the music of the North American Blackfoot Indians.[71] Beyond that specific area, his writings, however, offer an impressive presentation of the history and main areas of research of the discipline of ethnomusicology.[72] Some of the elements essential to ethnomusicology as defined by Nettl shed considerable light on our own area of research, and as far as I am aware, Catholic theology has neglected to integrate many of these questions and findings into its own reflection on music.

Nettl situates the beginnings of ethnomusicology, along with historical musicology, in the 1880s, with two scholars: Carl Stumpf and

---

71. Cf. Nettl, *Blackfoot Musical Thought*.

72. Cf. Nettl, *Theory and Method in Ethnomusicology* (1964), *Folk and Traditional Music of the Western Continents* (1973), *The Study of Ethnomusicology* (1983). This last book is his most well known.

Alexander J. Ellis.[73] In its process of development, it has dealt mainly with three kinds of music: the music of nonliterate (or preliterate/primitive/tribal, depending on the terminology used) societies, in which no system of reading or writing in their own language has been developed; the music of the Asian and north African high cultures, who have a long and complex history of music, albeit without such a complicated notation system as European music; and folk music (although not accepted by all musicologists): the music of oral tradition in areas dominated by high cultures. It is, however, difficult to define the field, and entire articles have been written simply on the definitions of ethnomusicology,[74] described from the different standpoints of the material they study, the activity they involve and the ultimate goals they have. It is a field still in the process of identifying its own intellectual, methodological and theoretical issues. Nettl's own attempt at defining or explaining ethnomusicology is the following:

> We can summarize the consensus in stating that ethnomusicology is, in fact as well as theory, the field which pursues knowledge of the world's music, with emphasis on that music outside the researcher's own music and culture, from a descriptive and comparative viewpoint.[75]

This definition clearly reveals one of the underlying creeds or convictions of ethnomusicology, which directly challenges any assumption of cultural superiority or classicist appreciation of a particular style of music: all music is to be received and studied on its own terms, and considered as equally valid and valuable. The invitation to an almost impossible neutrality is formidable:

> Needless to say, in all approaches, objectivity, avoidance of value judgments based on the investigators own cultural background, and the acceptance of music as a part of culture are essential.[76]

---

73. Cf. Stumpf, "Lieder der Bellakula-Indianer"; Ellis, "On the Musical Scales of Various Nations." Both writings are an important exercise in a specific area of fieldwork and comparative research.

74. Cf. for example, Merriam, "Definitions of 'Comparative Musicology' and 'Ethnomusicology,'" in which he identifies over forty.

75. Nettl, *Theory and Method in Ethnomusicology*, 11.

76. Ibid.

> Fundamentally, ethnomusicologists must be relativists.[77]
>
> [T]hey regard all musics as equal. Each music . . . is equally an expression of culture.[78]

I read this attitude as analogue to the paradigm shift Lonergan invites us to when calling to recognize that theology can no longer continue to reflect and express itself solely in reference to Western European culture, as if it were the only one existent or implicitly superior to others (an approach he calls "classicist") in order to become pluralist in its understanding and expression.[79]

The context that music is born in and listened to must be taken into account in seeking to receive and comprehend its meaning and function. In reflecting on studying music as a part of culture, Nettl identifies three possible stands: music in its cultural context (standard musicology, yet with a call to more awareness of context) the study of music in culture, which applies a more unitary role to music (involving history and ethnography); and music as culture, in the sense of music as both expression of culture and instrumental in influencing it (which is an anthropological specialty).[80] The first is the most straightforward, meaning that in the moment that one studies music, one needs to take into account the context in which it is born and played or performed. The second implies a theory of culture, and is therefore more complex. The third adds to this the double awareness that culture affects music and music can affect and "create" culture. From this standpoint it is understandable that Nettl underlines the usefulness of ethnomusicology both to musicology (albeit simply, via comparison, in understanding Western musical styles) and to cultural anthropology.[81] In practice, ethnomusicologists have ended up being

---

77. Nettl, *Ethnomusicology*, 10. The term "cultural relativity," and specifically "musical relativity," is to be understood in this context and in sociological writings in this sense: "One must accept the idea that different collectivities of people order and assess their music by quite different principles and that therefore one cannot say that one collectivity's music is better or worse than another's." Dasila et al., *Sociology of Music*, 16.

78. Nettl, *Ethnomusicology*, 10.

79. Cf. Lonergan, "Theology in Its New Context."

80. Cf. Nettl, *Ethnomusicology*, 131–32.

81. We are aware of the diversity of schools in this area, but to develop would exceed the limits of this book. Sufficeth to underline the link Nettl makes between the two and the importance of ethnomusicological studies in relation to the same.

considered as a cross between a "special" kind of musicologist and a "special" kind of anthropologist, studying the specific field of music of other cultures. And yet, mainstream musicology would benefit from listening more closely to the approaches and presuppositions of ethnomusicology:

> [Ethnomusicologists] have worked in an area adjacent to musicology at large and also to cultural anthropology. Musicology, defining itself as the field which involves the *scholarly* and *objective* study of music of all types and from all approaches, has actually given the lion's share of it attention to the music of Western urban civilization, the music of the European written tradition.[82]

The emphasis I have given above to the words "objective" and "scholarly" is intended to question the pretension of musicology to objectivity and scholarship, whenever its research fails to recognize its own premises and possible biases. It is interesting that Nettl identifies the lack of an ethnological approach to the music of Western culture, apart from folk music, as did Seeger. He suggests that such a study would look at:

> the role of music in culture, the problem of performance practice, those of descriptive versus prescriptive notation, the procedures and methods of describing music (which have barely been touched in Western music.) . . . [since] the historian of Western music, being a member of the culture he is studying, has not always had to be so concerned with objectivity, and the approach of the critic rather than the scholar is still felt in many of his publications.[83]

Many of the studies on popular music that have surfaced and continue to surface in the area of cultural studies and sociology take this approach, looking at performance, oral and written dynamics in music making, issues of "high" versus "low" aesthetics in the production of music, as well as popular expectation and demand.[84] The complexity of the current cultural situation due to globalization

---

82. Nettl, *Theory and Method in Ethnomusicology*, 1. Emphasis mine.

83. Ibid., 12. Seeger also thinks that ethnomusicology has overlooked taking in European music as an area of study, and that the maturity of musicological research depends on it being done. Cf. Seeger, "Toward a Unitary Field Theory," 117.

84. Cf. Frith, *Performing Rights*.

and the ever-increasing rate of racial interaction, emerges clearly in these studies on popular music. Contemporary music is plural and complex, not only due to the growing contact with the music of other cultures but because of the mixture provoked in music making as those cultures come together. One example of this kind of complexity can be found in the influence of the music of immigrant minorities in the music of the mainstream culture in which they find themselves. George Lipsitz,[85] studying various examples of threshold situations between mainstream and immigrant music, shows how given musical trends can not only manifest cultural changes, but also be a means of helping people in a time of rapid change to find their identity, through making music that combines their cultural origin and that of the mainstream ambience in which they find themselves—an eloquent example of music *as* formative of culture. He emphasizes here the need to not underestimate the power or role of creative people in the understanding of the culture and 'powers that be." In the current context, "migrant workers, immigrants and exiles take on new roles as cross-cultural interpreters and analysts."[86]

These are themes that ethnomusicology has been addressing for decades, albeit not applied to contemporary European music. Their methods and findings must be of use to us. In particular, Nettl outlines four underlying "beliefs" in the work of ethnomusicologists that help to understand their work and that offer significant light towards a balanced theological approach to music:

   i. The study of total music systems, and this in a comparative approach, i.e.: music considered typical to a culture and "owned," as such, by that culture,rather than the individual composer or idiosyncratic music type.
   ii. The study of music as a part of culture, a product of human society, and therefore of how music changes in a culture.
   iii. Research based on and nurtured by fieldwork, in a face-to-face concentrated confrontation with music makers and performance.
   iv. Research in which the ultimate aim is the study of *all* the

---

85. Cf. Lipsitz, *Dangerous Crossroads*.

86. Ibid., 5. We will revisit the significance of such an understanding when we look at how Nattiez analyses music. The figure of the "interpreter" is underestimated and limited in most musical analysis.

world's music, in extension and time.[87]

These "beliefs" or premises, especially the first one, stand in contrast with the more "modernist" view or assumption, sometimes implicit and at other times expressed, of truly good music appealing to the minority and being recognized (as a classic) only with time. The emphasis given to individual creative genius and innovation, as a result of modernity, despite its obvious positive aspects, could be said to have overshadowed other areas of musical culture, which ethnomusicology has focused on. The greatness of any composer and how he or she is received, is situated in the wider framework of their social context in which they compose. In the dynamic of creativity, there is always something given and something innovated or created.

> It is obvious that one cannot deal only with the musician's work, his concepts and techniques, but must also address the ways in which the values of a society are expressed in a people's evaluation of what is new and what is good in music.[88]

This draws our attention to contemporary, rather than past, music, and its meaning within the culture in which it is born and for the people who are playing and listening to it.

In the light of its study of music in all human cultures, ethnomusicology questions the very way in which music is, or has been, understood in Western thought. There is a difference between the "definitions" of music one will find in a dictionary and those expressed 'on the street." Nettl suggests that the emphasis most European dictionaries give to stressing tonality above any other function of music, such as rhythm or harmony, is surely culture-specific. The value of music in a society seems to be a major factor in determining the breadth of its definition of music. The widely held view of music as simply a "type of sound" is too narrow a basis of operations for acceptance by ethnomusicologists. In this regard, he integrates the aforementioned threefold description of music offered by Merriam, including concept (its importance, power, and function), behavior (musical and non-musical behavior of musicians), and sound (which we usually call music itself).[89]

---

87. Cf. Nettl, *Ethnomusicology*, 9.
88. Ibid., 35.
89. Cf. ibid., 22–23.

There are three themes Nettl deals with which are particularly pertinent to this chapter, as they present us with important elements of musical meaning: universals, musical notation and the attitude of the researcher. In brief:

Universals

We have already mentioned the theme of music as a universal language and the quest for universals. Opinions on this issue have come full circle over time: starting out with the consideration of music as a universal language, understandable by all, convictions swung to the opposite pole—as a result of the appreciation of the immense diversity of music in human cultures. This fed the view that to refer to music in this way was abominable and ethnocentric. We have, however, since the late 1960s, returned to the quest for universals. The discovery of the fascinating variety of musics available in different cultures lead to the "liberation" of these musics from the "dictatorship" of Western primacy, slowly leading to reflection on the underlying similarities. Parallel journeys can be found in other areas of study, such as mythology or the linguistic capacity of the human person. The quest for universals in music is linked in ethnomusicology with the study of its origins. The underlying logic is simple: in the measure that we discover universals in musical praxis—aspects that *all* humans do with their music, if they are indeed so ubiquitous among the far-flung peoples of the world then it makes sense for us to believe that "it has always been so."[90] For example: "the close connection of dance with music everywhere makes the idea of rhythm and physical movement as generative forces of music tentatively possible."[91] The widespread use of song in ritual suggests the birth of music as a mode of communicating with the supernatural. The refusal to consider music a universal language leads us to the theme of studying music as a non-universal language, that is to say, a form of communicating specific to different cultures. As we have seen above, Charles Seeger is indeed the author who deals with this more comprehensively, and refers to it as using "the speech mode of communication" for discourse about music. Nettl gathers

---

90. The definition of exactly how one understands and defines a "universal" is a still debated one in ethnomusicology.

91. Ibid., 164–65.

the questions around this theme in the following paragraph, which is worth quoting in full:

> Can one establish a way of viewing music that will work for all imaginable musics? Is description necessary or can music not somehow speak for itself? What, indeed, is the difference between analysis and description? Should there be a single procedure for analyzing music, a sort of paradigm of ethnomusicology? Or can one safely rely on the characteristics of each music to guide one, or on the way in which a society conceives of its own musical structure? Or again, should one act the scientist, able to produce replicable statements, or *should analysis be much more a matter of personal interpretation*?[92]

Oral versus Written Notation

The theme of oral music and written music is crucial for ethnomusicological work. Ethnomusicology in general re-evaluates oral composition and improvisation as complementary elements of musical creativity, alongside written music according to Western notation. Many forms of world music have been passed on orally and either do not have any form of written transcription, or have a form of notation that is very different from Western notation. For this reason, transcribing music in order to understand it has been considered one of the main tasks and quasi-proof of an ethnomusicologist's expertise. We already touched on the hermeneutical issues surrounding notation, but there is another one relevant to our theme: is writing music down an adequate way of dealing with it? Are there not essential difficulties created by that process? Seeger thinks there are: "A hazard of writing music lies in an assumption that the full auditory parameter of music is or can be represented by a partial visual parameter."[93] This is important for our theme from the moment in which popular contemporary music, very often, is not written down in the form of musical notation which musicological studies are accustomed to. Does this make it less "professional" or less valuable, from a musical point of view? It certainly implies that evaluation and understanding cannot be addressed solely by means of transcription and study of that writ-

---

92. Ibid., 83. Emphasis mine, as I wish to highlight how important the theme of interpretation is in this field, an area we shall look at in chapter 2.

93. C. Seeger, "Prescriptive and Descriptive Music Writing," 168.

ten form. But then one could ask the question of whether that would be the case with any kind of music: why is there the assumption that one can only study it once it is written down?[94] My own opinion is that if we are to integrate music fully within theological aesthetics as a form of theological praxis, then the act of listening to music, and not simply training people to be experts in writing it down or reading it, must be part of that process. In the same way that one would consider talking about visual art without ever contemplating a painting incomplete, so "writing down music" is a specialized form of listening to, and understanding music, which cannot exhaust the process. Even if a good musician can "hear" the music in his or her head as they write or compose, listening to the music itself has to add something to the experience. We will come back to this theme in chapter 4 on epistemology.

Hermeneutics—"the Researcher and Empathy"

Coming back to the theme of who is qualified to study the music of a particular culture, the centrality of fieldwork in ethnomusicology opens interesting points of reflection. Good fieldwork is vital to ethnomusicology.[95] The assumption is that analysis and discernment imply personal experience, empathy and openness as prerequisites of knowledge. It is significant that in this context, the notion is linked by Nettl with issues of hermeneutics and the relationship between researchers and the people or cultures they study. Researchers are meant to be "objective" and yet enter into a meaningful relationship with the culture being studied.

> Although they may wish to study their subject dispassionately, they are in the end often unable to avoid the results of extended contact with humans and their works in a foreign country.[96]

Is that "right" or "wrong"? In the beginning of this discipline, it was always someone from outside any given culture that studied their music, and yet soon afterwards researchers from non-Western countries became accepted experts in the research of their own musics. And who is the most adequate person to study the music of a given culture—the

---

94. Cf. Nettl, *Ethnomusicology*, 65–66.
95. Cf. ibid., 3–4.
96. Ibid., 10.

insider, who understands the *emic* of that musical language, or the outsider who can describe without bias the *etic* of each sound? Could it not be, as with all other areas of self-understanding and knowledge, that we need a healthy dose of both: internal perception and external comparison and complementation? A healthy disposition to come to know any music both on its own terms and in relation to other types is perhaps the only wise way of moving forward in the current plural and global world we find ourselves in. It also interesting that an experience of fieldwork is valued in ethnomusicologists, not just because of or by the quality of the data collected for study, but because of what the contact with a "strange" culture achieves in the researcher, both to the benefit of his or her own research, as well as that of other researchers or students who will learn from that approach and openness. It appears that someone who has been able to open to and appreciate a different kind of music will be better able to teach another person to do the same, and to deal with the difficulties that arise in doing so. The parallels with many areas of Christian music in the universal church are obvious, offering keys which would aid in moving forward towards greater understanding and discernment.

John Anthony Randall Blacking

> In a world such as ours . . . it is necessary to understand
> why a madrigal by Gesualdo or a Bach Passion,
> a sitar melody from India or a song from Africa,
> Berg's Wozzek of Britten's War Requiem,
> a Balinese gamelan or a Cantonese opera,
> or a symphony by Mozart, Beethoven, of Mahler,
> may be profoundly necessary for human survival.
>
> —John Blacking[97]

The last person I will present briefly is John Anthony Randall Blacking (1928–90). Blacking was born in Surrey, Britain, educated in Salisbury and Cambridge, lived and worked in Malaysia for a short period, and in South Africa for many years. If Nettl emphasized as essential to the identity of the ethnomusicologist having done fieldwork outside his or her own culture, in Blacking we see this ethos in action. His time

97. Blacking, *How Musical Is Man?*, 116.

of getting to know from within the culture and music of the Venda people in South Africa lays the foundation for his thought and teaching with regard to music, as he himself admits:

> the Venda of South Africa . . . broke down some of my prejudices. They introduced me to a new world of musical experience and to a deeper understanding of my 'own music.'[98]

He became well known on his return to Europe for his work at Queen's University, Belfast, where he founded the Department of Ethnomusicology (although he himself taught anthropology). He also founded the ESEM (European Seminar in Ethnomusicology). His premature death at the age of sixty-two left us with a rich but unfinished framework of thought, as we shall see, starting with a reflection on music inspired by his life and work in South Africa, moving towards

> a view of ethnomusicology as a synthetic social science drawing on linguistics, cognitive structuralism, psychology, philosophy, and biology, as well as musicology and social anthropology. His writings . . . were remarkable for their attempt to form a synthesis which had the power to explain why people make music, and what this tells us about the innate dispositions of the human species.[99]

I present Blacking's thought last as I think his way of understanding the analysis of music is a helpful bridge to the two main authors I draw from in chapters 2 and 3: the hermeneutical approach of Jean-Jacques Nattiez and Willem Speeleman's musical semiotics. Blacking insisted on an anthropological approach to music, as did Merriam, although Blacking felt the former had not gone far enough in bringing social and musical analysis together. Describing music as "humanly organized sound," he believed that musical analysis implied looking at more than its "sounds." Indeed, seeking to understand a music solely based on its sonic structure, according to Blacking, may be the reason for so many differing interpretations of one melody or piece of music, all of them laying claim to be the authentic one:

---

98. Ibid., vi.
99. Byron, " Ethnomusicology of John Blacking," 15.

This procedure is very common in analyses of European music and may be one of the reasons why musical journals are so full of contradictory explanations of the same music.[100]

Blacking called for a "context-sensitive analysis,"[101] which would recognize the importance of the context from which music is born and in which it is lived and understood. He was deeply critical of Western musicology's division between "art" and "folk" music, for its implicit and explicit elitism, as well as its pretension to objectivity, precisely for that reason:

> Paradoxically, their laudable aim to be context-free and objective fails precisely because they minimize their importance of cultural experience in the selection and development of sensory capacities.[102]

Indeed, he seems to epitomize the essence of that which in ethnomusicology stands in contrast with "classic" Western musicology. Stravinsky's famous declaration that "music means nothing outside itself"[103] finds its direct opposite in Blacking, for whom music conveys everything but itself.[104] And yet they are both seeking to understand why music is vital in human life, that is to say, its meaning. However, the paradigm or horizon of comprehension in which they situate themselves is different. Albeit a simplification, I suggest Blacking's is wider or more universal. For this reason, Blacking thought that musicological studies had a lot to learn from the research and advances in ethnomusicology:

> Ethnomusicology has the power to create a revolution in the world of music and music education, if it follows the implications of its discoveries and develops a method, and not merely an area, of study . . . it could pioneer new ways of analyzing music and music history.[105]

His specific quest was for what he called a unitary method of musical analysis, which could be applied to all music, taking into ac-

---

100. Blacking, *How Musical Is Man?*, 93.
101. Cf. Blacking, "Problem of Musical Description," 69.
102. Blacking, *How Musical Is Man?*, 19.
103. Cf. Stravinsky, *Poetics of Music*, 76.
104. Byron, "Ethnomusicology of John Blacking," 26.
105. Blacking, *How Musical Is Man?*, 4.

count and explaining sound itself and musical behavior as well. He saw this as one that would recognize and identify the link between musical structure and its function in cultural behavior, including both biological and sociological elements:

> Functional analyses of musical structure cannot be detached from structural analyses of its social function: the function of the tones in relation to each other cannot be explained adequately as part of a closed system without reference to the structures of the sociocultural system of which the musical system is a part, and to the biological system to which all music makers belong.[106]

Once again we are dealing with the balance between the absolutist and referential dimensions of musical meaning. Music has to do with a certain structural way of thinking about the world. The structure of music tells us much about how human beings organize themselves. That is why, he says, changes in musical style have generally been reflections of changes in society,[107] because music is an expression of the reality that it is born of. Therefore to approach music in isolation from the context in which it was born and within which it is played, sung or/and understood is unintelligent or short-sighted. In this respect we shall see a clear parallel with the structure of musical analysis that Nattiez offers us.

One final point I would highlight of Blacking's thought that is of interest in our own theological stance, developed from chapter 3 onwards, is his emphasis on corporality in relation to cross-cultural meaning in music. If music is so culturally conditioned, both in its making and in its reception, he asks, can there be any cross-cultural communication through music? And if so, how do we explain it? He does so referring to one of the notions of linguistics, the differentiation between deep and surface structures, relating them to the experience of corporality in music. Although skeptical about the possibility of comparison between music and verbal speech, he sees a possible future to comparative studies, borrowing the notions of "surface structures" and "deep structures" from linguistics.[108] He says that "many, if not all, of music's essential processes can be found in the constitution

---

106. Ibid., 30–31.
107. Cf. ibid., 76.
108. Cf. Nettl, *Ethnomusicology*, 64.

of the human body and in patterns of interaction of human bodies in society,"¹⁰⁹ and that at the level of deep structures in music there are "elements that are common to the [human] psyche, although they may not appear in the surface structures."¹¹⁰ He suggests the possibility of cross-cultural understanding through a common experience of corporality and empathy through our bodies:

> Perhaps there is a hope of cross-cultural understanding after all. I do not say that we can experience exactly the same thoughts associated with bodily experience; but to feel with the body is probably as close as anyone can ever get to resonating with another person.¹¹¹

The essentially corporal nature of music is emphasized by Speelman, the musicologist I will move to shortly, and embodiment is central to the theological framework we will introduce in chapters 4–6. Both Oliver Davies and Rosemary Haughton underline the need to "regain" a solid and integrated vision of our corporality in theological thought. Let us at this stage simply note that at times our quest for verbal or linguistic understanding relegates bodily empathy and corporality to an inferior level that does not do justice to the Christian vision. The symbolism of music is corporal and relational. Blacking, over his years of research, came to be aware of this. In researching music, he also studied the properties of human intersubjectivity: how music works as a medium of communication between people, and how it brings them together. He saw music as a kind of language that is culturally rooted and socially enacted, whose purpose is to convey meanings. It is a special kind of language, however, for it is only partly capable of conscious expression: music is also *felt* as well as made and heard: it induces and invokes the participation of the whole person, body and soul, not just the processes of intellectual reason.¹¹²

Perhaps it is for this reason that he thought it could be of essential use in one of the more basic tasks each human person faces: that of learning to love! He makes a very interesting if surprising link between how all our behavior is culturally learned, except for the dynamic of loving, in which each generation starts from zero. In this,

109. Blacking, *How Musical Is Man?*, vii.
110. Ibid., 109.
111. Ibid., 111.
112. Byron, "Ethnomusicology of John Blacking," 1.

music, he says, can help. Referring to Kierkegaard's book on *Fear and Trembling*, which reflects on how in being human, in learning to love, each generation has to start from scratch, he says: "The hard task is to love, and music is a skill that prepares man for this most difficult task."[113] Once again, during this book we will reflect on how the nature of music can help us to re-understand or re-interpret both our understanding of reality, of love, and of God.

Insights and Relevance of their Contribution for a Theological Comprehension of Music

After this overview of some of the authors from the fields of musicology and ethnomusicology, many "doors" and "windows" have been opened; it is impossible to explore all of them. And yet open doors and windows let the light in, and perhaps it is not a question of using them all so much as allowing them open and illuminate our minds, increasing our awareness of just how rich and complex our theme is, and how necessary it is to take into consideration and value its different aspects. It is important to notice how much more advanced this field is in integrating thought on culture and the plurality of cultures in the world than many Christian or theological writings concerning music.

To conclude this chapter on meaning in music, let us highlight the themes that have emerged as constants, and are distinguishing between themes that have emerged in Europe-based musicology studies and those from ethnomusicology, albeit recognizing certain overlap.

Musicology[114]

Musical Meaning and Emotion

This seems to be the theme that has polarized thought on music for decades: the link between music and human feeling, and how it can

---

113. Blacking, *How Musical Is Man?*, 103.

114. Writings on music in philosophy and theology are on the increase. By way of example, cf. *Philosophie de la pusique* (*Philosophy of Music*), Revue Internationale de Philosophie 60/238 (2006), and *Journal for the Scientific Study of Religion* 45/4 (2006), both of which gather a series of interesting articles on the current philosophical issues with regard to music. From the perspective of spiritual theology, and integrating themes of the philosophy of music and its role in culture, cf. *La Musique*, Christus 223 (2009).

be articulated. The two main opposing positions are those mentioned above and described as Formalism and Expressionism. The former identifies the importance and value of music in its structure and overall harmony. The latter accentuates the importance and value of music in its capacity of expression, understood mainly as emotional rather than cognitive or rational. The current debate on what is called "concatenationism" versus "architectonicism" has echoes of the same underlying issues, since the former considers the key source of musical appreciation to be found in following the flow of music, rather than in understanding it conceptually, in contrast with those who would place its appreciation in the architectonical perception of the piece as a whole, which would resemble a more formalist stance.[115]

Imagination and Emotions

The theme of the emotions unfolds into complex reflections on the nature of musical expression of emotion, such as the relationship between musical expression of emotion, the imagination and musical value; the possibility of emotional arousal in music; potential rewards of emotional involvement with music; the relationship between the expression of emotion in music with expression of emotion in the composer or/and the performer (interpreter), and if music can express states of minds or qualities.[116]

The Metaphysics of Music

There are various themes that come under this heading, such as what *is* music, its origins, whether it is a human creation or an element of the natural world, and the relationship of music with time and temporality.[117] With regard to the origins of music, one of the underlying philosophical questions is whether music is a human creation, born of the human mind or way of interaction, or whether it is born of the natural world, essentially similar and in continuation with, for ex-

---

115. This issue is an ongoing and well-documented debate between Jerrold Levinson and Peter Kivy. Cf. Levinson, "Concatenationism, Architectonicism"; and Benjamin, "Music through a Narrow Aperture."

116. Cf. Trivedi, "Imagination, Music, and the Emotions."

117. The work of theologian Jeremy Begbie focuses on this aspect of musical meaning, as we shall see in chapter 5.

ample, the sounds of creation and the animal world, such as birdsong. If music is a creation of the human mind, then it is cultural, and affected by the cultural conditionings of all other human activities and modes of communication. We have no proof of the origins of music, but some theories place it in the communication between mother and child, which is prosodic (or intuitive) in nature, rather than syntactical, or structured.[118] Others talk of the existence of an undifferentiated form of communication before speech and music,[119] and still others postulate music as prior to verbal communication.[120] In any case, despite some hypotheses comparing and linking birdsong to human music making, there appears to be more evidence supporting the intrinsically human, and therefore culturally conditioned character of music making: "Music, in particular, is an infallible indicator of human presence since music, properly speaking, is a human creation that does not otherwise occur in nature."[121]

Creativity as Discovery or as a Process of Composition

Creativity as discovery favors a platonic understanding of the universe and being, whereas emphasizing the process involved in composition highlights the positive nature of human freedom and collaboration with God. I have found that the underlying philosophy of each Christian theology profoundly affects the ensuing conclusions in this area. Various books and even ecumenical conferences on the themes of beauty, music, and revelation through music tend to draw conclusions from the way they understand human and divine interaction in creation and redemption, as well as their comprehension of truth, human and divine.[122] This is linked with the theme of creation and improvisation, and how we draw the line between the two.

---

118. Linguistic analysts differentiate between prosodic and syntactic elements of human language (i.e., stress, pitch, volume, emphasis, etc., as opposed to grammatical structure and literal meaning).

119. For example, Bruno Nettl, who proposes three stages in the development of music: undifferentiated communication, followed by differentiation between language and music, with music still in a highly elementary stage, and finally differentiation between various musical styles. Cf. Nettl, *Primitive Culture*, 136–37.

120. Cf. Steiner, *Real Presences*, 181–82.

121. Zuckerkandl, *Sound and Symbol*, 2:15.

122. For example, Best, *Music through the Eyes of Faith*. The book asks all the right questions, and its pastoral and musical sensitivity is remarkable, but from the

Interpretation and Performance

What is it that constitutes good music, and how do phenomena such as electronic recording and private listening to music as opposed to public concerts affect musical apprehension?[123] What is the role of the performer and how can one assess the validity of each interpretation?[124]

Music and Contextual Meaning

Here the aforementioned dichotomy between an absolutist position and a referentialist one continues, with the ever growing awareness of the influence of context on music and that of music on its surrounding environment, in the light of cultural and sociological studies.[125] If, as mentioned above, music is a specifically human invention or phenomenon, then it is essentially culturally conditioned, and has potential, in turn, to affect and influence cultural development.

The Universal or Transcultural Nature of Music

Can we identify universal elements present in music that offer keys to the intelligibility of our common human nature? The affirmation of music as a universal language on one level, "makes sense" in that music is an intrinsic part of all human life. However, as a definition, it is inaccurate. One cannot assume that there are specific types or traits of music that are universally recognizable. This leads necessarily to the issue of the understanding of diverse musical traditions and how we approach them.[126] There are writers and musicians who assume that the Western tonal system has universal validity, and yet studies in ethnomusicology and scientific studies on the nature and measurable vibrations involved in sound and music challenge this assumption. The tonic scale that our ear is used to and that we tend to call "universal" or based on natural laws, is learned. "The harmonic series is certainly a universal, since it is based on invariant acoustic phenomenon which can be mathematically described and measured,"

Catholic perspective, there is too much separation between human and divine action.

123. Cf. Frith, *Performing Rights*, 203–21.

124. Cf. Thom, "Towards a Broad Understanding," especially 402–7; and Predelli, "Platonism in Music."

125. By way of example, cf. Lynch, "Role of Popular Music," 486.

126. Cf. Higgins, "Cognitive and Appreciative Import."

but what is that harmonic series? We are inclined to think it is the triad—major and minor—because our ears are used to this, but in actual fact the third is only the fifth overtone to any base note, and even then it is not the major tone we are used to, which is slightly sharper than a pure third.[127] In Western music, we are used to relating a minor third to "sad" or more thoughtful music, and the major third to music reflecting happy states of mind, but evidence seems to point towards this being a culturally conditioned preference. How seriously do we take the cultural dimension of human existence? And where do we focus in order to understand if there is some universal dimension to music or music making?[128]

Ethnomusicology

The Importance of Culture in Musical Research

Research into music of traditions other than the Western one challenges us to open and enrich our own understanding of and taste in music. The questions it brings up are many and varied, such as what sounds we can actually call music, and how do we understand and define what, indeed, it is; what is its function in human life and culture, and what does it provoke; and what comparative studies in music and the discovery of certain universals could teach us about the origins of music.

Hermeneutics and Methodology in Musical Research

Two different but overlapping horizons or perspectives open as we look at contemporary music. One is geographical: the plurality of musics that exist, even within one and the same geographical location. The other is temporal: the dynamism over time marked by the three moments of music's composition, performance and reception—a dynamic that is never static, especially in its third step, as from one listener to another and one performance to another the musical event is never solely repetition. This second one leads us to the need for a hermeneutical approach to musical comprehension and analysis. As with the hermeneutics of any written text, neither the author of a text,

---

127. Cf. Storr, *Music and the Mind*, 56–64.
128. Nattiez's approach will lead us to some important insights in this area.

nor the text itself nor the reader, has the monopoly on the meaning of that text. Truth and meaning are played out in the interaction between them. In music, the same reality of meaning as a complex event played out in these three dimensions needs to be explored.

In synthesis, there seems to be a profound need to bring together musicology, ethnomusicology, and cultural studies. Shepherd and Wicke lament that the approaches of musicology and studies in sociology, communication and cultural studies have remained so separate:

> Neither approach [musicological studies and those situated in the area of cultural and social studies] seems capable of discussing a *relationship*, a set of *processes* between music's sounds and music's meanings wherein sounds are significant, but meanings are the consequence of the socially and culturally mediated character of this relationship.[129]

They identify the core issue as lying in the fact that although music is not referential, in the way linguistic communication is, this does not imply the lack of a dynamic of meaning making that needs to be explored:

> The real issue seems to lie in confusing a form of human expression that does not obviously refer outside itself to the world of objects, events and linguistically encodable ideas with one which makes no appeal beyond itself in the process of generating and evoking meaning. While it can be accepted that music falls within the former category, it cannot sensibly be said to fall into the latter.[130]

Once again we are looking at the need for an integrated and balanced approach to musical understanding that attempts to bring together the various levels involved. The work of Wicke and Shepherd is one attempt to bring together musicology and cultural studies, inviting musicologists to welcome the questions cultural studies present them with and feed back into cultural studies their answers and analyses on the significance and meaning of sound. My own work in this book seeks to add the quest for a theological paradigm in which to situate such reflections. It is significant, to my mind, that they mention as positive both Ferdinand de Saussure and Jean-Jacques Nattiez, who are both key thinkers in the approach offered here. De Saussure

---

129. Shepherd and Wicke, *Music and Cultural Theory*, 16. Emphasis original.
130. Ibid., 11–12.

is the theoretical backdrop from which Willem Speelman works, the author presented in chapter 3, in whose approach to musical semiotics we will find many points of access for the theological understanding of music the book presents. Jean Jacques Nattiez will be our guide in the coming chapter, whose approach aids us in building a hermeneutical approach to musical meaning. As this chapter has helped us appreciate, understanding meaning in music is more complex than one would imagine, and theological discourse on music needs to take this into account. Nattiez's form of musical analysis provides us with a useful instrument with which to do this.

2

Towards a Hermeneutical Understanding of Music

> *The elegance of structuralism has given way*
> *to the shifting charm of deconstruction.*
> —Jean-Jacques Nattiez[1]

The Importance of Context

LIEVEN BOEVE PRESENTS THE CHALLENGE OF CONTEXTUALIZATION as an intrinsic one for Christian theology of all times. Each and every generation must reflect on "the internal comprehensibility and the external credibility of the Christian faith."[2] And yet, he marks with particular clarity the profound shift from the modern context to the post-modern one:

> The modern context, however, has passed into history . . . The overlap between human existence and Christianity as a provider of meaning has become smaller. Fewer and fewer people are interested in the Christian message. Others prefer to see it as a sort of wisdom teaching, the inspiration behind which is also to be found outside the Christian narrative.[3]

It is the same underlying perception that Nattiez pinpoints in the above quotation talking about musical semiology: the paradigms are shifting, from structuralism to deconstruction. How we apprehend meanings is not the same, and in order to communicate, across the generations, so to speak, we need to be aware of these differences.[4]

---

1. Taken from Nattiez, "Musical Semiology," 4.
2. Boeve, *God Interrupts History*, 3.
3. Ibid., 5.
4. There is a similar concern to be found in Lonergan's research and writings.

Nattiez is dealing with understanding musical meaning at a time in which meaning itself "charmingly" but evasively shifts and changes according to rules or patterns we don't always comprehend. This book brings together the concern for musical meaning with that of the transmission of Christian faith in the contemporary cultural situation, suggesting music's capacity to transmit Christian meaning and seeking to clarify how and to what extent. For this reason, Nattiez's reflections, born of similar situations and concerns, are insightful and useful.

We are not the first to find his work useful in dealing with music in a faith context. Michael Jan Joncas[5] has fruitfully applied his semiological method to the understanding of liturgical music.[6] However, his field is that of liturgy, and the knowledge and use of this method has not been developed, or even really known, in the realm of theological aesthetics. The aim of this chapter is to present the method as an invaluable form of approaching and comprehending music. We have already begun to see the complexity of the issues facing musicology in chapter 1. In the plural context we are living in, the need to learn to integrate into theological thought on music perspectives from beyond Western culture is indispensable, and is an exercise that may well help us to open our minds to new forms of music emerging even within our own culture, which do not automatically correspond to our own tastes or musical experience. Although synchronic and diachronic perspectives are different, they can, I believe, aid one another, as they help us open our experience and understanding beyond the horizons of comprehension we normally inhabit. Jean-Jacques Nattiez, to my mind, can help us to bring together and mediate these two areas of thought.

Born in France in 1945, Nattiez is a musical semiologist, semiotician and professor of Musicology at the Université de Montreal, Canada. His writings manifest an impressive understanding of both Western musicological thought and recent explorations in ethnomusicology. He offers a framework or instrument that aids in comprehending the immense variety of judgments and opinions within musical analysis, as well as a method or tool of analysis for future work

---

5. Known not only as theologian and author but also as composer of many liturgical songs, including "On Eagles' Wings."

6. Cf. Joncas, "Liturgical Musicology and Liturgical Semiotics," and "Semiotics and the Analysis of Liturgical Music."

in that field. Why is it of particular interest to us? I would immediately identify two aspects of his approach that suit our theme of research.

Firstly, the question of whether contemporary music can mediate faith, and, if so, how, has a very complex object of interest—music of many genres, styles, with words or without, written in notation form or simply recorded or performed; music that is evaluated and commented on by listeners of all ages, musicians, composers, ministers, theologians, and parish priests. How can we hope to come to any clarity? Ignoring its complexity and simply exhorting or effusing about the transcendence of music is too simplistic to be helpful. Nattiez, to my mind, takes seriously the complexity of this challenge, and offers a very useful paradigm or framework within which to work, which without offering immediate results, allows us approach the issues with a certain amount of precision and thoroughness.

Secondly, Nattiez deals with the issue of method: he does not give all the answers, but he does ask many of the right questions. Method is a contemporary question in theology as well. Lonergan identified the main achievement of Vatican II as that of marking the entrance of history into theology.[7] As a response to what he saw as the fragmented world of theological disciplines, he dedicated himself to finding a method that would enable it respond to the challenges of our times. One of the main points of his reflection is the shift he marks from the content of theology to the person of the theologian. Without relativizing the former, he focuses on and studies the latter, as the only way forward towards clear and unified thinking. Nattiez has a similar approach in the area of what he calls his musical semiology.[8] He draws on the thought of historian Paul Veyne and his concept of the "plot" that informs and conditions the selection process in history telling.[9] And he asks of any musicologist that they identify their methodology, procedures, and even their underlying principles so as to be able to comprehend, and therefore compare, integrate, or critique their findings, all with the aim of furthering solid analysis and comprehension, thus "rendering possible a permanent critical debate and a progressive accumulation of knowledge."[10]

---

7. The expression has been explained and developed amply by Frederick Crowe in "All My Work."

8. I will explain his choice of terminology shortly.

9. Cf. Nattiez, *Music and Discourse*, 176–80.

10. Ibid., 30.

> In this way, methodology can be rigorous: musicological analysis must offer explicit data, as well as the justification of how that data is obtained, the theory that is used to explain it and the principles of selection by which it is interpreted.[11]

It is not hard to see a parallel with Lonergan's notion of method:

> A method is a normative pattern of recurrent and related operations yielding cumulative and progressive results.[12]

That both authors deal with the issue of methodology in their work is more than a coincidence or even an extrinsic parallel between the study of music and that of God (musico-logy and theo-logy). It reflects the current moment of human knowing, and our awareness of the situated and contextual nature of knowledge, even when dealing with themes of faith. That Nattiez works within that awareness makes him a worthy dialogue partner in a book we have described as "an exercise in communications."

Another of Nattiez's underlying concerns also coincides with Lonergan's and is intrinsic to theological thought: the quest for truth and therefore concern about the differences and even contradictions of opinion to be found on the same theme. It is interesting that neither of them question the normality of plurality in approach. Lonergan's eight functional specialities in themselves represent different ways of approaching and thinking theology. Nattiez would say that the very complexity of the musical fact (and that of any other symbolic form) demands a variety of methods for its analysis, as no one method or analysis will ever say it all. Yet both insist upon the need to be able to dialogue and come to an understanding between these different approaches. The concern is the pursuit of truth: how do we advance in our grasp of the same? Can we, indeed, even talk about it, and if so, how? In taking a step back and asking about how we are going about our quest for understanding, we are entering into the area of hermeneutics and, as we shall see, Nattiez's quest for a right interpretation of music unfolds into a specifically hermeneutical endeavor.

Herein lies the originality of Nattiez's research, in that he not only talks about music as a symbolic form (the meaning of which I will clarify below) but examines the very nature of musical analysis.

---

11. Ibid., 43.
12. Lonergan, *Method in Theology*, 4.

"Discourse about music is a *metalanguage*,"[13] he states—that is, "a language used to talk about language."[14] Although the term is one for which Nattiez has been criticized, and it does perhaps evoke unhelpful assumptions of music as linguistic, what does he mean by this? An analysis, he says, states itself in the form of a discourse—spoken or written.[15] He draws on the concerns of Charles Seeger, one of the first musicologists he perceives to have identified and written about the delicate problem of speech about music and the need to address it, as we have seen in chapter 1. This difficulty is familiar to musicians and music lovers: "Lamentations over the insufficiency of analytical discourse in comparison to the 'real' music that we all love are quite numerous."[16] And yet, paraphrasing Ricoeur, he recognizes that analyzing and understanding that which we live by is part of human nature: "as soon as someone dances, sings or plays an instrument, someone else gets up and talks about it."[17] We are cultural, historical, symbolic creatures, inserted in many overlapping "worlds of meaning" that color and condition our reading of reality and any "language" or "word" spoken to us. Our "real world" is ourselves in the midst of the world we make sense of by way of the explanations we give ourselves. Music is no less part of that complexity. So where does the problem lie? "We reproach discourse about music for its inadequacies precisely because we have not reflected on the semiological and metalinguistic status of that discourse."[18] This is therefore what he sets out to do. And the form he takes is one that I would call a hermeneutical approach to music. Under the influence of the semiologist Jean Molino, who developed what is called the "tripartition theory" or method for the analysis of symbolic forms, and of whom he was a student, Nattiez applies tripartition theory to musical analysis. Rather than focusing solely on the music itself, he widens the picture to look at the intention and dynamic of composition of a given song or piece of music, the

---

13. Nattiez, *Music and Discourse*, 133. Emphasis original.

14. Cf. *Merriam-Webster's Collegiate Dictionary*, 11th ed.

15. And although there are major differences between the spoken and the written word, for the point Nattiez is making, they follow the same dynamic. Ricoeur recognizes this when speaking about the word, as we shall see in the next chapter. Cf., Ricoeur, "Naming God," 220–21, and cf. *Testimonianza, parola e rivelazione*, 57.

16. Nattiez, *Music and Discourse*, 152.

17. Ibid., 183.

18. Ibid., 153.

finished product or work in itself, and the process of its reception, differentiating each moment of analysis. I cannot but perceive a parallel here with the development of hermeneutics in the last century, from the quest to understand the mind of the author (behind the text), to the importance of the text independent of origin or interpreter (in the text), to the importance of the reader and their interpretation of the same (in front of the text). Understanding is not to be found in one of these areas to the exclusion of the rest. And discourse about music needs to take this into account.

The importance of hermeneutics for theology has received extensive attention in recent years,[19] as the plurality of approaches to the various areas of theological research increases, and the very foundations of how we interpret have been brought into question:

> [A] proper hermeneutical training may well be an appropriate *starting-point* for any journey towards a more adequate understanding of God, the human self and the mystery of our being in this world.[20]

As yet, however, there are many areas of theological thought that remain relatively untouched by the insights it has to offer. Music as understood in and by theology is one of them. This is not only unfortunate but detrimental to its development, as the context and process of our interpretation influences the results, whether we choose to recognize it or not.[21] This is why we seek to introduce this hermeneutical

---

19. Cf. the writings of David Tracy and Hans Kung, especially Tracy, *Analogical Imagination*. For a thorough overview and evaluation of the importance and role of hermeneutics for and in theology, cf. W.G. Jeanrond, *Theological Hermeneutics*, especially chapter 7, "The Development of Theological Hermeneutics (III): Hermeneutics and Christian Identity."

20. Jeanrond, *Theological Hermeneutics*, 182. Emphasis mine. It is interesting to note that Jeanrond illustrates how approaching Scripture and doctrine with the use of hermeneutical tools was normal praxis in the church for centuries, only being challenged in the seventeenth century with modernity and the development of the human sciences. This is the same era, as we shall see in chapter 6, in which the church lost touch with a fuller a more living comprehension of a truth of faith we consider central to our theme: the ascension of Jesus. That the retreat into more dogmatic forms of defending Christian truth emerged historically as result of our losing touch with the embodied presence of Christ in the world merits reflection. We will continue this theme in chapters 4–6.

21. An example of fruitful application of hermeneutics to a particular area of theology, which I found insightful in order to apprehend the possibilities of applying hermeneutics to specific areas of theology, can be found in a book by J. Carlos

tool for musical analysis in a book in which theology is seeking to understand music. Addressing these concerns at this early stage of our reflection aims at overcoming some of the confusion surrounding theological debates on music, and placing a clear and critical foundation for our research.

> [H]ermeneutics has proven to be not an optional tool for sophisticated theologians, but a vital necessity for any theologian who understands his or her task as a critical service to the church, the world and to the pursuit of truth.[22]

In the following sections I will present Nattiez's thought and method of analysis. I do not expect theology itself at this stage to assume and implement the musicological analysis he advocates, as they imply formation and expertise in that area. I do, however, invite theologians who seriously wish to ask questions about musical meaning to understand and learn to recognize the different viewpoints and nuances involved in such research, as a step towards fruitful interdisciplinary work. The effort to understand the framework offered to us by Nattiez provides us with an immensely insightful tool or instrument with which to navigate our way through the maze of opinions and reflections on contemporary music presently coexisting in our church. To this end, and in order to do justice to these aims, I will present Nattiez's thought with a certain degree of thoroughness.

Coupeau, SJ, on the dynamics of hermeneutics applied to the Ignatian Constitutions: *From Inspiration to Invention: Rhetoric in the Constitutions of the Society of Jesus*. Another is *The Revelatory Text: Interpreting the New Testament as Sacred Scripture*, by Sandra Schneiders, which implies hermeneutics to biblical theology.

22. Jeanrond, *Theological Hermeneutics*, 181.

Tripartition Theory: Background, Aims and Terminology

> "What does one hope to gain by talking about talk about music when even just talking about music uses a language that is in itself metamusical?"
>
> —Benjamin Boretz[23]

We have already mentioned Nattiez's underlying aim to enable discerned dialogue and understanding between different forms of musical analysis. His immediate background and intellectual stance is also important: he describes his own endeavor as that of constructing a musical semiology "aimed at moving from a structural conception of music and semiology to a dynamic, open conception of musical function."[24] Semiology as a term is drawn directly from Jean Molino, founded on the concern of both for understanding in symbolic analysis:

> We can say, faithful to what is essential in its impulse, that it is semiology—the study of signs and their organization—that ought to control the study of signifying objects. This is certainly not a question of turning semiology into the general science of human facts, but of taking the problem of signification seriously: every human science has a semiological dimension.[25]

The core insight Molino had, which Nattiez assumed, was the need to differentiate the viewpoint of the person analyzing any given fact:

> Molino feels that praxis in the human sciences constantly confuses the poietic, neutral and esthesic levels, such that scholars appealing to the same matrix of thought can reach divergent, contradictory and arbitrary conclusions: "we cannot advance in our knowledge unless we keep these three dimensions separate. There will come a time when we can put them together again, and offer a synthetic construction. . . . Before, there is

---

23. Quoted by Nattiez in *Music and Discourse*, 155. Benjamin Boretz is an American composer and music theorist concerned with the nature of metalanguage on music.

24. Nattiez, "Musical Semiology," 4. Structural meaning would be related to an absolutist position on meaning in music, as explained in chapter 1, in contrast with a more referentialist one.

25. Molino "Pour une histoire de l'interprétation," 287, quoted in Nattiez, "Musical Semiology," 33.

confusion. After, there is synthesis. Between the two, there has been descriptive analysis."[26]

We will explain these terms in full shortly, but the point being made by Molino in relation to musical analysis is that, in studying any human activity, one needs to differentiate between the person inventing or initiating that activity, the activity in itself (if and how it is separable from the former in order to be analyzed), and the observers or recipients of that activity. This distinction is far from theoretical or a source of unnecessary complication. A novel may be timeless in the interest it provokes, but the author's intention, the meaning of the book in its finished state, and the sense each individual reader or group of readers over time make of the book, are not the same. To bring it closer to the theological field, the experience and intention of the inspired authors of Sacred Scripture, the resulting book or books that were the fruit of their writings, and the changing (or growing) understanding of its readers over the course of history all form part of the theology of inspiration. Ignoring any one of these aspects, or confusing it with the others, only leads to confusion.

The same needs to be said of musical analysis, and the same again of the theologian or pastor or liturgical director who "analyses" or comments on music in the service of faith transmission. According to Nattiez, here lies the key to overcoming so many contradictions and confusion in musical analysis. When a musicologist studies a given piece of music, what "point of view" are they taking? What are they looking at and for? Is he or she talking about what the composer wished to express, and the experience from which the music was born? Or is that which the listeners experienced the point of reference? Or do they believe they are taking the music independent of the context of its composition or reception, and if so, what form of analysis are they using to identify it? Overlooking these areas in reference to our own theme is the source of an infinite number of misunderstandings and confusion. Any attempt to grasp the meaning or discern and evaluate music's role in the transmission of Christian faith will only lead to dissension if it does not take into account these three areas: the birthplace, context and intention behind its composition, the piece of

---

26. Nattiez, *Music and Discourse*, 30. We shall explain these three dimensions shortly.

music as it is passed on, and the ever-changing variety of listeners or interpreters, who "receive" and reinterpret it.

Widening our vision implies taking into account a complex series of elements that too often are overlooked, and that Nattiez seeks to address by identifying an adequate structure for its analysis. Is semiology a synonym of hermeneutics, then? It seems to me that musical semiology situates itself within the wider hermeneutical endeavor, at the same time as integrating some of its findings. The aim is clarity of intention and perspective in the person who analyses or discerns Christian music, not the composer or musician themselves. In our contemporary postmodern context, few composers or interpreters would presume the meaning they give to a particular composition to be the only valid one. Similarly, with regard to its reception, enthusiasm to share what a given song or melody means to someone rarely comes attached with the insistence that another person experience the same. However, such freedom is not always apparent when reading a more academic assessment or critique of music. The problem, to my mind, is not always that of a lack of tolerance, as if having a strong opinion about a given piece of music were unacceptable. Perhaps "taking position" on whether a certain kind of music is "good" or "helpful" for a certain occasion or not would waylay what at times can be described as the progressive deterioration of the quality of Christian music. The issue is the lack of clarity of where the critique is coming from and what exactly it is aimed at; that is to say—the context of the analyst and the object of his or her analysis. Such analyses lack weight because they lack critical foundations.

Nattiez says his thought could be called poststructuralist, or even better *trans*-structuralist, as he integrates and completes rather than refuting structural analysis, as would a deconstructionist approach. He recognizes that we are in a stage of thought that is both postmodern and poststructuralist. However, he does not do away with structuralist thought in his musical analysis—he simply finds it insufficient, as it avoids social and cultural contexts, and is a-chronic, a denial of time.[27] However, he recognizes, albeit with nuances, that music in some aspects lends itself well to and even needs structural analysis, due to the particular mode of referral it entails, in comparison with verbal

---

27. Cf. Nattiez, "Musical Semiology," 16–17.

communication and the visual arts.[28] This balanced approach is of immense value for our theme. Structural thought announced the death of the author, but it did not work: he or she came back to life with a vengeance, and interest for the person of the composer or the interpreter and the meaning of a given piece of music for him or her often takes centre stage. The phenomenon is not always healthy, as obsession with the musician can and does at times become more important than the music itself, but from the moment we are interested in music as a means of mediating faith, encouragement (and concern) for the life, faith, and capacity of expressing themselves of Christian composers and performers is natural and necessary. The "shifting charm" of our postmodern environments, to quote Nattiez's expression, relativizes the danger of making any one point of view absolute, and invites us to value "what the music says to us," and how it is relevant above and beyond the formalities of its composition. Each moment of the analysis proposed by Nattiez takes into account a necessary point of view, allowing us to work towards informed and balanced discernment in relation to musical analysis. The quest is for its capacity of mediating meaning: what does a given piece of music actually "say" or do? Can we find that out? Indeed, in what sense can we talk about music as communicating? What kind of a "sign" is music?

Signs and Meaning in Relation to Musical Semiology

In order to understand Nattiez's tripartition and the methods he proposes, one needs to start from the very base of his thought: his understanding of what a "sign" is. Now, semiotics and semiology are notorious for their complexity, so a certain amount of effort and patience in arriving at conclusions is asked of the readers, but these are necessary areas of study and reflection, if any real understanding is to be accomplished. "All theories of semiology, general or applied, are based on the definition of a sign."[29] There are two basic understandings of what a sign is in the history of study on the subject: that of Ferdinand de Saussure and that of Charles Sanders Pierce, each of them highlighting different aspects of how the human dynamic of

---

28. We will explore the specific dynamic of musical semiotics and form of relationship with reality in chapter 3, with the help of Speelman.

29. Nattiez, *Music and Discourse*, 3.

signification works. Willem Speelman, the semiologist at the core of the next chapter's description of musical semiotics, takes de Saussure's understanding of the sign in verbal communication as a point of comparison for and with the dynamics of musical semiotics. Nattiez, however, albeit recognizing truth in much of what de Saussure says in relation to linguistics, emphasizes the originality of certain aspects of Pierce's thought on signs and semiosis as fruitful for thought on music. Understanding the positions and basic differences in their understanding of the sign will be helpful as a foundation for the conclusions they reach. Let me briefly present both.

Ferdinand de Saussure

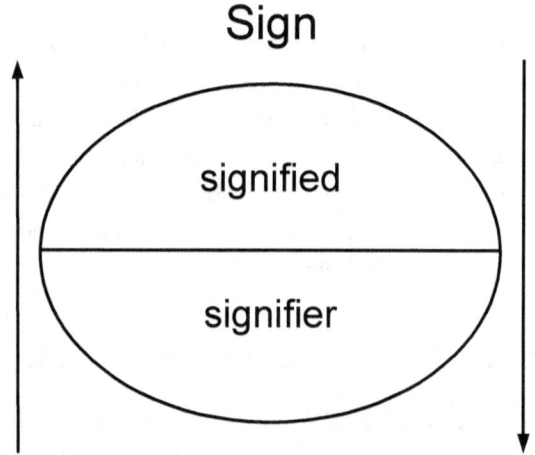

Figure 2.1[30]

Ferdinand de Saussure, as seen in figure 2.1, describes the sign as being made up of two elements: the "signifier" and the "signified." The signifier is the word or sign that mediates our understanding of the signified, which is the *concept* the object makes present. For example: the word "song" (\'sóŋ\) is the signifier, and our concept, our understanding of what a song is, would be the signified. They relate to one another through a process of referring (*renvois*), often called semiosis (which is linked with scholastic thought). According to de Saussure, this relationship is stable and bi-univocal, but arbitrary, in the sense

---

30. Adapted from de Saussure, *Course in General Linguistics*, 113.

that the meaning of a given sign is established by convention, rather than by any external relationship with the concept signified. It has meaning in relation to the other signs in the system of signifying signs, and therein lies its value: in relation to the system in which it exists, and to the other signs in that system, by way of "opposition to and difference from other signs in the same system."[31] Thus he distinguishes *langue* from *parole*:

> Synchronic ↔ System ↔ *langue*
>
> Diachronic ↔ History ↔ *parole*

He is thereby considered to be a precursor of structuralism, although he never used the word.

There are two aspects of his thought that to my mind are insufficient: one is the closed system of relations of the sign within the semiotic system that gives it meaning: how does the relationship with the world beyond the concept take place? How do we explain it? We need to take into account that neither the signifier nor the signified, in de Saussure's understanding, mean the object in themselves: the former is the word or sign that mediates our understanding of the latter, which is the *concept* the object makes present—*not the object in itself*. When we apply this to musical semiotics, which, as we shall see in the analysis of Speelman, are intrinsically relational and even corporal, it seems to verge on nominalism. Another aspect, and one that Nattiez himself challenges, is the *stable* relationship between signifier and signified. Can signification be that stable or fixed? Does the same sign or word always refer to the same concept? Is it not truer to recognize that as a word, for example, is used in different contexts, albeit to designate the same concept, its meaning is enriched and can even evolve or change? For example, the very word "music" evokes different realities depending on which culture it is spoken in, and the comprehension of what music is, as we shall see in chapter 3, has evolved over time, progressively integrating rhythm, melody and harmony. Words can have multiple meanings that vary according to who is speaking, who is listening and the context of the phrase or sentence. Nattiez challenges this overly static understanding of how signification works,

---

31. De Saussure, *Course in General Linguistics*, 119. The original French version was not written by de Saussure, but two of his students from the notes he left: Bally and Sechehaye, *Cours di Linguiste générale*.

seeing it as coherent with a structuralist point of view, but insufficient to assume the dynamic nature of human meaning.

Charles Sanders Pierce

Pierce offers a different, although related, way of explaining the sign:

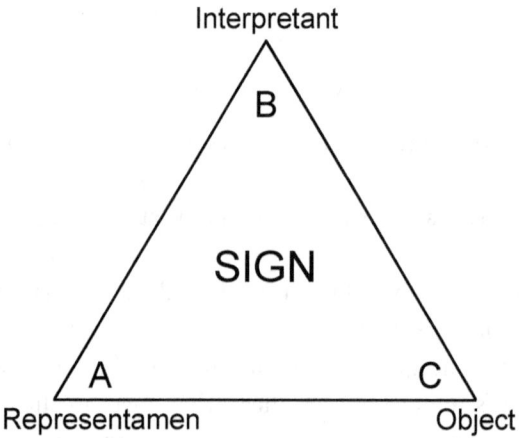

Figure 2.2[32]

The threefold explanation of the sign opens de Saussure's closed dual system to include the relationship with the external reality which the sign is representing. The "representamen" corresponds to de Saussure's "signifier," and the "object" is the thing or concept being signified, by which the sign relates to something other than itself, inserting Pierce's thought in a scholastic "realistic" line of thought. To this Pierce adds another element: that of the "interpretant," and here lies his greatest originality. The interpretant is not the interpreter (the person doing the understanding) but the sense made of the sign. And this interpretant is not only one: as sense is made of the sign, Pierce postulates a multiple and infinite number of interpretants in the process of signifying. Nattiez describes this in another way by saying that the experience of the sign's user enters into the interpretant, and therefore opens it up *ad infinitum* to more interpretations, as one person's perspective is never the same as another's in the same way as one's understand-

---

32. Adapted from Deledella, *Charles S. Peirce's Philosophy of Signs*, 47.

ing in one moment may be very different at different stages of one's life. For example: in Pierce's structure, the word "song" (\'sȯŋ\) is the representamen, the concept of what a song is for us in any given moment, is the interpretant, and the song itself is the object. Therefore, as soon as my understanding of what a song is enters into the equation, it also becomes part of the process of making meaning, reflecting the dynamic nature of the same. Every concept has a date of birth and a history, and in Pierce this is taken into account. For the dynamics involved in hermeneutics and meaning in general, as well as for our theme, the consequences are important.

Nattiez gives tremendous importance to the difference between de Saussure and Pierce in this regard, as he thinks it constitutes an intrinsic difference, opposition and incompatibility between the two forms of understanding the sign:

> Meaning cannot simultaneously be both the relationship between signifier and signified (the first step in a chain of interpretants) and a fixed, stable position within a system. . . . Semiological events . . . cannot be simultaneously open and closed.[33]

His approval of the notion of a sign in Pierce increases when applying it to music:

> In our domain [music], the Piercean terms of "sign" and "interpretant" are always to be preferred to the Saussurian opposition "signifier/signified," to avoid suggesting that semiological relationships in music are analogous to those found in language or literature.[34]

He is referring, above all, to the signifying relationship with the external world that verbal communication has and music cannot be presumed to have.

---

33. Nattiez, *Music and Discourse*, 23–25. In fact, he analyses and criticizes Eco's semiology on that basis, who despite having the intuition of the importance of multiple interpretants and the consequent ever-open process of semiological interpretation, which he calls, in act, "semiosis in progress," maintains the existence of fixed and closed local structures in which signs can only be understood in a type of "opposing terms" relationship presented by de Saussure. To do this Eco talks of "the semiological process" as "a succession of closed and formalized universes" (ibid., 25). Eco's later emphasis on the role of the reader is read by Nattiez as his realization that the semiological process cannot be based solely on the immanent level of analysis.

34. Nattiez, "Musical Semiology," 33.

It is interesting to note, albeit advancing some of the reflection of future chapters, that Alejandro García-Rivera, one of the more well-known theologians who worked and wrote in the area of theological aesthetics, also identifies the importance of Pierce's understanding of the sign and symbol, both in the integration of the notion of the "interpretant," and in the opening *ad infinitum* of this concept to other interpretants; thus, sign leads to sign. García-Rivera calls this "the community of the True," and in his own words, claims that "the uniting category for a theological aesthetics is not form but sign or symbol."[35] This is an important distinction which draws the attention of aesthetics to the epistemological understanding of our apprehension of beauty. Chapter 4 focuses explicitly on this point, as "how" music is apprehended and can be involved in our reception and assimilation of Revelation needs attention.

The Sign in Musical Analysis

So where does this leave our theological reflection on contemporary music? With two more keys for its grounding: the first is a key to understanding symbolic activity that is *in relation to the world*, which we will draw on in chapter 4 when talking about epistemology. The second is a much more complex and closer to the truth understanding of how human meaning and therefore also musical meaning, works. Meaning is an event. It is always an interaction between reality and human apprehension of the same, in a given moment of time and history, and as such is dynamic and in evolution. We shall see that music is a particularly dynamic symbolic form, provoking interaction with reality and between those making and listening to it, in a variety of

---

35. García-Rivera, *Community of the Beautiful*, 33. The whole book relies heavily on the importance of this distinction, in conjunction with the author's own Hispanic background, which he integrates into a framework of theological aesthetics. He invites theological aesthetics to move from the notion of the form, offered by Balthasar, to that of sign, in the tradition and mode of understanding of American pragmatism (or pragmaticism), of Pierce and Royce. García Rivera thinks that Balthasar, to a certain degree, is epistemologically lacking, in that his theology leads us to the frontier of reason and faith, but without teaching us to discern how beauty, in the manifestation of the form, appeals to our beings, as if there is no room for ambiguity. Pierangelo Sequeri identifies a similar gap in his thought, albeit offering a different approach and attempt at a solution. Chapter 5 will look at both.

ways. It is never simply the transmission of a message from producer to receiver.

At the root of Molino's and Nattiez's thought is the distinction between semiology and communication. The pattern they are using is not the standard conception of communication, which, although out-dated in philosophical circles, continues to be the way we perceive communication on a day to day basis:

> "Producer" → Message → Receiver

Figure 2.3

But rather the following:

> Poietic Process   Esthesic Process
>
> "Producer" → Trace ← Receiver

Figure 2.4[36]

In this scheme, the importance obviously lies in the inverted arrow, and its significance goes beyond simply understanding the communication process as more than a one way process. The point is that communication is only one possible result of symbolic functioning.[37] Both producer and receiver are involved in a complex form of symbolic interaction which is more than the one-sided transmission of a message which counts on a common code. In the next chapter, Speelman will take this a step further in its application to music, talking about the differentiation between "sending and receiving" and "sharing." Meaning is a shared event that is created and recreated as it happens. When talking about music, Nattiez talks about what he calls "communication utopia," the illusion by which one thinks that that which is in the intention of the composer can be perceived by the ear of the perceiver. This is simply not true, since "the *normal situation* in musical, linguistic, or human "communication" in general is precisely the *displacement*

36. Adapted from Nattiez, *Music and Discourse*, 16–17.
37. Ibid., 16–17.

between compositional intentions and perceptive behaviours."[38] This is problematic if our understanding of musical semiology is limited to that of "communication" according to figure 2.3. Does this mean one renounces on anything being communicated? Rather than renouncing, it means our understanding of the way in which meaning is transmitted needs to broaden. Nattiez refers to it as a "symbolic web,"[39] in which music has both internal and external referents, numerous "interpretants" and levels of meanings which overlap and interact, and invites us to integrate this more complete and complex framework in our understanding of music as a symbolic form.

This may sound difficult, but it is in fact the way our daily lives unfold as meaningful, and how musical meaning "takes place." We shall talk briefly about composition in the last chapter, but sufficeth to say here that when a musician composes a song, he or she may have some inkling or sense of what inspired it, but most musicians (and indeed artists in general) are aware that what they create or compose emerges from somewhere beyond or below their conscious rationality, to be embraced, perhaps enriched, but not always to be fully understood.[40] One may well seek words that seem to correspond to or "fit" with the music. Are they the only words possible? Probably not. Would someone else hearing that music put the same words—very doubtful, as the "miracle" of creativity passes through the human personality, sensibility and historical-cultural background of the artist. And when the music is played—the listener hears it in a context which may well mark the meaning of that song in that person's lived experience for every other time he or she hears it.[41] Or as life changes, what

38. Ibid., 99.

39. Ibid., 102.

40. Bono's description of how he composes is interesting in this respect, which is less focused on the words than on the music (sounds, rhythm, harmony, etc.): "The thing about song lyrics is: with the cadence and the way the melody falls, they can be more articulate than any purely literate response. This is something any non-English speaker knows. It's a funny thing, but when U2 songs are written, I don't write them in English. I write then in what the band calls "Bongelese." I just sing melodies and the words form in my mouth, later to be deciphered . . . so pop lyrics, in a way, are just a rough direction that you sketch for where the listener must think toward. That's it, the rest is up to you. Which is why pop music becomes the folk music of the next era. Feelings travel better than thoughts." Bono, *Bono on Bono*, 195.

41. For an interesting analysis of how the context in which music is heard conditions its meaning, and how it is not always innocent and can be manipulated:

the song evokes may change or be transformed. When a whole people give a meaning to a given song, is it right or wrong? Silvio Rodriguez's famous song "Ojalá," for example, is reputed to be about Fidel Castro. Hearing people sing that song in concert along with Silvio is profoundly moving, as you sense the heart of a people professing themselves. And yet, Silvio Rodriguez says it was birthed as a simple love song for the woman he loved. Can both "interpretations" be right? Are they not part of the full web of meaning that song evokes?

Behind this way of thinking is Nattiez's desire to defend an authentic hermeneutical endeavor with regard to music. The definition of meaning that Nattiez offers us, based on Pierce's notion of infinite interpretants, is the following: "all the kinds of interpretants, whether concerning intrinsic or extrinsic relationships, to which sound material gives rise,"[42] and the levels of meaning he is referring to, without being exhaustive, range from meanings immanent to the music, those experienced by the composer, the local meanings as perceived by the performer and by the listener or group of listeners, musical strategies the composer or musicians have access to or knowledge of, and hidden or unconscious layers of meaning within the persons playing or writing this music. All these elements and more are part of the event of meaning that takes place in the performance (or recording of and listening to) of any given piece of music.

So can we talk about correct interpretation or true understanding in the face of this complexity? Recognizing this web does not, according to Nattiez, imply giving up all hope of finding what he calls "local" or "provisional truths." Here, although welcoming some of the achievements of postmodern musicology, such as the non-exclusion of any musical style based on the exclusion of minority groups, or the questioning of "value scales" in musical historiography, he distances himself from what he calls the "cultural relativism" it has introduced. If Taruskin sounded a battle cry that musicology be a hermeneutical approach that allows music to be: "cumulative, multiply authored, open, accommodating, above all, mess, and therefore human,"[43]

Pouthier, "La musique au risque de l'histoire," 303–9.

42. Cf. Nattiez, "Musical Semiology," 33.

43. Cf. Taruskin, *Text and Act*, 192, quoted in Nattiez, "Musical Semiology," 30.

Nattiez talks about music being a "total social fact"[44] that must give us the possibility of analyzing it, even where no analysis could ever claim to be either exhaustive or definitive:

> In historical and cultural interpretation, just as in musical analysis, it seems to me essential to reinstate the idea of "fact" and to emphasize that some interpretations are more valid, indeed more true (let us not be afraid of that word!) than others.[45]

Nattiez's combination of the quest for truth with the recognition of the complexity and contextual nature of our apprehension of meaning touches the core of what is at stake in many discussions on music in Christian circles and theology: eternal truth in history. We can neither give up on the quest for truth nor ignore that its apprehension is complex and incarnated, in circumstances that are contingent.[46]

The Semiological Tripartition

At this point let us explicitly present the model Nattiez offers. Working with models is helpful when we take into account their purpose, conscious of their usefulness as well as their limits. In theology, the work of the late Cardinal Avery Dulles in organizing various areas of theological research in the form of models[47] has become known, valued, and widely used in the teaching of theology, due to its clarity in laying out a sort of map which identifies the main points and tendencies of the theme in question. The danger of such clarity is a risk of over-simplification or that of losing sight of the nuances that don't immediately enter into the structure presented. With a theme such as music, it can also seem removed or overly abstract. However, precisely because of

---

44. The expression is taken from Marcel Mauss; cf. Nattiez, *Music and Discourse*, 42.

45. Nattiez, "Musical Semiology," 39.

46. By way of example, an insightful analysis of the real issues behind a contemporary debate on rock music can be found in Ardui, "Truth, Rock Music and Christianity." In it, Ardui analyses the positions of a theologian, Joseph Ratzinger, and a rock journalist, Steve Turner, on rock music, looking at the underlying positions on truth and context coloring their opinions.

47. Explicitly those of revelation, ecclesiology, and faith; cf. Dulles, *Models of the Church*, *Models of Revelation*, and his work on models of faith in *Assurance of Things Hoped For*.

the nature of our theme and the often dissonant variety of voices that one hears speaking about music, there is a need of such clarity and methodological organization, so as to allow for and facilitate critical dialogue. The effort to take distance from our instant reactions and opinions, so as to find and follow a method, is indispensable. Before presenting a graphic representation of his framework of analysis, let us describe the three levels he presents and differentiates. As said above, Nattiez is drawing on the thought of Molino, in relation to what he called the "semiological tripartition," which identifies three levels or dimensions of the symbolic phenomenon. He calls the first two levels processes, and the methodology of their research "explicative," and refers to the third as a "quasi-structure" (as to his mind, the only real structures are mathematical), the analysis of which is "descriptive," as it is the analysis of a completed work.

The Poietic[48] Dimension

This first level focuses on the composer and or interpreter of a piece of music, and the process by which their music comes into existence. "[E]ven when it is empty of all *intended* meaning . . . the symbolic form results from a *process of creation* that may be described or reconstituted."[49] It is interesting that Nattiez notes that there may not be an explicit intention or "intended meaning" in the composer, as more literal, verbal expression would imply. The poietic process needs to be explained "as it happens," on its own terms, so to speak, and, in part, it will be in listening to and seeking to understand that process that theology will advance in its understanding of music at the service of the communication of faith. The term "poietic" itself is taken by Molino from Etienne Gilson.

---

48. Poïesis is etymologically derived from the ancient Greek term ποιέω, which means "to make." This word, the root of our modern "poetry," was first a verb, an action that transforms and continues the world. In the Western tradition its understanding has covered a wide range of meanings, from the general theory or intention behind all human activity to the more specific and literary one of a "theory of poetry." Cf. "Poetics," in Preminger and Brogan, *New Princeton Encyclopedia of Poetry and Poetics*, 929–37. In this thesis it refers to the creative process involved in the birth or making of music.

49. Nattiez, *Music and Discourse*, 11–12. Emphasis original to author.

> By "poietic" I understand describing the *link* among the composer's intentions, his creative procedures, his mental schemas, and the *result* of this collection of strategies; that is, the components that go into the work's material embodiment.[50]

As we will see in our last chapter, reflecting on the poietic process of music is a potential source of light and insight for theology since, in the context of Christian artists, it allows us focus on their experience and understanding of faith in its bond with musical expression, the source and evolution of their creative process and inspiration, and its link with prayer. It raises questions about the connection point between the artistic and the Christian vocations.

The Esthesic[51] Dimension

This second level focuses on the dynamic of meaning as it happens in and through those who receive or listen to a piece of music. "Receivers" or "constructors," "when confronted by a symbolic form, assign one or many meanings to the form." "Receivers" is a deceiving word because it implies clear intentional meaning on the part of the "creator" or "producer," which may or may not be the case, and also infers that the one receiving is passive in the process. Nattiez also seeks to widen the breadth of those he includes in this dimension to include the various types of people to listen to, receive and make sense of music. By "esthesic," therefore, he understands:

> not merely the artificially attentive hearing of a musicologist, but the description of perceptive behaviors within a given population of listeners; that is how this or that aspect of sonorous reality is captured by their perceptive strategies.[52]

This is important, as we cannot confuse the perceptual process of listeners "in real time" with that very different perceptive process of the musicologist; as is normal in any scientific study or research, the

---

50. Ibid., 92.

51. The word "esthesic," taking its meaning from αισθησις, the faculty of perception, is a neologism coined by Paul Valéry in an inaugural lecture for the Collège de France in 1945, who preferred it to "aesthetic" on etymological grounds. According to Valéry it includes: enjoyment, contemplation, reading, as well as scientific and analytical approaches.

52. Nattiez, *Music and Discourse*, 92.

scholar's perspective is different. Both are valuable and necessary, and therefore both need to be listened to, discerned and even put in relation to one another. This is relevant for our theme, on two counts: firstly, the evaluation of "professionals," and those without formation often varies, and overlaps with tastes, cultural or generational differences, and diverse spiritual traditions. These differences can enrich and inform one another, but if ignored create confusion or errors of judgment.[53] Secondly, it raises the issue of "learning" to listen and the importance of formation in aesthetic sensibility and music. We cannot hope to recuperate, grow in or maintain good musical quality without attention to this area. However, such formation needs to respond to the universal and plural nature of Christian faith and therefore its music.

The Trace

This third level or "quasi-structure," as Nattiez calls it, is that of the piece of music in itself, independent of whoever wrote it and those who listen to it. Molino suggested calling it the "neutral level" or "material level," as the poietic cannot be immediately accessed and the esthesic is dependent on the lived experience of the "receiver." It is also referred to as the "immanent" level, which is the terminology we have chosen. Molino calls an objective analysis at this level the "analysis of the neutral level." Without doubt, this level originated in structuralism, which has the merit of having shown us that a text possesses a dimension or structure beyond and independent of its biography or historical origins. He says this level is descriptive, and that the form it takes is paradoxically that of a fixed graphic object, which contrasts with the "infinite and fleeting character of the interpretants that it attempts to trace."[54] On this level of analysis, Nattiez identifies what he calls the "Tower of Babel" to be found in musical definitions at the present time. He talks of "fuzzy and ill-defined terminology" that

---

53. P. Sevez offers some interesting thoughts on this theme in "Rock, Rap, Slam."

54. Nattiez, *Music and Discourse*, 32. Interpretants here is to be understood in the sense Pierce gives it, not the "receivers" but the "sense made of the sign," the meaning of the piece of music at each moment of its being received or interpreted by any receiver or producer of new meaning in its reception or reinterpretation.

demands some form of precision for research to advance.⁵⁵ From there he talks about the different forms of analyses in use.⁵⁶

Some commentary on the implications of each of these three levels or stages is necessary:

Musical Analysis at the Three Levels of the Tripartition Theory

Analysis of the Immanent Level

Analysis of the neutral level is indispensable, according to Nattiez: "The link between poietic intention and esthesic perception is the material trace. There is no other. Such information is supplied by analysis of the neutral level."⁵⁷ This aspect of his thought is inherited from structuralism: messages manifest a level of specific organization that must be described, even if they are not enough to explain the whole. The issue of where we locate the trace, that is, what the material element is, on which we perform an immanent analysis, is core to our theme, because a lot of contemporary music is by its very nature, fluid. It is written by one person, completed by a band or an arranger, and enhanced by recording facilities. Some contemporary music includes in its ethos space for the improvisational skills of those playing it. Yet this level seeks to analyze the piece of music in itself, independent of human interaction or interpretation: the song, the sonata, the score, the recording—an objective and attainable "object" that one can analyze in order to grasp and understand it. Nattiez defends the indispensable role of the written score. He bases this opinion on the

---

55. Ibid., 159.

56. In the context of a theological study, it is perhaps not necessary to present fully the various forms of musicological analysis pertaining to this level. I will simply say that Nattiez identifies two main approaches, and a third method that combines these two, which can be described respectively as (a) non-formalized analyses, which do not appeal to resources other than language, and include impressionistic analyses, description in paraphrases, and hermeneutic readings ("explication de texte"); (b) formalized analyses, which simulate music, analyzing a chosen variable of music so as to create a model (modelization), of which there are two types, global (analysis by traits or classes, in a more structural way) and linear (describing the piece in terms of time and the real succession of the musical event); and (c) intermediary models that combine the two. His own approach combines these options in order to admit the complexity of the musical fact.

57. Ibid., 99.

issue of interpretation and multiple interpretants: if there is no score, notation, material and fixed, then the poietic process continues until the end of the performance, because its performance is indeed part of the creative process of the work. If we analyze the written graphic, that sign precedes interpretation. He concludes:

> multifaceted analysis of a work—to which musical semiology aspires—cannot be realized without the intermediary of notation, or . . . of transcription; music analysis must have the capacity to apply itself to a symbolic substitute for the sonorous fact. Musical semiology is in effect rendered possible by musical notation.[58]

Contemporary music, however, more often than not, is not written in a score, even where composers' rights and copyright protection imply they should be.[59] According to Nattiez, it is part of the work of the musicologist to identify, and if necessary to construct a way of "transcribing" a work of music that is not yet notated, in order to be able to analyze it, in what he calls an "unambiguous way." This notation, however, is descriptive rather than prescriptive, in that the aim is not to limit future interpretation (presenting a score which must be faithfully adhere to) but to provide a tool for analysis independent of or before future interpretations or developments. He recognizes that the semiological analysis of contemporary works or music of the oral tradition is much more difficult, for this reason, although not impossible, and that the task implies finding empirical techniques that are capable of delimiting and constructing these units.[60]

The challenge, therefore, within our own theme, is how we analyze the music we look at, so as to overcome the sense of distance between the material level and the actual music we are dealing with. I think the very fact that it is rarely fully written down says something about contemporary music and a cultural change of perception we are moving through. At the very least, that fact needs to be taken into consideration, in the attempt to understand its significance. Nattiez is convinced that music needs to be analyzed in its written form. Our

---

58. Nattiez, *Music and Discourse*, 72.

59. It is worth noting that SIAE, La Società Italiana degli Autori ed Editori, currently admits musical recordings where musical annotation is too difficult for a faithful reproduction of the piece in question.

60. Cf. Nattiez, *Music and Discourse*, 81 n. 8.

own opinion is that each particular analysis will have to mark its method, but that potentially, the analysis of musical recordings could be fruitful as a valid "trace" for this analysis of the material level. The integration of music analysis within theological discourse is necessary to be consistent and faithful to our attempt to reflect on music in and as theological *praxis*.[61]

Esthesic Analysis

As mentioned above, in analyzing music's reception, attention needs to be paid to the differences between the modes of listening of a composer, an analyst and a listener, as well as to their cultural context and background. At this stage, Nattiez talks about the relationship of music with time: "sound unscrolls itself and manifests itself in time . . . as living process, energy in action."[62] Music affects people in and over time in different ways, according to the context they are living, as well as their sensibility, which changes over time. It is one of the aspects Speelman will emphasize in chapter 3, as well as other theologians in chapter 5. He warns against the tendency of the description or explanation of a musical experience becoming normative—which can happen very easily.

Poietic Analysis

Analysis at this level seeks what the composer can reveal about his or her compositional process. In doing so, a composer is revealing the sources of her or his selection and inspiration. They are testimonies to the history of musical facts. However, in listening to them, Nattiez underlines, one must take into account various elements, in order to guarantee greater precision in one's reflection:

- The attitude toward language in general in the culture to which the composer belongs;
- The attitude toward discourse about music in that culture;
- The circumstances of the discourse;
- The speaker's personality.

---

61. In this regard Willem Marie Speelman's book *The Generation of Meaning in Liturgical Songs* is paradigmatic.

62. Nattiez, *Music and Discourse*, quoting Michel Chion.

Once again, it is not a question of considering the composer or musician's perspective as truer than the listener's, but of recognizing and receiving it for what it is. The aim is to provoke "dialogue," between researcher, composer, musicians, and listeners.

Based on the recognition that these three levels or dimensions are essential elements of any piece of music or musical experience, Nattiez unfolds and describes the various possible forms of musical analysis that can be found. Let me present his scheme of analysis, along with some examples or applications of how they can be found underlying theological or pastoral reflections on music. He describes six:

Explanation of Tripartion Semiological Method

	Poietic Process	Immanent Structures of the Work	Esthesic Process
(I)		X Immanent analysis	
(II)	X ← Inductive	X Poietics	
(III)	X → External	X Poietics	
(IV)		X → Inductive	X Esthetics
(V)		X ← External	X Esthetics
(VI)	X ←→	X ←→	X
	Communication between the three levels		

Figure 2.5[63]

---

63. The figure and its explanation are taken from Nattiez, *Music and Discourse*, 140. Reprinted by permission of Princeton University Press.

1. *Immanent Analysis* looks only and independently at the work in itself, tackling "only the immanent configuration of the work." So in our context this would look at a song or piece of music in itself, ignoring the life or inspiration of the author, as well as how that song is received. In general, this form of analysis has entered little in theological circles, as it implies a level of musicological knowledge or interdisciplinary collaboration which is as yet not common in theological endeavors.[64]
2. *Inductive Poietics* proceeds "from an analysis of the neutral level to drawing conclusions about the poietics. . . . It is one of the most frequent situations in music analysis." Here the musicologist or student traces, from recurring patterns in a work, the thought of the composer, obviously drawing from their knowledge of other works along with that of the historical or cultural context. In this case from the composition or compositions of a given composer, we deduce the meaning he or she must have had. Usually this implies what is called "seriation process": placing the piece in the context of other stylistically related works.[65]
3. *Deductive or External Poietics*: Type 3 is what he calls "external poietics" and is the reverse of the previous analysis, where one takes "a poietic document—letters, plans, sketches, explanations of the composer, and analyzes the work in the light of this information." Therefore the accent is placed on the experience

---

64. There are some interesting initiatives using music without theological interpretation which we will mention further in chapter 4, such as Esagramma, in Milano, and Theology and the Arts, in Britain and the U.S.

65. One could situate some of the enthusiasm in theological reflection for the music of Mozart in this area, albeit recognizing their starting point is not a musicological analysis of his works, but the perceptive assessment of accomplished musicians, which is worthy of attention. Mozart was not a particularly religious or pious Christian, by which it is not possible to attribute explicit theological intention to his works. But as we mentioned above, explicit intentionality is not the only element of the poietic process. Besides, it is his secular work that is being acclaimed as "theological" by theologians such as Balthasar, Barth, Ratzinger (before becoming Benedict XVI), and Sequeri. From their perception of the luminosity and brilliance of the work of Mozart, they present the music as a celebration of creation and eschatological hope, not because this was explicitly in the intention of the composer but because it colors much of his work. There is an element of inductive esthetics in these writings on Mozart as well.

and intention of the composer.⁶⁶

4. *Inductive Esthesics* is the most common form of analysis, and moves from the analysis of the work's trace to how it is, or should be, heard and received. Grounded in "perceptive introspection," or in a certain number of general ideas concerning musical perception, a musicologist uses an analysis of the work as a foundation and then describes what he or she thinks is the listener's perception of the passage. The danger here is the musicologist or "expert" sets themselves up as the collective consciousness regarding a given piece. Unfortunately, this is not uncommon praxis and remains one of the reasons of tension between contemporary musicians and music critics.⁶⁷ When presented respectful of context and of the limits of professional analysis, it can, however, be a useful and valid form of approaching and learning to listen to and appreciate music.⁶⁸

---

66. Cf. Nattiez, *Music and Discourse*, 141. For example, this is the form of analysis used by musicologist Pier Paolo Bellini in a recent Conference organized by the Italian Bishop's Conference: Dio Oggi in Rome from December 10th to 12th 2009, in a presentation called "Dio nella Musica di Ieri e Oggi," in which he presented on the music of yesterday, together with PierAngelo Sequeri, who focussed on music of 'today'. Bellini presented a Sonata of Schubert, accompanied by and described in the light of broader writings of the composer, not specifically written for or about the Sonata in question. The papers of Bellini and Pierangelo Sequeri are on music in relation to God and faith, and include live music in their presentations, are available, not to be read, but to be heard and seen online. It is, surely a more appropriate way of preserving "thought on music" than solely in written form: cf. Bellini, "Dio nella Musica di Ieri e Oggi," given at the Conference *Dio Oggi* on 11 December 2009, Online:http://www.cci.progettoculturale.it/questionedio/progetto_culturale_/iniziative_a_cura_del_progetto_culturale/00008605_Mediacenter.html. Another example, applied not to one piece but to the work of various composers in relation to their explicit faith stances, can be found in Dieuaide, "Du spirituelle en musique. Présentation de Compositeurs contemporains," 319–29.

67. An example of two polarized positions in this dynamic is that of philosopher Roger Scruton versus the British band Pet Shop Boys, whose notorious conflict of opinion went to the courts in 1999, resulting in Scruton having to apologize and withdraw his statements on the band made in his book *An Intelligent Person's Guide to Modern Culture*. Cf. "Pet Shop Boys versus Roger Scruton," online: http://www.petshopboys.net/html/reviews/news4.shtml.

68. Sequeri's presentation at the aforementioned conference, *Dio Oggi*, is an example of how learning to hear what is actually in the music can help to receive or grow in appreciation of what music has to offer. In the conference, Sequeri successfully managed to open people to listen to the music of Messiaen with appreciative ears. For many, it would have been the first time they could appreciate a type of

5. *External Esthesics* starts "from information collected among listeners, to attempt to understand how the work has been perceived . . . obviously the manner in which experimental psychologists would work."[69] I would add that this plays a large part in the evaluation of music nowadays, in which the opinion of the "fan" or listener, has a greater role than in former times. One could argue that this is conditioned and even manipulated by other factors, including economical interest, but nevertheless, public perception is taken into account and highly appraised in the analysis of contemporary music. From a theological point of view, the value of understanding what music is being listened to, and how it affects, helps or otherwise in a person's apprehension of or journey into faith, is indispensable.

6. Type 6 relates all three levels in both directions. It is "the case in which an immanent analysis is equally relevant to the poietic as to the esthesic."[70] Although it may sound simple, it is indeed very complex. Here the finished product says something about the intention and meaning held within the creative process, which in turn illuminates how that music could (and perhaps should?) be played. Its reception also helps understand the piece in itself and perhaps illuminates further interpretations of the same. In music of and within faith circles, the ideal will be this sixth approach, in which the piece in itself, how it is received over time, and where it was born of come together in evaluating and discerning its impact in the present moment and its capacity of helping mediate and transmit faith.[71]

---

music and tonality that until then had seemed alien. Cf. Sequeri and Bellini, "Dio nella musica di ieri e oggi."

69. Nattiez, *Music and Discourse*, 142. Important work has been done in this field, bringing together musicology and music therapy in the Esagramma project, pioneered by theologian Pierangelo Sequeri and presented in scientific form by Licia Sbatella in *La mente orchestra*. The aim is educational but should have lasting effects in philosophical thought on aesthetics in the future.

70. Nattiez, *Music and Discourse*, 142.

71. An example of an author who is aware of the difference involved in these approaches, albeit without any explicit mention of Nattiez, is Hal Lingerman, whose book *The Healing Energies of Music* includes chapters explicitly divided to serve that purpose. Chapter 8, "Music and Global Spirituality," takes into account the composers perspective and how that influences his or her music, and chapter 9, "Gallery

Most readers of this book will never personally have to analyze music at any depth, but it necessary to be aware of the differences they present. Therefore, the first aim in differentiating these levels and forms of analysis is to help train our perception and understanding for the discernment and evaluation of music in theology and ecclesial realities. When we read or hear about the appropriateness of a given piece of music for a certain event or public, our first question should be to situate where the assessment is being made from, and thus to understand, and perhaps complement it, with the other perspectives. Another factor to keep in mind, before we draw conclusions, is that Nattiez, in general, is dealing with the analysis of music, *not* the understanding of music and text together. Very often, in Christian discourse on music, attention towards discernment is focused on the words, rather than the music, and more often than not without differentiating adequately between a critique of music and that of text, before one reflects upon how they come together.[72]

Additional Conclusions for our Theme

Precision and Depth in Our Analyses

The main conclusion that emerges from these reflections on Musical Semiology is the call to take a seriously nuanced and informed approach to musical analysis and evaluation. It is clear that we can no longer indiscriminately identify a style or genre of music as incapable or not worthy of transmitting something of Christian faith, without a proper and comprehensive research into the different levels of meaning that it may hold or the meaning as event it may be a part of. I do not necessarily think this always, or even first and foremost needs to imply a full scale musicological, linear or paradigmatic analysis, which would be daunting, but if in our evaluations and opinions, we learn to recognize what we implicitly take as normative, and to give

---

of Great Composers: Composer Keynotes," gives importance to the experience (appreciation and enjoyment) of the person listening.

72. Many studies on contemporary music focus as much or more on the words as on the music. Cf., for example, the recent book by Gilmour, *God and Guitars: Seeking the Sacred in Post-1960s Popular Music*, which includes an analysis above all of the "texts" of popular music. The author, thankfully, is aware of this, and integrates it in his introduction.

space to the "voice" of other aspects of the musical event, we are on the right path. The wisdom of our discerning and decisions will grow.

The Question of Universals

Nattiez addresses a theme we have looked at before: that of the universals in music. Our interest in the quest for universals is obvious from the very title of the book, *Music as Theology*, and this in regard to contemporary music *in general*, not of one particular type, but the phenomenon of music as it appears in culture. The question itself *is* universal. In the introduction, I have stated clearly that my own experience limits me to talking about Western music, and that premise remains, but the aim is to offer foundational tools and a framework within which one can begin to approach and assess contemporary music *tout court*. This aim is underlined by the reality of our global world, in which, due to its moving boundaries, music types overlap and cross-fertilize continuously. Is there common ground and truth in our music making, with all its plurality and diversity?

The tripartitional method is immensely insightful in giving light to this issue, in that Nattiez states that universals are not to be found in the acoustic side of the analysis, nor in the immanent level, but in the poietic prospective. In other words, it is not so much in the styles of music, or how they are listened to and received, but in the very *making* of music that we will find our universal keys to understanding music from a theological perspective. Drawing on thought from Blacking and psychologist Dane Harwood, Nattiez refers to the deep structures Blacking talked about to understand the importance of music across various cultures, concluding that: "the universals of music must be sought not in immanent structures, but in the *behaviors* associated with sound phenomena, particularly in poietic strategies."[73] He is moving the accent from what the "sounds" may have in common to the activity of making music and the compositional endeavor, that which Boilées called "the attempt to behave musically."[74] It is a shift from content to those "expressing it." Nattiez's takes things a step further with his notion of the concept of process—the process of making music and that of reception (poietic and esthesic levels): "the process

---

73. Nattiez, *Music and Discourse*, 65.
74. Ibid., 65.

of understanding and engaging in musical behavior may be more universal than the content of musical knowledge or action."[75]

As we seek to open doors to understanding music and musical composition as a means of mediating Christian faith, this is a clear invitation to place the emphasis on the side of the composer, the musician and the dynamic created in listening to music, rather than on that of particular styles or genres of music. It is an invitation to go beyond a static analysis of types of music, to the dynamic one of human beings in "musical action." Theologically speaking, it is consistent with the basic Christian doctrine and theology of all human beings being made in the image and likeness of God, and therefore doted with the capacity to emulate and collaborate with the Creator in their activities, music making included. To my mind and for the purposes of this book, this is coherent with the dynamic of evangelization and faith development, by which, as faith is assimilated in people and cultures, the normal and expected result would be that musics of different styles and types be born to live and express the faith that has been received. It also opens ways of reflection for a coming together in music making of different cultures and sensibilities.

The Person of the Scholar

Nattiez, as well as Lonergan, gives great importance to the self-awareness, and (if we could use Lonergan's term) "self appropriation," of whoever does the analyzing. He identifies various elements that need to be examined in the quest for a thorough and grounded analysis:

- The "historical-cultural" background of the person analyzing. For example, it is not indifferent if the person is from the culture of the music in question, or how familiar they are with it, as it will provoke a more *emic* (from within) or *etic* (from the outside) approach. In theological reflection, this is applicable in time *and* space; that is to say, our awareness of how culturally situated as are, and how the differences in cultures across the world *and* over generations, affect us. It could perhaps also apply to people from different religious belief.
- The underlying principles and a priori assumptions of the analysis, especially what he calls "transcendent principles." These

---

75. Ibid., 66, quoting Harwood, "Universals in Music," 523.

would be the underlying philosophical positions that color and condition options to do with variables and analysis—the "plots" underlying how we approach and describe what we think. At times these principles are easy to see, and at others they are not, but we must try to trace them, so as to understand the presence and importance of certain variables as opposed to others in a given analysis. Nattiez talks of "the (more or less) conscious assumptions that are orienting the analytical operation." He recognizes his own:

> Obviously the tripartition is a transcendent principle, based on an ontological prejudice concerning the nature not merely of music, but of all human symbolic productions. This book begins with the theory of the tripartition for this very reason, in an attempt to explain the underlying axioms that inform my own enterprise.[76]

As we shall see in chapter 4, it is hard to overestimate the influence of these underlying conditioning factors and assumptions of the person analyzing in the area of theological and philosophical aesthetics. We will explore how there is always an implicit philosophical and epistemological stance in every theory, the unawareness of which only confuses or weakens the possibility of understanding and dialogue. I finish my analysis of Nattiez where I started, with the person of the researcher. It seems to me of immense importance that we learn to be clear about the underlying context, principles and the "plots" by which we evaluate the music we approach.

---

76. Nattiez, *Music and Discourse*, 174.

3

An Approach to Musical Semiotics

"Music and silence—how I detest them both!" Screwtape

—C. S. Lewis[1]

What is Music?

*If I could tell you what it meant,
there would be no point of dancing it.*

—Isadora Duncan[2]

THE AIM OF THIS CHAPTER IS TO "FOCUS THE LENS" MORE CLOSELY on music in itself, in order to understand its symbolic action and potential in and at the service of Christian revelation. Much of what we have written up to now has underlined the importance of context in musical apprehension, but music is also a specific aspect of human behavior, usually situated within the area of human art, which has particular characteristics and needs to be studied as such. For this reason, we need to try to describe, albeit briefly, *what music is*. Nattiez, one of the authors on music who best integrates musicological and ethnomusicological perspectives, leads us into this issue with the clear and provocative question at the basis of the analysis we have just presented in chapter 2: "Do we really know what music is?"[3] It is a "street-level" version of the issue of universals in music that we mentioned in chapter 1,

---

1. Lewis, *Screwtape Letters*, 102.

2. Cf. *Creative Chords*, xiv. Isadora Duncan (1877–1927) was an American dancer, considered by many to be the mother of modern dance.

3. Nattiez, *Music and Discourse*, 41.

as few people would question that they know what music is for them, but what the essence of music is, what makes a given sound *music*, rather than simply sound(s) or even noise, is not so easily definable. That which some people consider noise, others hold in high esteem, and the division is more than a generational difference of opinion. The gradual growth of knowledge of the music of other cultures has lead western European thought to acknowledge this fact. It can no longer be taken for granted that the notion of music is univocal for different cultures. In some cultures, the "concept" of music as we understand it, does not even exist. The phenomena we would call music is situated in other areas of human behavior and with different aims than those we would understand as musical. Even within the same culture, and this is definitely true for western culture, what is accepted as music or not, changes.

So what are the basic elements that make music be, in fact, music? Nattiez, in his quest to identify the phenomenon we call music, states that sound is an irreducible given of music even where it is only alluded to or implied. It may seem strange to have to affirm even this much, but John Cage introduced silence into the heart of musical understanding with his groundbreaking work, "4'33."[4] "4'33" is a three-movement composition composed in 1952 for any instrument (or combination of instruments). The score instructs the performer *not* to play the instrument during the entire duration of the piece throughout the three movements (of thirty seconds, two minutes and twenty-three seconds, and one minute and forty seconds, respectively). Rather than four minutes and thirty-three seconds of silence, however, the content of the piece, according to Cage, is that of the sounds of the environment that the listeners hear while it is performed. "4'33" became for Cage the epitome of his idea that any and all sounds constitute, or may constitute, music. Cage stated on more than one occasion that "4'33" was, in his opinion, his most important work. In this piece, sound is implicitly alluded to. Silence, however, is just as important an element of music as sound, in a similar way as listening is intrinsic to speech. Although not usually named as one of the basic elements of music, I would contend that silence is indeed, an intrinsic element of music, not only because without it, the sounds in a musical piece cannot be appreciated, but also because it is an intrinsic element of rhythm: the

---

4. Cage, "4'33," 1952. The premiere was given by David Tudor on August 29, 1952, at Woodstock, New York.

space between marked sound. For this reason, I include it in the description below of the elements generally recognized as intrinsic to music.

Another distinction is needed, between noise and sound, as the difference is not clear and has provoked many debates, serious research, and enormous creativity in the twentieth century in the realm of musical composition, pushing the limits of our thinking on sound, noise, and music.[5] Nattiez differentiates between noise and sound, although once again refusing to make an overall, "valid for all peoples and all times" definition:

> [J]ust as music is whatever people choose to recognize as such, noise is whatever is recognized as disturbing, unpleasant or both. The border between music and noise is always culturally defined.[6]

This book works in the belief that, although the line between sound and music is not always clear, it is discernible, as long as a truly hermeneutical and context-sensitive approach is used in that discerning, such as the one presented in chapter 2. Once again here, it is interesting to see how our understanding and definitions of music as opposed to noise, and the sounds that integrate it can be looked at from three different possible perspectives: compositional definitions, acoustic definitions and perceptive definitions.

---

5. One only has to think of some of the pieces of futuristic music, and the use of noise in musical performance.

6. Cf. Nattiez, *Music and Discourse*, 47–48. We could take examples from non-Western cultures, but for the limits of this thesis, one closer to us is the moving line or continuum between speech and music, and what has been called its "intermediary" forms, for example: chant, proclamations, auctioneering, horse-racing commentating etc.

Poietic Level (Choice of the Composer)	Neutral Level (Physical Definition)	Esthetic Level (Perceptive Judgement)
Musical Sound	Sound of the Harmonic Spectrum	Agreeable Sound
Noise (Non-Musical)	Noise (Complex Sound)	Disagreeable Sound

Figure 3.1[7]

Nattiez analyses the composers that have worked on the borderline areas of sound and noise, and explains how understanding them implies seeing where they situate themselves.[8] He alludes to Blacking's definition of music as "humanly organized sound," completing it thus: "The 'musical' (as there is not a music, but many musics) is any sonorous fact constructed, organized, or thought by a culture."[9]

Having acknowledged the basic complexity in identifying the phenomenon of music, we need to identify briefly the main elements commonly used in music making in Western culture. Peter Dufka, in a thesis on *L'arte Musicale come Espressione e Stimolo della Fede: La Passione secondo Giovanni di J. S. Bach*,[10] identifies various musical elements that influence Bach and that he integrates into his music: rhythm, melody and counterpoint, harmony (homophony and polyphony), modality, tonality and tonal color, or what he refers to as the "colours of sound."[11] Aaron Copland, in a simple but clear book called

---

7. Taken from ibid., 46 fig. 2.1. Reprinted by permission of Princeton University Press.

8. Cage, for example, takes the perceptive viewpoint of the listener; Edgard Varèse, who wrote the first piece ever written for percussion alone, [within the known musical tradition], "Ionization," saw things from a compositional perspective: "people call them instruments for making noise. I call them instruments for making sounds." "The more you realize the sounds of the external world are music, the more music there is." Ibid., 52.

9. Ibid., 67. Note the three elements of tripartitional analysis.

10. *Musical Art as an Expression and Stimulus of Faith: The Passion according to John of J. S. Bach.*

11. Cf. Dufka, *L'arte musicale*, 42–50; 186–97; 254–58.

What to Listen for in Music,[12] names four elements: rhythm, melody, harmony, and tone color and timbre. To both lists I premise that of silence. In brief:

- *Silence*[13]: an intrinsic element or background of all music. In music, silence is not empty: it is a space for listening, for an attentiveness which is expectation and a sort of "tuning" of all one's senses to the present moment and the sounds that are taking place or are about to. It involves the whole person, as music heard, played, composed or danced to, involves the whole body.[14] It is both the backdrop against which one hears the sounds and the space between, which makes them what they are. In a Christian perspective, when dealing with music born and played in order to express or share God's presence, silence is never empty, but is presence, welcome, and communion, even when no "words" are spoken.[15]

- *Rhythm:* the rhythmic scene is made up of meter and rhythm. "Most historians agree that if music started anywhere, it started with the beating of a drum,"[16] although the measuring off of rhythm in metrical units as we know it now only took place around 1150, when "measured metric" was introduced into Western civilization. Copland emphasizes just how important this move away from unmetered rhythm has been for music, both freeing it from its dependency on the word[17] and limiting it at the same time:

---

12. This book provides a simple but clear explanation of the basics in music for someone wishing to understand more the dynamics involved.

13. P. Goujon has insightful reflections on the relationship between silence and listening in music in his "L'écoute e silence intérieur": "L'interprétation musicale, pour ne rien dire de la création, est une expérience d'écoute autant que d'expression" ("Musical interpretation, to say nothing of its creation, is an experience of listening as well as expression," 340).

14. As we shall note later in this chapter, even when music is not explicitly danced to, movement of the body is part of all kinds of music. Observation of any orchestra, even as they silently read a score, confirms this point.

15. For an interesting study on the voice and revelation that touches on some of these aspects, albeit without reflecting on music, see Gaburro, *Voce della rivelazione*.

16. Copland, *What to Listen for in Music*, 27.

17. Up to that point, music followed the natural and unfettered rhythm of prose or poetic speech, from the time of the Greeks to the time of Gregorian chant.

> It supplied music with a rhythmical structure of its own; it made possible the exact reproduction of the composer's rhythmical conceptions from generation to generation . . . it was responsible for the subsequent contrapunctual, or many-voiced, music, unthinkable without measured metric units. . . . Yet it would be foolish to underestimate the confining influence that it has had on our rhythmical imagination, particularly at certain periods of musical history.[18]

- *Melody:* "only second in importance to rhythm in the musical firmament."[19] The importance and meaning of each musical element is a matter of opinion, and as such, debatable. Copland relates melody to mental emotion, whereas rhythm to physical motion, giving great importance to the identification of the melody, and the following of it in an "intelligent" appraisal of music, but such a clear division is simplistic and begs for further reflection on epistemological issues, such as how we apprehend music and its relation to our knowing in general. In the context of western music, it is important to note the generalized tuning of our musical ear to the seven degree tone system, with tonal center. This was of course challenged by Schoenberg, with his twelve-tone expansion of the scale and method of composition, which has become known as "atonal," although the name is not truly accurate, as it suggests the absence of any melody or form. He himself called his twelve-tone technique "developing variation" in which he sought ways of developing motifs without resorting to the dominance of a centralized melodic idea, using an ordered series of all twelve notes in the chromatic scale. In this sense, his challenge to the overriding musical sensibility of Western music still stands. It has not, however, been assumed into popular music culture, which still basically works out of the tonal system.

- *Harmony:* according to Copland, if rhythm and melody are natural developments, harmony is an evolution of an intellectual conception, unknown before the ninth century. It involves the interrelating of notes with each other, and takes on various forms, for example:

---

18. Ibid., 28.
19. Ibid., 39.

- *Organum:* the first true example of harmony, organum is a means of greater emphasis, or of reinforcing the sound to carry through the larger churches. It consisted of adding a voice that exactly paralleled the original melody at the interval of a fourth or fifth.
- *Descant:* from Latin *discantus*, "song apart"; "countermelody either composed or improvised above a familiar melody. In late medieval music, *discantus* referred to a particular style of organum featuring one or more countermelodies added to a newly rhythmicized plainsong melody. *Discantus* in this sense is usually spelled "descant" in English."
- *Faux-bourdon:* French for *false bass*, it is a technique of musical harmonization used in the late Middle Ages and early Renaissance, which involves three voices, two of which are written, and another added or improvised. In its simplest form, *faux-bourdon* consists of the *cantus firmus* and two other parts—a sixth and a perfect fourth below.
- *Polytonality:* developed primarily by French composer Darius Milhaud, it is the simultaneous use of two or more different tonalities or keys in a piece of music.

- These three elements (rhythm, melody, and harmony) are the main three identified when talking about music. As we shall see in chapter 5, they are the three mentioned by Balthasar in an early writing of 1925, when he analyses what he refers to as "the musical idea" and its development, in which he adds the significance of their genetic and historical evolution. Copland adds a fourth:
- *Tone color and timbre:* tone color, according to Copland, is about the available instruments and the "color" of their sound. Each instrument or group of instruments has a different timbre and quality of tone, which are chosen by composers or musicians in relation to the kind of sound they wish to make, and even the meaning they sense that particular sound carries or evokes.

He also talks of two other musical characteristics that are useful for listening to music. The first is musical texture, which can be monophonic (one melodic line—Gregorian chant), homophonic (melodic line and chord accompanying), or polyphonic (various melodies together). The second is structural principles, such as repetition, non-repetition, and free forms.

In the context of the present book, this brief and somewhat simple description of music's main elements can help us understand our main author of this chapter, and indeed the musicologist I consider most apt to help us enter music into the heart of theological thinking: Willem Marie Speelman, who brings together in his expertise the areas of semiology, musicology, and theology. It should be clear at this point that the music we are looking at, contemporary music in Western culture, makes ample use of all the characteristics described above, albeit remaining mainly within the seven-note tonal system challenged by Schoenberg and not shared in all cultures in the world. Naming the various elements that make music what it is will also be a helpful tool when we seek to listen to and "perceive" how music affects us and what it transmits to us. Whether a piece of music has its rhythm accentuated or not, which instruments are chosen and whether it is a lone voice or one used in harmony with others, all color our reception and "understanding" of it. Before we enter directly into Speelman's analysis, we need to situate it within the wider context of semiotics, semiology, and musical semiotics.

An Approach to Musical Semiotics

As noted already, there is as inherent difficulty or potential source of confusion involved in calling music a "language,"[20] the recognition of which is essential to understanding how musical symbolism can offer a particular entrance point to faith and theological "thought." My position is that music is a semiotic system, with its own dynamics and symbolic action, which are different from verbal semantics. Understanding music implies that we take music on its own terms and *listen* to *what* it is "saying" and *how* it is "saying" it. As long we try to approach music solely through the lens of verbal semantics, we are doomed to failure or misunderstanding, since its uniqueness and strength lie in the fact that it communicates in a different way. Theological discourse is so innately verbal that the concept of *logos*, or "word," and verbal expres-

---

20. There are those how would deny it carries any meaning in itself and others who defend it, but where its meaning lies and what we "mean" by "musical meaning" is still a complex theme without apparent consensus.

sion are often understood as synonymous. Our normal and assumed way of approaching and understanding communication, both in theological and pastoral terms, is verbal. And yet revelation (and indeed all human interaction and expression) is much more than verbal communication. Lonergan, when talking about religion, includes in the concept of the Word—not just linguistics but

> any expression of religious meaning or religious value. Its carrier may be intersubjectivity, or art, or symbol, or language, or the remembered and portrayed lives or deeds or achievements of individuals, or classes or groups.[21]

However, not only is such an acknowledgement rare, but the comprehension of just how to understand and integrate these other forms of communication into evangelization and theological thought is only in its beginnings. Indeed, even the knowledge of how verbal semiotics and semantics work is not widespread, and perhaps only becomes possible when we seek to understand a different form of communication such as music. This is why I give particular emphasis to comparing and contrasting verbal and musical semiotics. Such a comprehension is to a certain extent a "translation" of these forms into verbal expression, but I would like to consider such a translation as a kind of threshold that invites us to explore music in pastoral work and theology in a more conscious and useful way. Therefore, this chapter is dedicated to the semiotics of music, a discipline that is quickly establishing itself in the twenty-first century as an independent discipline, along with historical musicology. It is born, however, of the general field of semiotics.

The area of semiotics is notorious for the complexity of its discourse,[22] and it is beyond the scope of this book to attempt a comprehensive overview of that field of research. However, we need

---

21. Lonergan, *Method in Theology*, 112.

22. Justin Lewis notes that "its advocates have written in a style that ranges from the obscure to the incomprehensible"; Lewis, *Ideological Octopus*, 25. Daniel Chandler, responding to David Sless' challenge, in which he stated that "semiotics is far too important an enterprise to be left to semioticians" (cf. Sless, *In Search of Semiotics*, 1), calls the semiotic establishment a very "exclusive club", and in an attempt to make discourse more accessible, has written a concise and very useful book called *Semiotics: The Basics*. It is available online under the title *Semiotics for Beginners* at: http://users.aber.ac.uk/dgc/Documents/S4B/. The quotation mentioned can be found under "Introduction."

to draw on the reflection and conclusions of experts in that field recognizing that theological reflection in the area of communications as understood by Lonergan is by its very nature interdisciplinary. The importance of doing so could be expressed in this way:

> Semiotics is important because it can help us not to take "reality" for granted as something having a purely objective existence which is independent of human interpretation. . . . The study of signs is the study of the construction and maintenance of reality. To decline such a study is to leave to others the control of the world of meanings which we inhabit.[23]

Once again, we find ourselves looking at the broad issue of meaning and how it is apprehended. For that reason, some basic clarification of the diversity of approaches, authors and terminology is helpful.

Schools of Semiotics, Authors, and Terminology

Despite the importance of the area of semiotics, we cannot yet talk of a unified enterprise. There are two divergent traditions in semiotics stemming respectively from Ferdinand de Saussure and Charles Sanders Peirce.[24] The musicologist I have chosen as the main guide in this part of my research is rooted in the former. Semiotics, which de Saussure called "semiology," can be loosely defined as "the study of signs" or "the theory of signs." De Saussure defined it as: "a science which studies the role of signs as part of social life." Sometimes "semiology" has been used to denote the Saussurean tradition, and "semiotics" the Peircean tradition, but nowadays the term "semiotics" is more likely to be used as an umbrella term to cover the whole field. It covers the study not only of spoken or written language but diverse types of codes.[25] Semantics has been defined as "the study of meaning," and

---

23. Chandler, *Semiotics for Beginners*, "Introduction." The similarity with Lonergan's notions of levels or "control of meaning" is significant. Cf. Lonergan, "Dimensions of Meaning."

24. The work of Louis Hjelmslev, Roland Barthes, Claude Lévi-Strauss, Julia Kristeva, Christian Metz, and Jean Baudrillard (b 1929) follows in the "semiological" tradition of de Saussure, whilst that of Charles W, Morris, Ivor A. Richards (1893–1979), Charles K. Ogden (1989–1957), and Thomas Sebeok follows in the "semiotic" tradition of Peirce. The leading semiotician bridging these two traditions is the celebrated Italian author Umberto Eco. Cf. Chandler, *Semiotics for Beginners*.

25. As Roland Barthes says in his book *Elements of Semiology*, 9: "Semiology aims

some situate it within semiotics, as one of the three areas of linguistics that form part of the study of semiotics:

- *semantics*: the relationship of signs to what they stand for, or the comprehension of the preferred reading of the sign;
- *syntactics* (or *syntax*): the formal or structural relations between signs; and
- *pragmatics*: the relation of signs to interpreters.[26]

However, an exact delimitation of the areas of semiotics and semantics is difficult,[27] and more so in the moment that we are attempting an applied study to the specific field of music. For the purpose of this book, I have chosen to call the area this chapter looks at "musical semiotics"—as it looks specifically at the symbolical particularity of music. Chapters 1 and 2 have instead addressed the wider issues involved in the making of meaning in music, and have therefore been referred to more as situated in the realm of semantics: what music stands for and how to go about interpreting it, with particular attention given to hermeneutics and cultural context. The hope, in differentiating these semiotic and semantic aspects or layers within music, is double: first, that we can avoid hasty affirmations on the value and meaning of music, where adjectives such as emotional, transcendent, or universal are applied without clarifying their meaning and thus causing confusion in theological discourse and dialogue; and second, that we can

---

to take in any system of signs, whatever their substance and limits; images, gestures, musical sounds, objects, and the complex associations of all of these, which form the content of ritual, convention or public entertainment: these constitute, if not *languages*, at least systems of signification." A possible organization and division of the codes of semiotic study is offered by Chandler, who divides them into three typologies: social codes, textual codes and interpretative codes, relating them broadly to three key kinds of knowledge required by interpreters of a text, namely knowledge of: the world (social knowledge), the medium and the genre (textual knowledge) and the relationship between (1) and (2) (modality judgements). Chandler situates verbal language in the area of social codes and art and music in that of textual codes, a division I would consider too simplistic to convey the complexity of both "codes." However, the triple division of types of codes is helpful as a first approach to the theme's complexity. Cf. Chandler, *Semiotics for Beginners*.

26. Cf. C. W. Morris, who follows the threefold division of Pierce. Cf. Morris, *Foundations of the Theory of Signs*.

27. One formulation is that semiotics deals with how signs mean and semantics with what words mean. Cf. Sturrock, *Structuralism*, 22; but again, this is only one form of differentiating between them.

offer a clear, useful, and accessible understanding of what music is and how it works for use in theological thought and Christian spirituality.

Verbal and Musical Symbolism according to Willem M. Speelman

In our attempt to grasp the semiotics of music, I have chosen as my main source Willem Marie Speelman, a Dutch musicologist, semiotician, and theologian who teaches in and writes on the areas of musical semiotics, liturgy, and spirituality. As stated above, Speelman founds his thought on the school of Paris, drawing from Ferdinand de Saussure, Louis Hjelmslev and especially Algirdas Julien Greimas, in order to build his own approach to musical semiotics. My main sources in this chapter are his book on the generation of meaning in liturgical songs,[28] and a conference presentation he gave that I attended on music in worship in 2007, which has since been published.[29] The book presents the theoretical foundations of his thought, which he applies to the understanding of liturgical songs. In it he situates his approach as that of a musical semiotics, halfway between classical musicology (music as vibrating air) and ethnomusicology (music as a social activity), with an intermediary role between the two: musicology and social activities. He explains this approach in the following way:

> Musical semiotics is not involved with sound but with the musical image of sound . . . musical semiotics is not involved with social activities but with the musical competence of communication.[30]

This approach parallels my own quest to mediate theology and contemporary culture, in the area of faith communication through music. The semiotic school Speelman draws from has interesting points of contact

---

28. Speelman, *Generation of Meaning*.

29. The presentation, entitled "Words Can Be Understood, but Music Must Be Followed: Language and Music as Fundamental Categories of Liturgy" (hereafter cited as "Language and Music"), was given at a conference called *"Singing God's Love Faithfully"* (Notre Dame, April 12–14, 2007). The quotations in this chapter are taken directly from the full manuscript, which the author has very kindly given me. It has been translated into Dutch to be integrated in a book edited by M. Hoondert, as a chapter titled "Woorden kunnen worden verstaan" and a short version of the article was published as "Music and the Word: Two Pillars of the Liturgy" in *GIA Quarterly*.

30. Speelman, *Generation of Meaning*, 47.

with the theological approach outlined in the introduction. Greimas, on whom Speelman founds a lot of his thought, has a phenomenological starting point to his thought, focusing on perception—we perceive a signifying world. He recognizes that, from morning to night, from birth to death, we are surrounded by the omnipresence of signification.[31] There are parallels between the way he describes signification and common sense and Lonergan's description of the worlds or levels of meaning in which we are immersed. Another point of interest is his description of meaning as an event, as dynamic.[32] He relates this to the fact that if perception is the starting point or access point to semiotics, then as perception changes, so does meaning.[33] Hence we are dealing with a tradition of thought that recognizes and honors the dynamicity and complexity of human life, in its quest for and understanding of meaning.

Speelman's article builds on the foundation of his book to highlight the intrinsic differences between musical expression and verbal expression. Although his reflections on the value of music as a principle of organization of liturgy are highly innovative and suggestive, I am not dealing with the field of liturgical music at this time, and will therefore focus solely on the dimensions of musical semiotics he presents. Speelman offers the results of his research in a series of structural differences between language and music (the terms he uses himself). It is important to understand that he does not present these differences between language and musical expression as mutually exclusive, but rather as two principles, in the Greek etymological sense of *arche*: an abstract force underlying a given process, functioning as its source. They should therefore be understood as tendencies or accentuations that can in some moments overlap. For example, the first comparison he outlines is the aim of language to "send and receive a message," as opposed to that of music, which aims, instead, to "share." One could

---

31. Cf. Speelman, *Generation of Meaning*, 11; quoting Greimas, *Sémantique Structurale*, 8–9.

32. Cf. Speelman, *Generation of Meaning*, 12.

33. We have noted this point in our analysis of chapter 2, according to which, when one is attentive to the different viewpoints hermeneutics takes into account, shifts in meaning become easier to read and apprehend. There is also a very definite link between Greimas' thought on the making of meaning in relation to perception and Lonergan's notion of intellectual conversion, which I believe to be particularly relevant to the area of epistemology and aesthetics.

perceive an element of sharing rather than solely the sending and receiving of a message in the case of a chant in a public manifestation; and inversely, the blowing of trumpets in certain contexts, or the beating of "talking drums," although primarily musical, sends a very specific message for whoever is listening. However, the overriding intention in each case is quite clear and distinct: either that of creating music, or that of using a given medium for sending linguistic messages, by which the governing principle, verbal or musical, is patent. Examples taken from the line in which music and verbal communication overlap should not cloud the overriding dynamic of music in its more usual mode of use.[34]

His main concern in the writings I draw from is meaning as it manifests itself in contexts where verbal and musical expression come together, be it in liturgical songs or in the liturgy itself, which at its best brings together musical and verbal dynamics. He talks about how music and text affect one another, and that although we know this, we do not know how: "Although we feel that music and text contract a complex and effective relationship, we do not know how to describe this relationship."[35] For theology, the theme of music that brings together words and music is important, but as my interest is in drawing into theological discourse awareness and understanding of the existence of a "principle" or *arche* of music and how it works, in this chapter I limit myself specifically to musical meaning.

Now let us turn our attention to the aforementioned scheme of Speelman. Once again let us hold in mind that the differences are principles rather than direct oppositions.

---

34. I am also aware that this analysis overlooks completely the areas of poetry and narrative, which distance themselves in so many ways from purely conceptual or notional understanding. However, it is, I believe, necessary to simplify by taking more direct verbal or conceptual thought as our reference point in this comparison, in order to allow music's unique symbolism emerge.

35. Ibid., xi.

Verbal Dynamics	Musical Dynamics
1. Send and receiving	1. Sharing [and listening]
2. Disengagement	2. Engagement
3. Oppositions	3. Intervals
4. Images	4. Orientations
5. Static	5. Dynamic (movement)
6. To be understood	6. To be followed
7. Differentiating	7. Integrating (harmonizing)
8. Non-here	8. Omnipresent
9. Referring to Reality (and masking it)	9. Receiving reality

Figure 3.2[36]

Sending and Receiving/Sharing

Although the model of communication as that of sending and receiving a message has been questioned and enriched by different authors, and indeed even by the French school of semiotics itself, it still remains the most basic and common way of understanding verbal communication, and the one that informs our day to day living. Someone wishes to communicate something, and communication is only achieved when the other person has understood the message being sent, whether the message received is accepted or refuted.[37] Music, however, is not primarily about sending a message—it is about sharing the process of music as it happens.

---

36. Speelman, "Language and Music," 2. Reproduced with the kind permission of Professor Speelman.

37. Cf. Figure 2.3.

> The practice of musical communication is not so much a practice of a sender in opposition to a receiver,[38] as it is *an act of sharing*. Communication of music is not about anything else other than the sharing of the music itself.[39]

It is said that on a certain occasion when Beethoven was asked about the meaning of a certain piece of music, he sat down and played the whole piece again. This act did not constitute an explanation—it was a replay, a "resharing" of that piece of music. It is simple but significant that in verbal communication, two voices together are hard to listen to, while music allows for and invites participation, be it in unison, in harmony, or even disharmony. When people come together in music, be it a sing-song, a musical jamming session, or the creative arrangement of a song or a piece of music, almost instantly a connection is established, a togetherness in listening to the sound being produced. And the accent in music *is* on listening: "He or she is, as a musician, first and foremost a listener."[40] Why is it difficult to appreciate music (and even more difficult to play it) without a background of silence? Because both musicians and audience become listeners and followers of the dynamic of music as it unfolds, and there is a lot to listen to! Whether or not one is aware of it, even the simplest bars of music imply a combination of the elements we mentioned in the first part of this chapter: silence, rhythm, melody, tone color or timbre, and harmony (as even the absence of explicit harmony in music is significant).[41] It is therefore immediately both more simple and more complex than the "what I have to say and how I want to say it" involved in verbal communication. Even the elementary rule in choral singing, on the need to hear the voices of the people singing to your right and your left as much as your own, is an indicator of how much more importance is given to listening and togetherness in musical expression.

Disengagement/Engagement: Music and Embodiment

The issue underlying these terms is that of temporality and embodiment—engagement or disengagement with the reality of the present moment, or in other terms, our presence to reality in the here and now:

38. Or "in front of a receiver."
39. Speelman, "Language and Music," 3.
40. Ibid.
41. Cf. Copland, *What to Listen for in Music*.

> Because of the referential quality of language, linguistic communication presupposes a disengagement (*débrayage*) from the reality.... On the other side of the communication we find an opposite procedure, which is the engagement (*embrayage*) with the utterance. The process of reading [a letter] involves an engagement of the reader with the "you" in the letter. This engagement, however, presupposes a disengagement of the reader from his daily reality.[42]

By this, Speelman means that in the moment of expressing oneself linguistically (perhaps most clearly perceptible in writing, but equally true in speaking, as both are governed by the *arche* of verbal communication) one detaches oneself from the reality that is being described. The word I speak is not the same as the reality I am speaking of. For example, the "tree" I may write about is not the "tree" that grows in the garden—it is a concept that refers to it. The person I write about is a description of the person who lives, not the person themselves, and even the "I" writing a letter or a piece of prose is different from the traces that person leaves in the text he or she creates. Speelman describes this in terms of temporality and spatiality: verbal language is referential and draws our mind from the "I—here—now" reality to the conceptual understanding of the concepts the words refer to, therefore making us withdraw from the present moment and space we inhabit. In musical communication, however, engagement is more easily explained as it is lived in terms of corporality: our bodily presence or existence in the present moment.

> The human body, being the place where we can confirm who is I, where is here and when is now, is moved immediately by the movement of the music. Hearing music we may confirm what is here and now.[43]

The importance of the human person as embodied has been ignored or underestimated in theology, and this has particularly strong consequences in the understanding and appreciation of music in and as theology. A phenomenological way of describing my own experience of this reality is that when I move from solely thinking about

---

42. Speelman, "Language and Music," 4–5. Once again, at times a musical principle may animate a verbal form of communication. For example, the reading of Scripture in a liturgy: it is not read for the sake of gaining more information, but to celebrate and participate in the word given. Speelman's point is indeed that liturgy is *also* founded by the musical *arche*, not only the verbal one.

43. Ibid., 5.

something to listening to, playing, or composing music, the "centre of gravity" I work from internally shifts from my mind to my "gut": one listens with one's whole body, and the whole body (mind included) is affected by it. Speelman, quoting Tertullian[44] dedicates a separate part of his conference on the human body as the pivot of salvation, explaining how music is by nature connected to our embodiment and therefore apt to help us remain in this truth. He asks the question, which is at the core of our research:

> Thinking about the bodily realization of words and music, we come to the question of how language and music organize our senses. How do we perceive linguistically and how do we listen musically?[45]

In this light, the philosophical and theological background of Western thought has left us with an "uncomfortable" relationship with our bodies (and with the world, as Oliver Davies in *Transformation Theology* points out), and may be one of the reasons why we are uncomfortable with strong rhythms in a faith context. Our dualistic mind-frame, which favors abstract intellect over bodily sensations and lacks the tools to integrate and unify both, feels threatened, for example, by the powerful bodily awareness provoked by certain rhythms. We will come back to this in the next chapter, when talking about epistemology.

Oppositions/Intervals—Images/Orientations—Static/Dynamic

Speelman talks about the logical and eidetic (*eidos* = vision) qualities of language: language consists of logical oppositions and images. As we began to explain in chapter 2, Ferdinand de Saussure, the Swiss linguist who is considered to be the founder of semiology, taught that language is built on "binary oppositions": *langue* and *parole*, and signifier and signified, are two of the binary categories he introduced. At the very center of language we find nothing but logical oppositions. Lithuanian linguist Algirdas Julien Greimas, influenced also by the Aristotelian "logical square" or "square of oppositions," presented these oppositions in what has become known as the semiotic square:

---

44. "*Caro cardo salutis.*" Tertullian, *Treatise on the Resurrection*, 26.
45. Speelman, "Language and Music," 5.

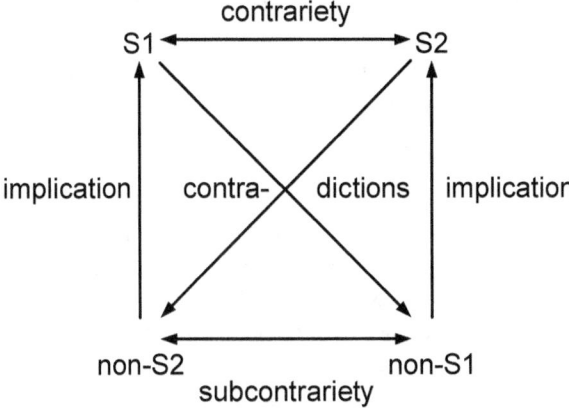

Figure 3.3[46]

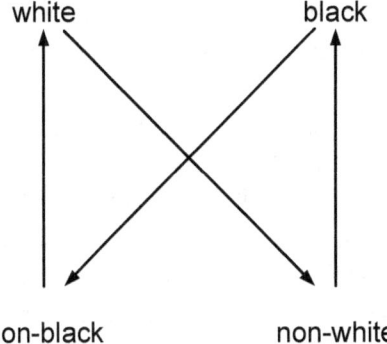

Figure 3.4[47]

This means that we understand the words we communicate with in terms of oppositions: white is not black, man is not woman, and so forth. Another factor to be taken into account is that, according to de Saussure, in verbal communication our brain works with images:

> Verbal expressions consist of *acoustical images* and the content of language consists of *images in our brains*, ideas, concepts. Verbal communication is making connections between acoustical images and cerebral images. The acoustical images are called phonemes and the cerebral images concepts or ideas.[48]

---

46. Speelman, *Generation of Meaning*, 20.

47. Speelman, "Language and Music," 5. Reproduced with the kind permission of Prof. Speelman.

48. Ibid., 6.

It is hard for us to understand this as normally we "imagine" that what we hear or "understand" is an acoustic sound, but it is not. A phoneme is an acoustical "image,"⁴⁹ which we connect with the ideas or concepts in our brain in order to understand them. Once again we are contemplating how verbal communication distances us from reality:

> Listening to speech is thus not listening, but *thinking*. And this is also true for the content of verbal utterances: they refer to *images*, not the reality. What is said in language is not what is happening in the world, but a play with images, or in other words: the medium is the message.⁵⁰

Apart from the obvious hermeneutical problem with which this presents us, the relevance of this fact for our study lies in the fact that images are static: in order to understand them, we "freeze" them, and then place them in context and in relation with other words, so as to grasp the whole. The movement is halting, from one image to another, no matter how quickly we do it, or how natural it becomes to us.

Musical expression has a different dynamic to it. Instead of oppositions, we listen to and "understand" musical tones in intervals, or what Speelman calls "intervallic" orientations. When we hear a tone musically we seek the relation to its fifth or third, major or minor. We "hear" it in relation to other notes. The semiotic square, when applied to music, is enriched with what he calls the category of the curve: "The musical operations that actualize the musical values form the category of the curve."⁵¹ In the musical world, things do not so much stand in opposition to one another as tend towards or from one another.

---

49. Ibid.

50. Ibid., 6–7. This position could perhaps be enriched with the Piercean understanding of the sign.

51. Speelman, *Generation of Meaning*, 49.

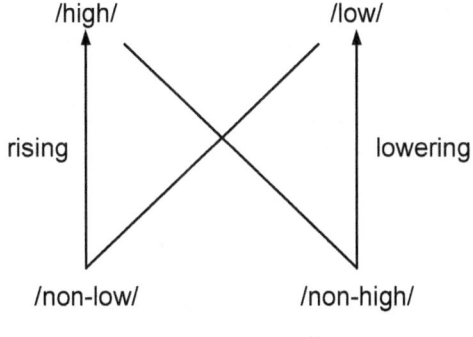

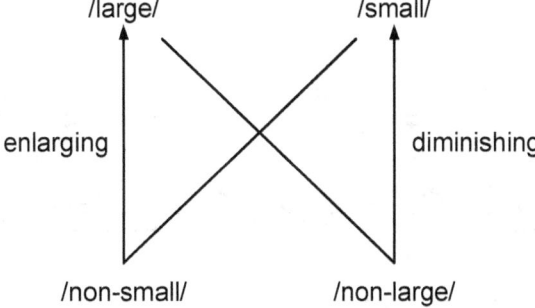

Figure 3.5[52]

In chapter 6 we will develop some of the implications of this aspect of musical symbolism, but it is not hard to imagine its creative potential for the transmission of faith in a God who is triune, and whose desire is to introduce us into communion with Themselves and with each other.

To be Understood / To be Followed

This leads Speelman to the following point: every note is oriented towards another one, be it in tonal relation or in timing: "each tone is a harmony . . . each duration is a rhythm and each intensity is a dynamic."[53] Therefore the fundamental dynamic provoked by music is that of movement. We do not grasp music by stopping it to "see" or "think" it. We follow, or are carried by it. To read music in a score is

---

52. Ibid., 48–49. Reproduced with the kind permission of Prof. Speelman.
53. Speelman, "Language and Music," 7.

to follow its movement adequately. That is why it moves us: listening to music, or reading it, even in silence, is hard to do without moving your body in some way. This is easily experienced if we seek to read a text, and then the text put to music. Our approach to "reading" differs greatly. For example, I invite the reader to read aloud the following text:

Meanwhile, slow down!
Wintertime is gone . . . move on.
You've been hiding safe, show me your face now!
The rain has gone—time to carry on!

Now, attempt to read this text in music:

Figure 3.6[54]

To read the text, we move word by word, extracting its meaning before moving on: "meanwhile"—while something else is happening; slow—you're moving too fast; wintertime—cold, rainy, not summertime . . . and so forth. To read the music, we move with its timing, and as a consequence the music moves us: "Literary utterances are to be understood, but music can only be followed."[55] This understanding of music coincides with that of other writers who relate music with time and the temporal nature of human existence, such as Bernard Lonergan, who, although he has only a few short writings on art, spe-

54. First bars of the song "Meanwhile," by Maeve Louise Heaney, 2007.
55. Speelman, "Language and Music," 8.

cifically relates music to time,⁵⁶ and Jeremy Begbie, who builds much of his theological thought around the notion of music as temporal.⁵⁷ Again, if we briefly anticipate some of the possible theological consequences of this fact, we could say that Jesus did not explain himself to his disciples—he invited them to follow him. Christian faith is better understood as a pilgrimage or journey (in the company of God and others) than as a set of beliefs, doctrines, or rules to be understood or obeyed. This corresponds with the widening of our understanding of revelation itself marked by Vatican II in the Constitution on Sacred Scripture *Dei Verbum*, which moved Catholic theology from a more conceptual notion of revelation to that of a plan of revelation realized by deeds and words with inner unity.⁵⁸

Non-Here / Omnipresence

> *Musical movement is omnipresent.*
> *We enter into a cathedral and hear a choir singing.*
> *I ask you: where is the music?*
> *Where is it not?*
>
> —Speelman⁵⁹

Once again we find the category of presence in the present moment. Music fills and penetrates the space it inhabits. You cannot "put it in the corner of a room": it is much more all-present and invasive than that.⁶⁰ Jeremy Begbie talks explicitly about how music provides us with an appropriate symbolic form to comprehend theological realities, precisely because it is aural and not visual. Talking about the Chalcedonian affirmation of faith, which seeks to defend the holding together of God's human and divine reality without confusion, without change, without distinction, without separation, he notes that when we seek to

---

56. "[M]usic is related to time; it moves one into another time . . . the time of the music"; he calls music "the image of experienced time." Lonergan, "Art," 216 and 227.

57. Cf. Begbie, *Theology, Music, and Time*.

58. Cf. Second Vatican Council, *Dei Verbum*, 2.

59. Speelman, "Language and Music," 8.

60. Hans Urs von Balthasar has some interesting reflections about the difference between visual and oral perception in the context of the liturgy. One point he makes is precisely this: one can close one's eyes to not see, but not one's ears. Cf. Balthasar, "Seeing, Hearing, and Reading." We are much more "open" and receptive in our hearing than in our seeing.

understand this truth of faith, our visual imagination struggles to hold together two "opposites" (humanity and divinity) in the same space:

> We are trapped in visual ways of thinking God's relation to the world. In a spatial model you can't have any two things in the same place at the same time, and a thing cannot be in two places at the same time. And this spatial model is applied to the relations between God and the world/God's presence to the world.[61]

Music, however, offers another approach. In a chord, one note is played with and through the other, and all the notes in a chord fill the room equally. Notes being played together, interpenetrating all the "aural space" there is, opens a different way of conceiving space to us—not mutually exclusive but overlapping and interrelated—they inhabit one another: without separation or confusion. This raises interesting questions about the preference of Gregorian non-harmonic chant in the liturgy, and the integration of polyphonic music, both its date and the motivation of this shift in practice.

Differentiating / Integrating (Harmonizing)

This point follows as a consequence of the aforementioned "intervallic" nature of music. We hear music in intervals because that is how our ears relate to the resonance it has. Music exists in harmonic relations. The musical tone itself is a harmony of different pitches, called "resonance-frequencies."[62] Music, therefore, is fundamentally harmonic:

> An acoustician may say that a specific tone is 440 vibrations per second, but a musician does not listen that way. The musical ear recognizes a tone only in relation to other tones in a scale: A is the fifth of D and so on.[63]

Even a melody without accompaniment in Western music is written in a particular musical key and is related to its corresponding harmonic tones. It "exists" in harmony. This contrasts with verbal language, whose critical power is in differentiating, or distinguishing,

---

61. Cf. Begbie, *Beholding the Glory*, 142; also *Theology, Music, and Time*, 24.

62. This is why, for example, when tuning stringed instruments, the accuracy of the tuning is not only measured by the ear, but by the vibrations of the strings together while tuning.

63. Speelman, "Music and the Word," 15.

rather than relating. This may seem a rather simple, if profound affirmation, but Speelman applies it to different levels of reality, by which it opens more possibilities. Let me quote two:

> [T]he interval of the fifth is consonant, for the two tones share one frequency in which they sound together (*con-sonare*).

and

> [T]he pattern of resonance-frequencies is recognized as a tone color. Instruments, people and things are recognized by the color of their tone.[64]

Therefore, the harmonic integration provoked by music, according to Speelman, is not only on the level of notes within a key, but also in tone color. Tone color, according to Copland, is about the available instruments and the "color" of their sound: strings have a different tone color than brass instruments, and even within the same group, the difference between a violin and a viola has to do with tone color. Copland links the relationship between instruments and tone color with meaning, at least according to the perception of the composer: "[The composer] chooses the instrument with the tone color that best expresses the meaning behind his idea."[65] The concept of the "idea" of the composer is an unclear one, and I would not express it in this way, but the relevance of tone color in relation to the "meaning" being expressed is an important one. Whatever the complexity of grasping meaning in music, Copland's observation does help us to understand what Speelman is pointing towards when he concludes: "Thus, harmony helps us communicate with reality." When one hears music, the ear registers its "resonance-frequencies" and resonates with the pattern of its movement. It resonates differently with different notes and different tone colors, but always resonating with and moving with the musical tones:

> Music makes our ears resonate with her harmony. To hear is to **harmonize** with the sound. Thus, the human enters into the harmony and meets the reality presented by it.[66]

---

64. Speelman, "Language and Music," 8.
65. Copland, *What to Listen for in Music*, 64.
66. Speelman, "Language and Music," 8.

Discernment in the use of music, therefore, would need to look at how it resonates and what it provokes in its listeners as well as its composer.

Referring to Reality (and Masking It) / Receiving Reality

This final point of Speelman's scheme, which in some sense integrates the preceding ones, invites us to reflect on the profound difference in dynamic between the way language leads us to relate to reality and the way music does. In a theological context in which the concept of the revealing God is so central, to talk about verbal language "masking" reality is significant. And yet, precisely because the verbal word seeks to enable us grasp and comprehend the reality we live, it takes us one step "away" from our "experience" of the world around us that we might understand its significance.[67] Herein lies its strength. The affirmation does not undermine the importance of the verbal word in theology or religion. Lonergan, in the same context in which he talks about the variety of forms of expression that are included in the Word, says:

> [L]anguage is the vehicle in which meaning becomes most fully articulated, the spoken and the written word are of special importance in the development and clarification of religion.[68]

So how are we to understand this reflection on the difference between referring to or masking reality and receiving it? Language provides one level of accessing and experiencing reality, and music another. They are complementary. Here we are touching directly on the issue of meaning: meaning as it is mediated by language and the specific mode of meaning that music is an expression of. Although all his work tends towards clarifying that issue, Speelman offers two particularly clear statements about the disputed issue of meaning in music. He quotes Charles Seeger when he states that "music communicates itself *qua* fact and value; but it does not 'say' so,"[69] and in his conference on the various structural differences between verbal and

---

67. This reflection touches on aspects we will deepen further in chapter 4, when we reflect upon epistemology—in particular the epistemological approach of Lonergan.

68. Lonergan, *Method in Theology*, 112.

69. Speelman, *Generation of Meaning*, 55, referring to Seeger, *Studies in Musicology*, 47.

musical communication, he draws them to a close in the following conclusion:

> Entering into the harmony as a medium of sharing, we learn the specific *musical form of meaning*: music does not refer to anything outside itself, but brings us in contact with the reality by receiving the reality in its harmony and by receiving us in that same harmony. . . . Music receives the reality it refers to and receives the listener entering into her harmony. Music is *receptivity* for reality.[70]

Meaning in music is about the way it enables us to relate to reality. Where language emphasizes the "not-I, not-here, and not-now" referential meaning of words, masking the outside reality (and therefore opening us to the challenges of hermeneutics), music keeps us in the here and now. It "turns understanding [of words] into spirituality," movement, not because it helps us long for a better life "somewhere sometime," but allowing us to realize that this "better life is within reach: it is happening here and now."[71] In this way, music has a different relationship with reality than the word does. This is not to say it is superior, or to be kept separate from verbal meaning in the expression and comprehension of our faith. The aim, instead, is to suggest that as we understand the dynamics of musical semiotics, we are better prepared to make use of it in the living out and understanding of Christian faith. The interaction of these two principles is all the more effective if we can grasp their strengths and weaknesses, both taking their place in the understanding of the Word made flesh.

---

70. Speelman, "Language and Music," 9. Emphasis original. There is an interesting parallel between how Speelman talks about the different ways of relating to reality and Lonergan's understanding of the role of art in human life. We shall deepen in his understanding of our process of knowing and art (and music's) role therein in the next chapter.

71. Speelman, "Language and Music," 9.

Conclusion: Music, the Word and the World

> *La musique ne nous* dit *rien du monde,*
> *mais elle nous donne* d'habiter *le monde.*
>
> —P. Charru[72]

Drawing together some conclusions from this brief but dense outline on musical semiotics, we can say that musical expression opens us to a different way of perceiving and apprehending reality and ourselves within that reality. The symbolism at work in music accentuates embodiment, movement, harmony, and interaction—presence to the present moment in an openness that emphasizes listening, interaction with, and reception, or even welcome, of the reality we listen to. When we seek to understand the presence of music in our lives, we are approaching a form of expression that "affects" human perception, that in some way transforms us as we receive and are received by music. Another theologian and musician, Pierangelo Sequeri,[73] talks about the symbolic nature of music as being relational as opposed to semantic, and he calls this type of symbolism operational (*operatività*):

> [T]here is a dimension of the symbolic, which human beings more typically live from, which have instead the form of action ... it does not produce objects, it transforms subjects. It establishes invisible bonds, which cannot be reduced to a meaning, to a concept, to an idea. Nor to a sign. Because they are bonds that act as strengths of interiority, not as exterior forms.[74]

We shall develop at length the theological implications of Speelman's analysis in chapter 6 when looking at the theological understanding of music, but for the moment it may be helpful to underline one of the more central aspects which have emerged: music's relationship with time and its accentuation of the present moment and the space which we inhabit. Its importance lies in the fact that it highlights the very aim of this book: what music has to say about the word, (which cannot, perhaps, be said in any other way). In Christian terms, the "Word" is more than "words"—it is our personal God who

---

72. "Music *tells* us nothing about the world, but it gives us a way of *inhabiting* the world." Charru, "L'écoute musicale," 295.

73. We shall present Sequeri's thought briefly in the next chapter.

74. Sequeri, *L'estro di Dio*, 176–77. Translation mine.

enters into reality and changes it, transforming our relationship with reality at all levels. The point is touched on in some of the reflections of Oliver Davies, one of the theologians at the center of the theological paradigm we have chosen.[75] He addresses our relationship with reality: past, present, and future, and the role of the word in that relationship. He suggests that in the history of theology, although much attention has been given to the meaning of texts, little reflection has been given to the very act, in *this* world, that takes us into their meaning: the act of reading. This is significant, because our way of perceiving and thinking reality often leaves us in a place that opposes text to world, or affirms the priority of one over the other. And yet, there is a need to pay attention to both text and the world. He seeks to underline that it is essential to our faith to recognize the power of God at work in the text and in the world:

> God's power is authoritatively manifest both in *this* text and in the world. Text and world or text and real history are aligned on the grounds of the divine power which has shaped both of them and not on the grounds of some intrinsic priority of history over text or text over history. The Christian normative reading of this text, in liturgy under the conditions of a particular time and place, is the implicit acknowledgement that the God who speaks through this text is present also in space and time.[76]

Davies, therefore, in addressing the issue of the relationship between Scripture and theology, offers as an axis for its comprehension the underlying perception of the relationship that there is between the text and the world. One can place this quotation alongside an affirmation of Speelman with regard to music: "Music therefore is a necessary medium to engage in the Word *and* in the world."[77] If Davies offers a way forward accentuating the "act of reading" in this world, I would like to suggest that music is another way of linking text and world in

---

75. Most of his thoughts on this specific theme are taken from a conference called "Fundamental Theology and the Word," given in Italian at the Gregorian University on the occasion of the Giornata di Studio of the Department of Fundamental Theology in 2008. It is available online at http://www.unigre.it/Struttura_didattica/teologia/specifico/ dipartimento_fondamentale_it.php. The quotations are from the original conference, written in English, before its translation, and kindly given to me by Prof. Davies.

76. Davies, "Fundamental Theology and the Word," 3.

77. Speelman, "Language and Music," 9.

a form of symbolism that situates us solidly in the present space and time.

In this respect, I would also point out that theology would benefit from more reflection on the important differences between the word spoken (and heard), and the word written (and read). The relevance of these differences has already been brought to our attention by musicological studies, given the difference between studying music as written in a score or listening to it as it is played.[78] Rahner makes an insightful observation on the relationship between the word, thought, and our embodied existence:

> [T]he word is the embodied thought, not the embodiment of the thought. It is more than the thought and more original than the thought.[79]

The context of this affirmation is an eloquent article on the vocation of a priest in relation to his calling to preaching. Therefore, albeit implicitly, the accent appears to be on the spoken word, but differentiating them is not the aim of the article, which focuses rather on the power of the poetic word to offer "primordial words" to our everyday language, transforming our perception of reality and in some way reality itself.[80] Paul Ricoeur also addresses the issue, proposing that, despite their differences, the spoken and the written word coincide in what he calls the fundamental function of discourse, transcendence: that is to say, they do not end in themselves, both having (internal) sense or meaning (they talk about something), and reference to the external world (they are aimed at communicating to someone):

> The Hermeneutical thesis, diametrically opposed to the structuralist thesis—not to structural method and inquiry—is that the difference between speech and writing in no way abolishes the fundamental function of discourse (which encompasses these two variations: oral and written). Discourse consists

---

78. We noted in chapter 2 as significant the fact that contemporary music is very often not written down in a score, but recorded and passed on via "oral transmission."

79. Rahner, "Priest and Poet," 295.

80. Let me note here that there is an interesting convergence between Rahner's thought in this article and that of Oliver Davies in the article I referred to: they both talk about the supreme vocal act of the priest as the moment in which he pronounces the words of the consecration. Rahner, "Priest and Poet," 306; Davies, "Fundamental Theology and the Word," 5–8.

of the fact that someone says something to someone *about something*.[81]

Although I agree with the referential nature of all verbal communication, there are important differences between the dynamics of communication through the spoken word, the "act of speaking," and through the written word that would be helpful to note.[82]

Davies draws on the work of linguistic anthropologists Michael Silverstein and Greg Urban, on the concept of "entextualization," who describe how written texts precipitate out of oral communication, by which the act of speaking is primary. He talks about double polarity between speaking and writing, writing and reading:

> Once written down, texts become detached from their immediate oral contexts, at a specific point in space and time, and can move across the generations. But each time a text is read, it is reintegrated into the orality of the living present.[83]

In doing this he relates the dynamic of writing and reading with temporality: that which is written instantly becomes part of the past, which we access in the present moment:

> People speak (voice—to be heard), this gets written down (text—to be seen) and when the text is read again, it becomes voice again: it may be spoken aloud, or spoken silently within, or it may shape our speaking in other ways. To understand a text is to make it our own. A text comes to us from the past but, once read, it has present force again, shaping what we think and say.[84]

Although he does not relate this past/present dynamic solely to the relationship between the written/oral word, it is clear that both the act of reading and that of speaking is part of the present moment.

---

81. Ricoeur, "Naming God," 220–21.

82. Let me mention two contemporary theologians who approach this theme: Pierangelo Sequeri offers some reflections on the human voice, in the context of writing on aesthetics: "the living voice allows the true interlocutory meaning of the other's discourse to be understood with greater precision." Sequeri, *L'estro di Dio*, 222, in a chapter on "Listening, Music and Song" ("L'ascolto, la musica, il canto"). Other interesting thoughts can be found in Sergio Gaburro's book on the human voice in revelation, *La voce della rivelazione*.

83. Davies, "Fundamental Theology and the Word," 5.

84. Ibid.

In music we have seen how the accent and emphasis on the present, the here and now, is important and is reinforced by the typically embodied nature of musical semiotics. In a book on contemporary music, the differentiation between and understanding of oral and written takes on special importance. It is true that Beethoven continued to compose when he could not hear, and a musician *can* compose within his or her mind, hearing the notes that practice and habit make familiar, even without externalizing them, but the symbolism specific to music comes into play in the moment that music is played and listened to. It is in that moment in which the specific "power" or capacity of music to affect change or transform the atmosphere or reality within which it is heard becomes actual. This is of epistemological importance, as we shall see in the next chapter: all knowledge enters through the senses, but music is accessed through our hearing.

This present chapter on musical semiotics constitutes the center of this book, as well as the bridge between the musicological and hermeneutical approaches of chapters 1 and 2 with the rest of the book, which will explore the theological dimension of musical semiotics. To my mind, in the context of what is aiming to be a foundational account of music in theology, this implies two steps or areas: reflection on how the dynamic of musical symbolism and expression can be understood and integrated into theological epistemology (a term I shall explain in chapter 4), and the presentation of a theological paradigm as the context or backdrop within which the specifics of musical semiotics and semantics can find their place or home.

4

Towards a Theological Epistemology of Music

Faith comes through hearing

—Rom 10: 7

"Straight to the point" can ricochet, unconvincing.
Circumlocution, analogy,
Parable's ambiguities,
provide context, stepping-stones.

—Denise Levertov[1]

Music and Epistemology: A Theological Challenge

The Importance of Epistemology in Theological Reflection

We possess art lest we perish of the truth.

—Nietzsche[2]

THE TITLE OF THIS BOOK INCLUDES TWO INTERRELATED POINTS: music as theology, or theological praxis and music as a means by which we can listen to and receive the Word of God. The whole book is an attempt to "prove" or present the first one. The latter asks if and how music can mediate Christian faith. As noted in the introduction, the underlying criteria or touchstone for discerning if and how this happens is revelation itself, since the word, in Christian terms, is

---

1. Levertov, "Poetics of Faith," in *Sands in the Wells*, 110.
2. Nietzsche, *Will to Power*, 435.

Someone—our God revealed in the incarnated Christ. Christian faith is a response to the revealing God. It is faith in our triune God who has taken the initiative of creating the universe of space and time, in the desire of living in a loving relationship with human beings, and of coming to meet humanity in history, through the people of Israel, in and through the humanity of Jesus of Nazareth, and through the Spirit in the church.[3] Therefore it is this revealing God and the how of that revelation of God in history that must guide our reflection and discernment on any possible means of mediating and understanding the faith which is born of receiving and accepting that God.

The interaction of how music affects or colors our relationship with reality (the world, other people, ourselves and God), as outlined in our previous chapter, with how we come to faith leads us to the theme of this chapter, on what could be called a "theological epistemology"—that is to say: how do we come to faith, to know God? What process is or can be involved? What role, if any, do the senses have? And the mind? Is the body superfluous, a hindrance, or it is touched and transformed in the coming to faith, being indispensable to that process? The intent of these questions is not to seek to control a mysterious reality that also has to do with the unfathomable freedom of every individual person, who, once they have intuited or encountered the presence of the living God in their lives, can accept or refuse to entrust themselves to that God. Nor is it possible to simplify the many elements that can enter into the process of God's touching any one life, such as culture, family influence, ritual and friendships, or the more obvious ones of the witness of a community of Christians and

---

3. Even if each moment of the history of salvation seems to highlight more the presence and work of one of the three Persons of the Trinity (Old Testament, God as Creator; the Gospels, the Person of Jesus and after his death and resurrection, the presence and work of the Holy Spirit), our faith tells us all three are present in the actions of all, rather than one succeeding the other temporally. For the doctrinal position underpinning this book, it is an important distinction, as the truth of the ascension implies that the humanity of Jesus is not less present in the world after his resurrection and the sending of the Spirit. The time of the church is not only the time of the Spirit, but also that of the continued presence of the incarnated, risen and ascended body of Jesus Christ in humanity, in whom we have been assumed. In another direction, it is interesting to note that Lonergan, talking about our coming to know God, maintains that the "process" is actually opposite to how we imagine it to be: the Spirit poured out in our hearts as our first point of encounter with the triune God, the Word of Jesus Christ announced to us through the church, and finally God the Creator, from whom all flows. Cf. Crowe "Rethinking God-with-Us."

their "giving reason for their faith" by the explicit proclamation of the gospel.[4] But there is a "coming to know" involved in the process of faith: coming to know the gospel, the truth held therein, who God is and who we are as human beings, and the very person of Christ, through the Spirit. What I am asking is what the potential or actual role of music *in that process of coming to know and therefore believe, is*. Understanding if and how music can have a role in that process will lead us to comprehend in what way it can become part of our theological endeavor, and how.

The importance of epistemology in theology is not limited to music or theological aesthetics. The contrasting approaches of a more Neoplatonic-Augustinian understanding of how we know reality and that of an Aristotelian-Thomistic one colors the history of Western theology and spirituality. In the more recent history of apologetics, authors from different schools of theological thought have convincingly identified the negative consequences of the naïve integration of inadequate epistemological approaches in theological thought, and sought ways forward in widening our approach to the same. According the authoritative analysis of Michael J. Buckley,[5] in the wake of modernity, theology learnt to talk of God and defend itself with the tools offered to it from the largely empiricist philosophical apparatus of the time. Thus it ended up defending a God that had precious little content of the Christian God of revelation, a tragedy in which "theologians allowed themselves to be hijacked unto alien grounds."[6] "God

---

4. Paul VI, in his noteworthy Apostolic Exhortation *Evangelii Nuntiandi*, summarizes with insightful clarity the steps involved in evangelization and coming to Christian faith in four: the silent witness of a community of people, provoking irresistible question marks in those who see them; an explicit response, offering "the reason for the hope that you all have" (Cf. 1 Pt 3:15); the acceptance of that Word and entrance into a community of faithful in the Church; and that the evangelized person becomes, in turn, an agent of evangelization. Cf. Paul VI, *Evangelii Nuntiandi*, nn. 21–24. The postmodern world we live in now is very different to the one Paul VI lived in, and perhaps one could include other elements that were not relevant then, such as beauty, aesthetics and a commitment for justice. Chapter 5 looks at some of these aspects.

5. Cf. Buckley, *At the Origins of Modern Atheism*, and *Denying and Disclosing God*. For a summary of the thought presented in the earlier book on this subject, cf. Buckley, "Atheism—Origins."

6. Gallagher, *What Are They Saying about Unbelief?*, 49, talking about Michael J. Buckley's analysis of the phenomenon of modern atheism in *At the Origins of Modern Atheism*.

became incredible because God became small," is the way Michael Paul Gallagher describes the process of western culture's distancing itself from the God of Christian revelation.[7] The problem with this is not only the result—theology's defense of a false image of God, but is also the way people learned to "think" about how we come to know God; that is to say, epistemological: the assumption without discerning, within the theological task, of tools of knowledge and expression for the comprehension and defense of Christian faith taken from a worldview without faith. "The nature of knowledge had changed and theologians were caught unprepared."[8] Buckley clearly identifies in an inadequate epistemology many of the mistakes of theology in past centuries. Referring to Baron Friedrich von Hügel's treatise on the importance of including in foundational thought on religion the three dimensions of the rational-speculative, the affective-mystical, and the institutional-traditional,[9] he states:

> [I]f one ignores or brackets as *cognitively* unimportant this religious manifold and turns to other disciplines to give basic substance to its claims that God exists, one has implicitly admitted that religion—or that reflection upon religion for its evidence that we have been calling theology—possesses an *inner cognitive insubstantiality*.[10]

Pierangelo Sequeri, from within a completely different school of theological thought, also identifies the need for an intrinsic analysis of the epistemological bases and dynamic of faith. He describes how modernity was criticized for its closure, in premises and conclusions, to transcendence, but without addressing adequately its epistemological guiding criteria, which theology instead assumed and implemented. It is perhaps eloquently epitomized by him when he points out the falsehood of allowing "a small group of intellectuals ... decide that the irreligious condition of man is his natural condition."[11] The result was

---

7. Gallagher, *What Are They Saying about Unbelief?*, 41.
8. Ibid., 55, talking about the thought of Turner in *Without God, without Creed*.
9. Cf. Buckley, *Denying and Disclosing God*, 138, referring to von Hügel, *Mystical Element of Religion*.
10. Buckley, *Denying and Disclosing God*, 138. Emphasis mine. His analysis of the limits of a certain type of philosophical inference as foundational to religion and theology prepare for and converge with that of Paul Janz.
11. Sequeri, *Qualità spirituale*, 58–59. This statement also reminds us of the danger of centralizing theological discourse in western culture, overlooking the particu-

a theology convinced of the need to argue for the reasons of credibility, taking, however, the "conditions of the arguing reason" from outside of the believing conscience, or consciousness.[12] For this reason, theology has been lacking a systematic research into the structure of the believing conscience and religious faith.[13] In other words, for a complex series of reasons, theology has not paid enough attention to the multiform nature of how human beings come to believe and trust, limiting itself to conceptual rationality. A right understanding of music implies addressing this gap.

We shall see in chapter 5 how, even while recognizing and indeed founding our own reflections on the groundbreaking proposal offered by Balthasar's theological aesthetics, one of its identified limitations is in the lack of an adequate epistemological theory to sustain and apply its insights. For the moment, however, we shall begin to look at some the epistemological aspects of musical apprehension that such an epistemology needs to take into account and integrate.

The Brain, Human Knowing, and Music

> *For me, music is all about feelings and vibrations.*
> *Generally, I sense low sounds in my legs and feet*
> *and high sounds in my face and neck.*
> *So instead of hearing*
> *I am able to sense the music*
> *in order to understand the harmonic make-up.*
>
> —Profoundly deaf percussionist Evelyn Glennie[14]

Epistemological questions about music have already begun to surface in earlier chapters. The debate on musical meaning and emotion, for

---

lar historical process it has gone through, which does not reflect the understanding of other cultures and therefore cannot be universally applied to other cultural situations without critical discernment.

12. The translation of Sequeri's notion of "*coscienza*" is not simple as it evokes elements of the English meanings of "conscience," "consciousness," and "awareness"

13. Cf. Sequeri, *L'estro di Dio*, 21–22. This is one of the main elements of Sequeri's thought, which we will present more comprehensively in chapter 5, especially in regard to theological aesthetics and music.

14. Glennie is famous worldwide for the expertise and musicality of her percussion playing. Quoted in Begbie, *Resounding Truth*, 314–15.

example, about whether the key to valuing music is in its internal structure and harmony, and therefore perceived by the critical appraisal of the intellect, or rather in its capacity to refer to or evoke emotional response, touches on the theme of human epistemology: how do we know? What can we know—the essence of things, or only the external phenomena? What are the respective roles of the mind and the emotions in knowing? Is intellectual knowledge superior to emotional understanding, and are they really that separate at all? These are some of the questions that have begun to surface.

According to substantial neurological studies, there is no doubt as to the direct influence of music on the brain. "Music and speech are separately represented in the two hemispheres of the brain." Language affects the left one, and music the right, albeit with overlap.[15] The right hemisphere is the one that processes more emotions, the left one conceptual thought and logic. If we add to this discovery the hypothesis of art historian Wilhelm Worrington on the two different modes of perceiving or valuing art, applied to music, the consequences for debates on musical value are interesting. Worrington talks about observation by "abstraction," which implies distance in critical observation, and observation via empathy.[16] He says that modern aesthetics focus on empathy, the enjoyment received from art, whereas classic art criticism focuses more on abstraction. This would be corroborated by Joachim-Ernst Berendt, who noted that in Western musicians and composers trained in concert music, experiments showed how their appreciation of music was to be found in the left side of the brain, rather than the right:

> In most of the people examined their musicality had moved to the left side of the brain, which programs what we do with the right hand as well as with our sense of form and design, visually and metaphorically. Musicality is thus . . . deprived of its natural feedback from the heart and feeling side, and transferred to the realm of logic and functionality which are usually in the left half of the brain.[17]

Although the dualism in Berendt's presentation seems slightly extreme or at least simplistic, the direction of his research is interest-

---

15. Storr, *Music and the Mind*, 35.
16. Worrington, *Abstraction and Empathy*, quoted in ibid., 39.
17. Berendt, *Third Ear*, 174.

ing. It suggests that western classical music accentuates abstraction and intellectual appreciation of music, rather than embodied empathy or emotional appreciation. Without taking their findings too literally, or generalizing them into a non-realistic form of dualism, I believe this could explain some of the more polarized opposed opinions between high art criticism and contemporary popular music: the viewpoints are different. One side perceives and accentuates the intellectual enrichment to be found, the other the pleasure involved in its reception. Different points of appreciation can be mutually complementary where those offering them are aware of the fact and open to recognizing the positive aspects of each. If this does not happen, dialogue and mutual understanding becomes difficult.

Simon Frith, in his discerning book on the aesthetic value of popular music, with the intention, in his own words, of "taking popular discrimination seriously," talks about his discomfort with the assumption that a "high theorist can talk about the meaning of low music without listening to it, without liking it, without needing to know anything more about it at all."[18] Surely there can be no discerning without empathy?[19]

> The exercise of taste and aesthetic discrimination is as important in popular as in high culture but it is more difficult to talk about . . . in terms recognized by high culture authorities.[20]

I suggest this difficulty is also epistemological: the non-recognition of how listeners appreciate music, or even a lack of integration of the different factors of the human capacity of apprehension and knowledge. For example, if "intellectual enrichment" is taken to be more "spiritual" than the pleasure to be found in empathy, we need to ask the question as to what comprehension of "spiritual" underlies that appreciation, which anthropology is at work and whether it can be considered a valid understanding of Christian experience or not. Once again we find ourselves on theological ground: what are the consequences of a faith in which God becomes human? How do we

18. Frith, *Performing Rights*, 253.

19. Gallagher talks about three elements necessary for Christian discerning: disposition, direction, and decision. The first, an openness to know and understand a culture must also include some willingness to like it. Cf. Gallagher, *Clashing Symbols*, 141.

20. Frith, *Performing Rights*, 11.

understand revelation and what is the corresponding experience of faith that accepting that revealing God provokes?

This question overlaps with another: that of the body's involvement in music. Alongside the need to integrate intellect and emotions, there is the relevance of the body in both composing and listening to music: "It must be emphasized that making music is an activity that is rooted in the body."[21] Indeed, as mentioned above and noted also by Storr, according to Blacking, "feeling with the body" is the essence of empathy.[22] Of all the art forms, which in some way involve the coming together of spirit and matter, music is the most embodied.

> I can well believe that some people can find that their heart beats faster when they look at a beautiful picture, building or sunset; but I doubt if they experience the urge towards physical motion, the increase in muscle tone, and the muscular responses to rhythm which music induces. Pictures seldom make one want to dance.[23]

In this light, music's contribution to aesthetics is a challenging one: "the danger—the threat posed by music and dance to aesthetics—is not so much the absence of mind as the presence of body."[24] The significance of our human existence as embodied is central to Christianity, which, at its very core professes faith in an incarnated God, witnessing to the positive nature of our existence in the world as beings of flesh and blood. So important is the embodied nature of human existence that our faith professes a God who lived, died, rose and whose *body* ascended and lives, glorious, having somehow assumed, in Himself, our own humanity. This "bodily presence," both our own and that of Christ, is the focus point of Oliver Davies's thought in *Transformation Theology*,[25] which is one of the reasons I have chosen it as a theological framework with which to approach music in and as theology, as we shall see in chapter 6. The underlying intuition is not only that understanding music implies a renewed understanding

21. Storr, *Music and the Mind*, 24.
22. Blacking, *How Musical Is Man?*, 111, quoted in ibid., 29.
23. Storr, *Music and the Mind*, 149.
24. Frith, *Performing Rights*, 260.
25. This book is the first book, published in 2007, presenting this strand of theology. Other books that come under the umbrella of this approach have been and continue to be published by individual theologians. This one, however, coauthored by its three first representatives, presents the principles of their theological paradigm.

of our embodied existence, but also vice versa, that music can help in achieving and maintaining a healthy Christian comprehension of our living in the world. It is interesting that Schopenhauer, whose writing on music is acclaimed above all by musicians and composers, identifies two ways of accessing the inner essence of reality (which he called the Will), otherwise inaccessible to us: music, and the subject's self-awareness of the body from inside. Music, for Schopenhauer, is a non-representational and non-propositional art, and expresses the inner nature of the Will itself. A person's body is the space through which they can have a direct and intuitive apprehension of the Will in action.[26] I am not aware that Schopenhauer reflects on the link between these two realities (music and the body) as Storr does, but for the purpose of this book, it is significant to do so. There is, of course, in Schopenhauer's thought, a platonic element in that he postulates the existence of Ideas or Values in an otherworldly sphere, which may affect any further thought on the significance of corporality. I would prefer to suggest that we have access to the universal only through the particular as manifested to us in "this world," and as we shall see the next chapter, part of the problem is that our divided perception of the spiritual and the material in western thinking is not helpful for understanding music, nor indeed for our living out Christian faith in general.[27]

Human perception and thought process is a complex one. Storr says that "conceptual thought requires the separation of thinking from feeling, of object from subject, of mind from body."[28] I beg to differ, and would advance that the freedom or "detachment" that discerning or the discipline of thought implies is not about separation but about awareness and healthy interaction. It is reported that Freud detested *all* music.[29] It would merit serious reflection as to why, but I imagine it has something to do with the intrinsic link between music, the body, and sexuality. If our corporality influences in our thought processes,

---

26. Cf. Storr, *Music and the Mind*, 128–49, who dedicates a chapter on Schopenhauer's thought. He does not mention if Schopenhauer brings these two aspects of the body and music together.

27. Rosemary Haughton, our third author in this chapter, also speaks of this element of "particularity" as essential to our experience of love, including Christian love.

28. Ibid., 122.

29. "He despised music and considered it solely as an intrusion!" Harry Freud, "My Uncle Sigmund," in Ruitenbeek, *Freud As We Knew Him*, 313.

empathetic and conceptual thinking can complement and enrich one another. This is an area that theology and spirituality in Western culture has neglected.[30] More attention to it would better equip us to answer the questions raised about the role of music in faith transmission, how music affects us and therefore how apt it is as an instrument to be used in the attempt to communicate Christian faith. Can it can help in the specific moment of proclamation of the gospel, or as a form of preparation or pre-evangelization, before the word, or can it somehow accompany or complement the verbal word and form part of the *Logos* as it touches human life?[31] These questions, at least in part, are epistemological. They ask about how music interacts with our human knowing, and therefore what role it has in our "knowing" the Son of God, and therefore having life.[32]

The area of theology in which these questions are normally asked is that of theological aesthetics. Aesthetics, etymologically speaking, is derived from the Greek term αἴθησις meaning "perception of the senses,"[33] and has to do with the study of perception, or how we perceive. Therefore it is always, implicitly or explicitly, situated within a theory of knowledge. When that theory is not explicit, as is the case often, it is difficult to understand and discern the concrete expression of art being looked at, and its value or role. Hence the need to be very clear in our understanding of how we know, what we can know, and

---

30. And yet in recent times it is once again moving center stage. Contemporary interest in the spiritual senses is a symptom of this interest, and we shall reflect on its insights and limits in chapter 6. Other approaches, including interdisciplinary efforts to understand and reflect theologically on human embodiment are also beginning to emerge. Cf., for example, a recent book by Biancu and Pugliesi called *Il corpo: Teologia e saperi a confronto* ("The Body: Theology and Other Forms of Knowledge in Comparison"), which brings together a study on the same from different perspectives, including theology, philosophy, and anthropology.

31. A quest to understand the complementary role of art or music in evangelization does not seek to deny or undermine in any way the importance of the verbal word in Christian faith and its communication. On the contrary, it seeks to ground both in the reality of God's Word incarnated in Jesus Christ and emphasize the need for and possibility of complementary roles. The recent book of Javier Morlans, a theologian and singer-songwriter from Cataluyna, *El primer anuncio*, which is about the first proclamation of the gospel, reflects on this area in chapter 8, specifically in relation to Christian composers.

32. Cf. John 17:1–3.

33. Cf. Richard Viladesau's comprehensive treatment of the history of the concept in Western thought in *Theological Aesthetics*, 6–11.

how perception and intellect interact in that process, in the service of our reception of revelation. This epistemological clarity can then be better integrated into the area of theological aesthetics in order to reflect God as beauty, alongside the other approaches to God, as good, or as truth.[34] The next chapter will explore the return of beauty to the theological scene, and present the thought of some of the theologians of recent times in the area of theological aesthetics. Before that, however, we will present the epistemology inherent in our own approach, as a first step towards building the theological paradigm we consider most adequate for theological aesthetics and its comprehension of music, to be completed in chapter 6.

Since one of the motivations behind this book is the lack of an overall paradigm for the theological understanding of music, the epistemological framework I work with brings together elements from three different authors. Their combined insights provide complementary epistemological and theological keys that are helpful in the comprehension of music from a theological perspective and are compatible with the more specifically theological doctrinal approach to our theme presented in the following chapter. The authors in question are Bernard Lonergan, Paul Janz, and Rosemary Haughton. From the first, we will take his epistemological structure, his understanding of the role of art and music therein, and its relationship with what he understands as conversion. From the second, we will assume a particular philosophical and epistemological insight which we consider relevant for the understanding of musical apprehension. Although less known than Lonergan, there are areas in common between the two, and his understanding of revelation and human knowing are insightful for the theological understanding of musical apprehension, and its comprehension (or lack of the same) in the history of Western thought. With the third author, we shall seek to bring together the conclusions of both of these in a specifically spiritual and Christian framework, that bridges us towards why and in what way our apprehension of and interaction with music is an aid to Christian faith and theological understanding. Haughton acts a bridge to Davies thought in transformation theology, due to the convergences in her thought with Lonergan

---

34. As noted by John Paul II: "In a certain sense, beauty is the visible form of the good, just as the good is the metaphysical condition of beauty." John Paul II, *Letter of His Holiness to Artists*, 3.

in his assessment of the philosophical and epistemological heritage of Western culture,[35] as well as with Davies's thought and doctrine on the Christian God and Christian faith.

Theological Epistemology in Theological Aesthetics: Complementary Approaches

> *Man's artistry attests to his freedom.*
> Bernard Lonergan[36]

Intentional Analysis in Bernard Lonergan

> *Let me write a nations' songs,*
> *and I don't care who writes her laws.*
> —Proverb quoted by Lonergan

Few theologians give as much importance to epistemology as Lonergan does. It reflects not only one aspect of his thought but the very process of his life's reflection. Although there are various collections of writings gathered from different stages of his life, without doubt his two main contributions to Catholic theology are the books he wrote on epistemology, *Insight: A Study on Human Understanding*, and the nature of the theological task, *Method in Theology*. And these two cannot be separated, since after his comprehensive study of the process of human knowing, he moves on to reflect on method in theological thought, where he applies the axis of his epistemological findings (his "intentional analysis," which we will look at shortly) to the whole dynamic of theological method.[37] Therefore it is not only or even primarily his thought on aesthetics or music we are interested in, but his

---

35. Lonergan admits her influence on him explicitly in Lonergan, "Pope John's Intention."

36. Lonergan, *Insight*, 209.

37. This he applies to the functional specialities we spoke of in the introduction, in the two phases of theology: research, interpretation, and history and dialectics (mediating); and foundations, doctrines, systems, and communications (mediated). It takes the specific role of each area of theological investigation seriously, while recognizing also the need for them to collaborate and work together.

overall epistemological approach, which we take as foundational in relation to our other two authors and in relation to the overall approach of this book. There is a certain amount of patience required in the reading, assimilation and above all application of Lonergan's thought, as his thoroughness in treating any given subject leads him to prepare and ground everything within the whole structure of his analysis. Frederick Crowe refers to Lonergan as a theologian of the future, rather than of the present, precisely because instead of dealing directly with the doctrinal issues theology needs to address, he takes a step back to ask *how* they need to dealt with effectively, and builds towards addressing them.[38] In the context of this book, the patience required is that of understanding his epistemology and the relationship to reality it implies, before we can attempt to relate it to aesthetic experience and art, as well as to the particular form of artistic reality that is music.

To my knowledge, Lonergan has no explicit treatments of the theme of beauty,[39] and therefore is not an author who is usually brought to bear on themes of aesthetics.[40] He has written briefly but significantly about art in various places.[41] We will return to these later. Richard Viladesau, in his book on *Theological Aesthetics,* outlines an ap-

---

38. He describes Lonergan's work in the following terms: "To withdraw from the hunt when there is quarry immediately before one, to postpone the pursuit while giving oneself to the forging of a new and vastly superior instrument, to be willing, and entirely to determine, to spend one's entire life at that task (hoping the long-term benefit will make it worthwhile but knowing with certainty that one will not see the full harvest and realising that at best one's effort will be appreciated by only a small band of attentive readers and students) . . . ," describing it as "an act of notable self-transcendence." Crowe, *Method in Theology,* 57. Understanding and applying Lonergan's thought requires, perhaps, some of that same tenacity.

39. He is remembered, on the occasion of his visit to Milltown, as having said that beauty differed from the other transcendentals in that it involved "the whole person" (from a conversation with Professor William Mathews, professor of that institute.) However, he has written, albeit briefly, about art, which we will look at shortly.

40. One exception is Mooney's insightful study of Lonergan's thought in relation to von Balthasar: Mooney, *Liberation of Consciousness.* The book is a thorough, competent, and early study of a theme that has since become central to theological investigation, bringing together two major authors that have not usually been compared in relation to this area.

41. Cf. Lonergan, *Insight,* 207–9, 291–92, 410–12, and 647–48 on its role in human knowing and its liberating effect on human living, and *Method in Theology,* 61–64, 74, and 272 with regard to its role in human living and theology. He also has one short but important text on "Art" in *Topics in Education.*

proach to beauty and aesthetics in connection to Lonergan's thought and framework. He clarifies that for Lonergan, methodologically speaking, epistemology comes before metaphysics: how we know authentically is the only access point to what is real. Indeed, he points out that for Lonergan, the real and the true are equivalent. Viladesau insists that Lonergan's most radical innovation or "gift" to this area is precisely that: he "insists on the dependence of metaphysical terms on a prior cognitional theory."[42] This corresponds with my own concern about our tendency in theological thought on music to make general affirmations about the essence of music and its transcendence (both metaphysical terms!) without serious consideration of its interaction with our living and knowing in the world. An appreciation of the role and value of music, and indeed all art, in faith transmission necessarily implies attention to the world of space and time in which we live and believe. Moreover, the musical analysis of Speelman we have just focused on highlights precisely how temporal and embodied music, and our apprehension of it, is.

The Scholastics used the term "transcendental" to refer to what they considered to the essential properties or qualities of being. Beauty has sometimes been included in the list.[43] Lonergan, instead of treating the traditional concept of beauty as a metaphysical "transcendental," unfolds it into a threefold dynamic whose point of arrival, rather than starting point, is that of beauty as a transcendental concept. Viladesau describes Lonergan's threefold approach to the transcendentals as follows:

- Transcendental notions, which are those spontaneous operative heuristic anticipations that push us to know. They are a priori and not conscious, a preapprehension.

- Transcendental precepts, which express them, and in which these notions are operative: "Be attentive, be intelligent, be reasonable, be responsible, be-in-love!"

- Transcendental concepts, which are what we arrive at when the goals of these imperatives are reached. These correspond to the "transcendentals" as theology traditionally understands them.

---

42. Cf. Viladesau, *Theological Aesthetics*, 29.
43. We shall touch on this more fully in chapter 5.

In this light, beauty is the implicit notion that drives us, *in this world*, impelled by the imperative to "be attentive" in a deeper, fuller way, to concrete reality, and thus understand and apprehend the concept or "transcendental" that is beauty.[44] For me this has major consequences for theology, and perhaps especially for any theology of revelation. We cannot jump to theories about the essence of things, without passing through our apprehension of them, through our human capacity of knowing. And we can only know something about beauty because and in the measure that God wants us to, that God reveals beauty to us. Indeed, not only does this approach correspond with how we actually interact with reality, as we shall see shortly in looking more closely at Lonergan's epistemological structure, but it also reflects more faithfully than a strictly metaphysical one how contemporary sensibility approaches, receives or "understands" beauty.

Lonergan's quest and writings are born first and foremost from the desire to understand truth and its intelligibility (keeping in mind that for him, the real and the true are equivalent), and it is in the context of his understanding of the same that his thought on art and music can be situated. He believes that errors in this area of the intelligibility of reality and truth are at the root of many of the misunderstandings and differences in opinion to be found in theology. In fact, this perception that philosophical thought as it has unfolded over the last centuries has influenced negatively our living and our theological thought in Western culture is one that our three authors have in common. Rosemary Haughton talks about our being "so stiff in our categories, so laced up in corsets of eighteenth century rationalism, that we can scarcely bend, and even normal breathing is difficult."[45] Janz's main point with regard to the history of philosophical thought is that it lost sight of our embodied presence in space and time, and taught us to think and try and function within what he calls "inferential" categories, sidelining the causal and motivational ones which actually make sense of our everyday living. The result was (and is) the difficulty to comprehend and reflect upon revelation in history and the reality that we inhabit in an adequate way. Lonergan, in words that come close

---

44. The tone of Lonergan's transcendental precepts is similar to Janz's notion of causal authority experienced as "command" rather than idea or reason, as is explained later in this chapter. Cf. Janz, "Coming Righteousness," and further developed in his later book, *The Command of Grace*.

45. Haughton, *Passionate God*, 27.

to Haughton's ones, (and interestingly in an article on art), says that "philosophers for at least two centuries . . . have been trying to remake man, and have done not little to make human life unlivable."[46]

Therefore, he addresses the issue of a "right understanding" of how we live and know in this world. It is my belief that this "right understanding" is also the only way forward in comprehending music's role in life and Christian faith. Let us start with the main principles of Lonergan's analysis, before complementing it with our other authors and applying it to art and music. Lonergan's description of the human capacity of knowing is referred to as "intentional consciousness." He analyses the operations and process of human knowing, and classifies them into four stages: empirical, intellectual, rational and responsible. In the first we experience, in the second we seek to understand what it is we experience (*Quid sit? Cur ita sit?*), in the third we reflect on what has been understood to verify its truth and reality (*An sit?*), and finally we decide on its value, and on what we are going to do with it (*An honestum sit?*). Human knowing of the world is moved by these questions within the person, and is therefore a fruit of the intending subject in touch with the world. This position is described by Lonergan as "critical realism."

According to Lonergan, human knowing always follows this process, from the experience of any given data, presented to human understanding through the senses, internal or external, we seek to understand that which we have experienced, reflect upon it and decide what to do about it.[47] He comments that, while for many authors experience is a form of knowledge, for him is it an infrastructure of knowledge. He fits in with the line of Anglo-American thinkers that challenge the original notion of experience as that of objects, or self as object, to that of our experiencing ourselves.[48] Therefore "experi-

---

46. Lonergan, "Art," 232.

47. For example, one feels cold: one asks oneself is that really what the feeling is (*Cur ita sit?*); then one asks why: it may be that there is a drop in temperature, a window open leaving a draft . . .; we verify that discovery (*An sit?*); and finally, the question of what to do about it emerges (*An honestum sit?*): shall I close the window, put on a coat . . . ? With internal experiences, the same process follows, albeit with added levels of complexity: one feels negative, or down; one asks why, and seeks the cause of the feeling; when the possible cause emerges, the question of: is that really what is going on (verification)? Finally, the decision of what to do with this experience and understanding of the same is dealt with.

48. Cf. Moloney, "Person as Subject of Spirituality," 74.

ence" properly expressed, (which can be both external and/or internal), for Lonergan constitutes the first part of the fourfold process of knowledge. This understanding of the term "experience" in Lonergan explains why he rarely speaks of "experience of God" ("we have no data on God"),[49] but rather of "religious experience": experience of the divine or of grace. True and "correct" knowledge (and hence by inclusion, also knowledge of God) always implies the interaction of all four levels. Experience of music, therefore, and indeed of all art, primarily affects this first level of knowledge. It is on the fourth level that the reality of our decision and freedom comes more specifically into play. This process achieves its ultimate fulfillment in the "fifth level,"[50] "being-in-love" provoked by the Holy Spirit being poured out into the human heart (Rom 5:5), which he describes as "the efficacious ground of all self-transcendence."[51] This gift of God's love is the principle of movement behind the whole dynamic process, and therefore infuses them all.

This analysis allows us to begin to address the issues that surface about *what* experience of the divine we can have in the world, and if and how it can be transmitted through music? Within this process, where should we situate the experience of listening to or making music: on the first level? On the fifth? Christian faith is friendship with the God revealed in and through Jesus Christ which implies our entering into the very knowledge of God: "Now this is eternal life: that they may know you, the only true God, and Jesus Christ, whom you have sent" (John 17:3). If knowledge of and belief in God imply the interaction of all four or five levels, then how does the sensorial experience of hearing music, or internally bringing its memory to our mind affect that faith or knowledge? Music, according to Speelman, engages us with the present moment, opens us to an attitude of listening to and receiving reality, provoking in us a corporal, dynamic movement with rhythm and time, rather than trying to hold reality still and static. Could the awareness provoked in us by music not affect, and even increase, our potential receptivity to Christian faith (first level), and if so, how? Or could music born of the experience of the Holy Spirit

---

49. Oral tradition as having been said by Lonergan often.

50. There is some disagreement as to whether Lonergan understood this a fifth level or as the fulfillment of the fourth one.

51. Lonergan, *Method in Theology*, 241.

poured out in our hearts somehow facilitate our knowing God at *all* levels of our process of knowing, as it is not tied down to conceptual understanding? This could explain why, when a truth of faith that has been effectively preached and welcomed, is followed by a song that evokes and confirms its message, the result would seem to be one of greater adhesion to the truth in question. At the core of this whole process of Lonergan's intentional consciousness, or critical realism, is our presence to and relationship with reality. Art, according to Lonergan, is situated precisely in that same relationship, with the role or capacity of freeing our consciousness for a fuller, more real perception and living out of the same. We shall return to this point when talking about aesthetics in epistemology, but first we need to complete Lonergan's own thought on the subject.

Awakening to and integrating this epistemological "structure" in one's comprehension of knowing is what Lonergan calls "intellectual conversion," and is of major importance to him. It is not common. Most people live out their lives without ever asking themselves how they know what they know, or what is "real" for them. "Converting" to a more adequate and truthful understanding of reality implies a serious effort of self-awareness and internal growth. And yet, where philosophy and theology are concerned, so important to Lonergan is the right understanding of how we interact with reality, that he places the "intellectual conversion" of the theologian to critical realism alongside moral and religious "conversion"[52] as the indispensable foundation on which theology needs to be grounded in the present cultural context.[53] Intellectual conversion, therefore, situates itself on the level of our cognition and consists in overcoming the myth of empiricism, or a noncritical type of "realism" that would have us think that "knowing is like looking, that objectivity is seeing what there is to be seen and not seeing what is not there, and that the real is what is out there now to be looked at."[54] The *real world is me in the midst of the world*[55] with the

---

52. We shall explain further this threefold dynamic of conversion in relation to the person of the artist, later on and in chapter 6. At the moment, our focus is on intellectual conversion and its relationship with aesthetic sensibility and the human process of knowing.

53. Cf. Lonergan, "Theology in Its New Context"; and *Method in Theology*, 130–32, 267–70.

54. Lonergan, *Method in Theology*, 238.

55. I emphasize to note the similarity of expression with Davies and Janz in their description of how we inhabit the world.

meaning that I give it, which I don't invent or create either but rather receive from and in the midst of a community which transmits that meaning to me. Knowing involves all the capacities of the knowing subject, and intellectual conversion is coming to realize and being able to affirm that the world mediated by meaning is the real world.[56] The world we know is not *just* one we see and touch with our senses, but one we perceive from within according to views, opinions and values that "color our vision," and are often not taken into consideration in our world of pragmatic knowledge.

Lonergan's critical realism, strongly influenced by the realism of Aquinas, and before him, Aristotle, stands against both extremes in epistemological theories, from a naïve empiricism as described above to that of an abstract idealism which denies our capacity to truly know the world in which we live. With regard to the former, he acknowledges the significance of the "world mediated by meaning" that we receive from the horizons of meaning within which we live and understand. With regard to the latter, he insists in that it is the world that offers data to the senses and awakens the heuristic desire to know, standing against Kant's position of the world being unknowable. False data, and not just false interpretation of the same, will lead to erroneous conclusions. Neither one position nor the other do justice to the truth of how we inhabit and live in the world, and come to know it.

Applying such an epistemology to faith and music grounds questions on music in relation to faith, such as: how music affects our relationship with and experience of reality? Or how revelation manifests itself in the dynamic involved in making and listening to music? Lonergan situates art in the first level of intentional analysis: that of experience, in particular in aiding and indeed liberating our perception of experience. Before presenting his position on art, we will briefly present the points of Paul Janz's thought that converge with and emphasize Lonergan's approach, in that he underlines the need for theological thought to "pay attention" at the first level of intentional analysis, to the realm of our experience in space and time.

---

56. Cf. Lonergan, *Method in Theology*, 238–39.

Revelation Happens: Casual Reasoning in Paul Janz

> *The truth of the incarnation is indeed the incarnation of the truth.*
>
> —L. Boeve[57]

> *The shortest definition of religion is interruption.*
>
> —J.-B. Metz[58]

Reasoning from within Faith

Janz, a Canadian theologian born in 1951 in Alberta, Canada, was formerly a prominent singer-songwriter of pop rock music in the mainstream and contemporary Christian markets. He currently teaches systematic theology at King's College, and writes in the area of philosophical theology.[59] In fact, in the team of transformation theology, and the book presenting the principles of their thought,[60] he deals with the philosophical approach. It is philosophy worked out in the context of and at the service of theology. In his recent book, *The Command of Grace: A New Theological Apologetics*, Janz identifies his position as different from that of a Christian apologetics as it has been known of late, which has tended to defend the validity or plausibility of the existence of God based on arguments that are understandable and acceptable to people outside the realm of religious faith, in order to work inward to more Christian truths. Instead, he takes a completely different angle, defining himself as seeking to

> defend the accountability of Christian truth from the very center of what most indispensably and distinctively constitutes and defines it . . . in the full rigor of reason.[61]

---

57. Boeve, "Theological Truth, Particularity, and Incarnation," 346.

58. Metz, *Glaube in Geschichte und Gesellschaft*, quoted in Boeve, *God Interrupts History*, 203.

59. Apart from his collaboration with transformation theology, his books include *God, the Mind's Desire*, and *The Command of Grace*.

60. Davies et al., *Transformation Theology*.

61. Janz, *Command of Grace*, 1–2. As a member of the team of academics at the core of what is known as "transformation theology," the particular "difficult" truth of faith his thought seeks to think within and understand philosophically is that of the ascension, which we will look at in the following chapter.

Commenting on that same book, Denys Turner describes the approach as one of opening

> to the questioning of sceptics while working from its own ground within the central truths of Christian belief, as distinct from an older form of semi-rationalist "Christian Apologetics" hoping to persuade sceptics from supposed neutral territory ... a "nowhere" world of neutrality occupied by neither believers nor their doubters.[62]

It is an approach that tends to avoid the mistakes and dangers pointed out by Buckley when talking about the origin of atheism, as it takes its reference point from within a Christian understanding of faith and reason. It is also consistent with how Lonergan deals with the this area of thought, who points to a similar understanding of Apologetics, less a quest to prove something (often on a merely rational level) that is somewhat "external" to those listening (which history has proved in any case to be generally ineffective, or even self-destructive), and more one to facilitate people in integrating (and perhaps even identifying?) how God in fact works in our lives:

> The apologist's task is neither to produce in others nor to justify for them God's gift of his love. Only God can give that gift, and the gift itself is self-justifying. People in love have not reasoned themselves into being in love. The apologist's task is to aid others in integrating God's gift with the rest of their living.[63]

This approach is suitable for my own purposes for various reasons: firstly, my aim is also the *theological* comprehension of how music can help to mediate Christian faith, as I find it is first and foremost within theological circles that we are lacking the tools to understand what music is, and therefore if and how it has a role to play in faith transmission; as a consequence theology has difficulty in facilitating the intelligent use of music in pastoral work. Secondly, because the current cultural context is more receptive to an apologetic approach that situates itself humbly yet fully within its own paradigm of truth and belief. Postmodern culture at ground level is more open to the non-rational, or to that which cannot be fully grasped by reason, than

---

62. Review on back cover of *Command of Grace*.
63. Lonergan, *Method in Theology*, 123.

modernity ever was.[64] Perhaps theological thought needs the audacity to trust that trend and present and argue its own case in dialogue with it. Theology renounces on too much when it lets go of its own presuppositions in order to "argue" with academic thought "on its terms," assuming the questionable presuppositions of the Enlightenment of reason without faith being more objective than reason with it.[65] Finally, music is already an intrinsic part of many people's faith experience and understanding, both within Christian circles and beyond; the quest is to understand how and why. Music, by its very nature, is not a "reason" or an "argument" one can situate outside human or faith experience. It is more operative and invasive than that. Therefore this book is not seeking to prove music could help convince people about God and even to lead people to Christian faith, but rather to understand why, how and when this is actually the happening. With understanding comes the possibility of discerning, helping us to facilitate and encourage its right development and steps forward.

---

64. Cf. Gallagher, *Clashing Symbols*, ch. 8, "The Postmodern Situation: Friend or Foe," especially 104–14. Gallagher analyses the premises, not only of postmodernity as a form of thought or philosophy, but also as a "street-level" sensibility, in which we *can* find points of contact and openness to Christian faith. For an analysis of the characteristics of contemporary culture and aspects of the same that make it receptive to religious experience, including the retrieval of an aesthetic attitude towards the Absolute, and the postmodern critique of Christianity's depreciation of the body, the writings of José M. Mardones are insightful; cf. Mardones, "La fe Cristiana ante la modernidad," and *Postmodernidad y Cristianismo*. Mardones analyzes the postmodern critique of religion in *¿Adónde va la Religión?*, and mentions a form of religious cult through music, but focuses on the syndrome of group experience rather than the music itself; in this book he identifies the retrieval of the symbol and aesthetics as essential to Christianity now and for the future (cf. 204–5), a theme which he develops impressively in his later book, *La vida del símbolo*.

65. Cf. the first section on this chapter on the negative effect such an approach has had on the theological endeavor, as presented by theologians such as Michael Buckley and Pierangelo Sequeri.

Revelation "Happens" in the Human World of Space and Time

> *"Inference simply cannot substitute for experience."*
>
> —M. J. Buckley[66]

Revelation, therefore, is the starting point and guiding question of Janz's reflections: How does revelation happen in history? How does God come to encounter us? And how do we "receive" that revelation? Janz talks about revelation in terms of "divine disclosure and declaration" in a similar way to *Dei Verbum* 2:

> [Revelation is] not merely the disclosure of information or descriptive propositions "about" God, but is rather declared by the scriptures most fundamentally to be nothing less than the revelation of God himself . . . a divine *self*-communication to the world, which *as* divine *self*-disclosure comes to its fullest expression in the incarnation of Jesus Christ himself, in whom "all the fullness of the deity lives in bodily form" (Col 2:9).[67]

This, in effect, is what is being said in *Dei Verbum* 2 of the documents of Vatican II, when it says:

> In his goodness and wisdom God chose to reveal himself and to make known to us the hidden purpose of his will (cf. Eph. 1:9) by which through Christ, the Word made flesh, [humanity] might in the Holy Spirit have access to the Father and come to share in the divine nature (cf. Eph. 2:18; 2 Peter 1:4).[68]

Janz expresses this understanding of revelation in philosophical terms with the notion of "divine causality" (title of one of his chapters in the book presenting transformation theology), and laments that theology in the last few centuries, (especially in the nineteenth and twentieth century) has moved from understanding revelation as a "fundamentally causal communication to embodied human beings in the real world of space and time," to that of a primarily conceptual or mental communication.[69]

---

66. Buckley, *Denying and Disclosing God*, 138.
67. Janz, "Revelation as Divine Causality," 64. Emphasis original.
68. *Dei Verbum* 2.
69. Janz, "Revelation as Divine Causality," 67.

He is not the first to affirm similar views. Max Seckler's presentation of the different models or lines of emphasis in the understanding of revelation that various periods in history have embraced is well known,[70] and the shift from understanding revelation as propositional to personal and incarnated is, at least theoretically, accepted in theological thought. However, of particular interest are the underlying philosophical positions that Janz identifies as having provoked this change, which are still at least implicitly present in much contemporary philosophical and theological reflection, their consequences and challenges for theological. He expands and, at least in part, explains the comments of Lonergan and Haughton on the suffocating effect of a philosophy on Western thought and living, due to the fact that reason has been reduced to a narrow understanding of conceptual and inferential processes. Analyzing the *history* of philosophy with regard to epistemology and causality, he identifies one key factor as crucial: the loss of a distinction in our knowing between causal comprehension or reasoning and logical or inferential comprehension or reasoning. Janz says that there are two ways in which our mind seeks to give explanation for the things we are presented with by reality—causal explanations or conceptual explanations:

> Reasons will at bottom always be either *conceptual*, that is, having to do with explanations of connectedness in the relation of *logical* processes in *reflective intellection*, or they will be *causal*, that is, having to do with explanations of connectedness in the relation of *sensible* processes and events in *space and time*.[71]

Talking about the difference between these two kinds of authorities or explanations, he states that *causal* questioning and explanations about connections are *sensibly perceived*, based on dynamic sensible processes, and on relations of real proximity in space and time; and *conceptual* questioning and explanations about connections are *logically* or ratiocinatively perceived.[72] Conceptual questioning or reasoning works by inference, albeit different types of inference (deductive, inductive and abductive) and with varying degrees of reliability, but always via inference. Causal reasoning does not, however, work by inference: "That is, they are not reasons or explanations yielded or

70. Cf. Seckler, "Concetto di rivelazione."
71. Janz, "Divine Causality," 328.
72. Cf. Janz, "Divine Causality," 324.

produced by mental processes as conclusions which are drawn from premises or from items of evidence. *They are discovered rather through attentiveness to sequences and connections which are found to be encountered originally in sensible processes.*"[73]

Janz traces how this differentiation between these two types or ways of reasoning was clear in Aristotle, maintained by Augustine, and fortified by Aquinas and even somehow present in Kant, and was only lost with the unfolding of classic idealism and reinforced by the development of other philosophical movements, theology and the human sciences in the twentieth and twenty-first century.[74] Philosophy (and theology) were drawn into a type of reasoning that lost touch with an attentiveness to the causal authority of sensible reality in space and time. Awareness of sensible causality became subsumed in conceptual thought, and as such has affected philosophical and theological thought to the present day.

An example of this can be seen in how theology has dealt with the *Preambula Fidei*. In this area of fundamental theology, one of the key words is that of "credibility." As a term, and in most of its current use, it seeks to express reasons that make plausible the notion of Christian faith, but as a term it points towards conceptual and inferential motives. And yet are those reasons the ones that truly motivate people towards an option of faith, or are we moving in the realm of what Newman would call more "notional" than "real" reasons? In some authors or schools, the shift has been made towards the terminology of "significativity"[75] or "meaningfulness" with regard to the Christian truths of faith, and perhaps that was a move in the right direction, as it underlines the personal dimension of significance—the reasonableness of faith is in reference to "someone." However, as we have seen when looking at the symbolism in musical expression, it also depends on whether we open to types of meaning that go beyond (or before) linguistic signification, as central as that may be in Christian understanding. Worth mentioning in this context is Sequeri's invitation to understand and speak of the relevance of faith in human life in terms of "trustworthiness," valuing the affective and aesthetic dimensions of human sensibility as essential receptive areas for Christian revela-

---

73. Ibid., 330. Emphasis mine.
74. Cf. Janz, *Command of Grace*, 22–28.
75. Cf. Fisichella, "Credibility."

tion. The underlying point is clear: the way things are perceived, experienced, assessed, and valued has changed, and theological thought needs to take this on board, and to a certain degree at least, move with it. We need to integrate in theological reasoning a way that relates to the manner in which people inhabit and think about reality in the contemporary paradigm, even as we maintain a critical distance in order to discern the rightness or truth of the same from a faith perspective. This is not to say that theology should not have a solid philosophical foundation. On the contrary, it needs to proceed with rigorous philosophical conceptual thought, which is critical about the assumptions underlying its thought processes and where they came from. The quest is for that which *Fides et Ratio* would refer to as a "unified and organic vision of knowing,"[76] which will not be accomplished by ignoring or "retreating from" the world in its sensible authority.[77]

It is this call to attentiveness to that which is encountered in sensible processes, in our interaction with the world, which we consider important with regard to our own quest of seeking a theological understanding of music. This is not only because music involves the senses, (although indeed, music *is* experienced first and foremost as a "sensible process"), but because our perception and experience of Revelation takes place there also—in the world of space and time. Revelation "happens" or interrupts us,[78] more often presenting itself as a question, a problem to be solved or even as a "command" (in the words of Janz), than a reason or a concept.[79] It is not primarily an abstract phenomenon. Our God in Jesus Christ, comes to meet us in and through our embodied life, and we perceive and receive that presence through witness, through the Word proclaimed, through

---

76. John Paul II, *Fides et Ratio*, 85.

77. As we will see, this terminology echoes Davies's emphasis on the presence of the ascended body in this world, and his lament of the "pointing away" from the world of many theological and spiritual tendencies in contemporary Western culture. The common aim of both is to reappropriate the basic incarnatedness of Christian faith and that of a philosophy and theology that support it.

78. Cf., Boeve's notion of "interruption" as a theological category: Boeve, *Interrupting Tradition*, "Shortest Definition of Religion: Interruption," and *God Interrupts History*. The convergence with transformation theology's emphasis on the importance of the incarnation in theology is not insignificant; cf. Boeve, "Resurrection—Interruption—Transformation."

79. As mentioned in note 44 above, cf. Janz, "Coming Righteousness," and *Command of Grace*.

bread and life broken and shared, through beauty perceived, seen or "imagined," in our interaction with lived reality. It is not primarily an abstract phenomenon. Even the mystical experience of Christian faith is anchored in the historical reality of the incarnated person of Jesus Christ.[80] Revelation is God entering into communication with our world of history, space and time. The plenitude of revelation has been given and fulfilled in the person of Jesus Christ, transmitted to us by the early church as our foundational revelation. However, our continued understanding and deepening in that Revelation, which is our task in this interim time, demands that we be open and awake, as God continues to be present to our lives in space and time, albeit in a different way.[81] As Robert Doran says, "God is always doing something in the world, even independently of God's explicit revelation in Christ Jesus. . . . Revelation allows us to give name to this 'what God is doing,'"[82] and that in every present moment of history. Therefore the call to "attentiveness" to the reality that surrounds us is essential to Christian apprehension and comprehension of revelation.

This has consequences both for the living out of faith and for theology. As mentioned above when talking about Lonergan's epistemology, "we have no data on God," but we do have data on the fruits of God's presence in the world, signs of the times of a God who has chosen to live, act, and interact with humanity in the world of space and time, and has not withdrawn from the same after the resurrection and ascension. Attentiveness to that world, aided by any and all of the knowledge that we can have at our disposal, should be normal praxis for theology.[83] There is an ongoing tension or contradiction

---

80. The renowned statement of St. Teresa of Avila's *"Maestra"* of the Christian mystical experience is paradigmatic: *"Sin la humanidad de Cristo, anda el alma sin arrimo"* ("Without the humanity of Christ, the soul is lame"). Teresa de Jesús, *Obras de la gloriosa Madre Santa Teresa*, 607.

81. This will be the thesis developed by Davies, in chapter 6, with regard to the truth of the ascension.

82. Doran, "Lonergan and Balthasar," 69–70.

83. This has very practical and immediate consequences for theological reflection and research. For example, in my experience of participating in conferences on theology and art, where the actual content and dynamic of those conferences has allowed for an active participation of artists and musicians in the dynamic and debate of the same, the results were qualitatively superior. It is for this reason that I have sought to write this book in contact and dialogue with people who are active in the area of artistic creativity.

in relation to the sciences which theology is affected by. On the one hand, the process of conceptualization described above leads to the natural sciences being looked down upon as "positivistic" and inferior, in comparison to the "higher" and more intellectual activity in sciences not dependant on time and space.[84] On the other, there is the prejudice according to which only the positive sciences are seen as valid and "objective," relegating philosophy, theology, and other "non-empirical" disciplines to a position of inferiority. And yet, with the aim of an integrated and unified understanding of human knowing, most sciences need to have a dual type of attentiveness, both to data from the world and experience, as well as solid inferential conceptual thought.[85] Theology, as reflection on revelation, needs to do the same, seeking to proceed with rigorous philosophical thought, but not at the cost of ignoring or "retreating from" the world in its sensible authority.[86]

> Just as in the empirical sciences we recognize the requirement to engage in questioning and to give explanations in two fundamentally different ways—(a) *causal* questioning and explanations about connections which are at bottom *sensibly perceived*; and (b) *conceptual* questioning and explanations about connections which are at bottom *logically* or ratiocinatively perceived, so too theology demands both a causal or sensible attentiveness, and a conceptual or logical attentiveness.[87]

---

84. Janz relates this account of the development of philosophy and advance of the supremacy of the human sciences in relation to the natural ones, referring to Gadamer's analysis of the same. Cf. Gadamer, *Truth and Method*, chapter 1, on "The Sgnificance of the Humanist Tradition for the Human Sciences."

85. Strictly speaking, pure mathematics would be the only science in which purely inferential thought is acceptable, a distinction which Janz maintains despite an essay by Quine on "Two Dogmas of Empiricism," in *From a Logical Point of View*, which claimed to have done away with it, both because of his disagreement with the arguments offered therein, and based on the lack of long-term change in common use with regard to this very terminology.

86. This terminology echoes Davies's emphasis on the presence of the ascended body in this world, and his lament of the "pointing away" from the world of many theological and spiritual tendencies in contemporary Western culture. The common aim of both to reappropriate the basic incarnatedness of Christian faith and that of a philosophy and theology that support it.

87. Janz, "Divine Causality," 324. A parallel could be made with Lonergan, in which he compares the role of the scientist as the foundation of scientific method to that of the theologian as the foundation of theology. Cf. Lonergan, "Theology in Its New Context," 63–67; and *Method in Theology*, 267–71.

This not only refers to theology as a discipline in its own right, but also provides a solid motivation for the integration of interdisciplinary work alongside and *within* theology. Well understood, this not only implies theology opening to dialogue with other disciplines and sciences but that theology itself integrates in its method forms of attentiveness to the world that allow for a fuller apprehension and understanding of the same. The very order of this book (from studies on music to theological reflection) is an attempt to do just that, and is the reason behind its title: music *as* theology, not just as its partner.

As mentioned above, the call to be attentive to lived experience is common to both Janz and Lonergan, albeit recognizing that for Lonergan, this attentiveness is twofold: not only to the world but to the subject in that world as they experience. But the point is similar: attentiveness to the world of space and time and how we experience it, due to the very nature of revelation, which is, and continues to be incarnational—at the very centre of embodied life. And it is in our embodied life that we experience music. Indeed, based on Speelman's analysis, it is fair to say that music helps us experience fuller our embodied life, an intuition that is confirmed, as we shall see shortly, by Lonergan's reflection on the role of art in human living. To be open and receptive to Christ's continued presence among us now through art and music is a doorway to a transformed and transforming experience of life and faith; a transforming presence theology needs to both receive from and speak to.

The Role of Art and Music as Enrichment of Human Experience

> *It is all very well to devote oneself to much thinking, but not all thinking is fruitful.*
>
> —Hans Urs von Balthasar[88]

Lonergan's epistemology presents four steps: experience, understanding, reflection, and decision. It is at the first level of experience that Lonergan situates the importance of art, in which it has most influence or impact, in particular as an aid to our *perception* of experience.

---

88. Balthasar, "Theology and Sanctity," 191.

Lonergan identifies the role of art as one of freedom of consciousness, experience for the sake of experience, at the service of everyday living. He underlines the significance of art's role in the context of the present cultural situation, which we could perhaps describe in his own terminology as "in decline," and this, as noted above, as a result of Western philosophical thought as it has unfolded in recent history. Art has a role in making life livable again. The following quotation, although long, is worth transcribing in full:

> Art is relevant to *concrete living*, that it is an exploration of the potentialities of *concrete living*. That exploration is extremely important in our age, when philosophers for at least two centuries, through doctrines on politics, economics, education, and through even further doctrines, have been trying to re-make man, and have done not a little to make life unliveable. The great task that is demanded if we are to *make it liveable again* is the re-creation of the liberty of the subject, the recognition of the freedom of consciousness.[89]

"To make life livable again"! The simplicity of the statement should not attenuate the radicality or depth of what is being said: that life has become unlivable, that the way we have learnt to think has had something to do with that, and that art has the potential to help rectify the situation. The fact is that without having the theoretical framework to understand why, culture itself seems to intuit this by itself. The proliferation of concerts of both classical and contemporary music, as well as the *actual* presence of art and music in contemporary society, perhaps best evoked by mp3 and iPod culture, witness to the fact that, from an early age, most individuals in Western Europe spend a noteworthy portion of their day listening to music. Could it not be said that the omnipresence of music in the Western world (and in most of the growing churches) is doing precisely what Lonergan evokes in the above quotation, albeit without understanding why—seeking to make concrete living more livable?

The growth of literature on the meaning and importance of leisure for the recreation and health of the human person points in the same direction.[90] Its theological meaning is even more relevant to this

---

89. Lonergan, "Art," 232.

90. The theme is one addressed by various churches and Christian communities in different ways, according to both theological positions and their particular traditions. Cf. Hoover, "Toward a Theology of the Christian"; and Messenger, *Holy Leisure*. For

book, by which recreation or leisure, which many would consider listening to or the making of music to be, is considered to have meaning in Christian faith as a gift of God to humanity, rather than something one does "taking time away" from that which is more effective and therefore, "more important." More specifically, is has a role of humanization, and as this is within and towards a person's relationship with God, also of divinization.[91] "Leisure is a quality of subjective time which permits us transcend ourselves towards God."[92]

And yet, what is behind this audacious claim Lonergan makes that art can help make life "livable" again? He is talking about the first level of our process of knowing, that of experience, and the role of art in the freeing of our perception, the freeing of our process of knowing—from the pragmatic for the contemplative, we could perhaps interpret, or from the purely intellectual for a more integrated apprehension of human living. To understand this claim of art's role or capacity to effectuate this process of liberation, one must ask about how Lonergan understands art and what he means by freedom, in this context. Lonergan admits the explicit influence of Susanne Langer, one of our authors from chapter 1. Based on Langer's understanding of art, Lonergan defines it as "the objectification of a purely experiential pattern,"[93] where the emphasis is on the pattern being purely experiential, elemental, without interpretations or objectifications alien to it. What does he mean by something purely experiential? Remembering that, for Lonergan, experience is (only) the first stage of knowledge, I understand that he means that art expresses or perhaps even magnifies experience, in order to highlight it and invite others to enter and experience it, or even to identify and "taste" that same experience within themselves. Art puts us in contact with and "holds us" for a while in touch with what is essential in our experience before we move on, or return, *enriched*, to our understanding, reflecting and deciding. In relation to Janz's terminology, perhaps we could say that art accentuates and intensifies the reality of sensible and embodied living,

---

an insightful perspective from the point of view of Catholic spiritual theology, and one that touches on the area of sacred art in Christian leisure time, see Coupeau, "Espiritualidad del ocio."

91. Cf. Coupeau, "La Espiritualidad del ocio," 74; 80.

92. Ibid.," 80. Translation mine.

93. Lonergan, *Method in Theology*, 61. Although it has been noted that the exact definition Lonergan attributes to Langer is not found in her writings. The orientation of his understanding is, however, clearly in line with her thought.

before we conceptualize it in order to grasp and understand it. Art communicates without words and we "understand" also without them, either before we conceptually grasp what is happening or in a way that complements it. Lonergan eloquently states that, while we are having the artistic experience: "that experience not only is unknown to other people, it is not fully known even to the one who does experience it."[94] It is an experience of elemental meaning, not fully apprehended or understood yet. This "purity," or non-instrumentalized quality of art, is what allows it to be transforming, not only of the world but of the subject, a transforming of our awareness and perception. Once again we are in a space that is not conceptual, and therefore emphasizes our presence to and in the world, transforming it. Talking about the "elemental meaning" that art allows us participate in, he says:

> It is . . . a transformation of one's world . . . a transformation of the world . . . an opening of the horizon. . . . Some people will say that art is an illusion, others that art reveals a fuller, profounder reality. But the artistic experience itself does not involve a discussion of the issue.[95]

It is a transformation of the subject (in his/her world mediated by meaning), and therefore it transforms the world.

Therefore, music not only situates itself within reality as a particular form of causal symbolism, but is, according to Lonergan, a means of freeing our perception for our concrete living in the world, and transforming it. "Freedom" is a complex word, and is usually or superficially understood as "freedom to choose." A step beyond that involves coming to realize that we are "forging" our very selves as we choose—that is to say, we "become" who we are. Lonergan would call this "moral conversion." But there is another freedom prior and much more radical than this, and that is the freedom of our consciousness to perceive, to experience, to enter into contact with the world. We could perhaps relate it to what Newman referred to as quality of disposition. The freedom to apprehend the world, not as it is explained to us, but, as George Steiner would express it, "reading being anew":

---

94. Lonergan, "Art," 217. It is interesting to understand how Lonergan perceives the process of creating within the artist, but I will come back to that when talking about the person of the artist in relation to faith communication.

95. Ibid., 216.

> It takes uncanny strength and abstention from *re*-cognition, from implicit *re*-ference, to read the world and not the text of the world as it has been previously encoded for us (the sciences know of this bind). The exceptional artist or thinker reads being anew.⁹⁶

More than *strength* to read being anew, perhaps we should talk of freedom, (or even grace), and one would have to admit, such detachment from the codes we have been formed in, is rare.⁹⁷ Born as we are into a world of meaning, we get used to reading it as it has been explained and interpreted for us (ready-made subjects in a ready-made world),⁹⁸ and art is a medium of refreshing and re-reading that meaning. It moves us to a different wavelength. Therefore far from being a "privilege" of the elite or a pastime for those with a certain inclination in that direction, it is a means of enriching any and every human life. Art is an invitation to the observer or listener to withdraw from practical living in order, not so much to understand as to participate in, and "explore the possibilities of fuller living in a richer world,"⁹⁹ which, instead of being considered superfluous or illusory could rather be called more real and more true.¹⁰⁰ Once again, Steiner's eloquence expresses in imaginative and biblical terms that the aesthetic experience is basically life- changing:

> What do you feel, what do you think of the possibilities of your life, of the alternate shapes of being which are implicit in your experience of me, in our encounter? . . . The encounter with the aesthetic is, together with certain modes of religious and of metaphysical experience, the most "ingressive," transformative summons available to human experiencing. Again, the short-

---

96. Steiner, *Real Presences*, 195.

97. We could find a converging point of view in Rahner's understanding of the human person as "spirit in the world," and potential "hearer of the Word," the titles of two of his books, which could arguably be said to reflect his understanding of the human capacity for God and openness to grace. Cf. Rahner, *Spirit in the World*, and *Hearers of the Word*.

98. The need to move from a passive and unthinking way of living in the world is a central concern for Lonergan. He calls it "inauthentic" living, and calls for appropriation and various areas of conversion in order to move towards authentic living. Cf. Lonergan, "Existenz and Aggiornamento." Although he does not write much on art, it is significant that he situates its role at the core of one of his greatest concerns.

99. Lonergan, *Method in Theology*, 64.

100. Cf. ibid., 63.

> hand image is that of the Annunciation, of a "terrible beauty" or gravity breaking into the small house of our cautionary being . . . the house is no longer habitable in quite the same way as before.[101]

Steiner is talking about art in all its forms, but music invades more than visual art does. It enters "the small house" of our embodied self in a much more powerful way than any other form of art. It changes us. To not accept its potential at the service of a faith that is always experienced as Another entering one's life, be it in the invitation of a gentle breeze,[102] be it as an interruption or intrusion,[103] would be shortsighted. Music can touch, affect, change, and transform concrete everyday living. In what way?

Whereas Lonergan situates the effect of the various forms of art all in the realm of experience, it is interesting to note the difference between the arts as Lonergan identifies them. Whereas visual art, sculpture, and architecture are concerned with space,[104] Lonergan talks about music in relation to temporality, calling it "the image of experienced time."[105] In chapter 3 we noted how it is probable that the first element of music to appear in human culture was rhythm, making motion, the marking of passing time, the most basic element of musical symbolism. Once again we are presented with the profoundly dynamic nature of musical symbolism. Mardones analyses contemporary culture, identifying four unhealthy or "pathological" ways in which postmodern culture relates to time.[106] One could ask oneself whether contemporary pervasiveness of music is not an instinctive attempt to balance or heal these anomalies. Taking it a step further, into theological discourse, if we view this insight about the temporal nature of musical symbolism from within a Christian and theological perspective, it challenges the static way in which we have understood the nature of reality itself, as well as our apprehension of it.[107] It invites our

---

101. Steiner, *Real Presences*, 142–43.
102. Cf. 1 Kgs 19:12.
103. Cf. Jer 20:7 (NIV); "O Lord, you deceived; me, and I was deceived . . ."
104. Cf. Lonergan, "Art," 223–27.
105. Ibid., 227.
106. Cf. Mardones, *Adónde va la religión?*, 161–65.
107. The next section of this chapter looks at how Haughton reaches this conclusion about the nature of reality and how theology perceives it.

imagination (which, according to Newman, is an important vehicle for our apprehension of the real) to reach towards "seeing" reality as born of a triune, interrelational, dynamic God and therefore marked and sustained by this origin. Jeremy Begbie, another author whose position we will explore in chapter 5, also underlines the relationship of music with time.

However, not just its temporal nature but in each and every one of the aspects of Speelman's analysis that there are areas in which the intensification of experience through music can be felt: the way in which music engages us with reality, holding us in the present moment, instead of distancing us from it; the subtle or nuanced awareness harmony provokes, in teaching us to listen to and relate to other tones or sounds, instead of taking distance or separating ourselves from them; the dynamic nature of musical movement, which affects our corporal existence and "moves" us, quite literally; the variety of tone color and sound that is heightened through the manifold possible forms of instrumentalization; the depth and complexity that music's omnipresence trains us to experience . . . to name but a few. However one looks at it, music intensifies our experience of reality.

From Music in Epistemology to Music in Theological Epistemology

> *The most perfect kind of theology would be the one that appropriates these arts as an integral part of itself.*
>
> —Karl Rahner[108]

Having seen the role of music in our living and knowing, how can we understand its function in the two aspects that interest us in this book—music as revelatory of the Word and as theological praxis?[109] In the context of this chapter on theological epistemology and praxis, this section suggests that the intensification of Christian experience

---

108. Rahner, "Art Against the Horizon," 163.

109. The integration of art into theology is not a new idea. Karl Rahner, while not developing it into a form of theological aesthetics, in various of his writings on creativity or art invites us to reflect on how this can happen. Cf. Rahner, "Art Against the Horizon," "Poetry and the Christian," "Prayer for Creative Thinkers," and "Priest and Poet."

through art and music, well understood, is not extrinsic to theological thought, and that this could be in fact one of the main contributions of theological aesthetics to the rest of theology.[110] I will touch on two overlapping ways of understanding this. The first has to do with Lonergan's intentional analysis and its application to theological method, the second with his notion of conversion. Both of them are visually presented in the diagram below, which this section will unfold and explain.

From Epistemology to Theological Method

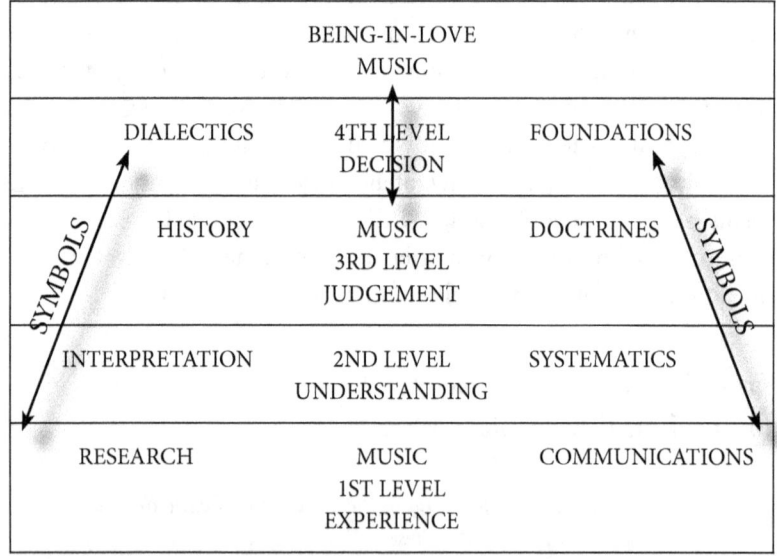

Figure 4.1

We have mentioned that Lonergan applies the stages of intentional analysis to methodology in theology. This correlation cannot be understood superficially. Following the diagram above: research is an application of our capacity to experience reality; interpretation, our quest to understand it; history follows the developments of our understanding during time in order to reflect upon and verify our understanding; dialectics challenges the differences in our conclusions on the basis of our threefold relationship with reality, (how we know

---

110. We shall follow the unfolding of this intuition in its main authors in chapter 5, from Balthasar through to contemporary writers.

it), authentic living (how we decide and choose), and God (how we believe and love). This fourth level invites us to an awareness and appropriation of the religious experience that is at the heart of theology, taking foundational position in relation to the particular area of theology we are doing. From there on we move to the aspects of theology that are mediated by this stance: doctrines reflects our mature (and "*aggiornata*") understanding of the truths of theology, systematics how each doctrine interrelates with the others, and communications the place where all the previous steps of theological investigation enter into dialogue with culture and lived religion. It is also important to keep in mind that while the first three stages of theological method can be done without faith, (or in collaboration with investigators from outside the field of theology), according to Lonergan, from dialectics onwards not only is faith indispensable, but how it is integrated and affects theological thinking is part of the issue dealt with in stages four and five, (dialectics and foundations). It is this link between faith and theological knowledge that is being defended in *Donum Veritatis*, when it refers to the faith and prayer life of the theologian as indispensable for his or her "supernatural sense of faith,"[111] and the theme of theological gnoseology is an important one in contemporary theology.[112] It is precisely because Lonergan's theological structure takes into account the specialization of knowledge in the sciences and their epistemological consequences in theology that I find it insightful for theology today and for our reflection on music.

Figure 4.1 above presents Lonergan's structure of method in theology enriched by Doran's invitation to attention to the symbolic.[113]

---

111. Congregation for the Doctrine of Faith, *Donum Veritatis*, 8.

112. Cf. for example, Balthasar, "Theology and Sanctity"; Martinelli, *Testimonianza*, especially chapter 1; Sequeri, *Qualità*[grave accent over a] *spirituale*; or volume 4 of Kern et al., *Corso di teologia fondamentale*.

113. I am grateful to Gerry Whelan, SJ, for pointing out this aspect of Doran's thought to me. It is not indifferent that our next author, Rosemary Haughton, is one who both influenced both Lonergan and Doran. Doran himself has described her main book as being full of the awareness born of psychic conversion: "Haughton's *The Passionate God* . . . is so replete with indications of the author's self-knowledge in the area of the psyche that it makes my methodological insistence seem to belabor the obvious." Doran, *Theology and the Dialectics of History*, Introduction n. 11. This book deals amply with the notion of psychic conversion and its relation to theology. For an explanation of psychic conversion in his more recent and comprehensive book, see *Theology and the Dialectics of History*, pp. 8–9, and chs. 2, 6, and 7.

Robert Doran, who worked with Lonergan and has developed this aspect, invites us to recognize and trace aspects of "thought" in theology and lived religion which are sometimes overlooked or underestimated, such as the dimension of the symbolic.

> [T]he mediation of religious meaning and truth in the present and into the future—theology's second phase—can be the work of a theological consciousness that can express its meaning in symbolic terms.[114]

This capacity of music in culture, religion and theology to help mediate faith and therefore the claim that it needs to be integrated into theological praxis is, in fact, founded on the importance of the symbolic dimension of human life and knowing for, and in, theology.[115]

However, how can the specific symbolic form that is music fit into this theological structure or method? Music, in this structure of Lonergan, could be understood as having a role on the first level of experience, widening and transforming human life, and therefore is related to the functional specialities of research and communications. Since we have explicitly focused our attention on contemporary Christian music, our theological reflection is more concerned with musical experience within Christian spirituality and lived faith (communications) and its subsequent integration into theology (foundations) than with music in general in culture (research).[116] We also noted extensively in chapter 3 the dynamic nature of musical symbolism. Hence the suggestion that music could be said to have potential to help "move" us from reflection to action or decision (levels three to four).

To "complete" our reflection on music in and as theology, a final aspect of interest is the notion Lonergan places at the core of foundations and dialectics, and indeed at the foundation of theology in the contemporary cultural context: conversion.

---

114. Doran, *Theology and the Dialectics of History*, 61.

115. For an impressive analysis of the power of the symbolic in human life and culture, and its need to be taken into account in theological thought, see the aforementioned book of Mardones, *Vida del símbolo*.

116. The gathering of some elements from musicology and music studies to inform our task is solely a small and necessary example of how communications does not work independently but in collaboration with research, interpretation, and history.

The Person of the Theologian in Conversion

The logical and structured way in which Lonergan writes can alienate us from the depth of his though in relation to the aesthetic dimensions of our existence, but well understood, the consequences are profound. The theologian "in conversion" grounds theological thought; in this light we could venture saying that the musician or composer "in conversion" is our inner path or link with between the estranged worlds of art and faith. The "unfolding" of Lonergan's notion of conversion by himself and those coming after him sheds tremendous light into music's role both in faith transmission and theological thought.

Lonergan divides the notion of conversion into religious, moral, and intellectual.[117] His thought on conversion is particularly helpful in the context of our reflection on a theological epistemology due to the way he understands and presents the notion of conversion or conversions, not only as a "spiritual" change, or an exhortation to more pious living and therefore to a "deeper" theology, but one that involves the "converting" of various dimensions of human living and knowing to a correct understanding of our apprehension of reality (intellectual conversion),[118] a responsible assuming of our persons and freedom (moral conversion),[119] and the horizon-changing experience of accept-

---

117. Lonergan does, albeit only on a few occasions, refer also to the notion of affective conversion. For example in "Natural Right and Historical Mindedness," 179, he seems to use it instead of religious conversion, albeit with a somewhat ample application. He is quoted by some as talking about four, rather than three, conversions. Cf. Doran, *Theology and the Dialectics of History*, 9; and Streeter, "Preaching as a Form of Theological Communication, 60. However, it is by no means as developed as the other three. It is taken up by other authors, and in chapter 6 we will come back to it, albeit accentuating more from a specifically christological point of view.

118. We already briefly explained intellectual conversion, which situates itself on the level of our cognition and consists in overcoming the myth of empiricism, or a non-critical type of "realism" that would have us believe (perceive and think) that "knowing is like looking, that objectivity is seeing what there is to be seen and not seeing what is not there, and that the real is what is out there now to be looked at." Lonergan, *Method in Theology*, 238.

119. Moral conversion, according to Lonergan, consists in the exercise of human freedom, which, far from being simply the possibility of choosing one thing or another, is the reality that we are entrusted with "choosing," with deciding over our very beings; the step from drifting to authentic living. The option for authenticity is another favorite theme of Lonergan, and one needs to vigil for both minor and major authenticity: the former being faithfulness to one's tradition, an option of personal deliberation and responsibility, the latter referring to a tradition's faithfulness to itself, of which history and God will judge.

ing the love of God flooding our hearts (Rom 5:5).[120] Furthermore, he presents this dynamic of conversion, or more precisely, the person of the theologian in conversion, as the foundation for theology in the contemporary cultural context.[121] It is the theologian who does theology. The divisions and contradictions or shortcomings of theology in mediating religion and culture will be overcome only by the right thinking of those who think theologically. Specifically in relation to the theme of this book, we will never have a fully theological understanding of music if its effect on our knowing and believing is not intrinsically understood by those who think theologically, which means not only understanding how music touches and affects human knowing, but also comprehending its role in the theologian's process of thinking and believing. This, in turn, implies relating aesthetic experience, and in particular that of musical apprehension, with the various areas of conversion presented by Lonergan and other authors who develop and complement his thought on aesthetics.

There are, in fact, a further three notions of conversion that are relevant to our theme: affective, psychic, and what is sometimes referred to as "aesthetic" conversion. The need to complement Lonergan's notions of conversion, in the recognition of their importance and in order to integrate aspects not addressed by Lonergan himself, has been identified by various authors. Robert Doran, working on the symbolic dimension of human living, introduced the notion of "psychic conversion" as complementary to Lonergan's thought. Lonergan admitted himself that it is overlooked in *Method in Theology*. According to Doran, psychic conversion refers to the healing of "sensitive consciousness," the affective "aesthetic undertow" of our spiritual being, and touches on aspects of the human experience such as affectivity, symbolic perception and intuition. Although a full presentation of Doran's notion of psychic conversion, and his integration of the advances of depth psychology with Lonergan's intentional analysis exceed the limits of this book, some convergence points are important. Doran relates the whole process of psychic conversion with the areas of feelings and values in Lonergan, and contends that the precariousness

---

120. In Lonergan's words, it is "being grasped by ultimate concern. It is other worldly falling in love. It is total and permanent self-surrender without conditions, qualifications, reservations." Lonergan, *Method in Theology*, 240.

121. Cf. Lonergan, "Theology in Its New Context."

of intellectual conversion is due in part to the need for more awareness of the psychic elements of our knowing, and that sustained growth in self-transcendence through the workings of intentional analysis is sustained also by the healing of our psyche.[122] He explicitly relates this aspect of conversion to the integration of our embodied existence with intentional analysis. We have already amply noted the importance of embodiment to music:

> A true healing of the psyche would dissolve the affective wounds that block sustained self-transcendence; . . . it would also render the psyche the medium of the embodiment of intentionality in the constitution of the person.[123]

Assuming Doran's perspective widens our understanding of self-appropriation in the person to include the symbolic, since psychic conversion "allows access to *one's own* symbolic system, and through that system to one's affective habits and one's spontaneous apprehension of possible values."[124]

Another development of the theme of conversion in relation to Lonergan's threefold one is that of Richard Viladesau, who talks of "aesthetic conversion" in terms of our spiritual level of intentionality, referring to a contemplative, appreciative, joyful, and perhaps less "practical" form of knowledge by which we apprehend reality, which even includes the erotic or psychosexual dimensions of life. He perceives it as underlying and even preparing intellectual conversion, and as teaching us to "value and judge" art, not solely by criteria such as skill, imagination and formal excellence, but also in relation to the revelation of the true and the good.[125]

Don Gelpi expands Lonergan's notion of "affective conversion," and unfolds moral conversion into two types: personal moral conversion and political conversion. He also develops the notion of religious conversion, presenting Christian conversion as exemplifying one form

---

122. Cf. Doran, *Theology and the Dialectics of History*, 52–53. He includes in the realm of psyche "our sensations, memories, images, emotions, conations, associations, bodily movements, and spontaneous intersubjective responses, and of the symbolic integrations of these that occur in, indeed are, our dreams" (p. 46).

123. Ibid., 62.

124. Ibid., 61.

125. Cf. Viladesau, *Theological Aesthetics*, 210. He relates aesthetic conversion to Robert Doran's understanding of psychic conversion. We shall briefly present his approach, as one with convergences and points of contrast with our own, in chapter 5.

of religious conversion.[126] It is interesting, for the theme of this book, that he relates affective conversion with the disciplines of psychology and aesthetics.

Coming back to the issue of a theological epistemology of art and music, how is it related to any or all of these aspects of conversion in theological appropriation? The answer to that question needs be differentiated between the apprehension or reception of music and its composition. My suggestion is that musical apprehension can be a powerful factor in the process of what could be called "aesthetic conversion,"[127] which is related to aspects of Doran's "psychic conversion," and that it can aid, prepare or even complement "intellectual conversion" due to the way in which it leads us to perceive and relate to the world we inhabit.

In Lonergan's article on art, without calling it by name, we find a clear description of perception when informed by intellectual conversion:

> Just as to think that we have to be looking at an object instead of thinking of the identity in act of seeing and seen falsifies the experience, so instrumentalizing experience in various ways can remove us from the primal mode of being that is proper to man and that is the normal level of human living apart from the differentiations of consciousness.[128]

The identity of act in seeing and seen; the mutual interaction of the knower and that which is being known, as inseparable elements making up the "real world"; the awareness of being alive in the midst of the world in that interaction, which Lonergan calls "critical realism."

---

126. In a recent book, Gelpi develops this thought in a systematic way, in the quest to apply it to contemporary Christology, and at the end offers a useful summary of definitions of the various types of conversion as he understands them: cf. Gelpi, *Encountering Jesus Christ*, 614–21. Gelpi both relates and differentiates his stance on affective conversion from that of Doran, insisting that "affective, intuitive thinking grasps reality in its own right and that most of the thinking which characterizes affective conversion engages affective, intuitive thinking rather than rational, inferential thinking." He considers psychic conversion to be more of a rational understanding of our affective and sensitive lives than his own emphasis on the affective and intuitive.

127. I present the term in this way in the recognition that it is a recent notion without a univocal definition.

128. Lonergan, "Art," 221. These words, indeed, were the one that initiated my own experience and comprehension of what Lonergan sought to express with the notion of intellectual conversion.

Intellectual conversion is awakening to the realization that being alive and knowing is a two-way, or better said, all-embracing presence of ourselves to and in the world around, before and within us. And the point Lonergan implicitly makes, and that I wish to emphasize, is that art can facilitate and perhaps even enrich that which he expressed by the notion of intellectual conversion. Artists live more aware of the world and our relationship with and within it than most. Poets would suggest that to walk through the world with that kind of awareness is what living is all about.

> *Are we, perhaps, here just for saying: House,*
> *Bridge, Fountain, Gate, Jug, Fruit tree, Window...*
> *oh, for such saying as never the things themselves*
> *hoped so intensely to be.*[129]

In saying "house," that normal everyday building we live in, I am not only realizing my own identity, (reason for being here), but also bringing the "object" I am pronouncing with my words into the intensity of what they are, in the here and now of their being named. Reality and the person perceiving it are in a relationship that affect both. I look at things and they look back at me, and we are both changed in the exchange.[130]

It is significant that this poem of Rilke appears in three different theological texts talking about the need for art in theology. Rahner quotes it in a piece in which he suggests the need for poets speaking primordial words, birthing language that we could know reality therein.[131] Viladesau quotes it when talking about art as mediating the sacred,[132] and Haughton to the backdrop of the understanding of reality as love, as exchange and God as passionate love. This is how reality is redeemed in contact with human passion.[133] This, she says, is the way

---

129. Rilke, "Ninth Duino Elegy," in *Duino Elegies*.

130. Cf. Paul Tillich's understanding of the human process of knowing in which the subject and the object become one, and somehow affect one another. "Life, as well as the mind, is creative." Tillich, *Systematic Theology*, 1: 77–78. In volume 3 of *Systematic Theology*, Tillich talks about the openness of each and every being to one another, by which "beings 'receive one another' and, by doing so, change each other" (pp. 62–65).

131. Cf. Rahner, "Priest and Poet," reference on 298–99.

132. Cf. Viladesau, *Theological Aesthetics*, chapter 5, "Art and the Sacred," reference on 141–43.

133. Cf. Haughton, *Passionate God*, 62–63.

saints and children see. Why? Because our relationship with reality is not passive, or is not meant to be. Neither is control or manipulation of the world around us the final word.[134] Serious questions are being raised about how our consciousness works in these "postmodern" times, and how technological culture changes the way we perceive and interact. The proliferation of "interactive art" draws light to this fact. It is not insignificant that the birth of art dates to where scientists identify creation's leap to human consciousness.[135] Artists seem to be given the grace of perceiving something of that, and of being able, therefore, to help us discover reality in that way. Colombian poet Orlando Gallo, having three of his siblings as missionaries dedicated to evangelization, wrote:

> Just as my brother and two sisters who are missionaries experience every act . . . of the routine of each day as a way of praying and of living thanks to God . . . so I, in a profane and heterodox way, *have sought, through and for poetry, to live a non-disposable relationship with things*, as, in a coincidental way, the understanding of the universe as a harmonic whole that celebrates itself has been given to me. And that has not happened in the midst of Great Ceremonies, but on the contrary, tying a shoe or brushing my teeth.[136]

Life, everyday "ordinary" life, lived perceiving the world as a harmonic whole, given to us, and establishing a "non-disposable" relationship with it! And not as a "special" or "strange" way of perceiving things, but as graced normality: how we *could* live—a fuller, more real living out of our daily existence, or to use Lonergan's phrase, more livable life! Aesthetics has the capacity of opening doors to perceiving reality afresh as God would have us perceive it. I am aware of the highly philosophical nature of intellectual conversion in Lonergan's presentation of it, and the element of "judgment" included therein which would seem alien to the artistic experience. And yet, when those theologians who assume and develop the notion seek to explain it, the form tends to be that of a colloquial or existential description of where and how it occurred (in similar terms of normal everyday

---

134. We know this from its consequences both in creation and in ourselves. The integration in theology of ecological concerns as part of understanding a "right relationship" between humanity and creation is part of this awareness.

135. Cf. García-Rivera, *Wounded Innocence*, chapter 1.

136. Gallo Isaza, *Siendo en las cosas*, 137. Translation mine.

life as the above poem), and the terms that emerge, such as "startling strangeness,"[137] or "lightness of being,"[138] are ones that could easily be used to describe certain aesthetic experiences. In Liddy's own words: "[T]he experience we are focusing on was primarily intellectual; but it had sensible overtones."[139] For this reason, I propose complementing Lonergan's emphasis on intellectual conversion with that of "aesthetic conversion," which includes some of the aspects Doran highlights, and that in this regard music has a special input to make. Furthermore, I suggest there is an even stronger link between intellectual conversion and the dynamic of aesthetic appreciation in the person involved in artistic creativity.[140] Perhaps the way to formulate it is art's capacity of widening its potentially intellectual reach to other dimensions of our sensibility and receptivity to the world we inhabit.

Aesthetic Experience and Conversion in Christian Spirituality and Theology: Rosemary Haughton

> *What happens if we take the Incarnation seriously?*
>
> —Rosemary Haughton[141]

It is in this line of transforming how we perceive that Rosemary Haughton, our third author of this chapter, is insightful. In the afore-

---

137. This is an expression of Lonergan, that is taken up by Richard Liddy to name and develop his thought. Cf. Liddy, *Startling Strangeness*, especially chapter 13, "A Shower of Insights," (in honor of the place in which the event of intellectual understanding began). The chapter contains not only his own insight into intellectual conversion, but that of others, as well as a lucid attempt at philosophical explanation of the same. What I believe to be my own initial experience of intellectual conversion occurred upon reading Lonergan's article on art. Cf. also Liddy, "Startling Strangeness," for a summarized presentation of the same, and his earlier work, *Transforming Light*, for his first work on the theme.

138. Liddy, *Startling Strangeness*, 206–9.

139. Ibid., 207.

140. For example, when Lonergan himself talks about the creative process in *Method in Theology*: "That meaning lies within the consciousness of the artist but, at first, it is only implicit, folded up, veiled, unrevealed, unobjectified. Aware of it, the artist has to get a hold of it; he is impelled to behold, inspect, dissect, enjoy, repeat it; and this means objectifying, unfolding, making explicit, unveiling, revealing" (pp. 63–64).

141. Haughton, *Passionate God*, 9.

mentioned book, *The Passionate God*, one of the most refreshing and spiritually mature books I have ever read, she unites similar intuitions with theological reflection. Haughton shares with Janz the centrality of the incarnation, not only to Christian faith but also to theology:

> This whole book is based on the idea that theology must spring from taking seriously the fact of incarnation—and this really does mean the *fact*, not just the *doctrine*.[142]

We mentioned in the introduction how she talks about the importance of language, and that a new "language" is sometimes necessary in order to express "certain fibers" of our being that are no longer containable in the philosophical and theological frameworks we work with. We suggested there that in the current time, music seems to be one form of expression which is doing just that. But why? Why is music an appropriate means to address the challenges of our time? Because it undermines the underlying compartmentalization in the apprehension of reality we have worked with (or tried to) for centuries, and which do not respond to how human life (especially our Christian understanding of it) functions.

Haughton talks of "a concealed model of reality [in which we use] ... the words 'material' and 'spiritual' as mutually exclusive categories. We can talk about their essential interdependence, or even oneness, but that is not how we 'feel' them."[143] We live internally divided and disassociated, when Christian faith is fully incarnational. For this reason, she says we need what she calls "a proper sensuality":

> The idea of the life of the senses as the stability of the spiritual body is one that may seem odd at first, but it is a conclusion from seeing creation in terms of incarnation. A proper sensuality must be the basis from which all upreaching of the spirit is possible.[144]

Not only does Haughton suggest we think about senses in a different way, she links it directly with our very understanding of being and God. She challenges us to think about being as dynamic, introducing three key words or images (as they are drawn from poetry and literature, more metaphorical than conceptual) to talk about the dy-

---

142. Ibid., 175.
143. Ibid., 20–21.
144. Ibid., 284.

namic as opposed to static nature of reality: spheres, exchange and breakthrough;[145] being as love, as gift donating itself. And she does not limit this dynamicity to the spiritual realm, but underlines how Christianity integrates the material world within itself. She offers the Body of Christ as the theological backdrop in which material and spiritual come and are held together, in relationship with Christ and each other.

If we stretch our minds to face these challenges, it is clear that there are numerous qualities of musical symbolism that emerge as significant, precisely because in music the sensual and spiritual are intrinsically united. Music can teach us to feel differently: to experience reality as dynamic and corporal at the same time. Understanding reality in this way is fully Christian. God is relation: three Persons in constant interaction with one another, and with the created world which is not far or distant, but somehow redeemed, assumed and loved within and as part of the Body of the Son. This is our faith. The growing awareness and presence of music in culture and the Christian churches could be read as one way in which the Spirit is pushing us towards a fuller living out of human life in Christ, and its understanding: the "language" of beauty as expressed though music, capable of leading or even introducing us into the realm of our triune loving God, who is beauty. *Not* to pay attention to this form of expression or communication when it is coming to the forefront of human life, or to neglect to welcome, discern and integrate it where possible into Christian living would be a lack of intellectual responsibility and, unwittingly perhaps, a stifling of the Spirit.[146]

As we move towards developing the specific area of theological aesthetics, I underline once again Lonergan's approach, moving from how we experience beauty to what beauty is, (that is to say, from epistemology to metaphysics), as the only coherent way to reason in contemporary theology. I would also point out that in this chapter we have focused on music (and indeed the aesthetic experience in general) as it is *received*: the "aesthetic conversion" it can provoke, and its aptitude to

---

145. I will simply mention that the inspiration she explicitly mentions as being behind the concepts of breakthrough and "spheres" is born of combination of Dante's journey through hell, purgatory to paradise, together with the last book of Lewis's *Chronicles of Narnia*, in which eschatology is described in terms of crossing through spheres.

146. Cf. 1 Thess 5:19.

reflect or express reality as Christian faith understands it. To complete our reflection on how music can actually mediate faith (and consistent with chapter 2, in which we reflected upon the need for a hermeneutical approach to musical meaning), some attention to the person of the artist and musician or composer themselves is necessary.[147]

Before that, however, we need to focus more on the return of beauty to theological thought, seeking to grasp both the context and reasons for its reappearance as well as its most important elements. In order to do just this, chapter 5 offers a brief introduction to theological aesthetics, and the presentation of some of its more important representatives in relation to our theme. Its panoramic overview of some of the contemporary theological reflections on our theme aims to allow the reader to familiarize herself with recent developments in the area of theological aesthetics, as well as to find points of comparison and contrast with my own position of chapter 6, which completes the epistemology presented in this chapter.

---

147. In chapter 6 we will explore more the relevance of Christ-centered affective conversion, in relation to the vocation of the artist and dynamic of musical composition, in the context of the theology of Davies as applied to the vocation of the artist in the Body of Christ.

5

Theological Aesthetics in Contemporary Theology

Contemporary Interest in Theological Aesthetics

> *This world was never meant for one as beautiful as you.*
> —From "Vincent" by Don McClean

> *The Risen One is as beautiful as the Crucified is ugly.*
> —Pierangelo Sequeri

The Power of Beauty in Post-Modern Culture

THE UNDERSTANDING OF GOD AS THE SOURCE OF ALL BEAUTY, AND natural beauty as an entrance point to perceive God is not new. The Sapiential writings in the Scriptures are a clear witness to that perception. One eloquent expression of this awareness is to be found in Wisdom 13:1–5, in the following words:

> For all men who were ignorant of God were foolish by nature; and they were unable from the good things that are seen to know him who exists; . . . If through delight in the beauty of these things men assumed them to be gods, let them know how much better than these is their Lord, for the author of beauty created them. And if men [and women] were amazed at their power and working, let them perceive from them how much more powerful is he who formed them. For from the

greatness and beauty of created things comes a corresponding perception of their Creator.¹

However, theology has not always remained in touch with this sensibility. For centuries it focused on truth and goodness, or morality, as its central concern, leaving beauty aside and "behind," on the margins of theological reflection, from Aquinas to the last century.² However, although not originally counted among the classical list of the essential properties or qualities of being which the Scholastics called "transcendentals," in recent times, God as beautiful has been rediscovered in theology and poetry, and beauty has become widely accepted as a transcendental quality of being, and therefore of the divine, alongside those of truth and good. God is one, good, true, and beautiful. Biblical terminology, with the different terms, *tob*, *kalos*, and *kabod*, points towards an interaction between the perception of good and beauty, and "the bond between theological aesthetics and divine revelation finds in the concept of glory [kabod] its most direct and illuminating application point."³

A superficial consideration of the notion of beauty could be tempted to consider it as slightly less important than the true or the good. After all, it is our decisions and our actions, based on solid reasoning, that make a difference in the world. Even the term "aesthetic," in the vernacular, can be used to evoke something that affects the surface, rather than the essence of things. And yet, one of the characteristics of our human life is that we are equipped with the capacity of perceiving beauty. The irony of the phrase quoted above from the song about artist Vincent van Gogh is precisely that we know the world *should*, in fact, be able to hold beauty, and perhaps especially people of beauty. And yet, the "Beautiful One" was crucified. Indeed, as we shall learn from the theologians presented in this chapter, the crucified and beautiful one was, and is, the very revelation of Beauty.

Theology and contemporary cultural sensitivity is drawn to reflect on beauty, and there is a common denominator in the way that sensitivity is awakening: the awareness of a paradox. Beauty can be found

1. This Scripture quotation is taken from the New Revised Standard Version (Catholic Edition), copyright ©1989 by the Division of Christian Education of the National Council of the Churches of Christ in the USA and are used with permission. All rights reserved.

2. Cf. Fisichella, "Beauty," 77–78.

3. Sequeri, *L'estro di Dio*, 84.

in very unlikely places and with very unlikely faces.[4] Contemporary Western culture is becoming conscious of this reality, and it is reflected in its music, which is often one of the first places where shifts in sensibility can be detected. In the last few years, songs specifically on the theme of beauty have not just been released, but have been immensely successful. To name but a few: "Beautiful," by Christina Aguilera, "You Are Beautiful," by James Blunt, and "Beautiful," by rap artist Eminem. In contemporary church music I observe the same trend.[5] A song that bridges both worlds is "Something Beautiful," by Sinead O'Connor, from her album *Theology*.[6]

The most interesting thing about these songs, to my mind, is that they are not "optimistic," light songs that address only the positive aspects of life. They all bring to the fore areas of pain, of paradox, of human ambiguity and suffering, as if to emphasize, despite it all, our need and our capacity for beauty, while somehow identifying in that kind of beauty something capable of redeeming. Recent films show the same trend: the award-winning, low-budget film *Crash*[7] has at its core the holding together of light and shadow, not in different people alongside one another but in one and the same heart, beautiful and ugly, at once. *The Secret Life of Words*[8] weaves, in a powerful way, the suffering and beauty of two lives, touching on the healing power of human presence and words in a world capable even of the horrors of the Balkan (and other) wars.[9] *Gran Torino*,[10] the story of a Korean War veteran in the States, is another more recent example addressing themes of

---

4. When my father died a few years ago, my brother and I, completely independently, wrote songs for him expressing beauty, the beauty of his life and of life itself, even amidst the pain.

5. For example, "You're Beautiful," by the Irish Christian community Emmaus: "I'm tearing, holding / Walls will fall, silent sigh. / I'm rising, glowing, washed in the wishing of You. / *You're beautiful, You're beautiful / I've never known anyone quite like You at all. / You're beautiful, You're beautiful, / Your love is calling me on.*"

6. The album is an interesting and, at times, hauntingly beautiful musical interpretation of Scripture.

7. *Crash*, directed by Paul Haggis, 2004.

8. *The Secret Life of Words*, directed by Isabel Coixet, 2005.

9. These films are quite mainstream and therefore well known. In the films of each country that are known to fewer people, this theme is much more present. For example, *Casomai* in Italy, directed by Alessandro D'alatri, or *Breakfast on Pluto* in Ireland, directed by Neil Jordan.

10. *Gran Torino*, directed by Clint Eastwood, 2008.

racism, violence, and friendship, as well as salvation, forgiveness, and the meaning of sacrifice.

This sensitivity towards the beauty of human life even within its inherent limitations and the suffering of the world finds an echo in the way in which theological and ecclesial reflection, returning to beauty and aesthetics as a pathway forward, is colored by that same awareness. For example, Cardinal Carlo Maria Martini wrote his pastoral letter *Saving Beauty*[11] for the new millennium against the background of the then-recent Balkan War and alluding to the unlearned lessons of a century marked by war and genocide. Pierangelo Sequeri starts his book *L'estro di Dio* of the same year, on the same note: the holding together of opposites: pain and joy, beauty and ugliness, identifying it as proper to Christian aesthetics from its very beginning, since Augustine.

> Two trumpets sound in a different way, but one and the same Spirit blows air through them. The first says: *Beautiful, the most beautiful of the children of man;* and the second, with Isaiah, says: *We have seen him: he had no beauty, no dignity . . .*[12]

How is this to be understood? Not only that beauty is indeed an access point for contemporary sensitivity to God, but that there are points of contact between how theological discourse and contemporary sensibility perceive it. In chapter 4 we spoke about how theology made a mistake in some of its attempts to "defend" God against modernity's rejection of Christianity, when its approach was extrinsic to Christian believing. In this very Christian understanding of human life according to which beauty can be found in that which is lowly, poor, and even weak, there is a possible point of contact or even entry for postmodern sensibility. Modern "man" believed "him"self to be capable, strong, and independent of God. Yet, this proclamation of the supremacy of the subject has revealed, in its unfolding, a very vulnerable, weak, complex, ambiguous, if loved centre of the universe; and one who is aware of that fact, at least at times. Nietzsche, herald of the reign of self, was a lucid prophet:

---

11. Martini, *Saving Beauty*, of which I prefer the original title: *Quale bellezza salverà il mondo?* ("Which beauty will save the world?")

12. Sequeri, *L'estro di Dio*, 3, quoting St. Augustine, *In Io. Ep.* 9.9.

> Who gave us the sponge to wipe away the entire horizon? What were we doing when we unchained this earth from its sun? Whither is it moving now? Whither are we moving? Away from all suns? Are we not plunging continually? Backward, sideward, forward, in all directions? Is there still any up or down? Are we not straying, as through an infinite nothing? Do we not feel the breath of empty space? Has it not become colder? Is not night continually closing in on us? . . . God is dead. God remains dead. And we have killed him.[13]

These words were ones spoken to superficial unbelievers in the marketplace. The tone is one of desperation, not triumph. And the unfolding of modernity into postmodernity has noted this passage: from confidence in our capacity to understand and fix things (to know the truth and act out the good), we have become painfully aware of our limits, disorientation and incapacity. With that awareness, our hope and confidence in our ability to change things is damaged and diminished. Therefore, the questions born now (including the ones about God) are quite different than those of rebellion and independence that modernity thrived on. No longer is rejection of God in the light of the situation of the world the overriding sentiment (with the implicit conviction that "man" would somehow organize things better!). When reality, with all its crudeness, hits our life, the question that surfaces when the dust settles and the anger subsides, is usually some form of this one: "What's the point?" It is as if one strand of postmodern sensitivity realizes we do not have access to the "whys," at least not the fundamental ones: a kind of "street-level" parallel to the "humility" of negative theology. There is more we don't know than we will ever be able to grasp and express. So the issue is about the now and seeking a way to move forward with meaning and decision, rather than scanning the past for whys and who is to blame.

This book is about contemporary music as theology and as an access point to the Word *now*, because it is in this present cultural climate that beauty, in its musical form and expression, has the power to reach and touch human hearts in a way that truth formulated in verbal concepts or moral exhortations struggles to do so. The authors we will look at during this chapter will help us understand why and in what way musical symbolism enriches theological aesthetics for its

---

13. Nietzsche, *Gay Science*, para. 125; quoted from *Thus Spoke Zarathustra*, 181–82.

understanding of God and Christian faith, but the ground we build on is this one: humanity's need for hope in the ever-growing awareness of poverty and sin, and music's capacity to help us access it. Songs, books, films, and cultural sensitivity in general have grown in the thirst and quest for beauty, and theology for some time, albeit in individual and prophetic voices, has begun to reflect on beauty as an access point to God. Why? Because, to paraphrase Balthasar, a world without beauty makes no sense:

> In a world without beauty . . . in a world which is perhaps not wholly without beauty, but which can no longer see it or reckon with it: in such a world the good also loses its attractiveness, the self-evidence of why it must be carried out.[14]

Beauty doesn't give us a rational or moral(istic) reason for living or believing. It opens a door and lets us see the same reality, with the same questions, in a different light. Or better said, its appearance in our world opens us to wonder at the very fact of life itself. Beauty reawakens our hope, and hope is something twenty-first-century Christians are in need of:

> The aesthetic is the recurring place of that question that the conscience rarely dares to formulate with the necessary seriousness: is this really the best of possible worlds?[15]

Beauty, art, and the aesthetic touch that part of us that knows there can be something better, different, whole, finished. It affirms our longing and our wondering, and therefore somehow our faith that there is more to life.

There is a parallel to be drawn between this reflection on beauty in Christian understanding and theological discourse and that of Clemens Sedmak, one of the theologians of transformation theology, who, when reflecting on world hunger, talks about the poor and the hungry as "a source of revelation, as a *locus theologicus*,"[16] and of pain, or the painful situations of the world, as a source for theological reflection.[17] He talks about the wounds of our knowing, in the sense

---

14. Balthasar, *Glory of the Lord*, 19.
15. Sequeri, *L'estro di Dio*, 14.
16. Sedmak, *Transformation Theology*, 115, in chapter 5, "Disruptive Power of World Hunger."
17. Cf. Sedmak, "Wound of Knowledge," 143.

that, as we open our eyes to the extent of the world's problems and the complexity of their causes, we become aware that they preclude any immediate solution. He calls this "epistemic vulnerability," which consists in "accepting the wounds of knowledge."[18] The essence of this vulnerability is double: the consciousness that the problem is too big and all-embracing to be "solved," combined with the awareness that no one is innocent. To live is to know one's guilt. There is no possible "justice" to be had, as the reality we live in is unjust. The move he suggests is one from justice to mercy:

> Living with this wound means having to live a life of "knowing rough" without the consolation of epistemic justice. If epistemic justice is not attainable, what is the alternative? The alternative is mercy, not justice.[19]

Nowhere in his reflection, to my knowledge, does Sedmak talk explicitly about beauty, but I suggest there is a parallel between his invitation to epistemic mercy as a form of perception and a motivation to action, and the presence and calling of Christian artists and musicians in the contemporary world:

> Epistemic vulnerability can make us say: it is in our weakness that we are strong. It is our weakness that reminds us of the task of transformation. Epistemic mercy is the attitude that prevents the wound of knowledge from losing its openness, its painfulness, its disruptive power.[20]

Art and music that seek to express beauty and pain together accomplish something of the same effect—they invite us to allow the beauty of the incarnated and crucified Son of God redeem our lost hope; the absurd trust that in the goodness, gentleness, and beauty of Jesus of Nazareth is the path to redemption. Despite all the weight of injustice and suffering that people carry, hope can be reawakened in the heart of those touched by beauty. God's justice is his mercy,[21] and the gratitude born of mercy experienced births a new song for the Lord.[22]

---

18. Ibid., 145.
19. Ibid., 146.
20. Ibid., 149.
21. Cf. Jas 2:13 (NRSV): "Mercy triumphs over judgment."
22. Cf. Ps 51, reputedly King David's response to God's forgiveness.

Theologically speaking, where creation is marred by the ugliness of human sin, beauty and mercy cannot be that far apart. The response to the question about the good is justice, whereas the response to the one on beauty is (at least more akin to) mercy. It is interesting that Richard Kearney, in his thorough and insightful analysis of human imagination over the ages, brings the two together,[23] calling for "an ethical-poetical imagination . . . radically de-centered in the sense of being opened to the demands of the other in the postmodern here and now."[24] The ethical imagination is understood by him as the fact that beyond the epistemological lies the reality of an "other" who forces me to take a stand. That this imagination be also poetical, in the sense of inventive, he suggests, would protect ethical imagination from becoming too puritanical or nostalgic.[25] It is interesting that one of the more conspicuous forums for challenging world hunger and injustice recently has been through concerts.[26] Perhaps the apparent "fragility" and freedom that art has is analogue to God's way of entering our world, as human, as poor, as vulnerable, as open-hearted, self-giving, crucified and risen to life by Another. Martini eloquently evokes this mystery at the beginning of his letter on the theme of "Saving Beauty" when he asks "how can a man who is so good and gentle put to rights a world that is so bad?"[27]

From Theological Aesthetics to Music as Theology

In the light of these introductory reflections, we can understand better the centrality of beauty and music as one of its channels of expression, in theology's task to mediate between faith and culture in the present moment. Humanity does not live by bread alone, and in the technologically powerful yet somehow "tired" world we live in, art, music, and theological aesthetics have something to say. This sensitivity to beauty as a source of hope and meaning, together with the current re-emergence of beauty in theological discourse is the context in which we

---

23. Cf. Kearney, *Wake of Imagination*, especially the last chapter; and *Poetics of Imagining*.
24. Kearney, *Wake of Imagination*, 389.
25. Cf. Ibid., 366.
26. Cf. the Live 8 concerts on July 2, 2005.
27. Martini, *Saving Beauty*, 25.

integrate the conclusions of the first three chapters of the book. Music is a particularly strong expression of contemporary culture's sensitivity to beauty and art. It accentuates sharing rather than answers, or the formal clarity of a message sent and received, because sometimes the message to be sent is simply not clear, and what remains and becomes the ground we walk on is human compassion and suffering shared. Reality does not work in the "right or wrong" contrapositions our minds have been trained in. Sometimes right and wrong, black and white, major and minor inhabit our world and make more sense played and held together than analyzed and differentiated to neatly organize our human existence. Music does this relatively effortlessly.

As we move further into the theological field, we seek to comprehend music as an expression of God's own being and beauty, and as an appropriate and potentially powerful means of bridging us into contact with the reality as Christian faith reveals it to us. This chapter presents a brief overview of some of the main forerunners and contemporary theologians writing in this field, so as to situate our own reflections firmly within and alongside contemporary theological efforts to address adequately the theme of aesthetics within theology. We cannot aim to be exhaustive in this summary, but to seek and offer some key authors who ground theological aesthetics and are relevant to our theme of music. Some of the various authors presented include reflections on music, others do not. However, in both cases, we offer a synthesis of their theological approach, so as to better highlight convergence points and differences in our attempt, not only to reflect on music in Christian spirituality, but to seek a solid theological understanding of music. To use a metaphor taken from contemporary music: the bass guitar is rarely "noticed" explicitly, but is, in fact, one of the most important instruments in present day music,[28] which marks the underlying rhythm and color of the sound, even in more gentle music. The invitation, therefore, in the rest of this chapter, is to "listen" to the theological bass/base of our authors as they write on aesthetics, as well as the "melody" of their more obvious conclusions or statements on art or music.

28. An interesting point of research for theology in the future would be to explore the epistemological and anthropological reasons why. The bass maintains both the tonal foundation to the chords and the rhythm. When it is missing, the lack of power or depth is obvious, by which, when organizing a musical event, it is the first instrument I look for.

Our first author, and the principal forerunner to theological aesthetics in contemporary thought is Hans Urs von Balthasar. His work has laid the foundations for the inclusion of theological aesthetics in theology for the foreseeable future. Although my own thought does not rest solely on his foundations, I recognize his work as the "condition of possibility" of my own. Of our other authors, perhaps the closest approach to Balthasar's theological aesthetics that addresses music is that of Pierangelo Sequeri. Our other authors include music in a wider concern for aesthetics, each from different paradigms: Richard Viladesau develops Lonergan's epistemological approach, offering the most comprehensive summary of current reflection on this theme. Alejandro García-Rivera enriches this theological field with reflections based on the combination of the sensibility of the Church in Latin America and the Hispanic or Latino communities in the United States with North-American philosophy. From an ecumenical perspective, Frank Burch Brown presents an insightful and pastorally concerned analysis of the field of discernment in Christian music, and Jeremy Begbie, from the tradition of the Church of England, deals explicitly and extensively the specific theme of music in and as theology. Finally Don Saliers invites us to "think" music beyond the sacred-secular divide we are used to thinking in.

Main Thinkers or Forerunners in Theological Aesthetics

A Return to Beauty: Hans Urs von Balthasar (1905–88)

Beautiful, beautiful, beautiful God

—Patrick Kavanagh[29]

God is not God because he is beautiful;
he is beautiful because he is God.

—Hans Urs von Balthasar[30]

---

29. "The One," in Kavanagh, *Collected Poems*, 159.
30. Balthasar, *Glory of the Lord*, 22.

Without doubt, the person who is responsible for bringing thought on beauty to the forefront of theological thought in contemporary theology is Swiss theologian and priest Cardinal Hans Urs von Balthasar, considered one of the most important theologians of the twentieth century. It is not possible to address the question of aesthetics with theological rigor without in some way situating one's thought in relation to his. His work is so vast in extension and depth that I will limit myself to briefly introducing his thought on theological aesthetics, albeit situated in the context of his overall theological framework.[31] His contribution to the field of theological aesthetics cannot be overestimated, and for this reason needs to be presented with a certain amount of thoroughness, as many of the theologians who write on aesthetics take his stance as their starting point, to agree with, complete or differ with him.

"One of the central concerns of Balthasar's theology is to recover the conviction that God is the supreme Beauty,"[32] and it is undoubtedly true that it is this aspect of his work that is most known.

---

31. For a clear general overview and as a valuable resource of his thought, I recommend the book *Hans Urs von Balthasar* by recently deceased John O'Donnell, SJ, by whom I had the privilege of being taught on the same subject at the Gregorian Pontifical University in Rome. The book, as were his classes, is a profound, concise, and insightful presentation of Balthasar's thought and relevance. Another eloquent overview of his theology and relevance today can be found in chapter 4 of M. P. Gallagher's book *Faith Maps: Ten Religious Explorers from Newman to Benedict XVI*, entitled "Hans Urs von Balthasar: The Drama of Beauty." Specifically on the area of theological aesthetics, two chapters of different books on his theology are particularly helpful: Leahy, "Theological Aesthetics," and Oliver Davies, our main author in chapter 6, offers an insightful introduction to Balthasar's entire work of *The Glory of the Lord*, specifically focused toward the Anglo-American reader, in his chapter on "Theological Aesthetics." Davies is particularly helpful in situating the underlying philosophical stances that influence Balthasar and to which he is seeking to respond. The main reference book of Balthasar himself is *The Glory of the Lord* volume 1, *Seeing the Form*, first published in German in 1962, together with other shorter writings, such as "Revelation and the Beautiful." The former work presents the foundational work of its author, and is followed by others volumes that continue the analysis and apply it. Volumes 2 and 3, on "Clerical" and "Lay" theological styles, apply his thought to the analysis of different styles of theological writings and literature. Volume 4 analyses the philosophical underpinnings of antiquity, which is continued into volume 5, looking at modern philosophy. Volumes 6 and 7 are very biblical in nature, analyzing Sacred Scripture from the point of view of his aesthetic thesis and approach.

32. O'Donnell, *Hans Urs von Balthasar*, 18.

> Beauty is the last thing which the thinking intellect dares to approach, as only it dances as an uncontained splendor around the double constellation of the true and the good.... Beauty is the disinterested one, without which the ancient world refused to understand itself, a word which both imperceptibly and yet unmistakably has bid farewell to our new world, a world of interests, leaving it to its own avarice and sadness.[33]

For theology to forget aesthetics, according to Balthasar, is to give up a good—if not the best—part of itself. Our apprehension of the beautiful, according to Balthasar, is not external or superficial, but rather united to our understanding of the good and the true. "The beautiful is beautiful only because the delight that it arouses in us is founded upon the fact that, in it, truth and goodness of the depths of reality are manifested and bestowed, and this manifestation and bestowal reveal themselves to us as being something infinitely and inexhaustibly valuable and fascinating."[34] It cannot, therefore, be understood on its own, and its comprehension is linked with our perception of being itself. According to John O'Donnell, one of the backbones of Balthasar's thought is "being as love," understood in Christian terms as God's dynamic triune love, open to and sustaining the world, in counterposition to German idealism, which would present being as Spirit, and God as Absolute Self-Presence. With this grounding thought of being as love, Balthasar follows the thread of the four transcendental attributes of being for his theological endeavor, writing seven volumes on beauty, (*The Glory of the Lord*), followed by five volumes on the good (*Theodramatik*) and three on truth (*Theologik*). "The transcendentals are inseparable... neglecting one can only have a devastating effect on the others."[35] Therefore, even though our attention will necessarily focus mainly on the first, it is important to understand that in Balthasar's perception and understanding of beauty, they are united.[36]

It has been said that Balthasar talks little of art itself in his work on glory, and indeed it is surprising that, being an accomplished musi-

---

33. Balthasar, *Glory of the Lord*, 1:18.
34. Ibid.
35. Balthasar, *Glory of the Lord*, 1:forward.
36. There is an interesting convergence in this aspect with Haughton's presentation of being as passionate and dynamic, although she develops it further what she calls her "doctrine of exchange."

cian, he talks very little of music.[37] This is because his underlying concern is not about art, but about faith and our approach to it. His is not a theology of art—it is a theological approach that sees in our aesthetic response to beauty an analogy of how God's self is revealed to us and how we respond to it. Herein lies his warning against the dangers of what he calls an "aesthetic theology," one that is drawn from aesthetics outside of the context of faith, and therefore limited. He favors instead a theological aesthetics derived directly from revelation. Theological aesthetics, according to Balthasar, is an approach to faith "that does not primarily work with the extra-theological categories of a worldly philosophical aesthetics . . . but which develops its theory of beauty from the data of revelation itself with genuinely theological methods."[38] He is responding, according to O'Donnell, to the valuable but limited attempts of some authors to address the beautiful in faith by comparison with created beauty and art. This, to his mind, is unacceptable. Although believing in the need to recover an aesthetic approach to faith and theology, Balthasar firmly rejects any attempt to take inner-world beauty as a measure for divine beauty: only revelation can set the standards for beauty. Christ is "God's greatest work of art."[39]

We can understand this better if we grasp that the underlying concern that moves Balthasar is theology's comprehension of the experience and drama of faith itself, and its ensuing consequences in how theology is done. He seeks to overcome a reduced understanding of faith as a mental act by which one "believes that." Faith is an act of the whole person, of surrender and obedience to the Father in Christ. It is faith in and through the faith of the Son (one of the more challenging aspects of his Christology, which, albeit from a viewpoint "from above," firmly defends that the human nature of Jesus meant he had "faith" in the Father, as witnessed in the Gospels).[40] Faith is an act by which Christ impresses his form on the believer, making them "Christoformic," and the role of the believer is one of active receptivity. Therefore, although he does not take human beauty as a path towards

---

37. Cf. Leahy, "Theological Aesthetics," 23–24. We will analyze shortly the writings he has left with us on the theme, but they are relatively marginal to his main approach to theological aesthetics.

38. Cf. Balthasar, *Glory of the Lord*, 1:79–117, quotation from 117.

39. Balthasar, "Revelation and the Beautiful," 117.

40. Balthasar, "Fides Christi," especially 52–58.

the understanding of God's beauty, he does use an analogy of the aesthetic experience to help us understand how faith works. Since our own quest is the theological understanding of how music aids faith, which in turn is rooted in the theological comprehension of aesthetics, an explanation of how Balthasar describes the act of faith is useful. So how does he unfold this reflection?

Faith as an Aesthetic Act:

Two core references mark Balthasar's understanding of faith: The first is taken from the Preface of the Eucharist for Christmas:

> Through the mystery of the incarnate Word the new light of your brightness has shone onto the eyes of our mind, that knowing God visibly, we might be snatched up by this into the love of invisible things.

The second is from the Johannine writings:

> That which was from the beginning, which we have heard, which we have seen with our eyes, which we have looked at and our hands have touched—this we proclaim concerning the Word of life. The life appeared; we have seen it and testify to it, and we proclaim to you the eternal life, which was with the Father and has appeared to us. We proclaim to you what we have seen and heard, so that you also may have fellowship with us. And our fellowship is with the Father and with his Son, Jesus Christ. (1 John 1:1–3)[41]

He relates this to the Christian call to contemplation, both that of every Christian and the theologian: "Christian theology is a reflection on what has been seen with the eyes of faith."[42] It is helpful to realize that the backdrop of Balthasar's thought is a dichotomy in the comprehension of faith introduced by Luther, by separating hearing and seeing.[43] Christian faith, according to Luther, was based on hearing

---

41. Taken from the Holy Bible, New International Version®, NIV®. Copyright © 1973, 1978, 1984, 2011 by Biblica, Inc.™ Used by permission of Zondervan. All rights reserved worldwide.

42. O'Donnell, *Hans Urs von Balthasar*, 19.

43. Could this maybe one of the reasons why Balthasar, and the majority of those who follow him in the area of theological aesthetics, have focused more on visual art than on music, giving more attention on the eye than the ear? Balthasar does write about the senses in faith, but relatively little of it applies to music.

the Word of God, not seeing, a dimension that was introduced in medieval times based on neoplatonic philosophy alien to Christianity. He "rejected on principle the idea of any aesthetic harmony in theology."[44] This influenced most Protestant theology, except for Barth, who went as far as affirming God as primal beauty, in a manner proper to God alone. Balthasar was very influenced by Barth, although he differed by defending the analogy of being, which Barth rejected,[45] although always situating it within Barth's understanding of the analogy of faith.[46] Therefore, with the backdrop of Catholic theology's reduction of faith to a narrow form of conceptuality and its forgetfulness of the patristic attention to beauty, philosophy's monistic conceptualization of being as spirit or as one, and Lutheranism's rejection of any aesthetic harmony in faith or theology, Balthasar develops his thought on faith as "contemplation of the form" of the glory of Christ.

His guiding hermeneutical principle[47] is that it is the theological object that gives the conditions of possibility of theological knowledge, in two steps: firstly the theological object takes form in divine revelation, through which God has revealed God's self in space and time; this form (*Gestalt*) in Christianity is Jesus Christ himself. Secondly, this form draws the beholder unto itself via a light that irrupts from within the form itself, not outside.[48]

> The Beautiful is above all a *form*, and the light does not fall on this form from above and from outside, rather it breaks forth from the form's interior.[49]

The aesthetic experience of faith, therefore, is the light of grace capturing our attention and revealing the object to us, drawing us into the depths of God's beauty. Balthasar is influenced in this aspect by Newman's illative sense, along with Rousselot's position on the role of grace in the act of faith,[50] defending that the mind "sees" aided by

44. Ibid., 19.

45. The analogy of being affirms the similarity between creature and Creator based on the fact that creation proceeds from the Creator and therefore in some way resembles the Creator.

46. According to Barth, this meant that the one point in which we see the unity between God and his creation is in Jesus Christ. Cf. ibid., 33 n. 5.

47. Cf. Dupré, "Hans Urs von Balthasar's Theology of Aesthetic Form," 309.

48. O'Donnell, *Hans Urs von Balthasar*, 21.

49. Balthasar, *Glory of the Lord*, 1:151.

50. Cf. Rousselot, *Eyes of Faith*.

grace through which evidence comes together to the apprehension of the form in faith. However, he emphasizes more the role of grace, over and above the subjective existential role of the person. "In the Gospel, the strength of the disciples' belief is wholly borne and effected by the Person of Christ, the locus of Revelation."[51] In this sense, "the power of synthesis comes not from the subject but from God."[52] In this way, contents and act of faith come together in one unity.

It is significant, to my mind, that this aesthetic approach to faith developed in his work on *Glory* be the entrance point Balthasar uses to his entire theological endeavor. It fully concords with my own conviction that theological aesthetics has an important place in fundamental theology. By focusing on aesthetic apprehension as one involving the whole person, it draws our attention to the fact that we do not "separate" our perception into reason, heart, and senses in the way that some approaches to faith and *preambulae fidei* would have us think. Balthasar does not, however, develop *how* this comes about. From the perspective of this book, we are missing some reflection or keys as to how our knowing integrates sense perception, heart, and reason as it opens to faith in the God who is Triune love reaching out to humanity. Pierangelo Sequeri, commenting on Balthasar's theology, says that assuming the perspective of aesthetics assures theology of three things:

- The primacy of the transcendental object (God's revelation);

- The experiential form of its apprehension (contemplation of the singularity of Jesus);

- The return to the original unity of conscience (which corresponds to the possibility of a phenomenology of truth).[53]

---

51. Balthasar, *Glory of the Lord*, 1:177.

52. O'Donnell, *Hans Urs von Balthasar*, 23, commenting on Balthasar's position in relation to Newman and Rousselot. Cf. Balthasar, *Glory of the Lord*, 1:175–77.

53. We shall present Sequeri's theological approach to aesthetics shortly, but let us simply anticipate that, by unity of "conscience" or "consciousness" (as the Italian term as used by Sequeri is not easily limited to either one of these two terms), he means the link between conscience and sensitive perception, which both allows and calls for a "*Christian theory of spiritual/sensible perception as condition for faith* (in which the 'eye-witness' accounts of the apostles and the patristic doctrine of 'spiritual senses' converge), the Christian doctrine of experience that derives from it." Sequeri, *Anti-prometeo*, 86.

This approach opens us towards a Christian theory of spiritual perception, (such as the patristic tradition on the spiritual senses), and Balthasar's call to restore the unity of the transcendentals in theological thought. However, in his quest to understand the structure of the believing "conscience" or "consciousness," Sequeri says that between the "perception of the form" that Balthasar highlights and a phenomenology of perception, there is the need for what he calls a "phenomenology of the truth."[54] We will come back to this when looking specifically at Sequeri's own approach, but it is very similar to an observation by Hilary A. Mooney, in a book bringing together Balthasar and Lonergan's perceptions of aesthetics:

> Current scholarship raises the question of the relationship between aesthetic perception and the affirmation of the truth . . . what is the status of the artistic form? What is its relationship to reality as we know it in other ways? Von Balthasar seems to identify the beautiful with the true without devoting much thought to these questions . . . it lacks integration with a critical, rational theory of cognition . . .[55]

This, in part, could be due to Balthasar's concern with avoiding any impression of an anthropological-transcendental foundation to his theological aesthetics.[56] This need for more development on how we come to know *and* believe through art is sought to be addressed by the reflections on epistemology developed in chapter 4 and integrated into chapter 6.

Art in Theological Aesthetics According to Balthasar

Balthasar's main focus is not on a theology of art. The process of his thought moved progressively from looking directly at art to the theological reflection on revelation and how it is apprehended, which would become its foundation and his main focus.[57] Furthermore, to say that

---

54. Cf. Sequeri, *Anti-prometeo*, 87. I understand that to mean the quest to understand how we apprehend, assent to, and appropriate as such the truth we perceive with heart and mind in an integrated way.

55. Mooney, *Liberation of Consciousness*, 223–24. The need to develop and complement Balthasar with elements of epistemology is also noted by Alejandro García-Rivera, as mentioned further on in this chapter.

56. Cf. Balthasar, *Love Alone Is Credible*, 31–50.

57. The growth of his thought, from *The Development of the Musical Idea* (1925)

the aesthetic experience is a valid doorway to the experience of faith is verging too close to the analogy of beauty Balthasar was adamant in avoiding, although he himself comes very close to doing just that in a short but very significant writing on Mozart's genius, which we will look at shortly.[58] The aesthetic experience serves as a reference point for Balthasar to explain the act of faith, in two ways. Firstly, he says that, in the same way as a true work of art is evident, and if one does not perceive its greatness or its meaning, the fault is in the perceiver rather than the work of art, so Christ is the revelation of God's beauty, whether one perceives that beauty or not. To the tricky question of how come many people did not and do not recognize in faith the form revealed in Christ, which should be evident, he offers two causes: the fallen condition of humanity and our perception, in need of healing, as well as the voluntary concealing of God as a consequence of his love and respect for human freedom.[59] The second way he refers to art in relation to faith is when he identifies a double dynamic or dipolarity in the aesthetic apprehension of a work of art: "perceiving the form is the experience of a fullness, [and yet] the perfection of the form initiates the perceiver into an experience of depth which is reflected in the inexhaustible character of a work of art."[60]

> The appearance of the form, as revelation of the depths, is an indissoluble union of two things. It is the real presence of the depths, of the whole of reality, *and* it is a real pointing beyond itself to these depths.[61]

---

to *Religion and Art* (1927), through "Revelation and the Beautiful" to *The Glory of the Lord*, bear witness to this process. Cf. Sequeri, *Anti-prometeo*, 88.

58. Cf. Balthasar, "Tribute to Mozart." It is one of the few places he talks explicitly of music.

59. Vatican II, in its Constitution on *The Church in the Modern World* (*Gaudium et Spes*), includes others: a critical reaction against religions, the Christian faith included, lack of care on the part of Christians themselves in faith instruction or even the false presentation of its teaching, or failure in life witness, which "conceal" rather than reveal the true nature of God. Cf. *Gaudium et Spes* 19.

60. O'Donnell, *Hans Urs von Balthasar*, 21–22. This corresponds to the dual structure of the beautiful, according to Thomas Aquinas: the aspect of form (from the Latin *formosa*, meaning "beautiful"), and that of splendor (*species/speciosa*). Cf. Balthasar, *Glory of the Lord*, 1:20–21.

61. Balthasar, *Glory of the Lord*, 1:120. This second aspect of pointing away is described by Balthasar as the movement of the whole person in and towards the invisible God.

He compares this to the experience of faith in which, as we contemplate the form that is Christ, we are drawn in by the light that comes from within Him, to the never-ending depth of his relationship with his Father.[62]

With regard to the first of these two applications, I think Balthasar is oversimplistic, in that the recognition of a classic is surely more complex and culturally conditioned than how he presents it. Is every great piece of art "self-evident"? According to whom? And does its recognition not imply a certain level of formation in the sensibility of the culture out of which it was created? This oversimplification can perhaps be explained in part by the fact that the obvious breadth of knowledge and culture that his writings portray are focused on Western culture, and the examples of classics in art are taken from what most would classify as "high" art. As valid as this may have been in the moment of his writing, for the current cultural and theological atmosphere it is incomplete and needs to be widened and applied.

With regard to the second aspect referred to above as the analogy of the aesthetic experience, and which is the more important aspect of his understanding of the act of faith as an aesthetic act, I consider it an insightful *intrinsic* way of approaching Christian faith and Christian art. Balthasar's theology is profoundly Christ-centered and contemplative. Continuing in that line of thought, if a work of art draws a person into an ever deeper experience of fullness in a similar way as the aesthetic experience of faith draws them into Jesus' relationship with the Father in the Spirit, then could not a work of art, or a piece of music, born in a Christian artist baptized into Christ and with their "eyes" of faith fixed on Him, lead us profoundly into the presence of Triune love? This seems to be the direction he is pointing in when he says:

> The beautiful, then, will only return to us if the power of the Christian heart intervenes so strongly between the other world salvation of theology and the present world lost in positivism

---

62. This unfolds into two aspects of the task of theological aesthetics, as Balthasar understands them: a theory of vision (which would be part of fundamental theology), and a theory of rapture (pertaining to dogmatic theology). He thus defends the thoroughly theological nature of both (as opposed to the *preambulae fidei* being situated prior to theological reflection) and their inseparability. Cf. ibid., 125.

as to experience the cosmos as the revelation of an infinity of grace and love—not merely to believe but to experience it.[63]

As we shall see in chapter 6, the way forward in Christian art and music is not only extrinsic, by learning to open to and accept newer or different styles of music, but intrinsic, by understanding and making room in theological thought and spirituality for the living faith of committed artists to express that same faith in ways that can draw contemporary culture with them. Understanding our faith in the terms described by Balthasar in his theological aesthetics can only help in that endeavor.

Balthasar's Writings on Music

> *How can it be possible to clarify in words*
> *something that cannot be expressed in words:*
> *and that we discover to be beyond words*
> *precisely because it appears to us*
> *as even more immediate than words?*
>
> —Hans Urs von Balthasar[64]

Balthasar was a passionate musician, reputed to have known some of Mozart's works on the piano by heart. Perhaps this accounts for his lifelong defense of beauty as an attribute of being and an entrance point to God. It is surprising, therefore, that music figures so briefly in his overall work.[65] Among the few reflections Balthasar has on music,

---

63. Balthasar, "Revelation and the Beautiful," 109; and Sequeri, *L'estro di Dio*, 102.

64. Balthasar, *Lo sviluppo dell'idea musicale*, 13. Translation mine.

65. I am aware of two authors who have sought to look more specifically at his thought on music, and to do so they have focused on different writings of Balthasar. The first is Pierangelo Sequeri, who draws primarily from the following four: "Katholische Religion und Kunst" (this article, and a similar one published a year later on "Religion and Kunst," have not been translated into English); "Revelation and the Beautiful" (first published in 1959/1960); *Die Entwicklung der musikalischen Idee: Versuch einer Synthese der Musik* (1925); and "Tribute to Mozart" (first published in 1955). He relates them, however, to many other works of Balthasar, including *The Glory of the Lord*. Sequeri is an authoritative interpreter of Balthasar, as well as developing his own theological thought on the subject. The second is Jorge Piqué Collado, in a thesis on *Teología y Música: Una Contribución Dialéctico-Trascendental sobre la Sacramentalidad de la Percepción Estética del Misterio*, which focuses on *Die Entwicklung der musikalischen Idee* and a chapter called "Die Wahrheit ist

there are two short writings in particular that are worth mentioning in this context, and which we have preferred to deal with separately for different reasons. The first is his very first book, published in Germany in 1925, when he was twenty, and called—with characteristic ambitiousness—*The Development of the Musical Idea: An Attempt at a Synthesis of Music*.[66] Although the book has points in common with his comprehensive approach to theological aesthetics, and indicates that which would later emerge, it is primarily a philosophical text, and is not representative of his mature theological synthesis—hardly surprising given that it was written more than thirty years earlier. It does, however, present interesting aspects of his early thought on art and especially music, and therefore merits attention. The second essay is a short but fascinating piece called "Tribute to Mozart." These short writings, often overlooked or underestimated fragments of Balthasar's thought, are potentially rich windows of insight for our theme.[67]

In the first book, Balthasar offers us an interesting and remarkably balanced synthesis of his philosophical understanding of music. He situates it within an understanding of the role of all art in relation to meaning, which constitutes their "prime matter." He says that all art tends to the perfect expression or realization of a spiritual idea, and although never reaching it fully, this fulfillment of meaning is that of the "objectification of the divine." It is divine light that inhabits the

---

Symphonisch." Cf. Balthasar, "Verità è Sinfonica Aspetti del Pluralismo Cristiano." For a guide to the Balthasar's first two as yet unpublished writings on art and religion, cf. Nichols, *Scattering the Seed*, 9–16.

66. Balthasar, *Entwicklung der musikalischen Idee*. It has not, to my knowledge, been translated to English, and therefore I have worked with the excellent translation by Pierangelo Sequeri, *Lo sviluppo dell'idea musicale*, facilitated by Sequeri's authoritative commentary (in which his expertise both as musician and an expert on Balthasar's theological aesthetics are invaluable), on the themes opened up by the Swiss theologian. In the same volume, Sequeri has published his own reflection on Balthasar's theological aesthetics in relation specifically to music, *Anti-Prometeo*, from which we have also drawn some insights and will focus on further when we look at Sequeri himself.

67. The aforementioned thesis by Piqué Collado, in relation to his first book, notes what he perceives to be the three characteristics of music identified by Balthasar: the ineffability of music, which can be translated as inapprehensibility, its reference to meaning (as in all the arts), which is what allows us to "talk" about music in words, and finally its capacity to "give form" to the divine, in which form is understood as the entrance of the divine in the categories of space and time. Cf. Collado, *Teología y música*, 131–41.

centre of the circle which is the core meaning of all the arts, and whose divine light is irradiated into space and time through the arts.[68] "It is a partial process of that great movement of 'discovering meaning' that is the very aim of the world."[69] In this direction, he underlines the intrinsic relationship between truth and beauty:

> The truth, which is thought, becomes, in its material dimension, beauty. This latter aspect is therefore only an analogical expression of the truth, and both are identical, inasmuch as they designate the divine.[70]

Music is special among the arts in that it is, according to Balthasar, more apt than the other arts as it acts in a more penetrating and immediate way.

> Music is the most incomprehensible art because it is the most immediate one. It questions us more directly, penetrating deeper in us than the others. But is it not perhaps this closeness that makes it an eternal enigma, which has always moved us to fix its limits, to regulate it, to force it into numbers and express it endlessly in laws?[71]

However, its role is, like the other arts, that of giving form to the divine, where form is understood as "the insertion of the divine in spatial-temporal categories, as the normal means of its accessibility."[72]

Due to his role as our main forerunner in theological aesthetics, let us briefly complete his analysis, particularly as it underlines his attention to many of the aspects noted in chapter 1 on the meaning of music. When explaining what music is, he says it is a specifically human phenomenon, even where its lowest level can be found in some birdsong, but cannot truly be considered such due to the lack of consciousness. He divides music's elements into three, corresponding to their evolution in time: rhythm, melody, and harmony.[73] His analysis of the three is both historical and genetic, in the sense that he notes their appearance over time, considering it to be organic: melody appears after

---

68. Cf. Balthasar, *Lo sviluppo dell'idea musicale*, 13–15.
69. Ibid., 16.
70. Ibid., 37.
71. Ibid., 13.
72. Ibid., 17.
73. Three of the essential elements of music as noted in chapter 3.

rhythm, and integrates it, as does harmony both melody and rhythm. Talking about rhythm, and drawing on Aristotle, he says that rhythm in music has two principles: an organic one (relating to the body and its heartbeat), and a spiritual one (related to the human consciousness of order in the cosmos). In this context, he defines music as "the expression of the instinct of order, accompanied by pleasure, in the kingdom of sounds."[74] "Melody," derived from *melos*, meaning "style," "atmosphere," intervallic structuring, or expressive arrangement, is the most noble part of music, but also the most incomprehensible and hardest to analyze. "In melody the whole is truly bigger than the sum of the parts."[75] Finally, harmony is the third aspect that over time has developed in the musical idea. Balthasar shows a wide breadth of understanding of the relationship between music's development and cultural awareness in the history of Greek and Western culture. With regard to this third element of music, for example, he explains how neither perspective (painting) nor time (past) had importance for ancient Greece: only the present and its eternal actuality, in proximity to us. For the Western world, on the contrary, the notion of relation and the relativity of all things (including the universe) gradually comes into play, as well as that of space. It is these concepts of "relation" and spatial depth that Balthasar relates to the element of harmony in music. The move to harmony was one from a linear understanding of music to the perception of its depth: the relation of notes between and with each other, and he notes that this development of harmony in music happened alongside the great discoveries of Western culture, including the changes in its cosmological understanding. Harmony, he says, opened "the space of music."[76] This coincidence of cultural changes, our growth in awareness of our existence in time (history) and space, and the appearance of harmony in the history of music anticipates interesting questions in relation to chapter 6, where we shall talk more fully about the theological significance of our changes in perception, and the potential role of music in mediating faith in such a context.

It is this gradual evolution of music over time that leads him to talk of the organic nature of the development of what he calls the "musical idea": an organic unfolding or revealing of the metaphysical idea

74. Ibid., 21.
75. Ibid., 26–27.
76. Cf. ibid., 30–32.

it seeks to in-form. Music is particularity apt to do this because it is a temporal art: it moves, proceeds, or returns, and as such is "a symbol of the industrious dynamic development of the world,"[77] capable of "representing concentration and expansion, intensity . . . the dynamism of God, precisely beyond the intellectual, visible, verbal dimension, as immediate pure form of truth."[78]

On the basis of this comprehension of music, he talks of the limits of music and its values. With regard to the former, he says that music cannot directly represent emotional content or intellectual content, without associations to extra-musical realities, such as thought, memory, emotions, and sensations.[79] In this sense, he takes an admirably balanced position in the (still ongoing) debate about whether to consider music a form of language or not, and about its having extra-musical significance or not. In the quest to understand music in faith transmission, perhaps most relevant to our theme in this context is his insightful suggestion that in the same way as music can enrich our understanding of words, similarly words, or the thought-frame and associations with which we come to music, can also help to understand music as a whole.[80] This is relevant to our discussion in chapter 2 in which we considered the relevance of context in musical appreciation, and the importance of being aware of how we approach it.

With regard to the values, and consistent with his highly metaphysical understanding of art, he says that the true value of music is of universal validity, and subordinates the worth of any individual musical form to the measure in which it reveals something new of the idea, of the divine. Therefore, the value of music can grow and be enriched but not surpassed. Each new musical form is a step forward in the understanding of the divine, and must be understood and integrated organically as such. Theoretically, it appears to be a foundation

77. Ibid., 34.

78. Ibid., 37.

79. It is important to keep in mind that Balthasar is always talking about "absolute" music, in the sense of music without words. Even where he talks of program music, it is music that, without the aid of words, seeks to represent something of the extra-musical world.

80. Cf. ibid., 40–41. Piqué Collado, quoting Sequeri, considers this to be a contradiction in Balthasar, in that it allows music to have representational significance. I would differ, seeing rather Balthasar's quest to understand how we approach music "in association" with other forms of apprehension, such as the verbal or pictorial.

for a balanced historical integration of the development of music over time. However, the underlying framework seems much influenced by German idealism, and the role of the individual artist totally subordinated to music in itself: "Since the artist is not important, only the creation. He is only the coincidentally personal instrument of the evolution of the immanent meaning of the world."[81] Having said this, although the personal aspect of musical composition is not important, the presence of that which is human in art is of the utmost significance, and it is in its reflection of humanity that art finds its greatness.

The phenomenological audaciousness of Balthasar's analysis of music in this small book is impressive, as is the depth of philosophical implications. For the purposes of our own quest for the relevance of music in theology and contemporary faith transmission, I would underline his insightful awareness of the interrelated nature of musical and cultural developments.[82] He extends this to talk, albeit briefly, of the complexity of the different cultural ways of musical expression and "in-forming" of the metaphysical idea behind the form. Varying human cultures mark the form music gives to the idea in diverse ways. He talks about how these "gaps" between cultures cannot be easily bridged, and his solution is to suggest that the development of the musical form needs to reach a pinnacle in each culture before being able to "cross-fertilize" fruitfully. This could be said to reflect a certain ethnocentrism in his appreciation of music, although, being that the text was written in 1925, it is understandable, and even then displays breadth of thought. I would only add that in contemporary praxis, the breadth of cultural overlap is too wide to consider the development of music as Balthasar does. Cultural and musical genres and styles cross-fertilize each other constantly, in a much more organic way than Balthasar could have seen or perhaps imagined.[83]

A few words are necessary on the short piece on Mozart. In his "Tribute to Mozart," Balthasar "lets loose" (as there is no other way to describe its tone) an uninhibited "Ode" to the musical genius of

---

81. Ibid., 45.

82. Albeit aware that we do not have a comprehensive analysis of the "theory of culture" implicit in Balthasar's writings. Cf. Sequeri, *Anti-prometeo*, 91.

83. Piqué Collado identifies three words by which theology and music come together in Balthasar: "form," "recognition," and "metaphor." The form would be that which, according to Balthasar, permits recognition, and musical metaphor is the expression of the ineffable in God and theology. Cf. Collado, *Teología y música*, 147–48).

Mozart, whose music (in particular his non-religious music) captured the essence of human life in its origin and its ultimate end. In this music, according to Balthasar, as in no other musical classic, we can "hear" the echo of creation transfigured and redeemed.

> Mozart serves by making audible the triumphal hymn of a prelapsarian and resurrected creation, in which suffering and guilt are not presented as faint memory, as past, but as conquered, absolved, transfigured present.[84]

This unadulterated celebration of human life and *eros* seems to rise above the "Christian" awareness of sin and the fall, reminding us of the paradise we were born of and will one day know. In no other place does Balthasar expound the power of music with such strength, not only to present us with theological realities, but to enter us into the experience of them. Sequeri sees in the text "the supreme freedom of a spirit that recognizes a theological *typos* in a particular *personal* form of musical experience."[85] He laments that the intuitions present in this short writing of Balthasar were not taken up by him and integrated into his theological aesthetics.[86] It is a tribute, and as such stands as a witness of one of the most outstanding theologians of the twentieth century to the power of one specific composer and musician to "mediate" Christian faith.[87] My own sense of Balthasar's thought on music is that, although insightful, it does not reflect the depth of his theological thought found in other areas. His earlier writings on music reflect a philosophical understanding of reality that seems to be strongly in-

---

84. Balthasar, "Tribute to Mozart," 399.

85. Sequeri, *Anti-prometeo*, 70.

86. Sequeri suggests that Balthasar in his statements about Mozart's music goes further in the appreciation of the theological potential of art than he ever does in his more comprehensive theological aesthetics. Cf. Sequeri, *Eccetto Mozart*, 75–90. Sequeri goes as far as to affirm that Balthasar did not (or could not) draw the consequences of this piece into his theological framework. His musical thought "stayed in the shadow of his youthful exploration." In Mozart and only there, Balthasar accepts what he would never accept of the theological word: the theological and Christian quality of a theology of *eros* without words that carries over the separation of spiritual and sensible, worldly and Christian elements. "As if in music there was space for the evocation of a Christian truth that, falling under the control of concepts, would fatally change into a heresy." Cf. Sequeri, *Anti-prometeo*, 71, 129.

87. It is, of course, significant that there are not a few important theologians that have a similarly high opinion of the music of Mozart, among them Karl Barth, Joseph Ratzinger, and Pierangelo Sequeri.

fluenced by German idealism, rather than that of the Trinity as love, which emerges later.

Other Aspects of Theological Interest

There are other aspects of Balthasar's theology that are worth mentioning for their convergence with my own approach to be developed in chapter 6. These are not separated from Balthasar's theological aesthetics, but rather form an integral part of them.

i. *The embodied nature of human life:* his positive understanding of the senses, in that, healed by faith, they can lead us to acquire a "taste" for God present in sensate realities, and into the contemplation of Christ, which is in and through the world. "One of Balthasar's favorite words is 'bodiliness.'"[88] This is linked, of course, with Balthasar's entire approach to the incarnation as *Gestalt*,[89] and the theme of the faith of Jesus, direct consequence of his kenosis.[90]

> Christian faith cannot bypass the senses, for both philosophical and theological reasons . . . as Revelation is in and through Christ, our access to God is always mediated by the humanity of Jesus.[91]

ii. *The world as the space in and through which we find God:* any approach to the divine that seeks to bypass the world is con-

---

88. O'Donnell, *Hans Urs von Balthasar*, 57. Significant in this regard are the writings he has on the senses, in which he brings together biblical and patristic sources, Ignatian spirituality on the application of the senses in the Spiritual Exercises and contemporary theologians. Cf. Balthasar, *Glory of the Lord*, 1:365–425; also "Seeing, Hearing, and Reading," and "Seeing, Believing, and Eating."

89. Apart from his writing in *The Glory of the Lord*, cf. "God Speaks as Man," and also "What Is Distinctively Christian." For his fully incarnational understanding of the truth, see "Truth and Life." The centrality of the incarnation and embodiment leads Balthasar to address themes such as the living out of sexuality in its varying forms or states of life: cf. his explicit writings on options of life and the evangelical counsels, such as in "Theology of the Secular Institute" or "Celibate Existence Today."

90. Cf. the aforementioned essay on the faith of Christ. Albeit without direct reference or even use of the expression, Haughton's description of the life of Jesus of Nazareth is a lucid presentation of the human-divine existence of Jesus, in which this aspect of his theology finds eloquent expression.

91. O'Donnell, *Hans Urs von Balthasar*, 25–26.

demned to failure, for such an approach would neglect the concrete realm where men and women live.[92]

iii. *The image of God as passionate and dynamic love:* Balthasar challenges any rationalized or logical understanding of God or explanation of his actions, in the face of the utter freedom and commitment witnessed in Scriptures. The God of Christians is not a God without passion but a God of divine *eros*.[93]

> It is impossible to rationalize this vitality of God, which at the same time is demonstrated and hidden in the tensions of salvation-history . . .[94]

iv. *The world assumed in the Body of Christ:* Balthasar's teaching on the Body of Christ is rich, and is another convergence point with Rosemary Haughton and transformation theology, as we shall see in chapter 6.[95]

> So deep is the reality of the Body that one member of the Body can always pray for the others as well as suffer for them.[96]

Balthasar dares to say that God allows himself to be influenced by our prayers.[97]

Despite these areas of doctrine which would converge with points Davies presents in transformation theology, which we will present in the next chapter, it is only fair to mention Davies's own perception of the limits of Balthasar's theology:

> For all the greatness of his achievement, von Balthasar's commitedly historical theology of the *Theodramatik* masks a conceptual and perhaps also idealist approach to history as

---

92. Ibid., 11.

93. Ibid., 32. Cf. Balthasar, *Glory of the Lord*, 1:121. This evokes Benedict XVI's statement in his first encyclical of our being able to call God *eros* as well as *agape*; cf. Benedict XVI, *Deus Caritas Es*, 10. Albeit with different styles, there are many similarities between how Balthasar describes Dante's sensibility in *The Divine Comedy* in "Eros and Agape," and a chapter of Haughton's book *The Passionate God* called "The Face of Beatrice."

94. Cf. Balthasar, *Glory of the Lord*, 1:655–59, quotation from 657.

95. Cf. Balthasar, "Who Is the Church?"

96. O'Donnell, *Hans Urs von Balthasar*, 59. Cf. Balthasar's book *Prayer*, an eloquent work on the role of prayer in the Body of Christ.

97. Cf. O'Donnell, *Hans Urs von Balthasar*, 73.

fundamentally idea and narrative rather than incarnational, spatio-temporal act.[98]

Theological Aesthetics: a Survey of Contemporary Debates

FAITH, THE AESTHETIC CONSCIENCE AND MUSIC: PIERANGELO SEQUERI

> *Listening to music is also a spiritual sense,*
> *music is also theological.*
> *This is not romantic.*
> *It is simply Christian*
>
> —Pierangelo Sequeri[99]

Pierangelo Sequeri, born in 1944 in Milan, a son of two musicians and himself a composer and musician, is a diocesan priest and theologian. Vice president of the *Facoltà Teologica dell'Italia Settentrionale*, he is an ordinary professor of fundamental theology there and teaches theological aesthetics at *L'Accademia delle Belle Arti di Brera*, as well as collaborating pastorally in the diocese of Milan and pioneering pastoral initiatives such as the "Orchestral Music Therapy," with children and young people with learning difficulties, a project called Esagramma. Sequeri is one of the best known and respected Italian theologians at present, and is renowned for his creative and original contribution to the theology of faith, among other areas. He is not well known in the English speaking world.[100] His thought on music is rooted in his overall approach to theology and theological aesthetics. We will therefore briefly look at four elements of his thought: the background and concerns of his theology, his particular theology of faith, which we could call the re-comprehension of the "believing conscience/

---

98. Davies, "Transforming Theology," 26. Cf. the aforementioned article of Davies on the theological aesthetics of Balthasar for an explanation of the underlying philosophical premises of Balthasar's thought.

99. *Anti-Prometeo*, 129.

100. The only piece I know is a recent article introducing his thought on faith: Gallagher, "Truth and Trust," a thorough and insightful presentation of his thought within contemporary theology and above all in relation to developing a theology of faith adequate for our times.

consciousness,"[101] his vision of aesthetics and art, and his understanding of music therein.

Background and Underlying Concerns

Sequeri is concerned with the spiritual quality of human experience, culture, and faith. He expresses the need for a redefining and reconstruction of what *spiritual quality* is, in order to contribute to cultural reconstruction.[102] He situates the causes of the present situation in the double separation operated in the arrival of modernity and subsequently romanticism: the separation between reason and faith, and theology and spirituality.[103] He identifies the coexistence of calculating reason and uncontrolled sentimental and emotional thrust, and is critical of these tendencies.[104] A sentimental thrust that does not integrate the bonds of *agape* worthy of human loving is not a valid paradigm for human—never mind Christian—living. The result is the type of "paralysis" of the conscience we referred to in the introduction, which becomes incapable of discerning and even less of deciding.[105]

This is not only lived at an individual level. With regard to the interaction of personal-social, he criticizes the coordinates of the present cultural (and political) situation in which the conscience is at the same time privatized and universally legitimized, and by which the individual decision is "always right," irrespective of the quality of the conscience that decides. This has a double effect of emptying and disempowering faith,[106] on the one hand, (either faith has external effect and influence or it is rendered useless and therefore meaningless), and on the other it leaves "culture" without a valid "interlocutor" to chal-

---

101. The translation of Sequeri's term *coscienza* is not straightforward, and could perhaps be covered by the intersection of the terms "conscience," "consciousness," and "awareness," with the inclusion of both perception of truth and justice (meaning) and that of what he calls "the order of the affections." For that reason, in explaining Sequeri's thought, at times I have chosen to use the original Italian term.

102. "In realtà che cosa possiamo pensare tutti insieme quando diciamo 'vita spirituale' e spiritualità?" ("In reality, what can we all think together when we say 'spiritual life' and 'spirituality'?"). Sequeri, *Sensibili allo spirito*, 4.

103. Cf. Sequeri, *Qualità spirituale*, 7–18.

104. Cf. Sequeri, *L'estro di Dio*, 14.

105. Cf., Sequeri, *L'oro e la paglia*, 110.

106. Cf. Sequeri, *Sensibili allo spirito*, 9–13.

lenge its values and ethos. The resulting effect on religion itself is that of a "politically correct" framework that is detrimental to both religion and culture:

> There are images of inter-religious dialogue that seem based more on disinterest for the quality of religion than on the common passion for truth. It is one of the effects of the so-called "political correctness," already quite devastating for anthropological quality and for culture.[107]

We noted in chapter 4 that he situates the cause of this situation in the philosophical development of Western culture, and sets about rethinking the notion of faith and how we come to believe in a systematic way. I point out the cultural awareness that colors Sequeri's thought as it echoes my own attempt at offering theological reflection in dialogue with and sometimes as a response to the contemporary cultural situation. Lonergan, talking about the mediating role of theology, and identifying the stages of meaning in history as those of common sense, theory, and interiority, calls for a theology based on interiority, as one thought out and expressed in purely theoretical and metaphysical terms is no longer adequate. I perceive Sequeri to be a contemporary theologian who is doing precisely that, with elements of a theology of music as part of that endeavor.

Towards a Re-Comprehension of the Believing Conscience

Sequeri rethinks faith in the light and awareness of the goodness of God, reflected among other places in the kenosis of the incarnation, (Phil 2:3–8), and our capacity of recognizing that goodness. The "background music" to his theological thinking and structure is the image of God as *Abbá*, as presented, for example, in his *Il timore di Dio*,[108] which overflows into his other writings explicitly, or implicitly, leading him to invite us to talk of God in terms of trustworthiness, rather than credibility. Although his theology is renowned for its complexity of style, and therefore at times this foundation can be hard to

---

107. Sequeri, *Qualità spirituale*, 61–62.

108. An inspiring and well-written book of what could be called "narrative" biblical theology, in which I perceive an understanding of God that continues, albeit implicitly, in his more well-known and ambitious ones: *Il Dio affidabile* and *L'idea della fede*.

perceive, Jesus' faith in the goodness of God, and in that belief the provocation of our own faith, is core to his thought. God is a passionate God, whose tenderness and anger (as presented to us by Scripture) are expressions of a passionate love for humanity. Sequeri eloquently challenges our lame notions of God, speaking of the "depth of an affection that sweeps away the impassive marmoreal profile of the dignity of God" or that "senile tolerance we dare to call mercy."[109] Therefore Job is applauded for not accepting an image of God that is not worthy of Him,[110] and Jesus is amazed at our lack of trust! In fact, distrust is presented as the root of all sin. "God considers immoral a faith that lacks intimate persuasion."[111] Although the centrality of the *affectus fidei* to faith may not seem immediately related to our theme of music, I contend that its importance cannot be underestimated. The widening of our understanding of the movement of faith to include areas of our being beyond a narrow understanding of reason helps to provide a context in which to situate music's "effect" on us, and in us, both in our knowing and believing. We will come back to this point when we talk about affective conversion, but firstly, let us look at Sequeri's understanding of human consciousness and how we come to faith.

As human beings, we are equipped with the capacity of perceiving and understanding the love of God. Implicit in Sequeri's thought is a basic trust in the human capacity for recognizing truth and justice, despite its being wounded or incomplete, which he calls "the truth of our experience."[112] Sequeri identifies in our sensibility to love a place from which to begin for a re-comprehension of faith, for the believer and for the dialogue with non-Christians, calling it the "order of the affections." It is in this place that God's gift to us takes place. In Sequeri's understanding, the unity of human perception of meaning, truth, and justice, that is to say, of the cognitive and affective potentials of human living, is of vital importance. He talks about the disciples "recognizing

---

109. Sequeri, *Il timore di Dio*, 75.

110. Cf. ibid., 39–50.

111. Ibid., 75. Although I am unaware that Sequeri has had any contact with the thought of Rosemary Haughton in *The Passionate God*, there is a similar approach to and understanding of the historical person of Jesus of Nazareth in these two profound and stimulating books—an insight to the quality of his human life that is (unfortunately) rarely so clearly expressed.

112. Cf. Sequeri, *Il timore di Dio*, 156.

themselves as recognized,"¹¹³ by which they believe Him, revisiting his memory and giving credit to the revelation of God in him. That happens enacting the same human capacities that come into play in all our contact with and appreciation of reality, and it is in this unity of our anthropological faculties that the importance of the aesthetic in the act of faith lies.

He criticizes the epistemological heritage of the *analysis fidei* in apologetics, arguing for a re-comprehension of the human capacity for and process of coming to believe. Theology, in his opinion, has been lacking a systematic research into the structure of the believing conscience and religious faith.¹¹⁴ In Sequeri's analysis of the believing *co-scienza*, which he identifies as a universal human reality, he offers two fundamental elements: the perception of its finitude, and the feeling of the "unfounded," by which it apprehends the world as given, in the desire and quest for meaning. This conscience is capable of receiving a *notitia Dei*, with a *ratio metaphisica* and capacity of posterior christological commitment. The *notitia Dei* can come either in the form of an aesthetic mediation, by which the "reality" appears "loveable," or that of an ethical mediation, by which truth convinces freedom of its "justice" or that of the sacred. He defines the "aesthetic *coscienza*" as the place where the "promise" of a complete revelation of the being, always missing in the reality, shows through; "ethical *coscienza*" as the judgment about the "justice" of every possible revelation, and "believing *coscienza*" as the conferment of credence given to the trustworthiness of every promised justice. It is the aesthetic mediation we are interested in this chapter. He gives major importance to the "symbolic" nature of this evidence.

> The believing conscience lives its own relationship with the truth according to modalities essentially mediated by an aesthetic and ethical appreciation: that is from the trust/ confidence and consent given to an appreciated justice of the truth that is shown in the form of symbolic evidence.¹¹⁵

---

113. "To actually see Jesus coincides with a resonance induced by being intentionally looked at and affectionately summoned by Him." In Frazão de Jesus Correia, *Penser la dynamique croyante de l'humain*, 86. Frazão has since published his doctoral dissertation on Sequeri in dialogue with other theologians: *Risonanza affettiva, appello etico, stile relazionale. Tratti di una fede vivibile e visibile* (Roma: Aracne, 2010).

114. Cf. Sequeri, *L'estro di Dio*, 21–22; and *L'idea della fede*, 47–52. We already spoke about the consequences of such a situation in theological thought in chapter 4.

115. Sequeri, *Estetica e teologia*, 9–11.

Up to now, the analysis applies to all human consciousness—how does the step to Christian faith take place? The *coscienza* becomes constituted in Christian faith through the recognition of the truth and justice of the foundational event of Jesus Christ, accessed through the witness of the testimonial faith of the church, (through the orders of the Word, fraternal relationship/community, and the sacraments). In this way, through what he calls "mediated immediacy" it becomes historically situated (*forma fidei*). Diverging somewhat his own reflection on music, this analysis allows for an interesting interaction between music's symbolism and the use of the Word/words in evangelization. The proclamation of the gospel will never be complete, nor will Christian faith be "consummated," without explicit knowledge and acceptance of who Christ is. However, the process towards faith can pass through stages which music can help mediate and facilitate. How does Sequeri develop this understanding of aesthetic mediation?

The Aesthetic in Human Life and Faith[116]

When talking about aesthetics, Sequeri is not only referring to art, but to our very apprehension of reality, and is critical of an understanding of aesthetics that limits itself to art, thus reserving it for "the few" who appreciate art as we understand it, rather than recognizing in aesthetic appreciation a place where reason and feeling are experienced together. For this reason, he sees as important the cultivation of aesthetic perception, not as a pastime but as a necessity within a Christian "spirituality of the sensible." According to Sequeri, the aesthetic is the place that asks the question about the world we live in: given its limitations, "is this really the best of possible worlds?"[117] The answer the aesthetic experience gives to this question is both yes and no, because it does not accept that beauty cannot reflect itself in this world, and yet it pushes the limits of the same, rejecting the trappings of the world, through what he calls: "the realism of the 'spiritual' imagination that takes form corporally."[118] Beauty awakens, in a way that words no longer seem to be able to, the awareness of another beauty. For this reason

---

116. Sequeri's main writings that refer explicitly to aesthetics (apart from those focused explicitly on music) are *Estetica e teologia* and *L'estro di Dio*.

117. Sequeri, *L'estro di Dio*, 14.

118. Ibid., 15.

he gives importance to the relationship between aesthetic experience and our believing consciousness:

> The study of . . . the bond between aesthetic experience and believing intelligence promises to have special importance in the slow reformation of a new way of considering the religious roots of Europe.[119]

He is very influenced by Balthasar, as can be seen from his writings and commentary on Balthasar above. Indeed, some of his work can be understood as an attempt to continue or complete what he senses is missing in Balthasar's immense achievement. Of particular relevance to our theme is how he addresses the theme of the person of the artist in Christianity and contemporary culture. Referring explicitly to Balthasar, he talks about the similarities and differences between the artist and the religious person.[120] I welcome Sequeri's perceptive understanding of the real issues in the ongoing debates on art and Christianity, as well as his sense of how to move forward. Against the backdrop of discussions on appropriate art forms, he calls for an unprejudiced new opening to the universe of artistic creation, and, rather than the imposition of one particular style or genre of art, its development, by "convinced believers of passionate faith and real talent and formation," who are allowed to work and draw with them the interest of a culture.[121] The same point is made more explicitly in reference to music, when he points out the intrinsic link between Christianity's being assimilated and the evolution of its musical expression in different and contemporary styles:

> After all, it is also the sign of the aptitude of the Christian form to affirm itself in a vital way. . . . Embarrassment should come, theologically speaking, from the impulse to freeze this process, not from the normality of its metabolism.[122]

This quotation is taken from a book on Mozart's music, proclaiming not just its brilliance but its theological significance. Even alongside

119. Ibid., 26

120. Cf. Sequeri, *Anti-prometeo*, 72, commenting on the early work of Balthasar found in "Katholische Religion und Kunst." This concern with the dynamic of integrating the Christian vocation and the artistic one is at the heart of this book, and we develop it further in chapter 6 and in the Appendix.

121. Cf. Sequeri, "Coscienza Cristiana, ethos della fede e canone pubblico," 29.

122. Sequeri, *Eccetto Mozart*, 11.

his obvious approval of "classical" music of the past, he takes a clear stance against the tendency of a nostalgic or biased defense of music from Christianity's past heritage, "against" more contemporary styles. Furthermore, he situates the progress of Christian art and music as intrinsic to its health, giving a radical (in the sense of rooted) foundation to the place of contemporary music in the church and contemporary culture. With regard to music, Sequeri goes even further, offering insightful reflections on music's symbolic form and its history in Western culture.

Musical Symbolism in Sequeri's Thought and Praxis[123]

> *The prophecy of Nietzsche—*
> *"Art raises its head where the religions withdraw,"*
> *has not been very listened to in music.*
>
> —Pierangelo Sequeri[124]

Although Sequeri is a musician and composer, with some of his liturgical songs being well known in the Italian Catholic Church,[125] his

---

123. His main writings on music and theology, apart from those dealing with aesthetics in general are: *Anti-Prometeo, Musica e Mistica, Eccetto Mozart, La Risonanza del Sublime*, and various articles published in *Erbamusica*, some of which are reproduced in the aforementioned *Anti-Prometeo*. *Anti-Prometeo* accompanies the excellent translation and commentary of two of Balthasar's writings on music with a reflection of his own, inspired by Balthasar, but moving beyond that which Balthasar writes and presenting his own considerations. *Musica e Mistica* is an extensive study of the points of contact between religious practice and music in the history of Europe. In it, he applies his theological conviction of the "friendship" in Christianity between spiritual and the sensible to a reading of history of music, offering what he calls "an instrument of knowledge and analysis" of the same. *Eccetto Mozart*, written on tho 250th anniversary of Mozart's birth, is an amplified and updated version of a previous essay: *Divertimento per Dio: Mozart e i teologi*, written together with A. Torno, and studies the significance of Mozart for music and theology, commenting on the many authors who have taken an interest in his music. *La risonanza del sublime* continues the reflection of *Musica e mistica*, with the specific aim of the series of books in which it is published (on Contemporary Christian Spirituality) to reflect upon spiritual issues in contemporary culture. In order to do so, however, he gathers some of the analysis of the history of thought and praxis of music up to the present time, and offering four examples of what he considers to be an new "revisitation" by contemporary music of the overlap between musical thought and religious or spiritual reflection for creative musical thought.

124. Sequeri, *Risonanza del sublime*, 11.

125. For example, "*Symbolum 77*" is one of the more well-known and used songs

reflection on music is not situated in the area of sacred or liturgical music. In fact, he has little time for the debates in that field as he perceives them at the present moment, seeing them to be lacking serious reflection on the complex issues at their foundation, such as ecclesiological perceptions and historical differences.[126] He talks about a "badly posed question" about the purity of music, instead of about the real possibility of whether religious meaning can manifest itself in music, and if so, how.

> [I]n what way does *religious meaning* manifest itself in musical work? And correspondingly: how is it possible to recognize and evaluate a particular form of religious *feeling* in the compositional style of a determined author? And finally, by what authority, if there is one, can music aim to have a singular capacity of reflecting a religious *faith*?[127]

He observes a two-way bond between music and faith, in that religious inspiration seems to fascinate musical composition,[128] and faith, in turn, has never renounced on a special relationship with music, and is at the core of much of its greatness.

> The contribution of the Christian Religion to the musical history of Occident is more profound, and propulsive, constant and decisive than in any other manifestation of the aesthetic.[129]

However, the level of reflection on music in theology in general, in his opinion, is very low. He perceives three ways of approaching music (and beauty) in the history of theology: music as a servant of the Word, music as the resonance of the sacred origins of the world and therefore harmony in the world, and music (alongside beauty) with the symbol of the crucifix at its center. I agree with his opinion that in all three approaches more relationship with musical semantics is lacking.

---

in Italian churches today.

126. "[V]ery often, apparently technical arguments over musical quality feed on overtly ideological foundations." Sequeri, *Risonanza del sublime*, 8.

127. Sequeri, *Eccetto Mozart*, 11. Emphases original.

128. Sequeri, *Anti-prometeo*, 109.

129. Ibid., 122. His aforementioned *Musica e mistica* develops this thesis in detail and with attention to many different composers in the history of Europe. For example, "A certain way of Christian understanding and evaluation of musical practice . . . in the realm of communitarian prayer contributed directly to the evolution of music as capable of autonomous semantic . . . : of expression, discourse, and thought" (p. 505).

There is some convergence between his understanding of the symbolism of music and my own, as drawn from Speelman. Our faith brings together many "dialectically opposite" realities: God and humanity, time and eternity, sin and redemption, the world and "heaven"—however we may understand those terms. At times, in the attempt to express these truths, words either fail or over-explain, and "suddenly the theological word pronounces something it shouldn't, and the conscience feels something it shouldn't."[130] Music has a way of expressing that gives us keys to overcome some of the difficulties that the necessary, meaningful but limited conceptual word has. It takes symbolic meaning in a different direction: rather than explaining, it puts meaning into action, making it resound and be recognized in our interiority. Music does not produce objects; it transforms subjects.[131] For this reason he identifies in music a valid means or instrument for "saying" the essentially Christian truth that matter and *eros* are good and that they are blessed.[132] This is true despite their dialectical relationship over history, during which the temptation or tendency has been to give priority to one over the other. Christian faith has always returned to and defended the goodness of both. This balance or integration is not easily maintained or expressed, and yet, according to Sequeri, music says it without becoming a heresy:

> Music, in itself, puts structurally in practice the *oxymoron* that represents the background of that truth of the Christian *logos*, but also its necessary effect: *the senses are also intelligent*, not only obtuse; *the spirit is also sensitive/sensible*, not only incorporeal. The Christian *logos* is not a naked truth without style.[133]

This integration of spirit and matter, senses and intelligence, is another central point of convergence between Sequeri's point of view and that of this book.

The amount of work dedicated to Mozart demands some mention, as his first reflections on music seem marked by this composer.[134]

130. Sequeri, *Anti-prometeo*, 107.
131. Cf., Sequeri, *Estro di Dio*, 176–77.
132. Cf. Sequeri, *Anti-prometeo*, 107.
133. Ibid., 107.
134. In these writings, Sequeri recognizes and gives importance to the fact that Mozart has drawn the attention of a number of important theologians in their writings, such as Kierkegaard, Henri Gheon, Karl Barth, Hans Urs von Balthasar, and Joseph Ratzinger, a fact that cannot be overlooked.

Mozart is acclaimed as a genius by musicians and theologians alike, not only for his sacred music or for how the text is ennobled by his music, but for the music itself, sacred and profane. Sequeri sees in his compositions an example of "theology in music," which celebrates creation and our eschatological hope. It is a music that maintains *eros* and *agape* together, bridging between matter and spirit, and therefore implies what he calls "a spirituality of the sensible." He points out that Mozart, while constituting a "stumbling block" for nearly two centuries with regard to his sacred music, judged not suitable for liturgy, is now hailed by cultured minds, including musicians and well-formed listeners for the religious and Christian quality, especially of his nonreligious music! He offers this reflection, in what I would call a spirit of grounded theological and pastoral wisdom, as a "concrete encouragement—narrative more than theoretical—towards a more easy frequentation between the worlds. For the new generations."[135]

This is the spirit that marks the aforementioned thorough and insightful study of the history of music and mystical-religious experience in Europe, *Musica e mistica*.[136] The book shows the author's competent knowledge of the theme, and suggests that the history of music has been moved by both the idea of music being able to initiate us into immediate contact with the divine, and the aim of representing or interpreting it in words, gestures, and drama. The decline or separation between the world of religion and that of music is a particularly Western phenomenon. Rather than interpreting this as a closed door, he suggests that it opens Europe to what he describes as a "third way," which, he says, "offers everyone something to think about."[137] This

---

135. Cf. Sequeri, *Eccetto Mozart*, 6–14.

136. One of the points Sequeri makes in this book, and in his following one, *La risonanza del sublime*, is the wisdom of Austine of Hippona in his approach to music. Although Augustine is not one of the authors we focus on, it is worthwhile pointing out two areas of convergence: the first his notion of "Jubilus," in his *On the Psalms*, 32, II, 1, 8: Ps 98, 6: 150: 8; the joyous outpouring of praise to God which goes beyond words; cf. Sequeri, *Risonanza del sublime*, 30–31. The second is the link Augustine draws between the body and song: the most eloquent music is to be found is in the risen bodies of the faithful! Cf. Sequeri, *Musica e mistica*, 74, commenting on Augustine's *De Musica*. Cf. also Sequeri, "Dio nella musica di ieri e oggi." For a thorough and insightful development of Sequeri's approach as applied to the musical analysis of Bach's *Cantata BWV 140, Wachet auf, Ruft uns die Stimmen* (known in English as *Sleepers Wake*): G. Osto, *Pentagramma teologico*.

137. Sequeri, *Musica e mistica*, 508; cf. *Eccetto Mozart*, 175–77.

"way" that he identifies is the notion of "creative thought," understood as the new "director" of the encounter between the sacred and art, which is neither simply destined to prayer, nor necessarily estranged from religion.[138]

> Creative thought, in the form of poetic invention, of reflective seeking and hermeneutical variation has generated a new space of aesthetic culture, focused on the bond between freedom and the sacred.[139]

The difficulty is that although the world of music visits the world of mysticism, it knows very little of the religion or faith that gives it meaning, and neither is the theological world familiar with the musical heritage and civilization Christianity itself has helped to create. However, it is interesting that Sequeri does not read the current situation in purely negative terms, lamenting this separation, but identifying its potential and a possible way forward. Therefore, the "solution" he presents is that of the creative and critical commitment of the "believing *coscienza*." He talks of this third way in terms of an opening towards "a new beginning. A purely sonorous space for invocation . . . in the search of a more sincere word: of Religion, but even for civilization."[140] This is all the more important given the plurality and differentiation of musical forms now in contrast with the past. The balance and wisdom of Sequeri's analysis, both cultural and musical, is hard to underestimate.

> The idea that music is perhaps already a step ahead, beyond the crossroads of Nihilism's fatality and beauty's mediocrity in which our culture flounders, does not seem to be too astray.[141]

One other point of interest must be underlined before we move forward: his commitment to a particular form of musical praxis, and the research born of that experience: a school of music therapy for children with learning difficulties, called Esagramma, and in existence for over twenty years, of which he is director. The theoretical foundation of this project is not that the enjoyment of "playing" with music brings emotional input and diversion to children who have difficulty in reasoning. It is much more challenging and insightful. Sequeri and

---

138. Cf. Sequeri, *Musica e mistica*, 507–8.
139. Ibid., 508.
140. Sequeri, *Risonanza del sublime*, 9.
141. Ibid, 11.

his team, in involving these children in concerts of classical music, have observed over the years that music aids the mind's thought processes. It is as if, where the mind reaches a limit in verbal linear thought, music helps to circumvent those blocks, and therefore helps them grow in their capacity of communication.[142] Licia Sbatella, the scientific director of the Esagramma project, has gathered and written about these insights in a book called *La mente orchestra: Elaborazione della risonanza e autismo*. The book draws on the musical theories of S. K. Langer, L. B. Meyer, and M. Imberty to reflect upon the experiences and praxis of years of work in this form of music therapy. To my mind, it is a clear witness to the power of music in praxis: a symbolic form that, in its working, transforms human life.

Overall, Sequeri's is a rich theological approach to music that integrates awareness of the cultural and philosophical causes of the contemporary situation, a lucid and integrated theological analysis of the act of faith which includes the aesthetic as an internal part of that process, and a knowledgeable presentation of the particular symbolic form of music.

Interwoven Traditions of Theology and Art: Richard Viladesau

Fr. Richard Viladesau is a professor of systematic and fundamental theology at Fordham University. He is one of the authors who deals with the theme of theological aesthetics more comprehensively, in the sense that, apart from his own stance on the subject, his books provide a solid and balanced introduction to the background of the theme, in its philosophical and theological premises and consequences, as well as an introduction to some of its main thinkers, both past and present. He clearly understands the aesthetic realm as a theological *locus*, and as such presents and develops his reflection.[143]

---

142. I am grateful to Prof. Sequeri for his time and attention on visiting him at the Esagramma project in Milan. These reflections are fruit of the conversation on that topic.

143. Cf. Viladesau, *Theological Aesthetics*, *Theology and the Arts*, *The Beauty of the Cross*, and *The Triumph of the Cross*. A valuable and summarized introduction to his thought can be found in the first chapter of *The Beauty of the Cross*.

Aesthetic Theology and Theological Aesthetics

Viladesau identifies three areas in the discipline of aesthetics:

i. Epistemology, which includes the study of sensation, imagination, and feeling in human knowing;

ii. Beauty and taste;

iii. Art in general or fine arts.

"Theological aesthetics," according to Viladesau, in a broad sense, is the practice of theology in relation to any of the three areas of the aesthetics outlined above; that is to say that theological aesthetics will consider God, religion, and theology in relation to sensible knowledge (sensation, imagination, and feeling), the beautiful and the arts.[144] Although the latter two overlap, one cannot, he says, automatically and a-critically relate them, as there are diverse aims or ends expressed and employed in art, which question its "obvious" relationship with beauty. One the other hand, the "disinterested" nature of beauty, present in Greek philosophy and taken up by Kant, is challenged in modern art, and on the other hand, religious art may indeed often have questionable beauty.[145] In the study of these three areas, there are two basic approaches: the first object-oriented, in which the study concerns a given class of *aesthetica*; the second subject-oriented, in which the determining factor is the "aesthetic frame of mind" or "aesthetic pattern of experience" (in the terminology of Lonergan). We will use the threefold distinction above as a guide to present his thought.[146]

In contrast to Balthasar, Viladesau talks of the need for an "aesthetic theology" without the negative connotation to be found in *The Glory of the Lord*, in an approach that opens theology to the consideration that human beings do not only think in verbal or conceptual terms, and that art and music are "ways of thinking" that can be complementary to conceptual thinking. He admits, however, that their relationship is ambiguous. He describes aesthetic theology as "an un-

---

144 Cf. Viladesau, *Theological Aesthetics*, 11.

145. Rahner has an eloquent essay on the meaning of religious art, which touches on the fact that the objectively "kitsch" nature of some religious art does not impede it serving its purpose in aiding people live out their faith and piety. Cf. Rahner, "Art Against the Horizon."

146. His first book, *Theological Aesthetics*, is where these foundations of his thought are to be found, which he later applies in the books that follow.

derstanding of faith that is reflective, but whose reflection is embodied in artistic modes of thinking and communicating."[147] This takes form both in liturgy and preaching, as well as in architecture, art, poetry, and music. The realm of aesthetic experience is a source for theology both when it is explicitly religious and as a part of human experience. In the first instance, its importance lies in that it complements the study of religion from written texts with that of its artistic expression, even when aware of its limits (reflection of educated minority, conservative limitations to "official" art, etc.). He suggests that, in the second instance, the artistic experience outside the explicitly religious realm, we find what he calls a "locus of revelation," a place of human consciousness that can open to and receive God's self-communication.[148] Therefore he underlines the importance of its use in the mediation of faith:

> There seems to be no doubt that experiences of beauty can lead the spirit to God and confirm people in devotion, and that therefore the aesthetic dimension is one that must have a place in the communication of religious truths.[149]

Epistemology

According to Viladesau, the basis to all our knowledge of God and all theological aesthetics is our being made in the image of God. In his reflections on epistemology, as in all his theology, the double influence of Rahner and Lonergan are clearly visible at different points in his explanations. He describes his approach as being that of applying the transcendental method to human knowing, according to which "the knowledge of the sensible reality takes place within the horizon of a non-objective pre-apprehension of being [mediated . . . by] symbols that arise in connection with sensible experience, synthesized by imagination."[150] He places a lot of importance on the notion of imagi-

---

147. Viladesau, *Beauty of the Cross*, 4.
148. Cf. Viladesau, *Theological Aesthetics*, 18–19.
149. Ibid., 104.
150. Ibid., 82. The influence of Rahner's transcendental theology on the a-thematic and unlimited horizon of God's being as the foundation and condition of possibility of all our knowing and loving, the mystery of being that is only afterwards reflexively identified with God, is clear.

nation and its role in our making and understanding of meaning: he links this faculty with the senses, taking what could be called a critically realist position, influenced by that of Lonergan, insisting on the connection of intellectual insight with sensible data and giving "a central place to imagination as the mediating moment between the two."[151]

> [T]raditional Christian anthropology has always clearly insisted that sense knowledge and spiritual knowledge constitute a unity, that all spiritual knowledge, however sublime it may be, is initiated and filled with content by sense experience.[152]

He also underlines the role of feelings and emotions in human knowing, criticizing the limitation of the purely conceptual:

> The higher feelings or affects . . . are the embodiment . . . of a latent, habitual actualisation of intentionality . . . —the "attunement" of the practical self to truths and values. As such they present a genuine form of rationality. . . . In Scholastic terminology, they are a form of knowing by "connaturality"—a "felt resonance of the *being* (*nature*) of the agent, a nature attuned by responsible action.[153]

Although Viladesau includes and integrates Lonergan's epistemology, he expands it in relation to art to include notions such as contemplation and enjoyment as part of the human dynamic of knowing.[154] It is also important to realize that, although we divide them for the sake of a better understanding, Viladesau's epistemology cannot be separated from his understanding of beauty as a transcendental notion. If God is beautiful, then the perception of that reality depends upon the disposition of the beholder, whose transformation at various levels is described with the notion of conversion. We have already mentioned something of Viladesau's understanding of Lonergan, and his integration of Lonergan's notion of conversion in his thought, which he complements with that of "aesthetic conversion." I will not repeat what has been developed already in chapter 4, adding only that Viladesau echoes Lonergan's awareness of the fragility of our beings, and talks about the need to learn to take pleasure in the "things of the

---

151. Ibid., 78.

152. Ibid., 77.

153. Ibid. 85, explicitly referring to Lonergan's *Method in Theology*, 30–41, on feelings and values.

154. Cf. Viladesau, *Theological Aesthetics*, 131.

spirit," a process in which there is an important place for both aesthetic sensibility and art. Here the notions of religious conversion, as giving us the ability to judge and feel value "from God's point of view," and aesthetic conversion, which includes the erotic in the psycho-sexual sense,[155] are important.

> The notion of "aesthetic conversion" implies one may make value judgments about art not only with regard to such criteria as skill, imagination, formal excellence, and so on, but also on the basis of its relation to the revelation of the true and the good.[156]

Art as communication can have a transformative effect on the person because it can literally give us a new way of seeing, hearing, feeling, and so on.[157]

Beauty

Viladesau's approach to beauty is a transcendental one, in the sense of seeking in the conditions of possibility of our knowing, a "way," if not proof of God's existence. He explains two basic positions with regard to beauty: that of considering it a quality of particular categories, or that of considering it as a quality of being as such. For his own purposes he notes the importance of taking into account the common characteristics to be found in beauty, be it perceived as pertaining to a category or to being as a whole. The way he approaches this analysis has its starting point and critical reference point in Lonergan,[158] beginning with "with a phenomenology of the subject in the act of knowing, [avoiding] both positivistic reductionism, on the one hand, and the problems of Cartesian or Kantian dualism, on the other."[159]

He clearly relates the notion of beauty with that of enjoyment or pleasure. "The essence of aesthetic experience is to be found in the affirmation of the joy of existence."[160] However, it is a joy that begs for

---

155. Ibid., 205.
156. Ibid., 211.
157. Cf. Ibid., 212, referring to Helmuth Vetter.
158. The insightful analysis Viladesau offers of Lonergan's approach to beauty has been explained more at depth in chapter 4, when presenting Lonergan's epistemology.
159. Viladesau, *Theological Aesthetics*, 120–21.
160. Ibid., 135.

a clarity that goes beyond the senses. The analysis of our experience of beauty shows that it is tied to our own finitude, and therefore fragility. In this way he echoes questions raised by Steiner and others about the eschatological nature of art and beauty, and its capacity to awaken hope and longing. He proposes that the condition of possibility for the experience of beauty—in the sense of the joyous affirmation of the "form" or desirable intelligibility of existence, even in its finite limitation—is the implicit and unavoidable co-affirmation of an ultimate Beauty:

> But my contention is that beauty points to the fact that being is in essence joyous: self-presence with delight. And the condition of possibility for finite beauty is the existence of the Beautiful as such.[161]

In this sense, it is no surprise that he expresses the need for a fundamental theological aesthetics, in the sense this chapter began by underlining: beauty is a potential access point to faith, which as such needs to be studied and discerned by theology. Such a discipline would have as its task the questions of the criteria of theological-aesthetic judgments, the source of these criteria, their warrants, and their relationship to conflicting claims. He suggests such a task would complement and perhaps serve as a corrective to Balthasar. It would be situated in what Tracy would call "foundational theology," whose audience is the academy, and would:

- Begin from below, inquiring into the conditions of possibility in humanity for the reception and of a divine revelation in beauty and art.

- Inquire into the criteria for beauty and for relating the categorical experience "beauty" to the transcendent beauty of God, as well as to God's truth and goodness.

- Ask whether and in what sense we may speak of the beauty of Christ, how it relates to what we otherwise consider beautiful, how and to what degree it can embody transcendental beauty, and how it compares with other experiences of the sacred and the beautiful.

---

161. Ibid., 138.

Aesthetic experience seems to play a major role—at least from some people—in the exercise of the practical judgement for belief in God—perhaps a great deal more so than the traditional "proofs" for God's existence set forth in apologetic theology.[162]

The Arts and Music

Finally, and consistent with the rest of his reflection, Viladesau applies his theological approach to the arts. Although it is fair to say that most of his work has focused on the visual arts, he has written about music, including a chapter on music in his book *Theology and the Arts: Encountering God through Music, Art, and Rhetoric* (which we will talk about shortly). He notes that before the modern period there was very little written about the arts, suggesting that perhaps its role was taken for granted, and therefore not reflected upon. In the West, art was mainly conceived as narrative: a pictorial form of understanding for those who could not read, although a few authors take a step further into what could be seen as the beginnings of a theory of aesthetics. On the whole, however, the arts were used and celebrated without explicit theological thought on that praxis. In his own reflection on the arts and the sacred, his aim is "to examine the ways in which the arts may embody or serve this categorical revelation of God," as transcendental revelation is always mediated by categorical revelation.[163] He says that religious art may serve at least three functions, and sometimes a fourth:

- The expression of explicit religious or theological content;
- Nonverbal communication of feelings and ideas, related to the message intrinsically, if not directly derived from it;
- The creation of beauty in a religious context;
- The self-expression of the artist (although he says this last characteristic is less frequent).

As an example of his own work in this area (related to the first function above), in recent years he has begun to publish a series of books on the concept and the symbol of the cross in Christian theol-

---

162. Ibid., 104.
163. Ibid., 146.

ogy and imagination, covering the periods from early Christianity to the Counter-Reformation. In his study of these different moments in history, he talks of paradigms, understood as "an entire constellation of beliefs, values, techniques and so on shared by members of a given community,"[164] and interrelates theology and art, not just as forms of "thinking" or apprehending, but as theological paradigms in connection with styles of art over the centuries. The way he goes about this is that of concentrating on the "classics" of each period.[165] He extends this notion to works that in themselves may not be classics, but that represent the way of thinking or feeling of a specific time or period, be it a way of thought in theology, or a style in art.[166]

One point of interest with regard to his methodology is that he correlates what he refers to as "two kinds of interpretation" of Christian tradition and human experience as they develop through time: that of theology as systematic thought, and that of the artistic affective and communicative images.[167] He calls both these forms "mediations," not in the sense that they mediate some prior message that exists apart from them, but as a "mediated immediacy": an encounter with reality whose meaning is mediated in the forms that we apprehend it. Art is one of these forms. Hence for Viladesau, the capacity of art to mediate the presence of God is clear. He goes as far as to place it alongside conceptual thought as one of tradition's ways of interpreting its faith experience. These two forms (art and conceptual reflection) overlap and influence each other, not neatly, or predictably, but in a complex way. This is one dimension of the conviction expressed by the title of this book, describing music as theology.

---

164. Kuhn's understanding and definition of a paradigm as applied to theology is offered. Cf. Kuhn, *Structure of Scientific Revolutions*, 132, 175, in Viladesau, *Beauty of the Cross*,13.

165. He uses the word "classic" in two senses: that of a work that represents a period, or in the sense David Tracy gives it, of a work of art or written theology that endures, lasting and influencing people beyond its time; he speaks of works that "involve a claim to truth as the event of a disclosure-concealment of the whole reality by the power of the whole as, in some sense, a radical and finally gracious mystery," and that have had lasting influence, proven by time, in challenging people with the truth they disclose. Cf. Viladesau, *Beauty of the Cross*, 17, referring to Tracy, *Analogical Imagination*, 163.

166. As we shall see shortly, Frank Burch Brown has a similar understanding of the notion of a classic. Cf. Brown, *Religious Aesthetics*, 168.

167. Cf. Viladesau, *Beauty of the Cross*, vii.

And what about music? In his reflections on music, he is influenced by various authors such as Van der Leeuw, Schopenhauer, and others. His understanding of music links it with the universe's original harmony, of which it is mirror and echo.[168] The medieval world, he says, was explicitly related to the divine, insofar as it reflected the order of the universe, the movement of the stars that praise their Creator. Another understanding of art is that of its *communicative function*. In this area, he seems to be influenced by authors who emphasize the emotional meaning of music, such as Susanne Langer and Leonard B. Meyer. He talks of music as "a tonal analogue of emotive life."[169] With regard to the uses of music, he differentiates between verbal and non-verbal music. Verbal music has different uses. The most usual and most obvious case is that of carrying the Word: the setting of texts in chant and song. "The purpose of such music is to create a scared 'ambience': to elevate the feelings, mind, and heart in the act of conveying the message, or a reflection on it, or a reaction to it."[170] He notes the four reasons in favor of the use of music in worship given by the Lutherans:

i. It can be combined with the Word;

ii. It enters the senses pleasantly;

iii. It moves the spirit directly;

iv. It aids the memory's retention of the texts.

Then there is *non-verbal music*. Once again, he refers to the non-representational form of communication that music is, conveying moods and feelings, rather than information, and notes the particular power of music to evoke and awaken us in this way.

> [Non-vocal] music . . . explains nothing directly. It can suggest, give rise to a feeling or state of mind, touch the subconscious, expand the faculty of dreaming, and these happen to be great powers: what it is absolutely incapable of doing is to "speak," in the sense of "inform with precision."[171]

He talks about the specific way music has of symbolizing reality:

---

168. Cf. ibid., 150.
169. Ibid., 151.
171. Ibid., 177.
171. Ibid., 178, quoting Oliver Messiaen.

> The musical analogy for darkness and semidarkness is silence and near silence. The musical "rest" is a kind of holding of the breath: "musical silence is therefore by no means a 'rest'" but the greatest possible tension. To be silent is not to be inactive, but is the greatest receptivity and the highest activity.[172]

He even enters into the relationship between music and spirituality, music and holiness:

> Spiritual music is music which is not only a revelation of the beautiful, but also of the holy, not through the subject matter of the text or the occasion for which it was composed, but through the fact that holiness and beauty have mutually interpenetrated. Such music can be church music or have profane character.[173]

In his book *Theology and the Arts*,[174] he looks at the history of the tensions between music and the sacred, with his focus primarily, although not exclusively, on liturgical or sacred music. He defends the possibility of beauty in music as an access point to God, and the need for the cultivation of an intuitive, aesthetic approach to God, which music can facilitate. This would complement, rather than supplant, the Word in our access to God. In this book, he gives the reader examples of music to illustrate his point.

Finally, Viladesau at least recognizes the importance of the person of the artist or musician, and their experience. He echoes Lonergan's placing of the artistic experience in the realm of experience, capable of widening or enriching that which language or conceptual thought may not fully grasp yet.[175] "Human consciousness itself, and especially artistic consciousness, is revelation: a self-manifestation of God through the creature."[176] However, he recognizes, as noted in chapter 2 of this book, the need to pay attention to context (cultural or otherwise), since the context of the writing can truly affect the comprehension, and even experience of the work of art. Viladesau's work is thorough and lucid, and where he takes on research into specific areas of art and

---

172. Viladesau, *Theological Aesthetics*, 197, quoting Van der Leeuw.
173. Viladesau, *Theological Aesthetics*, 181.
174. Cf. pp. 11–64.
175. Cf. ibid., 79.
176. Ibid., 156.

their relationship with faith expression and their value as mediation, insightful.

Popular Religion in Theology—a Prophetic Aesthetics: Alejandro R. García-Rivera

Alejandro R. García-Rivera taught systematic theology at the Jesuit School of Theology in Berkeley, California, and was a member of the Academy of Catholic Hispanic Theologians in the United States (ACHTUS). If the theological authors up to this point have written in and with reference to the world of Western art, García-Rivera moves us further afield. Based on his own Cuban background and later experiences, his work clearly manifests his Latino/Hispanic origins, and explicitly seeks to reflect upon his experiences in what he calls the "Latin Church of the Americas," referring both to the Church in Latin America and the Hispanic or Latino communities in the United States. These he places in dialogue and comparison with other approaches, in particular European theology and American pragmatism, in the quest to offer, not a theology *of* the Latin Church of the Americas, but *from* it. The two books that most relate to our theme are *The Community of the Beautiful: A Theological Aesthetics*, and his more recent *A Wounded Innocence: Sketches for a Theology of Art*.[177]

García-Rivera identifies a double principle or vocation at work in theology born of the realities that move him: the call for prophetic voices against injustice and one for innovation and inculturation, which takes on board the history and heritage of the signs and symbols of popular Catholicism in the Latin American Church. In this quest (and this aspect converges with the present book, albeit in a very different context), he brings together two theological traditions: semiotics and aesthetics. He places American writers Charles Sanders Pierce and Josiah Royce into dialogue and contrast with the theological aesthetics of Balthasar and philosophical and linguistic aesthetics of semiotics. This is complemented by his own particular form of thinking as influenced by the symbolic-cultural approach to theology of Virgilio Elizondo in Hispanic theology. The result is a thorough, creative, and challenging approach to theological aesthetics, which overlaps with our own quest in bringing together cultural, philosophi-

---

177. He has also co-written a book with T. Scirghi called *Living Beauty: The Liturgy of Art*.

cal and epistemological reflections with and in theological reflection.[178] Without the pretension of being comprehensive, I will point out the main elements of his theological aesthetics and his reflections on what he calls a theology of art.

From Aesthetic Nominalism to Theological Aesthetics

The foundation of his thought is presented in his first book, described by Don Gelpi as bringing "the Hispanic experience into serious dialogue with American pragmatism" in a systematic way.[179] In it, he defines aesthetics as that science which asks the question, "what moves the human heart?"[180] and identifies it as touching on the human experience of beauty. Theological aesthetics, he says, "recognizes in the experience of the truly beautiful a religious dimension,"[181] and is to be distinguished from a theology of beauty in that it pays attention to the reception of beauty, not just beauty as a theological reality. The capacity of human receptivity to beauty came into question in the eighteenth century, and for that reason epistemology has importance in understanding and defending, not just our apprehension of beauty, but that we can perceive God as beautiful. García-Rivera seeks to address what he describes as the polarization of philosophical aesthetics since modernity into an either/or position of objective beauty versus subjective appreciation, or even creation, of the same. Classical aesthetics defended the essentially metaphysical objective nature of beauty in itself. Modernity's turn to the subject transferred importance to the subject, both the artist and the observer or receiver of the work of art. And yet theological aesthetics needs to defend both. He talks of the holding together of the notions of glory and praise: the former referring to transcendental Beauty, with explicit reference to the theology of Balthasar, the latter to our own response. These in turn correspond to reality of the incarnation, and our response in freedom, signified in Mary's yes.

---

178. I am grateful for the time and encouragement received personally from Prof. García-Rivera, who sadly passed away last year, while doing research on the theme in Berkeley some years ago. His creative thought in this field will be missed.

179. Cf. García-Rivera, *Community of the Beautiful*, vii.

180. Ibid., 9.

181. Ibid., 9.

His critique of the philosophical premises or principles of modernity colors most of his work. The underlying concern about false dichotomies surfaces in various ways: Beauty versus the beautiful; the epistemological division between the intellect and the senses, which linguistically corresponds to positive and negative affirmations,[182] or *apophatic* Beauty and *kataphatic* beauty. These oppositions are systematically challenged by García-Rivera, usually by introducing or reminding us of a third element that opens a dual relationship into a triadic one. The subject-object dynamic becomes that of "object, medium and human imagination,"[183] the *apophatic* and *kataphatic* are mediated by human imagination, and the representant, object and interpretant, as we shall see shortly, in the understanding of sign and symbol. This threefold nature of aesthetics is a constant in García-Rivera's thought at different levels.[184] The very title of the book, *The Community of the Beautiful*, evokes the plural rather than dual nature of how he approaches the subject.

Theological aesthetics depends greatly on the understanding of signs and symbols that colors it.[185] Tracing briefly the history of its development, he values Duns Scotus's theory of the sign, and is highly critical of the influence of William of Ockham's thought, who reduced it to logical oppositions, and with whom "the anagogy of signs [became] a formal logic of relations."[186] This resulted in the philosophical outlook that is nominalism.[187] He makes a worthy case for the negative effects of nominalism on how we know, contending that it challenges or refutes the interconnectedness of being, at all levels: between things and other things, between objects and the subject knowing them, and between subjects, objects, and their creator.[188] His critique of its nega-

---

182. In the sense that the intellect defines based on that which one cannot perceive, the abstract, whereas the senses describe based on that which they can (positively) perceive.

183. Ibid., 13.

184. For example: *poeises, theoria,* and *praxis*, as corresponding to the three transcendentals of being:, the beautiful, the true, and the good, respectively.

185. We have already noted in chapter 2 the value of Pierce's triadic understanding of the sign, and how it is essential to García-Rivera's thought.

186. Ibid., 32.

187. Cf. ibid., 95–99.

188. This observation on how nominalism challenges our perception of reality converges with our own option for a critical realism based on the epistemology of

tive effects on art is also wide-ranging, coining the expression "aesthetic nominalism," which he develops more in his theology of art.[189]

Continuing his historical overview, García-Rivera laments that a possible contribution from the missionary church in America, in interaction with the symbols of their indigenous cultures, was lost,[190] and identifies in Charles Sanders Pierce the recovery of the notion of "difference" of Duns Scotus, leading him to enrich the classical dual understanding of sign with a third: that of the interpretant. We have already developed briefly the difference in this regard between the school of de Saussure and Pierce in chapter 2. It is enough here to remember that the introduction of the interpretant within the very understanding of a sign, and its opening *ad infinitum* to other interpretants, allowing the sign itself to grow and "gather" meaning, is more faithful to and reflects better the ways reality and meaning work. It is within Pierce's understanding of symbol that García-Rivera comes to "the startling claim that the uniting category for a theological aesthetics is not form but sign."[191] García-Rivera values highly the work of Balthasar in bringing the theme of beauty back to the fore of theological thought. However, he criticizes him, not his metaphysics, but rather his failing in epistemology,[192] in that he leads us to the frontier of reason and faith, but without teaching us to discern how beauty, in the manifestation of the form, appeals to our beings, and as if there is no room for ambiguity or complexity. He sees the field of semiotics as one element towards a remedy for this failing.[193] García-Rivera

---

Lonergan and Janz, and echoes somehow what was said earlier in the chapter on "aesthetic conversion," precisely underlying art's capacity of enriching our perception of the interconnectedness of reality and our presence therein. There is also an echo of the dynamic nature of being as proposed in Haughton's "being as exchange" in *The Passionate God*, in a notion García-Rivera develops and calls "metaphysics of relations," touching on themes such as the cosmological issues provoked between theology and philosophy as a result of its confrontation with Galileo and Darwin. Cf. García-Rivera, "Cosmic Frontier," and "Whole and the Love of Difference."

189. Cf. García-Rivera, *Wounded Innocence*, 26–30.

190. He refers to the work of Bernardino de Sahagún (sixteenth century) and Lafitau (eighteenth century).

191. García-Rivera, *Community of the Beautiful*, 33.

192. As noted above, Pierangelo Sequeri identifies a similar gap in Balthasar's thought, albeit offering an entirely different approach and attempt at a solution.

193. In this introduction of semiotics into theological aesthetics, there is an importance convergence with our own thesis, albeit colored by a different cultural context.

complements Pierce's understanding with that of one of his disciples, Josiah Royce, who introduces an ethical dimension into the theory of signs.[194] This understanding of semiotics and aesthetics opens the door for what could be called the potentially "subversive" nature of aesthetics, which he illustrates eloquently with the figure of Mary as presented through the Magnificat: the lowly are lifted up, the proud humbled.

This prophetic potential of aesthetics is particular to his thought, and faithful to the expressed intention mentioned above: a prophetic and inculturated theology, in line with the *aggiornamento* initiated with Vatican II:

> Mary's song gives voice to the redemptive nature of this theological aesthetics. God's beauty embodies itself as a "lifting up the lowly," creating the Community of the Beautiful.[195]

Under the inspiration of Virgilio Elizondo's revaluing of the symbols of Catholic culture in popular culture, García-Rivera discovers a major insight: culture is not so much a language as it is an aesthetics![196] Underlying this statement one can see a similar understanding of culture as we find in Michael Paul Gallagher's book on culture, where he describes it as "A cluster of assumptions, values and ways of life," the unrecognized ocean we live and move in.[197] Culture is a way of life, an implicit way of perceiving and assessing the world we live in, which sometimes and to a certain extent becomes explicit in language, but not always and never fully. In this sense, inculturated theological reflection cannot underestimate the value of the aesthetic dimension. This idea of a cultural aesthetics clearly colors and informs García-Rivera's work.

Beyond the content of García-Rivera, the very way in which he approaches theological aesthetics merits mention. In both books, his thought is inspired by and developed alongside the presence of poetry

---

194. Royce also discovered an aesthetic dimension to logic, in the relation between logic and geometry, which García-Rivera called "a great aesthetic discovery, the aesthetic underpinnings of logical order in the polyadic sign." García-Rivera, *Community of the Beautiful*, 35. He related it to Jan Mukarovsky's "semiotic aesthetics of foregrounding."

195. Ibid., 37.

196. Ibid., 60.

197. Gallagher, *Clashing Symbols*, 9.

or art, which, to my mind, give more credibility to the theological relevance of art within theology than many exhortations or explanations to that effect.

Towards a Theology of Art

> An artist's work ultimately becomes
> a sign of this relationship between God's creative freedom
> and the artist's human freedom.[198]

It is in his second book that García-Rivera applies this theological aesthetics to what he himself calls a theology of art, based on the metaphor expressed in the title, *A Wounded Innocence*. As we have already explained, the emphasis of his approach is that of moving from the dyadic relationship often found in theological aesthetics (work of art/beholder) to its triple dimension. In this book the triad proposed is that of: the work of art/beholder/artist. García-Rivera's aim is that of seeking to understand the spiritual insights to be found in and through art, as a way of offering concrete encouragement to artists to work in and for Christian faith. The integration of the person of the artist in his reflection echoes our own conviction that Christian theology and spirituality will only do justice to the area of aesthetics when the artistic calling is understood more intrinsically and assumed more fully into theological discourse.

García-Rivera focuses on how living symbolism and aesthetic expression inform theology, rather than solely what we could refer to as past "classics." The themes treated in the book are informed and enlightened by different works of art from a variety of sources, both historically and culturally. They range from the beginning of art to its end and eschatological dimension, moving through those of the theological dimension of art, its redemptive capacity, the power of popular art, even when it could be regarded as *kitsch*, and human freedom and creativity in the artistic endeavor. He develops the consequences of nominalism on art, identifying the following aspects:

---

198. García-Rivera, *Wounded Innocence*, 45.

- "The rupture of the bond between the aesthetics of a work of art and artistic innovation," when the freedom and inventiveness of the artist becomes an absolute.
- "The loss of general rules for artistic production," making discerning of art impossible.
- The loss of the belief in universals, including the transcendental of beauty, which separates artistic production from reality beyond itself.
- Art for art's sake, in which "exhibition" is the sole aim, without reference to human concerns and ends.
- Abstraction from the real, everyday issues and struggles of society and the world.[199]

In seeking to find the theological dimension of art, he distinguishes between religious art and spiritual art. In doing so, he says the first is iconic, in that it refers directly to the religious object, and latter not necessarily so. The spiritual dimension of art lies in the fact that something not specifically religious can move the mind and heart with some mysterious truth, without the object being intentionally or explicitly religious. The theological dimension of art, according to García-Rivera, is neglected in theological thought. In addressing it, he states that "the theological dimension of art . . . is the religious insight into the need and way of salvation that has as its source the beautiful in the form of a work of art."[200]

His reflection on the dynamic of the artist is insightful. The theological dimension of art emerges in the relationship between two freedoms: God's and that of the artist, which implies a struggle. There are echoes of the dynamic already highlighted by Balthasar and Sequeri of a double calling that is not always easy to integrate:

> For creativity involves both struggle and vision. The artist not only struggles creatively with the constraints of the medium of his or her art in order to give expression to the vision. The artist must also struggle with the constraints of his or her own

---

199. Cf. García-Rivera, *Wounded Innocence*, 26–30.
200. Ibid., 34.

> personality ... a struggle for a vision that is inextricably, intrinsically spiritual.[201]

This recognition of the intrinsic difficulty inherent in the combining of Christian faith and art is both insightful and necessary, precisely because it is intrinsic to artistic activity, above and beyond the cultural resistance that one can find in contemporary art circles (and their reception). Finally, in the quest to understand the revelatory dimension of a work of art, García-Rivera recognizes that the process of artistic creativity is not a product of intellectual inspiration, or an automatic translation of that which is in the artist's mind into an identifiable expression of the same, albeit in aesthetic form. In a recognition of the complexity of meaning, both the person's own grasping of it before he or she seeks to transmit the same, and the final result as it is perceived,[202] he eloquently describes what most artists or composers would probably identify as "the creative process":

> In fact, his final work is often very different from his original intention. Art, he finds, is a revelation to the artist himself. *Something from deep down inside is expressing itself.* As such, art, he feels, is a burden and a responsibility ... it is the burden of the prophet, the giving birth to something new.[203]

The emphasis is my own, and we will return to this dynamic of artistic creativity (and musical composition) and its importance in the next chapter. García-Rivera's explicit focus is mainly on visual art and its retrieval in theological thought, but his integration of the non-verbal symbolism of visual art explicitly into theological thought converges with one of the central aims of this book: theology can be expressed in non-verbal symbolism.

In a recent book coauthored with Scirghi, called *Living Beauty*, García-Rivera develops his thought into what the authors describe as a "liturgical aesthetics." It is an explicit attempt to bring together fundamental theology of the area of theological aesthetics and liturgical theology. García-Rivera touches briefly on the theme of music in the book, taking his starting point from the phenomenon of birdsong and relating it to church song and human song. Drawing on the thought

---

201. Ibid., 46.

202. A theme we have looked at extensively in chapter 2: the hermeneutics of musical expression and reception.

203. Ibid., 47.

of Charles Hartshorne, he says that birdsong is born of enjoyment and intensity of feeling; church song is an expression not only of delight (enjoyment) in life, but also of gratitude for the "memory" of who God is and who we are in God. Finally, human song is the expression of our human *habitus*, the way we inhabit and exist in the world. He therefore links song with the very nature of human living and culture.[204] Scirghi writes about music's "unitive" strength in liturgy, integrating Edward Foley's understanding of sound itself as a fundamentally uniting force,[205] (an aspect that Speelman also emphasizes). On the role of music in liturgy, he develops intuitions of Michael Jan Joncas[206] and Don Saliers[207] on the importance of shared song and harmony in assembly, and its capacity to transform and form dispositions and affections. Although his focus is on the liturgical significance of music, rather than on the symbolic form of music in itself, he does mention the capacity of music to bring to expression areas of meaning our rational understanding struggles to grasp, and Schopenhauer's theme of the capacity music has to touch the innermost dimension of our being.[208]

An Ecumenical Perspective: Frank Burch Brown

Frank Burch Brown is a contemporary theologian from the United States who currently teaches at the Christian Theological Seminary in Indianapolis and is well known for his writings on the area of theological aesthetics. His theology is born of and within a Calvinist context, although he respectfully and knowledgeably explores the writings of ancient writers such as Augustine and Plotinus, as well as those of other traditions, such as Karl Barth and Benedict XVI, insofar as they touch on this theme. As a musician and composer, active in the area of musical ministry, his writings are sensitive to the dilemma that inspires much of my own reflections, and lucid in many of their insights.[209] The

---

204. Cf. García-Rivera, "In Whom We Live and Move." The pages specifically on song are 75–83. Scirghi brings music more fully into his reflection, on which we comment below.

205. Cf. Foley, "Toward a Sound Theology," in which Foley talks about music as an "invitation to engagement."

206. Cf. Joncas, "Liturgy and Music."

207. Cf. Saliers, "Integrity of Sung Prayer."

208. Scirghi, "It Is Right to Give God Thanks and Praise," in *Living Beauty*, 105–15.

209. Indeed, I met Prof. Brown at a conference held at Notre Dame, Illinois, in 2007, on the theme of "Singing God's Love Faithfully" which brought together, which

clearest way of presenting his thought in relation to this book is that of offering the points of convergence in his theology with our own found, in chronological order, in the three books he has written on the subject.[210] These books represent a "reflection in process," moving from the foundations of his thought through its gradual deepening to his very pastoral and practical application to some of the dilemmas found in contemporary Christian culture and praxis. In this sense, his reflections have pastoral concerns as their motivation, but also address the theological and philosophical roots that provoke and sometimes sustain them.

In his first book, *Religious Aesthetics: A Theological Study of Making and Meaning*,[211] Brown's epistemological concerns echo our own. He is critical of the narrow understanding of the rational that has allowed theological comprehension discredit the subject of art in theology, as if it were less valuable or reliable, since "aesthetic forms in religion . . . affect ideas and volitions as well as the emotions and senses."[212] He says that "the very distinction between aesthetic and non-aesthetic is relative; it marks a continuum" from qualities of form, process, sense, and imagination, which are not grasped practically at all by any "logical, cognitive, semantic, practical, ethical or religious considerations," to the opposite position, that is, expressions and ob-

---

brought together both theologians and pastoral workers in the area of musical ministry, above all in the context of liturgy. Although this book has chosen to address Christian music outside of that context, for the reasons already given, the pastoral concerns and some of the theological keys of interpreting them that Brown offers show much convergence with my own reflection.

210. Cf. Brown, *Religious Aesthetics*; *Good Taste, Bad Taste and Christian Taste*; and *Inclusive Yet Discerning*.

211. In it Brown presents his aim as that of justifying the notion of "theological aesthetics" before the academia, which has thought aesthetics independently of, and somewhat hostile to, religion. To do so he identifies three areas of study: that of aesthetics from a philosophical point of view, the role of art and the aesthetic experience as part of religion in general, and finally how the integration of aesthetics specifically in the Christian study of theology would affect it. In the first, he suggests the implicit purist biases and Western emphasis of philosophical aesthetics has prevented it from developing more, leaving unanswered the questions of a possible relatedness between the world of art and religion, such as: why religion can be aesthetic, why some religious art is simply understood as such, and the value of non-religious art in religious or spiritual experience. The second approach seeks to discover the religious meaning of art in religion and rituals, in accordance with the tradition using them. The third addresses the relevance of art within a specific Christian tradition.

212. Brown, *Religious Aesthetics*, 1.

jects that are valued almost exclusively for "logical, utilitarian, moral, religious, or cognitive reasons."[213] However, these meanings or aspects cannot be separated fully in aesthetic appreciation, and often overlap. He is also very aware of the need to take our embodiment into account in theological thought, identifying one of the causes for the neglect of art and the aesthetic in theological thought in the lack of attention to our embodied existence:

> Undoubtedly, the widespread theological neglect of aesthetic factors in religion is related to the fact that over much of Christian history, the prevalent theological and moral climate has been such as to generate considerable ambivalence and suspicion regarding things sensory and bodily.[214]

In his second book, *Good Taste, Bad Taste, and Christian Taste: Aesthetics in Religious Life*, which addresses the theme of music more specifically, and above all music in worship, Brown develops the need for a renewed critical approach to the theme of musical quality. In order to do so, he addresses the issue of taste in and from a Christian perspective, because he recognizes that with regard to worship, "questions of taste . . . have become as vexed and potentially divisive as questions of doctrine."[215] This book focuses on music outside the liturgical field precisely because of my conviction that the underlying (and unrecognized) issue in many contemporary debates on liturgical music is one of taste, without enough attention given to the nature of music itself and the issues of discernment that Brown addresses in his theology. As the title suggest, he challenges the Christian and theological underestimation and neglect of the theme of taste. The clarity with which he approaches the theme is refreshing. He takes a balanced position between the extremes of an elitist appreciation of art, defended as "good taste" and necessary for "good" spiritual development, and one that gives absolutely no importance to quality whatsoever. He seeks "a concept and theology of taste that is both spiritually challenging and nonelitist,"[216] talking about the need to be wary of both a purist[217] and dogmatic approach to art on the one hand, and a relativist

213. Ibid., 12.
214. Ibid., 3.
215. Brown, *Good Taste, Bad Taste*, xv.
216. Ibid., 9.
217. By "purist," Brown means anything seeking to be self-contained and self-referential (unrelated to religious or moral values) rather than interactive.

one on the other, in favor of what he calls "critical pluralism." No one taste should be considered "Christian," but to consider musical quality as completely relative is to not understand the importance of the aesthetic in human life and religion. He proposes the cultivation and maintaining of a creative tension between openness to aesthetic diversity, while still seeking to be discerning and discriminating.[218] Such an approach would help to develop what he terms "ecumenical taste": learning to recognize aesthetic and religious differences without mutual alienation, to appreciate art and music to which one would not initially be drawn, and to seek common points in the aesthetic and religious quests.

The balanced approach of Brown's thoughts are clearly in line with aspects addressed in chapter 2 on learning to approach art and music within a hermeneutical framework that respects the context and sensibility of each type, at the same time as inviting to a discerning examination of its reception and effects. Sacred Scripture and Tradition witness to the fact that art can mediate a sense of grace and the mystery of God, and therefore it can be as important as other aspects of human understanding, such as reason and morality:

> [A]nd since art cannot mediate without the aid of *aesthetic imagination, response and judgement*—without taste, in short—we must consider the perhaps surprising possibility that taste at its most encompassing is no less crucial to religious life and faith than is intellectual understanding and moral commitment.[219]

Brown develops three aspects of aesthetic perception, aesthetic enjoyment, and aesthetic judgment in the terms of what he calls "apperception," "appreciation," and "appraisal," which are the processes by which we receive a work as it is, register our own reaction, (like and/or dislike), and judge in a way meant for public validity.[220] In brief:

i. Apperception implies learning to perceive music, especially that kind we are more unfamiliar with. He admits that there is training in art that can help us to listen, and that everyone is culturally conditioned in their perception, which implies constant willingness to be open to learn to listen.

218. Cf. ibid., xiv.
219. Ibid., 11. Emphasis mine.
220. Cf. Brown, *Religious Aesthetics*, 12–24; and *Good Taste, Bad Taste*, 13–23.

ii. Appreciation looks at the importance of enjoyment (or lack of enjoyment) of art and music. He raises the issue of the dualism that often underlies our fear of musical enjoyment, as well as the need to be very aware of context in our appreciation and discerning of music in any given setting.

iii. When talking about appraisal, he asks more questions than he answers (rather refreshing in an area in which strong opinions are rife), inviting us to critique not only our judgments but where they are born of and the direction these judgments lead us to.[221]

Throughout these three steps he defends the thesis that taste is also a Christian gift that needs to be developed, without which Christian life and faith is impoverished.

Clearly Brown's approach is one of theological thought applied to arts and spirituality. This approach is emphasized in his last book, not least by the title itself: *Inclusive Yet Discerning: Navigating Worship Artfully*. His underlining of the importance of reflecting on our forms of worship, and not only its content, is important and eloquent:

> Such things, which pertain to *how* faith is creatively expressed and enacted, and not only *what* is believed or done, has always been of religious significance. They have nonetheless rarely been a major part of training in Christianity of in theology itself.... But it turns out they matter. And the primary reason they matter is that the very "content" of religious identity and belief is something conveyed and shaped to a significant extent by the *way* it is imagined, narrated, pictured, and sung.[222]

Therefore, in this book, Brown applies his thought to various issues concerning art in and in relation to religion, such as: whether good art has a place in worship and liturgy, and if and how they can enrich each other; the need to be discriminating and discerning in our openness to secular art and music in the same; how to approach the musical and verbal dynamics in Christian and liturgical music in a balanced way; the need to approach art with a spiritual and theological view

---

221. For example: *should* music in worship be "relaxing," and to what extent? Is entertainment to be ruled out, or what does it say about a culture when that is the overriding type of music or worship being sought out?

222. Brown, *Inclusive Yet Discerning*, xv.

that integrates rather than sidelines embodiment, and how not doing so has marked Christian tradition in theology and praxis.

With regard to the specific theme of music, he raises the issue of needing to look at music on its own terms, apart from or alongside the words (which is one of the main aims of this book), affirming that although the importance of the text demands that it receive attention, not just to content but also to its literary qualities "discernment in Christian music means going beyond just the words, important as these may be, and giving due consideration to music's own ways of being religious."[223] His understanding of music having its own forms of interpretation and semantic meaning is significant:

> [I]t is now more necessary than ever to affirm something that the church has seldom clearly recognized: Music itself—and not least in the context of worship—has its own ways of interpreting the very meaning of faith, prayer and praise. The better forms of music go some places where words alone cannot. Even those whose ears are untrained can nonetheless learn to hear what the Spirit is saying musically as well as verbally.[224]

The convergence points between Brown's position and our own have been highlighted and will come to the fore as the next chapter evolves, but I underline the embodied epistemology he seeks in approaching art.

> [W]hether instrumental or sung, the music that has received the highest approval of theologians from the first century to the present has not been ecstatic or even animated. It has tended to be simple and restrained. . . . And in the past, at least, it has often been music that through its mathematical structure pleases the intellect even more than the senses.[225]

He traces many moments of latent dualism or lack of integration of our physical senses in theological reflection on the spiritual value of art and music. For example, in the context of examining Augustine's approach to beauty and music, he sees the tension of a person sensitive to beauty as mediating the divine, but who did not manage to integrate his embodied human existence in his spiritual vision: "What he does not see consistently or clearly is how much the vision of God

---

223. Cf. ibid., 90.
224. Ibid., 98.
225. Brown, *Good Taste, Bad Taste*, 39.

and the enjoyment of the spiritual senses remain indebted to, and in dialogue with, the physical senses and their aesthetic transformation."[226] Ultimately, Brown recognizes that the controversy about the use and value of music in worship reflects the wider issues of the relation of the church to the world and the physical to the spiritual.

Music and Temporality: Jeremy Begbie

> [W]hat would it mean to theologise
> not simply about music but through music?
>
> It is clear that music is one of the most powerful communicative
> media we have, but how it communicates
> and what it communicates are anything but clear.
>
> —Jeremy Begbie[227]

Jeremy S. Begbie, an ordained minister of the Church of England, is a musician, theologian, and a well-known author in the area of the arts and music.[228] The various books written or edited by him reveal not only his theological thought but also his approach to the arts in and as theology. From the first book published in 1991, called *Voicing Creations Praise: Towards a Theology of the Arts*,[229] Begbie expresses an interest in the bridge between the world of the arts, which as a musician he is immersed in, and that of the Christian gospel and theology. As with many of our previous authors, he analyses the heritage of European philosophical developments that have alienated art from Christianity, and seeks to rebuild an understanding of the same based

---

226. Ibid., 109.

227. Begbie, *Theology, Music, and Time*, 4.

228. Begbie has been the associate president at Ridley College, Cambridge, and associate director of the Centre for Theology and the Arts at St. Mary's College, in St. Andrew's University. He is currently the Thomas A. Langford Research Professor of Theology at Duke Divinity School, where he is director of "*Theology and the Arts*" (DITA). Cf. http://www.divinity.duke.edu/programs/dita/. This initiative continues a project called "*Theology Through the Arts* "(TTA), which was set up in September 1997 within the Centre for Advanced Religious and Theological Studies in the Faculty of Divinity, University of Cambridge.

229. This book approaches the theme from the perspective of Protestant theology, drawing on Tillich and Dutch neo-Calvinist writers. From that backdrop he develops his own theological understanding of art based on the themes of Christology, creation, and creativity as participation in the creative purpose of the Father.

on the incarnation and the redemption of the material and physical world. He also challenges the Enlightenment's predominately individualistic vision of human creativity as going against the intrinsically relational character of the Christian ethos. He defines art as "a vehicle of interaction with the world . . . through which we engage with the physical world we inhabit, and through which we converse with those communities with whom we share our lives."[230]

Begbie's work has often included, as we shall see, projects of theological reflection on the arts in collaboration with others, both artists and theologians. He has been involved with numerous projects involving the coming together of theologians and artists, both for the purposes of reflection and that of artistic creativity. Various books have emerged as a fruit of this collaboration. I have already noted my conviction about the fruitfulness for theological aesthetics of this kind of approach. *Beholding the Glory: Incarnation through the Arts* is a book edited by Begbie that brings together essays by artists, writers, and theologians, from the theological perspective of the incarnation. In this book, his chapter on "Through Music: Sound Mix" explores how musical symbolism gives us an alternative entrance point to core truths of our Christian faith. One example is taken from musical harmony: the fact that a chord is a series of notes played together, at the same time, and that all three notes "fill the space" we listen to without "encroaching" on each other, gives us a better understanding of the human and divine nature of Christ—"without *confusion*, without change, without *division*, without *separation*"—or of the Trinity (Three in One), than does a visual metaphor. According to Begbie, our difficulty in grasping how human and divine nature can both subsist in one person is because the "image" we use to "imagine" it is visual, and in visual terms two things cannot occupy the same space. It is a simple but effective example of what he calls theology "through" music.[231]

Sounding the Depths: Theology Through the Arts reflects this ongoing process, gathering the work of theologians and artists in the creation of an international arts festival in Cambridge in the year 2000, born of the research project "Theology Through the Arts" in Cambridge, of which Begbie was director. Underlying the surface of these initiatives is the conviction that "not only does theology benefit from the arts, but

---

230. Begbie, *Voicing Creation's Praise*, 257. Emphasis original.
231. Cf. Begbie, "Through Music," 144–48.

that it needs them."²³² Another example of such a form of approaching music in theology can be found in a book called *Creative Chords: Studies in Music, Theology, and Christian Formation*,²³³ in which, in a chapter on "Music, Theology, and Divine Communication,"²³⁴ Begbie relates the musical trait of repetition and meter, and the tension and resolution found in the various musical elements of motifs, phrase, dissonance to consonance, etc., with the dynamic of promise and (repeated) fulfillment to be found in Scripture.²³⁵ The inexhaustible nature of musical tension and resolution echoes the inexhaustibility of God.²³⁶ He also applies it to repetition in the liturgy and the Eucharist.

Begbie's most well-known theological reflection is to be found in *Theology, Music, and Time*, in which he emphasizes and develops the temporal nature of music. He addresses in the book the issues of what music is and its particular form of meaning, which he believes to be a combination of intrinsic, non-referential symbolism and association with external elements. He emphasizes, as we have in this book, the need to be careful with overemphasizing the links between verbal language and music,²³⁷ and identifies in the non-referential nature of music not a weakness, but a strength:

> Indeed, just because music is relatively weak in consistent referral, it is generally freer than, say, language to interact with its contexts in the generation of meaning.²³⁸

---

232. Cf. Begbie, *Sounding the Depths*, 6. This book brings together reflections by theologians such as Rowan Williams, Tom Wright, and Ben Quash, as well as composer James MacMillan. Of particular interest is the collaboration of Williams, Macmillan, Michael Simmons Roberts, and Michael and Megan O'Connor in the creation of an operetta called *Parthenogenesis*, a Scena for soprano, baritone, actress and chamber ensemble. Cf., *Sounding the Depths*, 17–53.

233. Astley et al., *Creative Chords*.

234. Begbie, "Play It (Again): Music, Theology, and Divine Communication."

235. Cf. ibid., 52. The underlying influence of Meyer's emphasis of tension and resolution in musical meaning is perceptible.

236. In this sense, he notes an interesting critique of tonal music as echoing, in its "tidy closures," modernity's supreme confidence in self and in human progress. Cf. ibid., 55, referring to Kermode.

237. He also draws from the Saussurian semiological tradition, as does Speelman, in his reference to the arbitrary nature of the words used in language, as well as from Barthes's definition of music as a "field of signifying, and not a system of signs."

238. Begbie, *Theology, Music, and Time*, 13.

This he relates to its "temporal" nature—it evolves in time: "Musical tones become meaningful . . . because they are dynamically and intrinsically interrelated to preceding and coming sounds," provoking temporality.[239] This emphasis on temporality on music is developed through the attention he gives to the rhythmic aspect of music:

> Temporality in music is principally manifested through rhythm . . . interacting with *metre*. Metre is the configuration of beats permeating a piece of music. In notated music it is usually written in the form of a "time-signature" at the start of the piece.[240]

Meter is not rigid; it is marked by the stronger or weaker accentuation of the beats. This element echoes Speelman's emphasis of the dynamic nature of music, in that it provokes moving involvement ("following") rather than static apprehension. Despite his emphasis on the temporal nature of music, Begbie challenges suppositions that music's temporality aids us to "escape" the limits of our temporal world, due to its "loose ties" with the physical world. Rather, it provokes a rethinking of time, as it provokes engagement with time as one aspect of our created being in the world.[241] His reflections touch on other important aspects of musical symbolism, identifying four ways in which music relates to the extra-musical world: it is a living practice; it engages with the physical world; it is "inescapably bodily"; and it "has very strong connections with our emotional life."[242] All four evoke elements that have been reflected on in the chapter on musical semiotics, and will be developed further in the next chapter.

If the leading question in these books has been what music can bring to theology, his more recent book, *Resounding Truth: Christian Wisdom in the World of Music*, inverts the question, asking instead, what can theology bring to music?[243] In this impressive book, the first half looks "backwards," seeking to explore how music has been understood in the Christian tradition of the past. Laying a double foundation for his thought, in the first chapter he asks what music *is* (and

---

239. Ibid., 12.

240. Ibid., 39.

241. Ibid., 66–67; cf. also Begbie, "Music, Theology, and Divine Communication," 64–65.

242. Cf. Begbie, *Theology, Music, and Time*, 15.

243. Begbie, *Resounding Truth*, 19.

answers by once again emphasizing its "bodily" nature),[244] and then moves in the second chapter to studying the biblical basis of his theme. It is interesting that the title of Part 1 comprising these two chapters is "Music in Action." The dynamic nature of music itself, as well as our comprehension of it, is implicit. He looks at some of the more significant voices on music in the Western tradition (such as Pythagoras, Plato, Augustine, and Boethius), before dealing with three Reformed theologians from the sixteenth century (Luther, Calvin, and Zwingli) and three from modern times (Schleiermacher, Barth and Bonhoeffer). Once again, Begbie's approach is rich in integrating theologians with musicians, from the past and the present, as he interweaves in his reflections chapters on Bach, Olivier Messiaen, and James MacMillan. In the second part of the book, he proposes what he calls a "music in a Christian ecology," in which he develops some of the themes we have already mentioned, and introduces others, such as the capacity of music to provide us with what he calls "emotional concentration," which he links emphatically with our embodiment, and music's relation to it:

> [M]usical sounds can be said to have emotional properties by virtue of their connection with bodily expressive behavior. . . .it is claimed that music embodies not emotion as such but bodily motions associated with emotion.[245]

This obviously converges with our own conviction of the unified nature of human living, feeling, knowing, and believing, and of music's potential to affect and transform us at those different levels. Other underlying points of convergence with this book are elements such as the repeated affirmation of the goodness of the created order, music as a calling, which he develops in relation to a theology of creation: music as a vehicle of discovery, development of the created order, healing and hope (linked with the themes of harmony and eschatological anticipation).

Although liturgy is a concern he touches on, his intention and focus converges entirely with my own conviction that we will only come to clarity in the world of liturgical music when we understand more the nature of musical meaning in its own right:

---

244. "Music is a very bodily business . . . it would seem that music's first appeal (but not necessarily its last) is to the body." Ibid., 47.

245. Ibid., 299.

> I am increasingly convinced that many of the dilemmas and difficulties currently plaguing music in worship will being to be alleviated only when we stand back a little and address the broader issues about what kind of medium we are dealing with, how it functions in different settings and how it links up with God's wider intentions for the world.[246]

Begbie's implicit and explicit challenge to theology is that of refraining from precipitated judgments on music (including its use in worship) before seriously engaging in understanding the complex nature of the musical event and the "meaning" to be found therein. It is worth keeping in mind that, as a member of the Anglican Church, Begbie has a wider exposure to the use of music in liturgy than most Catholics (including theologians), from classical music, to rap, to dance music from the (much discussed) "rave" culture. Although the theological paradigm offered by this book differs from his, the way he brings together theological thought, musicological reflection, and musical sensibility is impressive.[247] As a form of approach aimed at bringing together the world of theology and the arts, it is one of the most convincing I have found, opening interesting forms of application of the theological attentiveness and approach this book suggests.

Bridging the Sacred and the Secular: Don Saliers

We close this chapter with a brief mention of Don Saliers, a contemporary theologian who bridges the areas of thought between music in theology and music in liturgy. His relatively recent book, *Music and Theology*, although short, brings together various insights on music in and as theology. To mention simply the points of convergence, he recognizes Christianity's ambivalent relationship with the body as being at the root of many of its difficulties. Looking to its origins, he says that although the difficulty with music in Christianity was patent before Augustine, with him it takes on a philosophical slant: the conflict between body and spirit. His deep attraction to music and sensibility to the language of doxology born of the Psalms sits alongside an inherited Platonic and Neo-Platonic suspicion of physicality and the body.[248]

---

246. Ibid., 23–24.

247. Begbie has a forthcoming book precisely on the relationship between music, words, and theology.

248. Albeit, recognizing the truth of Augustine's struggle—that a discerning stance towards music in liturgy prevailed—in chapters 9–10 of his *Confessions*.

Theological reflection about the nature and role of music often turns on how strongly the boundaries between the material, sensate, and spiritual worlds are drawn. Strong distinctions between material and spiritual (body and soul) have consequences directly affecting the practice of suppression of music making within Christian communities.[249]

I relate this clearly with the theology of Oliver Davies and companions on the materiality of the ascended body, and its relevance to our living and perceiving. In this sense, albeit from a more ritual or liturgical point of view, Saliers emphasizes the senses in our experience of God, and how a text when enhanced by music, allows us to "taste" the presence of God in a more profound way. He calls this *synaesthesia*: "the engagement of several senses."[250] He challenges the radical divide between the sacred and the secular realms, highlighting the aspects of music that bridge and enrich the theological world. He names four such characteristics: its rootedness in silence and mystery, its essentially bodily nature, its capacity to express the inexpressible, and the "life-connection" it provides theology with, being an expression of cultural and social life.[251]

As we move towards completing our own theological approach to music, the words that come to mind are those of Balthasar: indeed truth is symphonic.[252] In music, no one note or instrument is the best, nor does any one thought about music explain that which cannot be put into words. But as we listen, we enter into harmony with each other, our deeper selves, and Christ, and are enriched. This chapter has wanted to recognize the thought of the people who alongside the attempt of this book seek a theological comprehension of beauty and music. However, as we move forward, the invitation is to allow them to remain as "background music," or a prelude to chapter 6, which continues with the position initiated in chapter 4 and completes it, in the light of our faith in the incarnated, risen, and ascended Christ, in whose continued body we live, move, and have our being.[253]

---

249. Saliers, *Music and Theology*, 15.

250. Ibid., 9.

251. Cf. Ibid., 61. Another, perhaps less theological and more accessible expression of this challenge of the sacred/secular division can be found in a book he co-wrote with his daughter, a well-known singer and member of the band Indigo Girls: *A Song to Sing, a Life to Live: Reflections on Music and Spiritual Practice*.

252. Cf. Balthasar, "Verità è sinfonica."

253. Cf. Acts 17:28.

6

Theology of the Body of Christ and Contemporary Music

> *Are some intricate minds nourished on concept?*
> *Resurrection, for them, an internal power,*
> *but not a matter of flesh?*
> *For the others, of whom I am one [. . .]*
> *can't open to symbol's power unless convinced*
> *of its ground, its roots, in bone and blood.*
>
> —Denise Levertov[1]

The Presence of Music in Western Culture and Theology

> *Put your ear to the ground and listen,*
> *Hold your breath.*
> *Free your inner antennas.*
> *The Lord is near.*
>
> —Helder Camara[2]

WE HAVE COME TO THE FINAL STAGE OF OUR JOURNEY. THE METHodology of this decidedly interdisciplinary book is that of listening to and allowing music and thought on music to inform and lead theology into a deeper understanding both of the nature of music and of theology itself: hence the order of the chapters, which move from studies

---

1. Levertov, "On Belief in the Physical Resurrection," 115–16.
2. Camara, *Desert Is Fertile*, 29, although the translation has been slightly changed to coincide more with the Brazilian original.

on music (musicology and ethnomusicology), through epistemology and theological aesthetics, to this chapter offering a specific theological paradigm for music.

Balthasar's presentation of faith as an aesthetic act in which Christ reveals himself to the believer, who in turn is "held" in the apprehension of the form that is Christ, lays the foundation for the creative understanding of art "from within" that this chapter seeks to affirm, albeit with different coordinates. Faith colors the way one perceives things. Revelation unveils, uncovers, dis-covers realities that may or may not be visible to the eyes of a non-believer but that take on new meaning when perceived in Christian faith. "Faith throws a new light on everything,"[3] and it is guided by this very light of faith that we look and listen. Some would say this impedes objectivity, and there is no doubt that at times the church has allowed certain ways of understanding its faith make it resistant to advances in human comprehension and science that seemed to be in opposition with that vision of faith. But "objectivity" is a complex word: we all live in and understand our surrounding world[4] guided by what Lonergan called "the worlds of meaning"[5] in which we live and within which we work out our comprehension. There is no human opinion or stance or even formulation of the truth that is completely devoid of the perspective of the one taking position or expressing themselves. Lonergan's critique of our imagining that which is real as being "out there," separate from human contexts and available to anyone who decides to "take a good look,"[6] is well known. To think in that way is both illogical and naïve: illogical, as the infinite wisdom of God would have found another way of creating human beings and the world we live in, had it not been part of their plan that living and knowing integrate our personal perspective; and naïve, as to seek an unattainable unconditioned absolute perspective

---

3. Second Vatican Council, *Gaudium et Spes* 11.

4. I am aware of difficulty of speaking of the "world," since our very inhabiting the world means we cannot truly conceptualize it "from without," and the ambivalence of the very concept "world" in its various uses over time in the Christian tradition has increased that difficulty. I will only say that in my own understanding it means the created order, good yet fallen, in which God inhabits and through which God manifests herself.

5. Cf. Lonergan, "Dimensions of Meaning."

6. We have explained this position more at length in chapter 4, while talking about intellectual conversion, which refers to the correction of this false understanding of how we perceive and know reality. Cf. Knasas, "Why for Lonergan."

within the moving world of history leaves us vulnerable to fundamentalisms and dogmatisms. Objective truth is found by and in shared authentic subjectivity.[7]

Christian faith is also a world of meaning, or "horizon of comprehension," that orientates and colors our interpretation of things. A right understanding of perceiving the world enlightened by faith calls for respectful and trusting attentiveness. In the prologue of their book *Transformation Theology*, Davies et al. criticize contemporary theology for being "in a broad retreat from the real world of space and time as the ongoing site of God's self-revelation today."[8] Perhaps in part as a reaction to the excesses of the past, perhaps also as a result of a somehow reductive understanding of its "subject matter," or even at times (as I intuit is the often case with regard to music), conditioned by a certain fear or protective stance towards the potential effect such an openness or receptivity could provoke, theology has too often embedded itself in the conceptual world, and left the "empirical world" to the human and natural sciences.

And yet, as has been argued in the previous chapter, the Christian, and more particularly the Catholic, worldview permits no such limitation. Christian faith is not a way of life that invites us to withdraw from the world, or to be suspicious of what is, after all, created by God and therefore "good."[9] Rather than fear of the created order, or the need to keep our distance from it in order to emphasize the superiority of the Creator, the Christian calling, and therefore also that of the Christian theologian, is to "keep our ear to the ground," as Helder Camara would describe it, to be attentive to the very rhythm of God that manifests itself in and through the world we live in. The Gospels present Jesus of Nazareth not only as their Lord and Master, but also as a man who was very much in touch with and aware of the needs, hopes, and dreams of the people around him, a man of his time. If the incarnated God could assume humanity in Himself without losing or giving up his divine nature, then Christian theology can surely listen to and learn from the different areas of human life without fear of losing depth. Indeed,

---

7. Cf. the as yet unedited doctoral dissertation of Woimbée, *L'objectivité de la raison théologique: L'intellectualisme de Bernard Lonergan et la crise de la vérité*, defended in the Gregorian on October 11, 2007.

8. Davies et al., *Transformation Theology*, 2.

9. Cf. Gen 1:3, 10, 12, 18, 21, 25, 31.

the danger in not doing so is the opposite: that in enclosing ourselves away from the real world of space and time in which people live out their lives, we run the risk of becoming at best, elitist, and at worst, irrelevant. The hope, in opening ourselves and listening in depth to what is happening through music in our world and how it is understood, is not just one of "non-contamination" but one of enrichment—the humble and serene hope of receiving and learning from others about the immense God we have certain and secure faith in. And if the process implies rearranging our concepts or our apprehension of things, in the quest for truth, so be it.

We have already begun to present why and how elements of musical expression offer themselves to theological thinking, as an enriching complement to verbal semantics. In this chapter we take a step further in the process: that of gathering these insights in a wider and, to the measure that it is possible, comprehensive theological paradigm to sustain and ground it. This is necessary because a disjointed, if rich, series of characteristics of music is simply not enough to understand the underlying reasons why art and music have been displaced from the centre of Christian self-understanding, nor to lay the foundations for a solid theological understanding of music and its (re)-integration in evangelization and pastoral work. This is the challenge underlying Benedict XVI's recent address in an encounter with 250 well-known artists, during which he renewed Paul VI's invitation for a commitment to friendship between the Church and artists, "analyzing seriously and objectively the factors that disturbed this relationship."[10] Only in this way can we build a solid foundation for the future.

The specific theological paradigm I have chosen to adopt, understood as both doctrine and methodology, is found in the recent development in theological reflection born in King's College, London called "transformation theology," whose doctrinal content is spearheaded by Oliver Davies. This choice should not be understood as "separate" or radically different from that of other authors writing in the area of theological aesthetics. In fact, the grounding truth of theological aesthetics, as seen in Balthasar, is that of the incarnation. Davies and his colleagues are also centered on the embodied existence of Jesus Christ, although they develop it in the direction of his continued incarnated presence in his Body, in the church, after the resurrection, ascension,

---

10. Benedict XVI, "Address to Artists."

and the coming of the Spirit. To that end, they focus on the ascension, and how this truth of faith has been understood and celebrated in the history of the church. It would be a misunderstanding, however, to see this emphasis as separate from the truths of the incarnation, resurrection, and presence of the Spirit in the Body of Christ which is the church.[11] It is the neglect of this aspect of the ascended body that leads the theologians of King's College to bring it into the heart of their discussion, and needs to be understood in relation to them, as the continuation of Christ's risen, glorified and embodied presence, in the world, in which we also, through baptism, have our existence.[12] To my knowledge, transformation theology has not developed the theme of aesthetics as yet, although Davies has written about poetics and art in a book called *A Theology of Compassion: Metaphysics of Difference and the Renewal of Tradition*,[13] and is soon to publish a book in which he integrates thoughts on the imagination, art, and artistic creativity, with some reference to music.[14] However, it offers an overall under-

11. Rosemary Haughton, for example, emphasizes many of the points that the theologians of King's College do, from the perspective of asking how we can understand and assume the resurrection in all its fullness into Christian theology and spirituality. Cf. Haughton, *Passionate God*, 174–212. Much of her understanding of the body of Christ is drawn from a short but comprehensive book on the Pauline understanding of the body: Robinson, *The Body*.

12. In this sense, it is interesting to note growth in interest in the theme of ascension, albeit with different emphases, doctrinal approaches, and intentionality than our own. Cf.: Abbaye de St-Andre, *Fête de l'ascension*, in which the issue of the difficulty of talking about "heaven" is addressed by Vincent Ayel in a chapter called "Peut-on parler du ciel aux homes de aujourd'hui?"; Torrance, *Space, Time, and Incarnation*; and Farrow, *Ascension and Ecclesia*, which has an impressive summary of how the doctrine was dealt with in patristic theology. Andrew Burgess's book *The Ascension in Karl Barth* not only presents his understanding of Barth's theology on the theme of the ascension but relates it to two of the above authors, Torrance and Farrow, on the subject. Cf. also Dawson, *Jesus Ascended*. Another book that I perceive as touching on many of the same issues in theology, albeit while dealing explicitly with the resurrection, is Kelly, *Resurrection Effect*. He underlines the importance of the bodily nature of our faith and salvation, bringing the doctrine of the Body of Christ into the picture. He also touches on the aspect of art and the aesthetic, although most references are to visual art, rather than music, which is perhaps to be expected given the visual nature of the resurrection appearances. Indeed, influenced above all by Balthasar, he has a chapter on the visual phenomenon of the resurrection as it opens to a wider sensory field and a deeper experience of faith. It is in Davies, however, that we find a reflection on the auditory nature of the apparition to Paul (of the ascended body of Jesus) in contrast to the visual nature of the resurrection appearances, as we shall see.

13. We present his findings later in the chapter.

14. Cf. Davies, *Touching God: Transforming Theology*, forthcoming. I am grateful

standing of Christian spirituality and theology in the history and evolution of European culture, within which it is possible to comprehend why beauty and music have been sidelined in theological thought (and Christian spirituality), as well as providing a theological horizon in which it is possible to situate a "right" understanding of contemporary music in faith mediation and theology. Although it is a framework of thought "in process," its essential characteristics are quite clearly outlined by the first authors who identify with the approach, and are fully in line with those presented already as motivating the introduction of music into theology.[15] Our reflections, however, draw extensively from this particular school, by the fact that they focus and develop one of the central truths of Christian faith, from its very beginnings. For this reason, in the measure that they are relevant to the study of contemporary music, these characteristics will serve as the structure and outline for this chapter.[16]

Davies refers to transformation theology as one whose method could lead it to be described as "reconstructive" theology. This method can be divided into two related but distinct moments: the first "critical" and the second "constructive."[17] The former involves a critical re-reading of Western theology, in the awareness that the present cultural moment is one in which many of the ideas or ways of thinking that have shaped Western thought, including theological thought, are no

---

to Prof. Davies for providing me with some of the chapters of the book while he is in the process of writing it.

15. I am referring especially to points made in the introduction and gathered from authors such as Lonergan, Pierangelo Sequeri, and George Steiner regarding the effect of recent cultural shifts on western culture (time of the *Epilogue*) and therefore also on theology.

16. The main source for this chapter is the book *Transformation Theology*. I also refer to other sources of each individual author, books or articles they have published that corroborate or offer some development on their respective areas. The two first chapters written by Davies are called "Lost Heaven" and "The Interrupted Body," and will be quoted as such in this chapter, which focuses primarily on Davies's contribution to the book. One complementary source is a conference by Davies in December 2008 in Leuven, called "Transforming Theology: A New Catholic Theology for Europe?," which has been recently published as "History and Tradition: Catholicism and the Challenge of Globalised Modernity." This quotation is taken from the original conference, kindly sent to me for research purposes by the author. This article is particularly helpful in identifying the aforementioned essential grounding principles of transformation theology.

17. Davies, "Transforming Theology," 5.

longer adequate. This is one of the perceptions motivating this book, as outlined in the introduction: the need to rethink theology in the current cultural context if it is to respond adequately to its mission, integrating the symbolic expression inherent to music as part of that *aggiornamento*. The latter has two dimensions. Firstly, a reappraisal of Christian faith in the light of the doctrine of the ascended body of Christ, one which implies the challenge of what Davies refers to as a moment of "penitential reflection" for the theologian, in order to return to the theological apprehension of the Lordship of Christ in the created order, "the presence of Christ in history . . . the one wounded and raised, in new ways and with a new openness of heart."[18] Secondly, Davies talks about what he describes as a "theology of the act,"[19] which he sees as not identical to "praxis" but related to it. Drawing on Janz's distinction between speculative reasoning and motivational reasoning, it focuses on the realm of human freedom as the place where salvation is played out, and on the specifically human dynamic of "acting" by which we are agents in history, rather than observers. This second dimension is not separated from the first, but is rather its consequence, in the sense that an encounter with the ascended Christ transforms our sensibility and commissions us to the proper activity of followers and disciples of Christ. It is in our acting (and we shall see later what is implied in this term), in each present moment that we have access to the embodied presence of the risen and ascended Christ. These three elements provide our theological framework for reflection on contemporary music in theology: the relevance of music in this critical moment for Catholic theology, the role of music in relation to the embodied presence of Christ, and a theological understanding both of the "act" of participating with music (creating music or listening to it) and the more radical "action" that is the option for music as one's life calling. These are the essential points of reflection for our theme.

Therefore this chapter will unfold in three moments: the first, in order to understand why and how it serves as an adequate framework

---

18. Ibid., 12. We will draw out parallels with Lonergan's emphasis on the conversion of the theologian as foundational to theology in the measure that we move forward.

19. Davies identifies convergences of thought or interlocutors in Maurice Blondel (*L'action*), Mikhail Bahktin (*Towards a Philosophy of the Act*) and Hannah Arendt (*The Human Condition*). I will relate it to the dynamic notion of being to be found in the writings of Rosemary Haughton.

for the theological comprehension of contemporary music, will explore the reasons behind the loss of spiritual and theological attentiveness to the world of space and time and the doctrine of the incarnated, risen, and ascended body of Jesus Christ,[20] together with its possible links with the theme of contemporary music. Without taking the comparison too far, there are interesting convergences between the contemporary crisis of Christian music and the historical development of Western thought with regard to this truth of faith. Understanding the implications of the gradual loss of importance of this doctrine sheds light on the possibility of a new awareness and openness to music in Christian spirituality and theology. In a second moment, through the lens of our focus on music, we will look at how the reconstruction of our comprehension of the embodied presence of Jesus Christ opens important perspectives both for the normal living out of Christian faith and for theology itself. We will reflect upon how music can be an apt means or aid in revealing God's Word and transmitting Christian faith, in that it can help us to "become present to body of Christ" in the present world and moment, and as a source of theological enrichment. Speelman's analysis of musical semiotics will be important in this regard, in particular his emphasis on the present moment and temporal dimension of musical symbolism. We will also reflect on how, from an epistemological point of view, the "conversion" Davies alludes to in the reintegration of the Lordship of Christ over the created order in theology is related to, and can perhaps even be aided by, Lonergan's development of the notion of the various conversions that should ground theological thought, especially affective conversion. Thirdly, we will reflect on the Christian vocation or commissioning that emerges in the encounter with the ascended Christ as it manifests itself in the vocation of the artist and/or musician. The risen and ascended Christ, Head of the Body of Christ which the Spirit vivifies, pours out gifts in the church according to its need. The vocation of the musician and composer is one that requires theological attention, reflection, and encouragement, both as a specific vocation and mission in the church and world today and as an integral part of our wider Christian calling.

---

20. My use of "Jesus Christ" when talking about the risen and glorified Christ is conscious, as I perceive sometimes in our abbreviation of the title to "Christ" we open ourselves to an implicit spiritualization of or even disassociation with the humanity of Jesus of Nazareth, as if it were somehow less present.

Davies's development of a theology of "the act" will be helpful when applied to the act of musical composition and music making.

The entire process aims to integrate, in as much as is possible, the dynamics of music as talked about in previous chapters with our chosen theological paradigm. As is clear from our exploration of other theologies on the theme of beauty and art, most approaches to theological aesthetics take the incarnation as their foundation, since the arts necessarily touch on the worthiness of matter as a means of bringing forth, or allowing divine beauty to emerge. However, Oliver Davies and his colleagues take our Chalcedonian faith in the fully human and divine nature of Christ a step further, in focusing explicitly on the ongoing human presence of Jesus to humanity in and through his glorified and ascended body, in a way that has far-reaching consequences both for theological thought and for the understanding of Christian experience and of contemporary music therein, in the present moment. It not only grounds in an explicit way the attentiveness to the world mentioned above, as intrinsic to theological methodology, but it demands it:

> [The] affirmation of Jesus Christ as presently real then also requires ... a fundamental transformation in theological procedure or method, and especially a transformation in original modes of theological attentiveness. Most essentially, this ... transformation involves the rediscovery of the real world of embodied sensible human experience in space and time as the ongoing and indispensable site of God's self-revelation today, and therefore as a primary and indispensable source of theological authority today.[21]

As we shall see, it is the accentuation of our "embodied sensible experience in space and time" that opens a field of exploration in the area of musical experience, both music making and its reception. For the sake of clarity and thoroughness, as we move forward and in the measure that it is relevant to our theme, we will seek to present briefly but clearly the doctrinal position taken by Davies and his colleagues with regard to the ascension, since it is a fairly recent development in contemporary theology, and therefore as yet not well known; this, however, within the limits that such a book with its own particular focus allows.

---

21. Davies et al., *Transformation Theology*, 4.

The Roots of an Estrangement in Space and Time

> *Resurrection is bodily or it is nothing...*
> *So what happened to material reality,*
> *What happened to bodies,*
> *When Jesus rose from the dead?*
>
> —Rosemary Haughton[22]

Our attempt to situate the present cultural moment together with the relevance of music will be divided into two parts, both looking at one form of division or disassociation. The first is our alienated relationship with heaven, which is formulated very often in the metaphorical terms of "height." The second is our intrinsic difficulty in holding together spirit and matter, which has left us bereft of interiority, provoking the current cultural thirst to compensate in various ways, searching outside and inside the Christian world view.

Heaven and Earth in Musical Mediation

We have already noted on various occasions that music and embodiment are intrinsically related. The central issue of transformation theology is also about embodiment: first and foremost that of Jesus of Nazareth, the nature and "whereabouts" of his risen body, but this reality opens up to ask about our own embodied existence as well, since the eternal life at the core of Christian faith is because of and *in* Jesus Christ risen. Therefore the question of our own embodied life, not just after death (as if eternal life could be understood as mere continuation), but here and now, in space and time, transformed in him, is part and parcel of this doctrine. This embodiment is the reality of the continuation of the incarnation in what has been called the Mystical Body of Christ, or "Total Christ."[23] We will explain this further in the course of the chapter, but the importance of understanding the link between Christ's embodiment, our own, and the role of music cannot

---

22. Haughton, *Passionate God*, 1. Emphasis original.

23. This truth of faith is more known in its application to ecclesiology, and its development or application to Church structures. The truth, however, is much greater than this application, and constitutes the underlying theological and spiritual truth which grounds this book.

be overestimated. Understanding the role of music in faith is linked with how we "feel" and understand our own corporality, and this, in turn, is related to how we "feel" and understand Christ's. Music moves our bodies, perhaps especially in regard to its rhythm, which has an organic link with human life, as was already observed by Aristotle and others. Andrew Louth begins a chapter entitled "Dissociation of Sensibility," from his book on the nature of theology, with the following words:

> A consciousness of division, a yawning gulf, that penetrates into our very heart and mind, a failure, an inability to relate: much of this is characteristic of modern culture and society.[24]

This is a phenomenon of "Western" modern culture and society, however, and I contend that it is part of the heritage left to us by the history of philosophical thought, and how its divisions have filtered down into lived culture. We have an estranged relationship with our corporality, a divided one, which has not always been helped by Christian theology. But music simply does not obey those rules, and therefore makes us feel life and our very selves in a different way. One could reasonably ask if this is the reason why certain liturgical trends have such an issue with rhythmical songs or instrumentation in their celebrations: the body has to become more involved. This division in contemporary sensibility between faith and embodiment runs totally contrary to the core of Christian faith, founded on the goodness of creation and the incarnation of God therein. Therefore, only a theological approach that brings together both our own embodied reality and that of Christ's is adequate, since we tend to project in our image of God that which we have difficulty grasping in human life.[25] Transformation theology seeks to address both, from the starting point of Christ's body, to our own assumed in him, in the following way.

Our faith states that the second Person of the Trinity became human, took on human flesh in a way that made Jesus of Nazareth one

---

24. Louth, *Discerning the Mystery*, 1.

25. An obvious example of this is that of a God who judges and punishes according to human weaknesses and prejudices, rather than one of mercy. Another would be the image of a God who is masculine, as the basis of a church with primarily male figures of authority. With regard to the integration of the spiritual and the material dimensions of reality, even the doctrine of the spiritual senses evokes a spiritual rather than sensible apprehension of God.

Person (*hypostasis*) with two natures, without division nor confusion, without separation nor mixture in such a way that in him humanity is transformed and becomes a new creation.[26] Therefore, the body of Jesus is still just that: both human and divine. In Catholic theology, this lead to the affirmation of what has been called the "local" existence of the body of Christ:

> Christian faith [commits us] to a belief that Jesus has risen from the dead, that he lives and is still fully human. And being fully human, as well as fully divine, Jesus must still in some sense have "local" existence and thus be in continuity with our own space-time reality today. The alternative to this possibility is either that the Incarnation has ceased (Christ is no longer properly alive, or properly human) or that the humanity of Christ has been absorbed into his divinity: a possibility which the early Church specifically rejected.[27]

However, the affirmation of the "local" existence of the body of Christ begs the question: where is that body and how do we perceive it? The normal response to this question tends to be the Eucharist, and in its sacramental form, this is true. But tradition has always affirmed what it has referred to as the "local" existence of the glorified body of Christ, fruit of the Paschal mystery, and source of our eschatological hope: Jesus' glorification and presence in heaven as the guarantee of our own future glorification. This is what we affirm in the reciting of our creed: he rose from the dead, ascended into heaven and is seated at the right hand of the Father, and will come again in glory.

This embodied existence of Jesus Christ touches on another aspect that was highlighted by Speelman in his observations on musical semiotics: the present moment. Davies notes that the statement on the ascension is the only one in the creed about the second Person of the Trinity that refers to the present moment: we evoke his incarnation, life, and death as it happened; we announce the hope of his return, in the future, but in that phrase we say something about the *present whereabouts* of the second Person of the Trinity, locating him "in heaven," as a result of his "ascending" there after his resurrection. So our belief in the ascended body of Jesus Christ has to do with his embodied presence in the *now* of history and, since humanity has been

---

26. Cf. Col 1:15–20; Eph 1:9–10; Col 2:17.
27. Davies, "Interrupted Body," 39.

assumed in him, also our own presence to his embodied person, *in our everyday life*. I emphasize the dynamic of everyday living, because it is not first and foremost the special modes of presence that we struggle most to comprehend, but his concrete, everyday presence to us.[28] In the Eucharist, we receive the sacramental presence of Jesus to us now, and we enter into and participate in his presence through the gathering of the faithful, the minister and the proclamation of the Word. These are all true and valid forms of accessing God's presence through Christ, but they do not answer the fundamental question about the whereabouts of the glorified body of Christ *in the world*, now, *in the present moment*. At the risk of sounding simplistic, the fundamental question is the following: Where is Jesus now?[29] How is he real to us, now? The answer to that question is the foundation on which one can talk about music as mediation, and it touches on two of the aspects of musical symbolism as noted by Speelman: the relevance of the present moment, and its influence on our embodied lives. Albeit indirectly, this suggests its possible potential for mediating Jesus' ongoing embodied presence.

It could be argued that the problem of presence is not only with regard to Jesus Christ, and that the same can be said of the Holy Spirit. Frederick Crowe, in the context of talking about God as Trinity and the process of our coming to know them, in prayer, identifies a similar type of confusion with regard to the Holy Spirit:

> Thus, if traditional Catholics were asked, "Was the Spirit really sent into the world?" they would surely and without hesitation answer "yes." "And is the Spirit really present in the world?" "Well, yes" (slight hesitation here for some). But press the

---

28. In effect, the sacramental nature of the Catholic worldview and theological reflection on the same has certainly addressed more fully the question of how Christ's presence is mediated through liturgy and the sacraments. Davies notes how the efficacy of the sacraments in Catholic theology as a means of birth to and growth in divine life was often founded on the efficacy of the ascended body in the world and Christ as Head of the Body of the church as their minister. This teaching was eloquently represented first and foremost by Augustine. Cf. on this point, Davies, "Lost Heaven," 17, 33 n. 41. What is lacking is its relation with everyday concrete Christian living.

29. This is not only asked by the theologians of transformation theology. Douglas Farrow deals explicitly with the question of where Jesus is in relation to space and time in chapter in relation to changes in cosmology and philosophical apprehension of the world in chapter 5 of the aforementioned book, *Ascension and Ecclesia*.

question a little: "Is the Spirit as really present now as the Son of God was nineteen centuries ago?"[30]

But even here the question is not theologically precise: Should we think the "real presence" of the Spirit is the same as how Jesus was "really present" during his time on earth? Does the Spirit then substitute the presence of Jesus, who is really gone, but present to us through the Spirit and the church? It is Davies's perception, in fact, that the Spirit and indeed the church are presented in Christian life and thought more as substituting Christ's presence than as mediating it:

> Thus what is undoubtedly an entirely fundamental relation between Spirit and Son, and Church and Son, is changed from being a relation of Trinitarian *mediation* to one of simple substitution.[31]

The importance of this substitution is clear once the relevance of the risen Jesus' corporal body and our own is taken onboard, and reaffirms that which has been said above about our divided sensibility: although we may find it somewhat difficult to grasp, it is easier for us to relate to a spiritual presence than a material one. However, it is obvious that things are somewhat confused or unclear. An interesting question in relation to our theme is why music is such a strong element in Charismatic Renewal, which precisely emphasizes and celebrates the *Spirit's* presence. My intuitive answer would be that the underlying reality being celebrated is that of the Spirit in the church, in Christ's Body, even where the explicit emphasis does not always recognize the link. However, developing this theme exceeds the limits of the book.

Having understood the importance of Jesus' embodied presence to us now, and its potential relationship to music, we can ask the questions: What has happened to our understanding of the importance of the Ascension? Why has it been lost? And what are the consequences of the same? The answer to these questions implies looking at the historical process of this truth of faith, as doing so explains better our current situation.[32] As a doctrine of faith, the ascension holds its place still

---

30. Crowe, "'Spirit and I' at Prayer," 302.

31. Davies, "Interrupted Body," 39.

32. Such an attempt finds convergence in the intentionality behind the functional "speciality of history," in Lonergan's structure for theological method, which seeks to understand "what is moving forward" in any given area of doctrine. This is important in order to detect both what is advancing and deepening in our understanding of revelation, and that which is in danger of getting lost, as is the case here.

in the list of dogmas that are essential to our faith, but what was once a key celebration and cornerstone in the Christian community's self-understanding has become, for all intense purposes, a metaphor we no longer relate to, but have not dispensed with, or have not yet translated to a more accessible or eloquent expression.[33] The reasons for the loss of relevance of this doctrine are, in the main, not faith-inspired, but scientific. The premodern worldview (including the biblical one, albeit with differences) conceived the universe as tiered, with three levels, at the top of which was heaven, the dwelling place of God. Jacob's Ladder on which the angels descended and ascended is an example of that understanding.[34] Therefore Jesus ascending and being taken away from them "upwards," was coherent with that worldview. It is important to understand, however, that no matter how high heaven was understood to be, it was conceived as being "in continuation" with the world and universe in which we live. Therefore, although out of sight, the glorified and ascended body of Jesus was somehow understood to be in continuation and in some way, in contact with the human world.

> However conceived, Heaven, where God dwelt and the saints with him, was always where it had to be: at the very highest point of all. Exaltation and physical height were deeply connected ideas in pre-modern cosmology. And however strange this paradigm may seem to us today, it secured the possibility of a *direct continuity between the heavenly above and the earthly below*, albeit under exceptional conditions, through the principle of superabundance or overflow.[35]

It is hard for us to imagine a pre-Copernican worldview, accustomed as we are to inhabiting a world that we know is but a point whirling in the midst of an immense universe, a universe, indeed, to which we have hardly even begun to have access. Therefore, to comprehend that something that is for us is an image, a metaphor, was for earlier Christians literal, is not easy. What is essential in the effort to

---

33. Davies presents a brief historical overview of the importance of the ascension for the early church (it is referred to thirty-five times in the Scriptures), both in its liturgical practice and writings, including St. Augustine and Thomas Aquinas. Cf. Davies et al., *Transformation Theology*, 15–23.

34. Cf. Gen 12:12,17; Davies, "Lost Heaven."

35. Davies, "Lost Heaven," 14–15. Emphasis mine. Davies quotes Thomas Aquinas as summing up this traditional belief that the ascended body of Jesus must be above all creatures both physically and spiritually, from the *Summa Theologiae*, pars 3, q. 57, art. 4 and 5.

grasp this change is to comprehend *just what has got lost* in the move from literal to metaphoric: *the sense of our [and the world's] presence to the glorified body of Christ in the present moment.* The notion or image of Jesus ascending, apart from conflicting with our knowledge of the earth being round and surrounded by space, leaves us with the sense of Jesus "going away." Jesus is in "heaven," but where "on earth" is that? The heaven whose whereabouts we do not know, is out of reach, beyond our world and our vision, spiritual, perhaps not even very real, but in any case, elsewhere. And this can be heard in our expressions about heaven, the afterlife, and also music, when applied to Christian life. The metaphor of height is still with us, but with very different implications. The move from a classical worldview to a Copernican one has shifted our imagination with regard to heaven and Jesus, in the words of Davies, from "pointing towards" a place *within* the imagined universe that overflows to touch and give us plenitude, to *pointing away* from earth to somewhere beyond anyone's reach:

> Whereas natural verticality for the pre-modern paradigm was a pointing *to* (that is, to God in heaven, which—according to Gn 1:1—was part of the first creation along with the earth), metaphorical verticality is only a pointing *from* (that is, from the world).[36]

So how do we find God? Do we need to move away from and beyond the world, or does God come to meet us here, infusing human life with fullness? Does our singing take us out of our bodies to experience God above, or open our embodied spirits to a greater presence of God within and through our transformed existence? Is it any wonder that expressions like "heavenly" or "transcendent," when used to describe things, and in the context of this book, music, leave us perplexed? If "heavenly" music means it comes from above, then where do the senses come in? Or if it is meant to inspire and elevate us, are our bodies touched and changed by the experience? And how can one know which music is heavenly and which is not? Perhaps it is music that does not affect us bodily that is more "spiritual" and "uplifting" (note the direction) than more physically involving or "incarnated" musical genres? And yet, if we try to reach the heart of these expressions with a direct question, such as: where is heaven and what are we trying to say when we feel something is "heavenly?," would the answer be that

36. Davies, "Interrupted Body," 43.

this music helps us live our ordinary lives more in touch with faith and committed to loving, or that it helps us forget, remove ourselves, and "take a break" from the mundane? The point is not to suggest that "taking a break" is negative, but to understand the underlying apprehension of faith, and discern if it is consistent with Christian living and knowing, or if it leads instead to estrangement and alienation:

> By the internalisation of such a metaphorical conceptual paradigm which points *out* of the world, the Christian self is drawn to live under alienation *within* the real world, of which there can be no real "outside." Thus we Christians who live by this paradigm, may find that we live but poorly in the world, and not at all in any other.[37]

If we apply this to our apprehension and experience of music, we are invited to question ourselves about how we understand and integrate music in our Christian lives, and indeed how it affects our living in the world. We only have one world to live in, and it is this one. Fullness of life, from a Christian point of view, cannot mean escaping from the world but plenitude of life now and forever. Only God can know what shape eschatological reality will take, but biblical images point more towards a transformation of the created order, assumed in Christ, than a leaving it behind:

> [N]ot a way out of the world but a way *into* the world, functioning not through abstraction or annihilation (in its more millenarian forms) but rather through a *transformation* of the real. It thus corresponds to what Paul Ricoeur refers to as "immanent" rather than "transcendent height."[38]

Reviewing our expectations in regard to the Christian experience alters how we integrate different tools or means of growth in the same, including music. It is not a coincidence that much of the more well known and used contemporary Christian songs evoke this reality of presence experienced. Two particularly famous examples are "Carry Me"[39] from Hillsong Church, Australia, and "Breathe"[40] from the

---

37. Ibid.

38. Davies, "Transforming Theology," 131.

39. Hillsong, *Forever*, which talks of the "courts" of the Lord as being the place "where dreams are made."

40. Martin S. Smith, *Worship*. "This is the air I breathe . . . Your holy presence living in me."

Vineyard Church. Both denominations are renowned in contemporary Christian culture for the quality of their music and music ministry.

Sensibility and Spirituality in Music

The change in our cosmological worldview went hand in hand with another shift of awareness that compounded the alienation mentioned above and directly affects our apprehension and understanding of music: a change in our comprehension of the relationship between spiritual and material realities. In looking back it is easy to underestimate the process and nuances involved in historical events, and one way of doing so is to consider the Enlightenment and atheism as one and the same reality. However, it was not the existence of God that was questioned, first and foremost, in the Enlightenment, but the relationship between the human and the divine, how spirit and matter interact, and indeed, if they can. The "loss" of heaven, as described above, brought with it the perceived loss of divine power over the material universe. In Davies's words:

> A further development in this period was the loss of an understanding of matter as being open to the Creator's power in such a way and to such an extent that it could undergo fundamental transformation.[41]

He identifies primarily two historical factors as having caused this change:

i. The development of modern science, specifically Newtonian physics; and

ii. The Idealism of the eighteenth and nineteenth centuries.

The first refuted the fundamental transformability of matter, since the natural sciences' seemingly unstoppable increase in understanding of the empirical world compounded the separation between the material order, which the human mind could access and organize, and the spiritual, which was inaccessible and therefore "relegated" to the realm of the metaphysical.[42] This provoked the counterreaction of the second,

---

41. Davies, "Lost Heaven," 29.

42. These developments led to what we have referred to in the previous chapter as naïve "empiricism": the real world was understood to be what is out there to see, touch, and feel. It is worth pointing out that science now, with the theory of relativity

with the polarization of the conceptual and consequent sidelining of the affective or emotional dimensions of human reasoning to a "non-rational zone" inferior to "reason."

The effects of these cosmological and scientific changes on our understanding of life and faith were real and still endure. It is not surprising that the result was what Davies refers to as "living poorly" in this world, as mentioned in the quotation above.[43] In practical terms, a chasm opened between everyday living and perceiving, on the one hand, and the faith inherited from the premodern church, on the other, which had the effect of loosening "the relation between the domain of sensibility (the life of the senses) and the actuality of faith";[44] that is to say, the relationship between our life of and in the senses and the experience and living out of our faith became estranged. It is this existential estrangement that makes it difficult for us to experience God in human life, and even to comprehend how this can happen. Part and parcel of that difficulty is how to open to and welcome the role music is taking on in Christian living. Paradoxically, it is precisely this chasm that music can help to bridge.

The dynamism of human life is somehow irrepressible in its quest for wholeness, and the Spirit joins with our human spirit in that endeavor.[45] Therefore, many and varied are the attempts to overcome this alienation and find some form of spiritual dimension to living in this world, from *Harry Potter* and *Twilight* vampire books to yoga

---

and quantum mechanics, is much more open to the transformation of the material, and the "imagining" of heaven in ways that are more akin to our current cosmology. Davies offers offer a contemporary cosmological account of "where the ascended Christ might be" in terms in which we understand the universe today, drawing on the "evolving-block universe" (EBU) of George Ellis and others, who oppose this model of an open universe to the "fixed-block universe" (FBU) of Newtonian physics. He explains that they argue that biologically complex organisms can in principle have free effects upon the nature of the world that emerges from quantum indeterminacy, and place great emphasis upon present time as the moment in which the universe is fixed as past, and the unlimited possibilities of its unfolding are realized as specific futural possibilities. Within this paradigm, the past is always known as past: we cannot know the present; we inhabit the present not as observer but as agent, in the actuality of our acting and becoming part of the universe as it becomes and opens possibilities of future. Cf. Davies, "Transforming Theology," 22.

43. Once again we find ourselves with the recognition of the impoverishment of life and thought in Western culture, as marked by Lonergan, Janz, and Haughton.

44. Davies, "Lost Heaven," 11.

45. Cf. Rom 8:26.

and martial arts or the heightened interest in Celtic spirituality, as well as contemporary fascination with music,[46] to mention but a few. As a positive Christian contribution in the midst of this sea of spiritual seeking, one has to recognize the imaginative writings of J. R. R. Tolkien and C. S. Lewis.

From the perspective of Christian spirituality and theology, one attempt to ground and orientate this trend to which we should give particular attention to is the recent reappearance of the theme of the Spiritual Senses.[47] Its importance lies in the fact that it manifests a serious attempt of Christian spirituality and theology to regain the lost link between the world we live in and the God we believe in. The teaching is an ancient one in Christian thought, present in the fathers of the church, starting with Origen and also found at least partially in Gregory of Nyssa, Bonaventure, and Augustine. The theme practically disappeared from the scene for centuries (and not by coincidence, I would say) during the Enlightenment and the unfolding of modernity, and is now once again drawing people's attention:

> Is there a sensible/sensitive experience of a spiritual reality? [1 John 1:1–4] The Word of God made flesh offers Himself to our senses, permeated by the Spirit, to be known.[48]

> Man can *learn* to feel God through all that he encounters: seeing, hearing, touching the Presence. And it is through the senses that man "witnesses the Divine."[49]

---

46. By fascination, I mean the multifaceted omnipresence of music in every dimension of our lives, both every day and in its more spiritual moments. There is no shop open without background music; the iPod culture rules sport endeavors and commuting workers; practically all spiritual ventures, from evangelical reborn churches to New Age experiments and holistic health oriented initiatives, include music of some form in their ethos.

47. For example, Gómez-Acebo, *Pregare con i sensi*; Campo, "Sensi spirituali"; Endean, "Ignatian Prayer of the Senses"; Gentili, *Nostri sensi ilumina*; Goettmann and Dürcheim, *Dialogo sul cammino iniziatico*; Pisarra, *Giardino delle selizie*; Rahner, "Spiritual Senses according to Origen," "Doctrine of the Spiritual Senses," and "Reflections on the Problem of the Gradual Ascent"; Rendina, "Dottrina dei sensi spirituali"; Rupnik, "'Sentimento religioso'"; Schneiders, "Spirituality on the Academy"; Špidlík, "Sentimenti spirituali nella tradizione patristica"; Tedoldi, *Dottrina dei sensi spirituali in San Bonaventura*.

48. Gentili, *Nostri sensi ilumina*, 9. Translation mine.

49. Goettmann and Dürcheim, *Dialogo sul cammino iniziatico*, 119. Translation and emphasis mine. There is a *learning* needed for this perception, as not all sense perception is necessarily conducive to God.

However, worthy as these attempts may be, the dichotomy that has been created is not that easy to overcome. Modernity has radically marked our world vision and perception. We cannot simply "turn the clock back" in the quest of lost innocence. The only way to move is forward, and theology needs to give an answer to the difficulties being experienced and the questions being asked, in order to reground the internal unity of our knowing and thinking. If not, the danger is that the whole issue be relegated to the realm of "spirituality": thought on the spiritual senses is one more instrument or area of reading that can be helpful for whoever wishes to take advantage, leaving "academic" thought enclosed in narrow forms of understanding. The very term "spiritual senses" too easily evokes a form of spiritual apprehension, akin to "intuition" or "contemplation," without taking on board the incarnated, bodily, or to use Haughton's terminology, fleshliness of our human living.[50] The spiritual senses are our same physical senses transformed and formed in Christ, not another set of more ethereal tools to which only the more enlightened have access. Properly understood, they evoke a way of being and living that is a specifically Christian way of taking life and the world seriously. Theological thought needs to address this re-comprehension of the relationship between the material world and the spiritual one. It is in this area that a renewed understanding of the doctrine on the ascension offers some serious answers.

A final word in this section on the historical backdrop of our faith in the ascension, specifically in relation to our theme of music in contemporary culture and theology: Is there a link? Did these cosmological and epistemological shifts affect Christian music and its development, or the lack of it? I would not suggest that the relevance of these changes in perception on our theme is *directly* that of cause-effect. I present Davies's thought more as a paradigm to help us to ground faith transmission through music than as an explanation for the current situation, but it is interesting to note the convergences. The crisis in understanding music's place in theology and Christian spirituality is a contemporary one. The worlds of faith and music have not

---

50. Haughton quotes St. Teresa of Avila's insistence that the humanity of Christ is at the core of all contemplation. The second week of the Ignatian month of spiritual exercises focuses on the life of Jesus of Nazareth, and is an invaluable source of spiritual experience and growth. My own pastoral experience witnesses to the fact that integrating contemplation and physicality, both that of Christ and our own, is still a (mental) challenge, but one that reaps enormous benefits when achieved.

always been so disjointed. This is not because the question of music's role in faith has not been raised beforehand. St. Augustine's perplexity with what to do with his emotional response to music in the liturgy is an early and authoritative witness to that fact,[51] and exemplifies the fact that the relationship between music and faith is an intrinsic one. The need to discern in what way, and to what extent, a particular piece of music or its use is appropriate or helpful for each person and in each moment will be with us always.[52] However, the radical shift from a scenario in which the church was one of the foremost sponsors of the arts to one in which most known music is composed outside of the church is a contemporary one. This is this same period that saw the disappearance of beauty as a core theme from the center of theological thought, in which the church gradually lost contact with the meaning of art and beauty in its praxis. Could it be, alongside the other influencing factors, that as the church lost the sense of its contact with the embodied presence of the glorious Christ, its artists and musicians lost the "home place" of their inspiration? Our whole reflection on the role of art in human consciousness and experience illustrate that art, to be art, has an intrinsic role with freedom, and cannot be "forced." Experience in and of art precedes understanding and judgment. Great art and music have something to say about what is truly important in human life and culture, even when that importance is not (yet) fully appreciated or conscious. That which is important will be expressed! As Christian faith lost touch with who we are, and life began to be played out in other forums, art followed; or if we are honest, in many cases it preceded, heralding the direction culture was to take.

---

51. Cf. Augustine, *Confessions* 9.6–7; 10.33. His obvious appreciation of the role of singing in his own conversion, and in uplifting the faithful, together with the awareness of the difference in need and appreciation as maturity in faith grows, is eloquent and thought-provoking for any discernment in the use of music in worship.

52. Discernment is intrinsic to the Christian living out of faith at all levels, be it applying St. Ignatius's rule of "in the measure that" (*in tanto e in cuanto ayude al fin*), or other guiding principles. An interesting study on the theme of discernment in spiritual life that could potentially be fruitful as applied to the use of art and music is Rupnik's work on discernment, *Il discernimento*. Based on Ignatian spirituality, it takes into account the different moments of the spiritual journey, as having diverse challenges and therefore requiring appropriate answers. This awareness in the use of music in ministry and faith mediation could be important.

The Embodied Presence of Jesus Christ: Three Keys for Christian Spirituality and Theology

> *May your inner eye*
> *See through the surfaces*
> *And glean the real presence*
> *Of everything that meets you.*
>
> —John O'Donoghue[53]

> *In Him we live, and move, and have our being*
>
> —Acts 17:28

Recovering the Essentials of the Doctrine of the Ascension

Having sketched the historical and cultural causes and process of loss of theological attentiveness to the truth of the ascension, and its consequences for our theme, it is time to focus on the specific elements this truth of faith introduces (or recovers), and apply them to the music and its use. What Davies seeks to do is to recover and reformulate the "essence" or core of this truth of faith, in a way that is understandable for contemporary theology and culture. The need to recomprehend and reformulate a doctrine of faith as history and perception changes is an accepted fact in theology, often referred to as the "development of dogma,"[54] but to do so implies a clear understanding of what it is the doctrine is seeking to express, so that its "translation" may be accurate. Davies identifies three essential points that the early church comprehended as part of or directly linked to the truth of the ascension, which can be summarized in the words "presence," "universality," and "mediation." Before we apply them to our theme, it is important to understand the point they emphasize.

---

53. O'Donoghue, "For the Senses," 57.

54. A key writing in the process of theological understanding of this theme is Newman's *An Essay on the Development of Christian Doctrine*.

The Ascension as Presence Rather than Withdrawal

The ascension does not mark a withdrawal of the presence of Jesus Christ to us, but rather his being present in and to the world in a different way:

> While the withdrawal of the body marks the cessation of its visibility (which is to say its objectifiability), it also marks its availability or presence *to the senses* in an entirely new way.[55]

I emphasize that the presence of Jesus Christ is a presence *to our senses*, for the reasons mentioned above, in relation to our difficulty in holding together the spiritual and the material world. That the ascension cannot mean withdrawal from us is often preached on its liturgical feast day each year, but not *how* that presence is felt, nor how to bridge the fact that he is invisible to our eyes and yet still here! Therefore, our imagining of that presence tends to spiritualize it: presence to our spirits or souls, rather than to our physical embodied reality in space and time.

The Ascension as a Universal Presence

This presence is one of universal impact, only possible after the resurrection, ascension, and sending of the Spirit:

> It is only through the new advent of the Spirit, that the presence of Christ in the fullness of his humanity becomes universally possible: to those to whom he is now known in the Spirit through faith.[56]

This universal presence of the body is described by Davies as his "world-body," in the sense that while the reality of the incarnation marks the entrance of the divine into the world, the resurrection, glorification, and ascension, with the coming of the Spirit marks the "entrance" of the world into the body of Christ. This world-body of Jesus Christ is "a body which contains the world, a body which the world itself can now be said to be 'in'; and thus we too, as part of this transformed world, can also be said to be 'in.'"[57] It must be understood that we are not talking about an either/or division, but the moving, dynamic of the process of

---

55. Davies, "Interrupted Body," 50. Emphasis mine.
56. Ibid.
57. Ibid.

our salvation. The world, created in and though the Word, carries that mark from its very origin.[58] From the moment of the incarnation, human nature comes to form an intrinsic unity in the Word with divine nature, and in the living out of that nature we see the gradual emerging in Jesus of Nazareth of this divine nature until, passing through the specific moment of his passion and death, that human nature is transformed fully by the power of the resurrection.[59] Humanity participates, in some way, in this change and transformation. This is the Pauline doctrine of what has come to be called the Mystical Body of Christ or the Total Christ, the former referring more explicitly to the church as Mystery of Salvation, the latter to the cosmic dimensions evoked by Paul of all creation assumed in and transformed by Christ, with eschatological perspectives.[60] The birth place in Scripture of the awareness of this doctrine is Saul's encounter with Jesus on the road to Damascus,[61] in which there is a direct identification between Jesus and his followers that Paul would later develop in his letters as the Body of Christ, with Christ as the Head.[62] This truth has echoes in the other New Testament writings: Jesus risen and yet carrying the mark of his wounds,[63] and the image of the vine and the branches.[64] This leads to the third aspect underlined by Davies: Christ's role as mediator.

---

58. Cf. John 1:1–5

59. There is an interesting parallel between how Davies perceives this process, coming to its culmination in the transfiguration, passion, and death of Jesus, and Rosemary Haughton's account of the same in *The Passionate God*. Her emphasis on the importance of the Jesus' embodiment, both historically and in its continuation in the Body of the church, passing through the resurrection, is eloquent.

60. Cf. Eph 1:3–14; Col 1:15–20.

61. Cf. Acts 9:4. Davies bases his analysis of the truth of ascension in part on the encounter of Paul with the risen and ascended Lord on the way to Damascus, in which Paul understands Jesus asking him the question, "Why are you persecuting me?" in direct reference to Saul's persecution of the early Christian church. He was not asked why he persecuted the church, or his followers, but "Why are you persecuting *me*?" This encounter is unique in the foundational post-resurrection apparitions of the New Testament, in that it is the only one that occurs after the ascension, and its characteristics are distinctively different to the descriptions of the other apparitions.

62. Cf. Col 2:10; Eph 1:10; Eph 4:15.

63. John 20:19–28.

64. John 15:1–5. Kelly eloquently brings together these biblical images or metaphors as applied to the doctrine of the Body of Christ in *The Resurrection Effect*, 35–39.

The Ascended Christ as Mediator

In biblical terms, it is Christ's entrance into the heavenly tabernacle that permits him to exercise his "priestly" function of mediator between God and humanity:

> Only because Christ has entered into the immediate presence of God can he perform the mediatorial functions on behalf of the humanity whose nature he assumed and which remains present in him.[65]

The universal presence of Jesus Christ to us, having assumed humanity and the cosmos in himself, has initiated therein a process of definitive transformation, of which he is the center, mediator, and catalyst: "in Him we live and move and have our being."

The next two sections of this chapter reflect on the significance of these three characteristics of our faith in the ascension, as applied to the two aspects of our theme of contemporary music: its revelatory capacity of the Word of God in the daily living out of Christian faith, and its place in and as theology itself; that is to say, music as mediation of faith and theological praxis.

The Ascension, Christian Living in the World, and Music

> *It is by this door [the humanity of Jesus] that we must enter if we want his supreme Majesty to reveal to us great and hidden mysteries.*
> *No other way should be attempted.*
>
> —St. Teresa of Avila

Keeping in mind this threefold dimension of our faith in the ascended body of Christ, in what way can or is contemporary music a means of mediation of faith?

Music as a Means of Presence to the Present Moment

The presence of Christ to our senses, in a different and fuller way than during his human life, teaches us not only to open our eyes and rec-

---

65. Davies, "Lost Heaven," 15–16.

ognize the value of the present moment, but also to draw a bridge between the historical life of Jesus and our faith in him today. How often do Christians committed to the following of Christ and the values of the gospel wonder what knowing him "in the flesh" could have been like? And yet the thinking through of this truth of faith allows us to intuit the limits of the historical "knowing" of Jesus in comparison to the participation in the newness of life open to us now. As amazing as Jesus of Nazareth must have been to see, listen to and come to know in his historical life, the "through him, with him, and in him" we live now, in the present moment, has to be qualitatively superior.[66] The full power of divine life by which we are saved is fruit of the culmination of his life in his passion, death, and resurrection, and only experienced as such after those events. We are in a privileged situation with respect to the disciples, enabled to live an intimacy with Christ in every present moment that they could not have imagined. Without realizing it, often our focus in Christian living is on faith in the past or hope in the future: faith in past events that truly happened, and that we "make memory of," as significant for the now, or hope in a future beyond death, a future that we do not fully understand or even imagine but which gives perspective (be it comfort or a conscience call) to our present and mortal lives. Growth in awareness of the embodied presence of Christ to us now would draw our gaze from past faith and future hope to present love or loving: eternity understood as depth of life in the present moment, rather than continuation (in horizontal) of the lives we live now, after death, which is neither fully appreciative of New Testament writings nor particularly appealing to postmodern sensibility.[67]

66. To begin with it is a universal presence, not limited to one person or place at a time, nor to the normal joys and sufferings of human friendship and love. The gospel is quite clear in the miscomprehensions that occurred between Jesus and his family, Jesus and his disciples, Jesus and the Pharisees. Human love lived at depth carries nearly as much pain as it does joy, not least being the very "mortal" nature of our lives and friendships, by which there will always be separation to face. Even in the Gospels the pain experienced as a result of separation is not hidden; to ignore that fact in the light of paschal faith would be to read the Gospels very superficially. For an insightful and thought-provoking approach to the Gospels in this respect, Haughton's aforementioned book is exemplary.

67. John's understanding of eternal life in John 17:3, as "knowing God," depth of presence to the Lord in the present moment, is more helpful to contemporary sensibility than that of a future without end. A life transformed by a love made new, the quality of life offered has a potential of fullness that is more easily imagined and

How can music help in this regard? One of the aspects we noted that Speelman underlined with most strength was music's capacity of holding us in the present moment of space and time, receptive to reality, rather than taking distance from it in order to understand it. If music's aim is not to send a message, but to open a space in which both musician and listener share in that experience, it is at least "reasonable" to ask about how that dynamic could open human sensibility to (and in) the presence of a triune and sharing God. If we bring to mind again what we talked about in our third chapter with regard to Greimas' semiotic square, enriched by Speelman with the category of the curve when applied to musical semiotics,[68] we can comprehend that when one listens to music (and even more so when one composes, as the listening factor is heightened in order to create) instead of "thinking" in oppositions, we "listen" to, resonate with, and are oriented towards other tones and harmonies. This is how music works. There is no other way to deal with music: *all* music, of any genre, implies this kind of dynamic. It creates a different relationship with reality than verbal understanding and expression does, which Speelman goes as far as to describe as receiving reality as opposed to language's dynamic of referring to or even "masking" it (thus introducing the need for interpretation). Music helps us inhabit the present moment in which we are living. That does not in any way mean that *all* music bridges to the presence of Christ: on the contrary, it is more precise to say music creates a bond with the reality of which it is born, before or beyond the words that may seek to "explain" it. Therefore we are talking more of the potentiality of a form of symbolic communication than of its direct use. However, if the person composing, playing or singing a given piece of music *is*, indeed, in contact with the living reality of Christ in the world, is it unreasonable to suggest that this connection is somehow accessed?

Music as Theodicy of God in and with Humanity

The universality of Christ's presence understood as "world-body" touches on an even more acute nerve of present-day sensibility towards

---

therefore, perhaps, more eagerly sought. This Gospel reading is consistent with and even evocative of the understanding of a possible "location" of heaven more compatible with contemporary science.

68. Cf. Figure 3.5.

faith and Christianity, to do with the justification of the existence of God in the light of the world's suffering and pain, which theology calls "theodicy." Although this question is intrinsic to religious faith, as witnessed to already in the Scriptures (especially Job and the Sapiential books), in the twentieth century it took on a density hitherto unknown. The extent of worldwide suffering and our universal access to information about it seems to have changed our perception of the world. Where is God? What are They, our triune God, doing, in the face of this situation? How can faith in a God of creation make any sense when that world is so tragically in pain? In Western culture, this situation is aggravated by the growing awareness of the complicity of the church in situations of suffering.[69] So the question of how can we hold together a fallen world, the extent of human capacity for cruelty and sin, with the profession of a God of love is at the heart of the church's call to evangelize.

How useful is the doctrine of the Mystical Body of Christ to respond to this crisis? In twenty-five years of missionary life in Europe seeking to "give reason for the hope that we have,"[70] I have found that there is no stronger motivation to let down barriers to Christian faith than that of discovering God's eternal loving commitment to this world, to the extent of assuming in God's very Self that reality, suffering in and with those who suffer. The truth of the ascension and the Mystical Body of Christ is just this: God's love is not distant; the Creator not only loved us enough to incarnate Himself so as to reveal and redeem, but also to remain implicated in the world, assuming us in Himself, in his Body. Although this truth of faith is, in effect, one that implies a vision of faith to grasp it, being inaccessible to reason alone, it is, however, "reasonable" in that it speaks of a God whose love takes Him to the extreme of assuming in Self the breadth of human pain in the world.[71] People may not grasp God, but they do understand

---

69. Be it through alliance with unjust political structures, or other forms. As I write, Ireland is still reeling from the publication of reports on child abuse on behalf of institutions belonging to religious congregations and by diocesan clergy, only a few years after evidence of similar stories surfaced in the United States, and the Church has been called to investigate its praxis by a United Nations Committee against Torture. The impression on people's mind-frame towards the Church has been radically affected by these events.

70. Cf. 1 Pet 3:15.

71. Once again we are faced with the fruitfulness of an apologetics that does not try to defend God from outside its own rationale, but is fully grounded in revelation.

the dynamics of human love, which includes just how far true love will go for a loved one: it is a comprehension that goes beyond or even before words, but where there is real suffering words are of little use, and the presence of Someone in the midst of that pain is not a solution, but it is an answer: it is life (and death) shared.

Music is a form of presence that does not seek to "give answers": it integrates player and listener in a common space. Those of us who are musicians know that when faced with people's pain, it is easier, and sometimes more appropriate, to express compassion or grief in song than in words, as it can touch without preaching and speak without patronizing. Benedict XVI, writing as Ratzinger before his appointment as pope, identifies the apologetic function of the Church's art:

> Next to the saints, the art which the church has produced is the only real "apologia" for her history. It is this glory which witnesses to the Lord, not theology's clever explanations for all the terrible things which lamentably, fill the pages of her history.[72]

He is referring to what he considers the great heritage of Western art, but the notion is applicable on a more everyday level to the role of music in helping people access faith, in the midst of their questions for and about God. "We are not alone in our loneliness," writes the Irish poet Patrick Kavanagh, "others have been here and known griefs we thought our special own."[73] And yet it is not easy to become present to another person's grief, or to allow them into our own. Music has often been a form of achieving that. Liam Lawton's song "The Cloud's Veil" was a source of consolation for many after the 9/11 tragedy. The Hymn "Abide with Me" evokes the presence of God upon the loss of loved ones more effectively, for many, than a Scripture reading, and although a poetic expression of the truths of faith we know is undoubtedly helpful, it is unrealistic to put it down solely to the words of the song. A good melody can move more than words; rhythm can uplift more than explanations, and when music has touched us in a given context, hearing it brings us back, helping us "make memory" more effectively, I would say, than any other means. Music is a form of shared presence, a non-intrusive human form of resonating with someone, and *resonating with* is, perhaps, the best way to describe it. The natural way in

---

72. Ratzinger, *Feast of Faith*, 124.
73. Kavanagh, "Thank You, Thank You," in his *Collected Poems*, 247.

which grief manifests itself is in corporal expression, be it crying, or wailing or in the body bracing itself to deal with the tension that is physically experienced, even when the "blow" is emotional. The capacity of music to touch, enter into, and "minister to" our embodied pain cannot be underestimated. Indeed, it is accepted with relative normality in cultures that have not assumed such a dualistic mind-frame as Western Europe has.[74]

Music as Mediating Jesus" Presence

This leads me to the third element: that of mediation. How can we reach God and how can God's grace actually touch and transform us? Can music mediate Christ's grace to our lives? That people feel the need to experience God's presence, even in our secularized Western Europe, manifests itself frequently, often in the simple but honest request (above all in moments of difficulty) for prayer. When offered respectfully, even to someone who professes not to have Christian faith, it is rarely refused. The unsaid premise is that hope is needed but God is distant, "somewhere else" other than where we are, external to our reality, albeit somehow close to those who "seem" closer to God. The implicit quest is for ways to have the distance mediated for them.

A right understanding of the truth we are talking about would present Jesus as the redemption of human freedom, that immense gift of God, mysteriously wounded and incapable of trusting God's all-embracing love.[75] Then the truth of the body of Christ becomes the final link in the chain of God's unbreakable love for humanity, which will stop at nothing to reach and save us. Rather than intruding on the dynamic of human freedom, God opens a path of newness *from within*, in the definitive union of Christ with humanity. In Christ, mediation takes on a different quality.[76] No longer is prayer, for oneself or for

---

74. For example, the laments of African culture, the bodily participation in gospel lament music, and the practically extinct practice of the keening at funerals, which apart from Ireland was known in Greek and Roman cultures, as well in as Israel.

75. The understanding presented by Sequeri of original sin as suspicion and distrust of God's immense love and mercy for humanity is the most convincing and coherent with the content of the Gospels that I have found, and has influenced my own reflections here. Cf. Sequeri, *Timore di Dio*.

76. The means for accessing this life are obviously perceived differently by the different Christian denominations. For an interesting approach to the theme in relation to prayer, see Lonergan, "Mediation of Christ in Prayer."

others, a plea from afar, but an opening, in mind and body, of oneself to the grace of God, which is the blood that runs through the body we are inserted in, or the sap that feeds the branches of the vine, to use the aforementioned image in John 15 of the vine and the branches. For the reality of the world assumed in Christ is not an individualistic one: we are members of the one body, branches of the one vine, whose dependence on God and on each other is intrinsic to our existence. We can mediate God's grace to one another. In this context, the meaning of our mutual interaction and communion, including intercessory prayer, so ingrained in Christian spirituality, takes on new depth.[77] In the words of Davies:

> Through the transformation effected in us . . . made present to us in his living or ascended form, the world is made in some small way more permeable and responsive to the order of divine grace: to the living telos of the world in whom we act and in whom we now live.[78]

Can music take on this dynamic? I believe it can. Paul, in the context of exhorting the first Christian communities to overcome tensions and live in love, called Christians to sing psalms, hymns, and inspired songs to each other.[79] It is fair to assume he was not considering it as a form of relaxation but aware instead of its spiritual potential. As a musician and singer, I intuit this has something to do with the physical act of singing, when united with conscious prayer and praise. The importance of breathing in the act of singing, and the embodied effort it implies to sing well, when done consciously and as an act of prayer, is spiritually and corporally very uplifting, as the whole person is involved. The truth of faith of our being inserted in the body of Christ in which the breath of God is its life can help us understand why this is so. The importance of music in Charismatic Renewal and Pentecostal spiritualities, which focus precisely on the resurrection and the new life given to us through the Spirit of the risen Lord, and on praise as a means of accessing it and of combating the presence of evil, would

---

77. Cf. The well-known quotation of Pius XII: "This is a deep mystery, and an inexhaustible subject of meditation, that the salvation of many depends on the prayers and voluntary penances which the members of the Mystical Body of Jesus Christ offer for this intention . . ." Pius XII, *Mystici Corporis Christi*, 44.

78. Davies, "Transforming Theology," 23.

79. Cf. Eph 5:15–19; Col 3:16.

seem to confirm this. To my mind this point, although not identical, is related to what various authors have identified as the eschatological potential of art and music,[80] that is, the capacity it has to reawaken longing for the world as "it might have been," or as it could be, even when we may be unaware we have resigned ourselves to its present situation. Yet, becoming conscious of our shared existence in the Body of Christ takes it a step further: not only does it awaken longing but somehow can infuse us with true Christian hope, which is not optimism but access to the new life we have already won in Christ.[81]

The Ascension, Music and Theological Thought

> *We must feel the pulse in the wound to believe that*
> *"with God all things are possible"*
> *taste bread at Emmaus that warm hands broke and blessed.*
>
> —Denise Levertov[82]

We now take a step further, and look at how this theological framework can illuminate music in and as theology.

THE PRESENCE OF MUSIC IN THEOLOGICAL THOUGHT AND TEACHING

If we take the first element noted above, the ascended body of Christ as a new form of presence or availability of the glorified body of Jesus Christ to our life in the senses now, what consequences does it bring for theological thought? We have already highlighted one such consequence sufficiently, both in this chapter and in the last one: the call to

---

80. In particular, George Steiner and Pierangelo Sequeri. Another author who emphasizes it in relation to art in general is Trevor Hart, director of the Institute for Theology, Imagination, and the Arts at the University of St. Andrews. In a conference I attended September 2–5, 2007, on the theme of "The Offence of Beauty," his paper was entitled "Ugly as Sin?: Beauty, Holiness, and the Crucified," and was related to other writings he has on eschatology.

81. This is the most coherent explanation I have found to the repeated experience of being told by people who listen to Christian music (my own and that of others), that it touches them, moves them, gives them peace, serenity, hope, or strength. And they are not referring solely to the words, but to the singing and the music that carries them.

82. Levertov, "On Belief in the Physical Resurrection," 116.

a greater attentiveness to the embodied world of time and space as a *locus theologicus*.[83] Yet there is another, which is more subtle, but no less important: the primacy of the world of the present moment over the text. Davies situates the emergence of narrative and hermeneutical theologies in the context of a waning faith in the historicity of the Scriptures, together with the changes in perception of the world that we have already mentioned. Without denying the value of research into narrative and hermeneutical approaches to theology, he claims that, when taken to the extreme, the text became

> an *alternative* world of sacred immediacy and saving meaning . . . [in which the real world becomes] a function of textual one. . . . Thus the field of the reader's sensible and embodied real, in which the sacred text itself is being read, became lost to view.[84]

The emphasis, for Davies, is on the present moment, and how people are present to us in a very specific way, different to that of a text. The very essence of a personal relationship is that the other is present to us as *given*: we do not have to call them to mind.[85] This concurs with Speelman's analysis of the dynamic of verbal communication, in which we are led to disengage from the reality we are living in, so as to "think" it, and understand it. We remove ourselves from the present moment and situation, in order to grasp and interpret the reality we are immersed in. The interpretation and performance of music implies involvement and interaction with the reality (music or song) being played or sung. We do not talk about reality, but rather open ourselves to receive it. Even in a hermeneutical approach to music analysis, such as Nattiez's one presented in chapter 2, the dangers signaled by Davies can be avoided due to the attention given to the person of the composer, the context of composition, the music itself and the world of the receiver. At each stage, the musical event draws us back to the

---

83. As noted in the introduction, Melchor Cano's influential description of the *loci theologici* included ten such "theological places" or sources. The most important of these are of course, Sacred Scripture and the writings of church tradition, but one of the complementary sources is described as "the lessons of history," one of the roots of the current theological theme of the "signs of the times." It is in this sense that I present music as a *locus theologicus*.

84. Davies, "Interrupted Body," 38. He is responding to George Lindbeck's statement that it is "the text which absorbs the world rather than the world the text." Lindbeck, *Nature of Doctrine*, 118.

85. Cf., Davies, "Interrupted Body," 49.

present moment, widening our viewpoint from that of the "content" of our faith to the presence, at least, of those transmitting it to us, if not also of the One in whom we believe, who lives in the present moment, through the dynamic and beauty of the music we are sharing.[86]

How this "presence" of music could inhabit our theological endeavors is an invitation to creativity. Perhaps simple can be effective, although it implies moving out of our comfort zones and risking new ways of doing things.[87] By way of example, I would offer the article of theologian Chris Pramuk, "'Strange Fruit': Black Suffering/White Revelation," which is a reflection on the eschatological significance and role of the oppressed black community in the conversion of white Americans, in the context of the United States. It starts with a reference to the song of the same name by Billie Holiday. The article was first presented in a conference, together with a recording of Holiday singing the song. The effectiveness of the speaker's input, as witnessed by some of those present, was greatly increased by that fact. Theology solely based on a verbal mode of communication risks placing the accent on accumulation of knowledge: both that of the student and the professor! Whereas integrating music or other art forms invites both to a more assimilated and integrated focus in learning.

Music as a "Thick, Deep, and Fresh" Form of Theological Expression

Moving on to the universal presence of Christ, in his human-divine world-body in which the created order is assumed: what are the theological implications and what role could music play therein? Talking

---

86. Once again I would note the relevance of Rosemary Haughton's challenge to change our understanding of reality and being itself from a more static form to a more dynamic one—the "hidden model of reality" that we implicitly live by and within which we think, which tends to separate spiritual-material as if they actually function that way.

87. If an image from shared cultural experience can help, the classic, if sad, film *Dead Poets Society* comes to mind, featuring a young professor with rather novel forms of teaching, who introduces his students to a love of literature and the challenge of learning to think for themselves. Such a lateral approach to teaching is only possible in one who has assimilated what needs to be transmitted and is as much concerned with the students' growth in learning as in covering the course's content. When theology adopts a similar ethos in relation to art and integrates it in its reflection and communication (be it in books or when teaching) the results are interesting and important.

about Christ's world-body invites us to consider what is referred to as "world music," meaning the plurality of the world's musical heritage in each particular culture. A question that needs to be asked is how attention to them could enrich theology, and one reply can be found in the thought of Clemans Sedmak of the transformation theology team.[88] Sedmak addresses the theological implications of the immensity of the suffering of humanity, and talks about theology's need for renewal in the form of what he calls "thick, deep, and fresh" concepts, in order to address adequately in its reflection the reality of world suffering. Integrating attention to the world's music into theological reflection would, I believe, help provide theology with such concepts. In order to grasp this it is helpful to understand what he means by each term. In his own words:

> A thick concept is associated with personal experiences and local examples. A deep concept is laden with emotions and shows not only a cognitive but also an affective content. A fresh concept is a concept that has provocative "sting" to it that calls for an ongoing *relecture* and reappraisal, a concept that opens up new avenues of investigation and invites us to take a fresh look at causal realities and conceptual frameworks.[89]

The underlying challenge is that of the reality of the world truly affecting and entering into theological praxis, on the basis that conceptual reasoning is not only insufficient, but can somehow keep the world's suffering distant from us, leaving us over informed and undercommitted:

> There seems to be a point where we could say: the more we know, the less we understand—if we take "understanding" to be a sapiential skill that translates into ordering and judging in a way that bridges the gap between the conceptual and the causal.[90]

88. Sedmak is the member of the team who deals with the ethical teaching and implications of transformation theology, with chapters entitled "The Disruptive Power of World Hunger" and "The Wound of Knowledge."

89. Sedmak, "Disruptive Power of World Hunger," 117.

90. Sedmak, "Wound of Knowledge," 149. In fact, Sedmak, coining the expression of *didedicy* (in parallel to "theodicy," in reference to a "justification of justice" in the face of so much suffering) asks whether or to what extent, in situations of extreme suffering and the apparent impossibility of a solution, "discourse" about ethics makes any sense, due to the danger of belittling the realities it seeks to address. A parallel sensibility and concern can be found in what is referred to as "theology after Auschwitz."

This echoes some of the semiotic observations of Speelman when talking about verbal communication. In order to grasp and understand the words, we take distance in order to abstract meaning and "make sense" of them. Theological attentiveness needs to find ways to open to and reflect upon the realities of suffering *as the very sufferings of Christ* in a way that thickens, deepens and refreshes our thinking. Conceptual reasoning is just not enough. Can music help in this endeavor, and if so, how?

Firstly, if "thick" concepts are "associated with personal experiences and local examples," then a theological attentiveness to music and musicians of *each and every culture and genre*, as potential sources of theological reflection, would "thicken" the density of our theological discourses, with the voice, presence, concerns and riches of this diverse and plural world we live in. Sedmak talks about the power of what he calls "disruptive" situations that resist solution and force us to "rough knowing and raw thinking."[91] Music can be disruptive, which is why it is often polemic. Dermot Lane, in an article about where theology has been moving to over the last fifty years,[92] identifies three major shifts, one of which is that of an Eurocentric theology to the recognition of its plurality in diverse contexts, according to the cultures and contexts in which it is born and done. One way of allowing that plurality to enter our minds and hearts as we think theologically could be attentiveness to the artistic and musical expression and experience of the cultural context we are working with. Music is not only such an intrinsic part of every culture that it can help us read and understand it, but it sometimes even occupies a prophetic role in helping us intuit cultural shifts before or as they are happening.[93]

Secondly, can music offer depth to theological reflection? In Sedmak's terms, "depth" touches on the affective and emotional aspects of our knowing. I believe the interrelational or "operational" symbolism of music is capable precisely of this.[94] We have noted how Sequeri

---

91. Sedmak, "Wound of Knowledge," 145. A "disruption" is a total turn-around of our reference points, that does not call for a solution, but for redemption, and above all to conversion and self-transformation. Cf. Sedmak, "Disruptive Power of World Hunger," 135.

92. Cf. Lane, "Fifty Years of Theology," reference taken from 400.

93. Cf. for example, the insightful book of Lipsitz, *Dangerous Crossroads*.

94. Recently, in a meeting of research students of the Gregorian University, we chose to share the state of our research bringing something of our work to that forum:

brings together the appreciation of the role of affectivity in faith and that of the symbolism particular to music. I suggest that exploration in how to allow music to bring its *affective depth* to theological discourse could be extremely enriching and fruitful, given the centrality of this aspect of human existence to contemporary culture.

Finally, could music help to discover *fresh* notions and concepts in theological praxis? We spoke earlier of how music could be approached as a form of expression or "language" for the current cultural moment, albeit with the qualifications of that term offered in this book. We have still to talk about the dynamic of artistic creativity, and in particular, musical composition, but I would suggest that music and in particular, the making of music, could help us to access areas of ourselves that are not automatically accessible to "rational" conceptuality:[95]

> There are "areas of concern" which are so ultimate that they are literally out of sight and can easily be not only out of mind but dismissed as not worthy of being in mind because they cannot be thought of in the way we think about breakfast, or geography, or pneumonia.[96]

Failure to access these underlying concerns ends up draining thought of its strength and its originality. Artistic creativity situates itself precisely in those underlying, prerational areas of human life that are not immediately expressed or even expressible. Gaining access to our "real reasons" is always life-giving. Talking about "the common language of ulterior depth," Roberta De Monticelli says:

> We are fragile, our energy is finite and it discharges easily. However there is no sleep, diet or thermal cures that are

---

personal reflections, a provocative article, or, as was my choice, a song that sought to express a particular theological conviction I wanted to convey. On sharing this song, the response was a "deep" and slightly uncertain silence, in which it was obvious that something had been transmitted, but as one of the participants noted afterwards, it was "something" they did not quite know what to do with. It alerted me to the need to cushion or bridge such moments with keys for its understanding, but I believe the depth or density was one of affective involvement with the song that we are not used to in a forum of theological reflection.

95. We could perhaps compare with Newman's distinction between notional reasons and real reasons. The latter are refreshing because they are, in fact, the real motivations behind our options.

96. Haughton, *Passionate God*, 5.

enough to regenerate the life of the mind, where the free gift of a "right" encounter is lacking.[97]

The encounter between music and theology is a right encounter waiting to happen.

When that contribution is present, the difference is notable. In a relatively recent conference on beauty in theology,[98] the difference between musical expression and intellectual reasoning was highlighted in the contrasting ways academics and composers present described the process involved in musical composition. A speaker who himself admitted to not being familiar with the dynamic involved in composing music, ventured a description of the creative process as that of moving from an idea the composer wishes to transmit to the form it finally takes; the group of composers in the audience, of different styles and genres, were unanimous in saying that they did not, in fact, follow the process of ideas through to music, but rather the opposite, allowing music to emerge, listening to and receiving that which it seemed to be expressing, while seeking to give it form. Fresh concepts will not be born of repeated or reformulated ideas, and while suggesting this is but one way forward, perhaps learning to expand our awareness to those zones of our person that are "under the surface," out of sight, or perhaps we could say "preconceptual," would help us to widen and refresh our thinking. Music can help in that process.

Furthermore, without doubt, collaboration and dialogue with artists of all areas would help theology to stay in touch with the culture it is meant to mediate to. Music, as we have seen, is a form of symbolic expression that is particularly prophetic for the church and theological thought in this moment. Learning to listen to it would lead us to fresh pastures. In a recent encounter with artists, Pope Benedict XVI said that without artists the work of the church is more arduous, and reaffirmed its prophetic capacity:

> [I]f we were deprived of your assistance, our ministry would become faltering and uncertain, and a special effort would be needed, one might say, to make it artistic, even prophetic.[99]

---

97. De Monticelli, *L'allegria della mente*, 63
98. The Offence of Beauty, St. Andrews, Scotland, September 2007.
99. Benedict XVI, "Address to Artists."

This would, I believe, evolve towards a further step: that of forming musicians with a grounded depth of spirituality that, with their God-given creativity, would work within and alongside theology at the service of evangelization and faith formation; but we will talk about this in the third section of this chapter.

The Sacramentality of Music as Theological Praxis

> *The world is charged with the glory of God.*
>
> —Gerald Manley Hopkins

Our third question is about the music's role in theological praxis in relation to mediation, and if music could help theology to think in terms of how this happens. As noted above, the mediation we are talking of, first and foremost, is not liturgical or sacramental, but encountering Christ in our everyday life. This can then be applied to liturgy, but only after understanding the presence of Christ in and for the world. How can music assist theology in understanding Christ's mediating presence?

In this section I would like to suggest that music can form an integral part of theology's reflection: the first, in relation to the transformation that occurs to a person in the encounter with Jesus Christ; the second, drawn from the particular calling of the artistic vocation, which needs to enter more fully into theological discourse. In order to understand how, we need to understand how Davies describes the "effect" of an encounter with the risen and ascended Christ. The body of Christ, and our belonging to it, is not known representationally, but though the transformation in sensibility that comes about through our encounter with the living and ascended Christ, and the act of commissioning that always accompanies that encounter. These two notions, however—the change in our sensibility as a result of the encounter with Christ and the ensuing mission—are neither separate nor separable, as the ascended body of Jesus is not objectifiable, and is known *only in and through* the transformation in sensibility that results from that encounter, and in which the particular calling of each person is born. In Davies's words:

> [T]he transformation of the world of which we ourselves are intrinsically a part. We do not know it directly, but we do receive it in the change that comes upon ourselves as part of that world, as we enter a new sensibility or come to a new condition of sensible existence, through the Spirit.[100]

> This new sensibility is our ecclesial existence, a new life of mandate and commissioning, which is the mode of our belonging in the world as it is irreversibly changed by incarnation.[101]

The encounter with Jesus Christ *changes* a person. Admittedly, the mission of a Christian is embedded, at least potentially, in her first experience of Christ, and a person often reading back on their life of following Jesus can trace the lines of where God was leading them, unknown to themselves. However, although encounter and commissioning are intrinsically united, they are not the same. The second aspect opens a theme we have touched on before without developing it: that of the particular call as artists and/or musicians at the service of the body of Christ, one of the many vocations and callings which the Spirit gives at will. Because of its importance, I will develop it separately in section three of this chapter. At this point I limit myself to the theological implications of the first: our transformed sensibility in Christ and music's role therein.

The first aspect, our transformed sensibility in Christ, marks our coming into the body of Christ, opening our eyes to see reality as loved by and assumed in Christ. It includes our being gifted with the *sensus fidei* that makes us part of a people who grow to discern the presence of Jesus in their life and world as real. How can music enrich theology's understanding of this encounter? Music has a role in helping us experience, remain and grow in this transformed sensibility. Contact between Christ and ourselves transforms our being in this world, and therefore our perception of and interaction with reality. Most people who come to Christian faith would describe their encounter as provoking a change in their perception of the surrounding reality, similar, albeit more lasting, to that of falling in love. It could be argued that, once there has been such an encounter with Christ, reality will never be the same. One cannot "unknow" Christ, even though one can change negatively, forgetting or even rejecting him. But our history

---

100. Davies, "Interrupted Body," 53.
101. Ibid.

and encounters are never fully lost. However, it *is* possible to live more or less in touch with that transformed sensibility, and herein lies the dynamic of Christian spirituality: growing in and maintaining alive and active a renewed presence of Jesus Christ in and to all things. This book suggests that music can be an important means of entering into and nurturing this transformed embodied Christian life. Davies himself notes that, although

> we have few resources which offer us a sense of connectedness to the living Christ *as embodied*, which is to say a relation with Christ in his continuing or living embodiment as ascended and glorified,[102]

art is potentially one of them.

> There are multiple mediations in Christian arts and culture. But however "mediated," the ascended body always remains directly active.[103]

Understanding how music can aid this transformed awareness and identifying ways of facilitating it is a task that theology needs to take onboard. Davies does not develop the mediations of art in the context of transformation theology,[104] but one of the concluding points of Speelman's semiotics that presents music as "omnipresent," as opposed to the "non-here" nature of verbal semiotics, can at least indirectly evoke music's potential to lead us to an awareness of an all-present reality, in which we live and move. I would also suggest that, when seeking to discern which music can and does help to mediate the Christian experience, it is our transformed sensibility in Christ that is the basis for this. That music can be appropriate for aiding the

---

102. Ibid., 44.

103. Ibid., 57.

104. He does write on the theme of poetics and theology in chapter 8 of *A Theology of Compassion*. He identifies there the need for fundamental theology to interact with aesthetic and modern art, in order to be faithful to its calling to give reason of its faith to those outside it. He focuses on the science of poetry, or poetics, and analyses the different semiotic process at work in poetry as compared to ordinary speech, and compares them to theology, identifying aspects such as ambiguity, origination (the issue of the origin, "author," and creative process) and a transformed experience of the world (or as he says, "the heart of things") as seen through the experience of the writer. Although he also notes the differences between poetry and theology, and in particular the historical nature of theological discourse, the convergence with Haughton's understanding of the need for a "poetic theology" is noteworthy.

experience of Christ's embodied presence in the world, by virtue of its particular symbolic dynamics, does not imply that all music, everywhere and at any time serves that purpose. On the contrary, as Christ is available to be experienced in the world through a transformed sensibility, and music does, in fact, affect our corporal existence with such strength, there is a strong need for discernment, and for tools in that task. Taking this fact seriously implies integrating the reality of *sensus fidelium* into theological reflection. Due to the plural nature of the world we live in, and the difficulty or impossibility of any one person or group of people understanding "all" types of music, the only way to assess the usefulness of a given style or piece of music to mediate faith is by way of an inculturized discernment. Criteria from one culture alone cannot be the rule, as even a transformed sensibility will have a cultural feel to the music it values. This does not imply that musical sensibility would not benefit from education—simply that any formation given must be soundly situated within the setting of a living, embodied and shared faith, as well as on the recognition of the plurality of musical styles and expertise in the church. The hermeneutical reflection on music in chapter 2 sought to offer light and a possible tool to address this plurality.

Another implication for theological thought is that of giving greater attention to the embodied sensibility of those in theological formation, alongside and integrated with their intellectual education. This is not simply about including music or aesthetically oriented courses in seminaries and theological colleges, although these can certainly do no harm. It is rather about addressing the underlying issue of a transformed sensibility, a "converted" sensibility, in theological discourse. We have mentioned Sedmak's call to the conversion or self-transformation of the theologian or ethicist in taking seriously the role of thought in the world we live in, and Davies's mention of the theologian's call to "penitential reflection," when presenting the foundations or requirements of transformation theology. This recalls something of Lonergan's development of the theme of the conversion of the theologian, as seen in chapter 4.[105] If we recall, one of the concerns underlying Lonergan's development of the theme of conversion in theology is that of differing and conflicting opinions with regard to Christian doctrine, as a result of false or erroneous positions. The various dimensions of

---

105. Cf. Lonergan, "Theology in Its New Context."

"conversion" he offers are an attempt to address this reality. What this book is suggesting is that some of the misunderstandings that we come across in the evaluation and use of music in spirituality and theology are also based upon contradicting understandings of reality on the part of those who profess them.[106] Musical formation can help theology to focus on the person of the theologian in her dynamic of conversion, rather than solely on theological content. And taking it further, understanding better the link between conversion and music will lay the foundations for a theological understanding of art and music in Christianity, and their role in faith.

Chapter 4 focused on music in its reception, and underlined the aspects of conversion which music and art could help facilitate. In the light of the truth of faith of the ascension, as presented by Davies, I would suggest that Lonergan's notion of religious conversion be complemented with that of a specifically Christian form of affective conversion, that is to say, conversion with a decidedly more Christ-centered approach. We could perhaps refer to it as "Christian affective conversion," in recognition of the fact that there could undeniably be an affective dimension to other faith experiences outside the Christian realm.

Why an emphasis on what I would describe as affective conversion within the Christ-centered doctrine of the continued embodiment of Jesus? For the reasons already touched on in chapter 4, embodiment is one of the key issues to be understood in music, and I believe it is often fear of or alienation from our embodied existence that leads to suspicion or misapprehension of what music is about. A theology that works to integrate that dimension into its perspective could help to develop a spirituality that would sustain and encourage Christian music. Too often the very passion involved in creativity and especially that of musical creativity is divorced from the living out of faith (perhaps above all in liturgy but also beyond) when this cannot integrate the whole human dynamic of living and loving in its self-comprehension. Properly understood, affectivity and corporality (and sexuality, an inescapable part of our being human) are inseparable.

---

106. For example, I think a Neo-Platonic epistemology does not do justice to how we apprehend reality and music. The corporal nature of human life, which music is born of and accentuates, is much better served by an epistemology of critical realism.

Returning to Rosemary Haughton: she bases her whole theological vision on the reality of romantic love, the passionate love between a man and a woman as *the most adequate* expression of love with which to "understand" God; in fact, not only as a comparison with God's love, but as an example of it. According to Haughton, the birth of "romance" in the courts of Provence in the eleventh century was not something alien or tangential to Christianity, but rather *caused by it*, despite its being developed on the margins of or even in opposition to the institutional church. Romance has imbued our understanding of life, making it hard for us to imagine a consciousness in which the image of romantic love is not at the center of human concerns (perhaps as hard as it is to envisage the worldview before Copernicus). It is even harder to separate it from the excesses or banality of the same as it is often transmitted in contemporary culture. However, Haughton challenges readings of human passion that would only underline or trivialize its sexual nature, while keeping the physical and bodily nature of love as intrinsic to that experience. Passionate love is embodied and particular, and it is such because of its reference to Christian faith and Christian worldview.[107]

Her theological ground for developing this approach to Christianity, once again, is the incarnation and the historical life of Jesus of Nazareth—not in the superficial way of trying to read into the life of Christ aspects of human love or romance that are not in the Gospels, but rather in taking that fully human life, in all its power and complexity, as both the starting point and the reference point for all posterior theological reflection. She invites us to keep our eyes fixed on the of person Jesus of Nazareth, who "loved the Lord his God with all his heart, all his soul, all his mind and all his strength,"[108] who always loved those who were his own in the world[109] (men and women), calling them friends and sharing with them all he had learned from his Father,[110] even in the midst of misunderstandings and abandonment. This Jesus is the one who calls us into a similar relationship with him

---

107. It is in the face of Beatrice that Dante sees Christ: cf. Haughton, *Passionate God*, 51–53.

108. Cf. Mark 12:30.

109. Cf. John 13:1.

110. Cf. John 15:15.

in his Body: "Remain in my love!"[111] Christian affective conversion, in my understanding, is that of understanding one's whole life and calling as a personal and intimate answer of love in and for him, with all one's mind, heart, soul, and strength; that is to say, with a similarly passionate love.

Haughton is not alone in considering romantic or passionate love as one of the core experiences of human life without which it is difficult to imagine or grasp God's very being and love:

> In the present configuration of the modern city, the only universally "sharable" consciousness of spiritual experience is today that which is written in the circle of individual emotion and feeling of love.[112]

Sequeri, as we have seen in chapter 5, is one of the authors in whom reflections on aesthetics, music, and the quest for an understanding of faith that does justice to our affectivity and capacity of trust, come together. Jeremy Begbie underlines both that music is "inescapably bodily" and has strong connections with our emotional life.[113] Don Saliers touches on the same in a chapter of his book *Music and Theology* entitled "Music and the Body: Christian Ambivalence." Music, embodiment, our emotive and affective life, and our faith belong together.

Attention to these areas of Christian experience and thought would widen the framework within which to talk about music, and provide a more solid foundation for Christian artists to live out their faith more fully. It goes together with our understanding of the incarnation as the center point of revelation, by which the humanity of Jesus of Nazareth, in its historical manifestation, is also at the core of theological discourse. This could potentially be very fruitful for Christian musical creativity, as it highlights the fully human "nature" of Jesus Christ, and could allow creative activity to expand and deepen. For example, it has been commented that contemporary Christian music is weak in "laments," which are such an integral part of the Scriptures. I intuit that one underlying factor in causing this gap is a fear-inspired

---

111. John 15:9. Taken from the Holy Bible, New International Version®, NIV®. Copyright ©1973, 1978, 1984, 2011 by Biblica, Inc.™ Used by permission of Zondervan. All rights reserved worldwide.

112. Sequeri, *Sensibili allo spirito*, 13.

113. Cf. Begbie, *Theology, Music, and Time*, 15.

tendency to find an answer before or without experiencing the problem. The very intensity and complexity of the life and person of Jesus of Nazareth could enrich our models of Christian music, leaving space for the doubt, suffering, and growth that form part of our human journey of trusting in God, as it did Jesus. Christian music that seeks to reach out to non-believers needs to address this without fear.[114] Attention to this whole area would come under what could be called "Christian affective conversion," and would be a fruitful investment for music in and as theological praxis. Composing music, as well as good interpretation of it, implies connecting with areas of our consciousness that are not purely conceptual. The sensitivity of artists and musicians, which is not infrequently considered to be "overdeveloped" or difficult to work with in Christian communities, is more than just a strongly developed "ego" or lack of maturity, but is part and parcel, the glory and cross of one called to artistic expression and creativity, with all the emotional and corporal energy that this implies.

The Ascension, Discipleship, and the Call of the Christian Musician

> *I always feel as if I stood naked for the fire of the Almighty God*
> *to go through me—*
> *and it's a rather awful feeling.*
> *One has to be so terribly religious to be an artist.*
>
> —D. H. Lawrence[115]

This leads us into the second aspect or consequence of the encounter with the embodied presence of the ascended Jesus mentioned above: that of the call or commissioning.

> There are many gifts, but it is always the same Spirit; there are many ways of serving, but it is always the same Lord. There are many forms of activity but in everybody it is the same God

---

114. In my conversations with various Christian composers and songwriters, one factor I perceived was a certain "embarrassment" or need to justify the existence of songs whose content was not very clearly one of convinced faith. This is, I believe, a misunderstanding of the nature of faith, and responds to a more fundamentalist view of Christian believing than a balanced and healthy one.

115. Quoted in Steiner, *Real Presences*, 228.

who is at work in them all. The particular manifestation of the Spirit granted to each one is to be used for the general good.[116]

According to Davies, the call or commissioning that unfolds as a result of the encounter invites theology to reconsider the notion of "act" as the defining place of human freedom, not comprehended, however, within a speculative form of reasoning but with a motivational one, as presented in chapter 4. Saul, after and through his encounter with Jesus on the road to Damascus, is already, at least potentially, an apostle.[117] We will develop this point here in relation to that particular gift of the Spirit which is the call to make music.

In the moment we encounter Christ, the transformation it provokes is received, but is not merely passive: we are called to participate in the building up of that body. The active nature of Christian life is rooted in the very life of Jesus of Nazareth. He called his disciples to follow him, and to participate in the proclamation and building of the kingdom; calling and mission go together.[118] Christian life continues to unfold itself in this dynamic: life in Christ at the service of the kingdom. What Davies suggests is that the nature of Christian "acting" needs to be developed more in Christian thought and theology. I believe doing so in relation to the particular calling of the Christian musician would be helpful both for theology and for the task of developing a theology and spirituality to support this particular vocation of being a Christian artist. We already noticed in Speelman's analysis of musical semiotics that by its very nature music is dynamic, rather than static, and that listening to, playing, and composing music imply "following" it, rather than holding it "still" in order to "see," grasp, or understand it better. This would suggest a natural empathy between music and a theology of the act, with a particular emphasis on our "doing" in understanding faith. However, there is a need to deepen in the specific nature of the Christian call to make art. Haughton, talking about Dante, says of him that "he was not only a great poet, but a great Christian poet (which is not the same as a great poet who is also

---

116. 1 Cor 12:4–7

117. Cf. Acts 9: 15–16.

118. Cf. Mark 3:13–14 (NIV): "Jesus went up on a mountainside and called to him those he wanted, and they came to him. He appointed twelve . . . that they might be with him and that he might send them out to preach."

a Christian)."[119] The expression is eloquent, because too often these two callings are lived and perceived separately. One could ask: why are there so many Christians in our churches who are excellent musicians, but few who perceive and present themselves as Christian ones? This is, at least in part, because the Christian calling and the artistic one are perceived and understood separately. The resulting gap between the quality of Christian art and music inside church circles and beyond them is a normal consequence—one that is not caused so much by the secular nature of the world as by our lack of understanding of the artistic calling in Christian life.[120] Since both the artistic and the Christian vocation come from the same God, surely such a separation is unhelpful and unnecessary. Should not our artistic gifts be one way of expressing gratitude and love to God for our sustained salvation? The elements Davies offers as intrinsic to our "commissioning" are eloquent when related to the artistic calling.

He talks of the particularity of the calling: it is unique for each person—one life, one calling, which is that person's and no one else's, to be unfolded in the concrete space and time in which he or she lives.

> It will not be a general commissioning but a particular one, worked out in the concrete circumstances of an individual life: precisely within and not at an angle to the sensible reality of each and every one who is touched by this commissioning.[121]

There are few callings in which the particularity of human life is more emphasized than in the artistic. Where else is the person acting and the product of their act so intimately linked? The very essence of the artistic calling is in the individual creativity of the one "creating" (composing, writing, painting). Not only can no two people compose the same piece of music, but music born of the same person usually tends to have some similarity, some element of the "creator" carved therein, even allowing for creative growth.

---

119. Haughton, *Passionate God*, 51.

120. As a musician and composer, this was my own experience for many years, during which the connection between the call to evangelize and the gift and vocation of being able to make music were lived separately. It is one I see repeated too often in those I work with pastorally. It is immensely liberating for people called to an artistic vocation to understand it as an intrinsic part of the way they serve, love, and follow Christ.

121. Davies, "Interrupted Body," 54.

Furthermore, when Davies talks about the act, he is precise in that it is not all human "doing" that fulfills that category. He talks about the act in analogous terms to those of Lonergan's fourth step of intentional analysis, and when he talks about moral conversion, emphasizing that the person "becomes" through their actions:

> For the act in its pure sense is not simply what we happen to do, far less is it what is done to us. An act always follows judgement, and decision. . . . The act is therefore the realisation of who we are . . . as embodied human beings, functioning within the causal flow, as an expression of our considered judgement and values. We are held responsible for what we do in this sense. Who we are, or more exactly who we become in the moment of the act . . . [122]

Once again, I submit that although limit situations in which we are radically defined by the choices we make may not be frequent for anyone, and the daily grind of habit-forming work needs to be as present in an artist's life with regard to their work as in any other, still it is true that in good creative work of any sort, we are more confronted with our "real" reasons and thoughts than in many other fields. One cannot write if one is not in touch with oneself at some "real" level. This, in my experience, is the essential reason why writing and composing is, at times, so difficult, because one cannot do it in a dispersed or distracted frame of mind, without interiorizing or paying internal attention. Coming back to Lonergan's understanding of the aesthetic experience, his description of the dynamic of the artist in the quest to express meaning is a lucid one:

> That meaning lies within the consciousness of the artist but, at first, it is only implicit, folded up, veiled, unrevealed, unobjectified. Aware of it, the artist has to get a hold of it; he is impelled to behold, inspect, dissect, enjoy, repeat it; and this means objectifying, unfolding, making explicit, unveiling, revealing.[123]

All in all, it is hard work, and implies quite an intense level of experience and self-awareness. In artistic work, the particularity of a person's calling and the call to act, are very united. In music, this

---

122. Davies, "Transforming Theology," 17.
123. Lonergan, *Method in Theology*, 63–64.

includes the dynamic not only of composition but of performance and our presence therein:

> Pure act has to take account not only of what is done, even deliberatively, but also of the way it is done: whether it is done as the *performance* of a pre-existing narrative or whether it is the *realisation* of our most fundamental and constitutive freedom in history. Whether and to what extent it is one or the other will depend upon the extent to which we put ourselves at risk in what we do, by acting personally, individually and freely.[124]

Although Davies in the above quotation uses the word "performance" in a different sense, its application to musical performance is related and valid: how music is played—its actualization in the present moment and its implications for the musician should not be underestimated. This is the daily dilemma of any artist, in every piece and performance: the total involvement of who they are in every performance, which implies taking the risk of doing things their own way, and implies a considerable amount of self-exposure and generosity.

Theological reflection on the creative process of the artist and the dynamic involved in musical creativity is necessary and even urgent, towards the formation and preparation of Christian musicians. It is interesting that although transformation theology has not yet developed a reflection on artistic activity in its understanding of the Christian act, other authors have. In a book on the centrality of the resurrection to theology, which echoes many of the intuitions or concerns of the writers of King's College, A. J. Kelly speaks eloquently of the potential of the artistic act to inform theology. Although the quotation is long, it seems an appropriate intuition with which to finish this chapter on contemporary music in and as theological praxis:

> I would suggest that artistic creativity is not simply an illustration of faith in an intrinsic sense, but more an inner dimension

---

124. Davies, "Transforming Theology," 17. Arendt herself links her understanding of the act with a person's individuality and personal reason for being: "With word and deed we insert ourselves into the human world, and this insertion is like a second birth, in which we confirm and take upon ourselves the naked fact of our original physical appearance. This insertion is not forced upon us by necessity, like labor, and is not prompted by utility, like work. It may be stimulated by the presence of others whose company we may wish to join, but it is never conditioned by them; its impulse springs from the beginning which came into the world when we were born and to which we respond by beginning something new on our own initiative." Arendt, *Human Condition*, 176–77.

of resurrection-faith itself . . . where a phenomenologically attuned theology and contemplative Christian art meet. For when faith is met with the phenomenon of this world-transforming event, however depicted or expressed, only an artistically conscious faith can appropriately respond to it by devising a form expressive of what originally disrupted all mundane forms of expression. Art is, as it were, an inner moment in the phenomenality of the resurrection, be it in music, painting or even poetic expression.[125]

---

125. Kelly, *Resurrection Effect*, 35.

Conclusion

> *Etrange duo où je parle à deux voix,*
> *recevant mon souffle des paroles de l'autre.*
> *« Ceci est mon corps », et sa voix est la mienne.*
> *... nos deux corps voisés.*
> —Jean-Pierre Sonnet[1]

> *And the world is alive with moving grace.*
> *Hold my hand in Your side, 'til*
> *Touching You, feeling You*
> *Tasting You, breathing You*
> *Knowing Your life is within my reach...*
> *Touching You, healing me,*
> *Tasting You, breathing me*
> *Flowing... Your life's running through my veins.*[2]

THE UNDERLYING IMAGE IN THE ABOVE SONG IS THAT OF JOHN 20:25–27, in which Thomas asks (and Jesus acquiesces) to be allowed to place his hand in Jesus' wounded side. A superficial reading of this encounter perceives a doubtful man needing the ultimate (and uncomfortable) proof of physical contact in order to believe the unbelievable: Jesus is not dead; the unspeakable tragedy that had unfolded before their eyes, has not had the final word: their beloved teacher is among them. There are, however, other readings:

> Thomas' obstinacy is not that of insensitivity, it is that of the super-sensitive person whose only defense is in disguise. He wanted—how he wanted—his beloved. He wanted Jesus himself, for himself. He got him. He got all that he had asked and

---

1. "Strange duet in which I speak in two voices, receiving my breath from the words of the other. 'This is my body', and his voice is mine [...] our two voiced bodies." Sonnet, *Le Corps Voisé. Petite Suite Eucharistique*, 17. Translation mine.

2. Chorus of M. L. Heaney, "Dancing in our Minds", the song that gathers something of the theological and spiritual backdrop I propose for the comprehension of music in theology. Cf. http://www.fmverbumdei.com/main/maeveheaney/index.html.

much more, he received the full flood of that passionate love that longs to respond even, and especially, to such demands as that of Thomas.[3]

In other words, in this scene we are perhaps not witnessing the return to the flock of the prodigal disciple, but rather a highly charged re-encounter of two people who shared a deep, felt friendship—a friendship Thomas was not willing to lose, and one Jesus was only too willing to confirm and even take deeper. We started this book with an awareness of the difficulty of faith transmission in the present moment, due the "paralyzed sensibility" of contemporary western culture. Our questions were: why is music so important in people's faith lives? Can it help mediate the Christian Word to us and if so, why and how? Could understanding music enrich theology? We finish evoking the image of a disciple so "in-love"[4] with his master that he cannot survive on the witness of others alone, but has to touch, with his own hands, the body of the One he is to confess as his Lord and his God! Music as a means of mediation of Christian faith, and Thomas' hand reaching out to Jesus' open wound: where is the link? In the words above of Jean-Pierre Sonnet: the voiced body. We live and move and breathe in the body of our God made flesh. Could it not somehow be this Body that is voiced and expressed when song or music emerges from a person immersed in Christ? Is that thought too audacious? Or is it simply Christian?

Our constant thread has been that of the Incarnation and music: taking the humanity of Christ seriously and to its last consequences—the presence of Jesus Christ embodied with and in humanity, from the moment of his Incarnation to the present, and until the end of time as we know it. This is our faith. This is also the stumbling block for many admirers of Christian values: the particularity of Jesus of Nazareth, in flesh and blood, as God's own Word spoken to us. "[D]ifficult to believe or not, the entire Christian faith nevertheless stands or falls on the premise that God became human in Christ."[5] Taking Jesus' hu-

---

3. Haughton, *The Passionate God*, 209.

4. The term is expressed with the underlying comprehension of Lonergan's "being-in-love" as the plenitude of our knowing, and the density of Haughton's analysis of the dynamic of human passionate love.

5. Boeve, *God Interrupts History*, 161.

manity seriously implies, in turn, taking our own seriously. As Rahner rightly intuited when talking about the body in the order of salvation:

> God is man to all eternity, so that to all eternity we cannot think rightly about this God or express him properly unless we add to our thinking what we men and women are as well.[6]

We are embodied creatures, and our relationship with God in Christ is in and through our bodies, *and* his. Finally, taking the Incarnation seriously also means that it is through that which is human that the living God meets us. "Is this not the ultimate meaning of incarnation: that the 'all-too-human' speaks for God, without diminishing God in the process and without assimilating humanity into God?"[7]

The human reality that "speaks" for God, in this book, is music—music as one way of bridging the link between the human hand that seeks to touch God, and God's love poured out into the world through the wounds of Christ. And contemporary sensibility *is* similar to that of Thomas, in many ways super-sensitive and reluctant to accept or trust anything that cannot be touched and experienced. Artistic sensibility definitely is. And although it is true that this sensibility is often frayed or disperse, and the need to feel can leave people paralyzed or trapped in a world of sensations, it is still part and parcel of our human condition as embodied creatures, and God is not 'out of reach' of humanity's grasp. Jesus can still 'take our hand' and place it in his side, precisely because our connection to God in Christ is real, intimate and corporal.[8] We have begun to appreciate here how can do just that through music, because music has something to say which other expressive forms do not, or cannot.

By way of conclusion, let me simply draw together what I feel has been addressed, achieved and the areas which I feel are either weaker, or simply beyond the scope of the book and therefore left open and in need of further reflection and research.

---

6. Rahner, "The Body in the Order of Salvation," 80.

7. Boeve, *God Interrupts History*, 172.

8. "[W]hen Paul says we are the body of Christ he is speaking not corporately but corporally. This statement is opaque to our rationalistic culture," Moore, *The Contagion of Jesus: Doing Theology as if it Mattered*, 197, quoting the study of Robinson on St. Paul's understanding of the body: Robinson, *The Body*.

From Spirituality to Theology: A Biographical Note

That which started as an intuition has become a conviction. Research for this book began based on an intuition about the capacity of music to reach the human heart with something of who God is, in a way verbal communication or preaching struggles to. It was an intuition based on years of pastoral experience, the "it is so, therefore it must be true"[9] we spoke about in the introduction. That intuition has become a theological conviction.

One way of describing my experience during its writing is with the image used by Chesterton, when he describes how his discovery of the truth of Christian faith was like that of the English yachtsman who, having gone abroad to discover new lands, found himself "discovering" England again, in Brighton.[10] This has happened at two levels, the first in relation to my Irish roots: Oliver Davies, author of the doctrinal aspects of Transformation Theology, is Welsh, and this cultural background colors his theological approach.[11] The particularity of the Christian world-view of those parts of Europe which were not reached by the Roman empire; a form of Christianity which did not internalize the over-riding tendency to separate (and often oppose) spirit and matter is one which echoes with my cultural background and artistic sensibility. The most well known example can be found in what is called "The Deer's Cry," known as the Breastplate of St. Patrick, although it was surely posterior to his time,[12] but "Celtic spirituality is a thoroughly embodied spirituality in its general theology, and not just in its literary genres."[13] Aside from the more superficial or uninformed aspects of contemporary interest in Celtic spirituality, its non-dualistic mode of apprehending and relating to reality remains a source of reflection and enrichment for theology in Europe.

Secondly, I have "found myself" in the Christian (and very Catholic) truth of the mystical body of Christ, one of the four sources

---

9. Cf. Haughton, *The Passionate God*, 274.

10. Cf. Chesterton, *Orthodoxy*, 2–6.

11. Cf. Davies, "An Introduction to Celtic Spirituality," 3–25. I am grateful to professor Davies for the personal conversations in which he brought this to my attention.

12 "I arise today through the strength of heaven; Light of sun, Radiance of moon, Splendour of fire, Speed of lightning, Swiftness of wind, Depth of sea, Stability of earth, Firmness of rock."

13. Mackey, in the introduction to the book *Celtic Spirituality* edited by Davies, xvi.

of spirituality of the missionary community I am a member of (along with the Indwelling of the Trinity, the Eucharist and Mary), and in many ways, my own spiritual "home." Within this truth of faith the notion of the person in the role of transmitting Christian faith, and that of the various forms of conversion presented by Lonergan and those who develop his work as a source of its effectiveness, come together:

> No means or method will ever achieve the same strength, conviction or vitality of the living, personal and direct word of the missionary who is convinced by and in love with Christ [. . .] The intimate union of the apostle with Christ will allow her to feel vitally linked with all her brothers and sisters with bonds which are stronger than those of flesh and blood.[14]

A theological understanding of the musical vocation within the same paradigm that grounds the calling to consecrated missionary life opens potentially fruitful avenues of future work in the area of spirituality and the arts.

Emphases Explored and Areas of Future Research

The reflections of this book do not claim to be exhaustive, and will surely need to be developed, contrasted and at times, I have no doubt, corrected. But they offer some necessary foundational reflections on what music is and how theology can situate, comprehend and be enriched by this particular aspect of human life and art form. The founder of the community I am a member of,[15] dedicated to prayer and ministry of the Word, gave us a (Spanish) rule for getting a point across when preaching, which I am going to apply in this conclusion: "Announce what you intend to say, say it, and then explain what you have said." Let me state once again that at the heart my understanding of music, and therefore at the centre of this book is the analysis offered by Willem Marie Speelman in chapter 3, as it is in his thought that we begin to appreciate the specific differences between verbal and musical "communication." If, in a Christian understanding of the Word, we are referring not only to linguistics, but to "any expression of religious meaning," including art, or symbols, as Lonergan reminds

---

14 *Constitutions of the Verbum Dei Missionary Fraternity*, 51.
15. Jaime Bonet Bonet VDMF.

us,[16] then theological discourse on Revelation and the Word needs to understand each semiotic system for what it is, in order to integrate them in its thought. Until music is truly understood and assumed by theological aesthetics, there is work to be done.

Every choice one makes includes the exclusion of another possibility. Bringing together two areas of research has implied a constant dynamic of comprehension and relevance of one to the other, which somehow limits the depth with which each area can be developed. This is the case both with the authors of the area of musicology and theology. For example, the need to open theology to areas of musical research beyond western music has implied *not* focusing on any one musicological author's approach, but integrating those of ethnomusicology as well. Each author would merit more time and attention. The same can be said of the theologians I have brought to the theme. I have not taken any one theologian as the only foundation. I have "stood on the shoulders of giants"[17] of the past, in order to see further into the issues of the present and the future. There are useful and even necessary studies to be undertaken on the thought on music of Augustine or even dealing more at depth with music in Hans Urs von Balthasar, from whom we have drawn our first reflections. The reasons I have not done so are clearly presented, but it remains a limiting factor.

Lieven Boeve talks about the challenge of contemporary theology to have both "contextual plausibility and theological legitimacy," as a method of going about theology, given that "the overlap between human existence and Christianity as a provider of meaning has become smaller."[18] The attempt to dialogue in an interdisciplinary way with the world of music and with thought about music is the reason for both chapters I and II. Catholic theology and philosophy are intrinsically linked, and therefore this book is enriched by the insights of leading academics in musicology and ethnomusicology. The attentiveness and clarity of their investigations enrich theology's attempt to understand music, giving us tools to analyze and critique the context and form of theology's discourse on music. Dialogue is always mutually enriching. A question that has emerged in the process of writing this book is that

---

16. Lonergan, *Method in Theology*, 112.

17. Famous aphorism attributed to Isaac Newton: "If I have seen further, it is only because I have stood on the shoulders of giants."

18. Cf. Boeve, *God Interrupts History*, 1;5.

of what theology brings to *musicological* studies. As I come to the discussion more from within the theological field, I only hope that future work and collaboration together will allow studies on music answer that question.

The reader interested in music will miss more practical examples from music itself. The choice not to focus on any one genre or composer within contemporary music was a conscious one, born of the realization at the earlier stages of research that we are, in fact, lacking in theological aesthetics a foundational discourse on the theological comprehension of music in itself. To integrate a specific analysis of any one piece of music would automatically focus attention on that style and on the areas of discernment and taste. To my mind, it would have been premature, and would have contradicted the explicit aim of the book to provide theological grounding for contemporary music in general. The few examples of my own music that are included aim to illustrate "from within," as it were, that which the book is trying to say, and I hope as such they do not distract. They also are fruit of the expression of a particular style and sensibility, and are in no way proposed as exemplar. However, as I finish writing, ideas for a project which would integrate examples and application of the research presented here are already emerging.

We have not dealt with two important areas of research into music. The first is the role and use of music in liturgy. It is especially significant when one realizes that most Catholic theology on music is focused in this area. However, the hope is that its findings will be useful in that field. In the words of Miram T. Winter, who does focus on music and singing in liturgy:

> [T]he discourse of the church for a long time has been separate from reflection in the musical world on the meaning of music. This division is no longer tenable.[19]
>
> Any theology of church music that arises out of the present time must be firmly rooted in an understanding of the music of this world.[20]

This endeavor would imply bringing together with theological aesthetics reflections from the fields of liturgy, ritual studies, ecclesi-

---

19. Winter, *Why Sing?*, 237.
20. Ibid., 22.

ology and missiology. The use of some form of musical analysis that takes into account the plurality of ways of receiving and appreciating music, such as Nattiez's model of chapter 2, would be indispensable in such a venture.

The other area we have not dealt with except in passing is that of the revelatory capacity of music beyond the realm of explicit Christian inspiration. Does God reach out to and touch human hearts in non-Christian art and music? How can or is God's presence felt or "known" in the creative process in which no explicit experience of Christ is present, at least, to use Rahner's terms, categorically? I have no doubt that some of the reflections on creative process in Christian composers would find an echo in the dynamic of creativity beyond the realm of Christian faith, as God rarely overlooks the natural human process of things in revealing Godself to us. However, I have not drawn out my thoughts in this area, and these are questions which cannot be ignored and imply further thought and reflection. I sense that the findings of this book could be fruitfully brought together with some of Rahner's intuitions on the universal gift of grace to human freedom, or Lonergan's teaching on the double mission of the Spirit and the Son (which he calls the inner and outer Word) in reaching out to the world.

There are different motivations behind all thought. Rahner wrote a piece on the nature of theological thought entitled, "a theology one can live with." Seeking to address the concern of whether there is, indeed, a theology that one can live with, he issues the challenge: "Really, just what kind of a life is actually meant?"[21] Art and music, by their very nature, are free. Music may exist, or it may not. Life can move on without music. And yet could we imagine life without music? Would we want to? This book is born of the desire to make life more livable, in Jesus, and the conviction that music is an invaluable gift and resource which the Church can and should understand better and make more use of. Aware that accepting that challenge implies more than just music but an openness to the wedding of our voices with Christ's and the "voicing" of our bodies, touching open wounds and drinking of his life poured out . . .

> Thomas wanted and needed to see and touch the wounded body of Jesus [. . .] This is where faith has to begin, that kind of faith which earns the title 'blessed' for those who embrace

21. Rahner, "A Theology One Can Live With," 99–100.

it, here, at that place where the human heart of Jesus marks the utmost centre,[22]

I pray:

Invoke your Holy Spirit upon them!
Raise up among us men and women endowed with creative powers, thinkers, poets, artists. We have need of them.[23]

---

22. Haughton, *The Passionate God*, 210–11.
23. Cf. Rahner, "Prayer for Creative Thinkers," 130.

Appendix

WE ENDED CHAPTER 6 REFLECTING ON THE ARTISTIC VOCATION AS AN intrinsic part of our Christian calling, one way of responding to Christ in the service of the Church, his Body. We noted the negative effect it has, both on music and on Christian faith, when these two aspects of our human and Christian life are divorced from one another. This appendix seeks to offer some primarily pastoral and sometimes personal reflections on the coming together of the two, drawn both from my own experience and from that of musicians and composers I know or have had contact with during the time of research of this doctorate, and who have been gracious and generous enough to share their experiences and thoughts on the subject. The thoughts of these pages are colored by their concerns, experiences and honesty.[1] The aim is to address one of the intuitions mentioned during the course of the book: that of bringing together in theological reflection the experience, work and perspectives of musicians themselves, as well as to open doors for future research. There are many areas which could be looked at, but we will touch on one: a reflection on the similarities and tensions involved in being a Christian "artist."

---

1. The reflections of these composers have been accessed either through face-to-face conversations, over the phone, or via email. This is a theme on which I continue to reflect, and on which, in relation to rock music, an essay of mine will appear in a book on that area shortly.

The Christian and Artistic Callings: Similarities and Tensions

> *But if all prophets are artists,*
> *then surely not all artists are prophets . . .*
>
> —Balthasar[2]

What happens when the Christian and the artistic calling come together in the one person, when an artist encounters Christ, or when an encounter with Christ unfolds into a mission in music or art? I would suggest a dynamic of tension and completeness. All of the composers I spoke with expressed the tremendous grace and joy involved in being able to live their musical gifts in the service of their faith, the sense of participating in something of the Creator's joy in birthing music, and in allowing God's grace somehow be expressed to others through their own unique artistic expression. Some of them also spoke explicitly of the difficulty there can be in living as Christian and artist, and the need to not sacrifice one to the other. As we have seen in chapter 5, both Balthasar and Sequeri bring into their theological reflection the similarities and differences between the artist and the religious person. As a similarity, for example, they identify the sense of calling and the fact that both are incapable of inscribing the absolute in the singular, although the call to do so underlies both! They also identify differences, however, and these differences are not coincidental or superficial, nor merely obstacles to be removed. Rather they are essential elements that come together in a life called to creative ministry. Understanding them is important in helping to facilitate the intrinsic (creative) tension that is part and parcel of being a Christian artist, tension which, when misinterpreted, can become a stumbling block. One of the differences mentioned, for example, is that the religious person receives his or her call in total obedience, whereas the artist, in the most perfect autonomy. The figure below identifies others which have emerged during reflection on my own creative process and that of others.

---

2. Balthasar, *Glory of the Lord*, 1:43.

Points of Tension between the Christian and the Artistic Calling

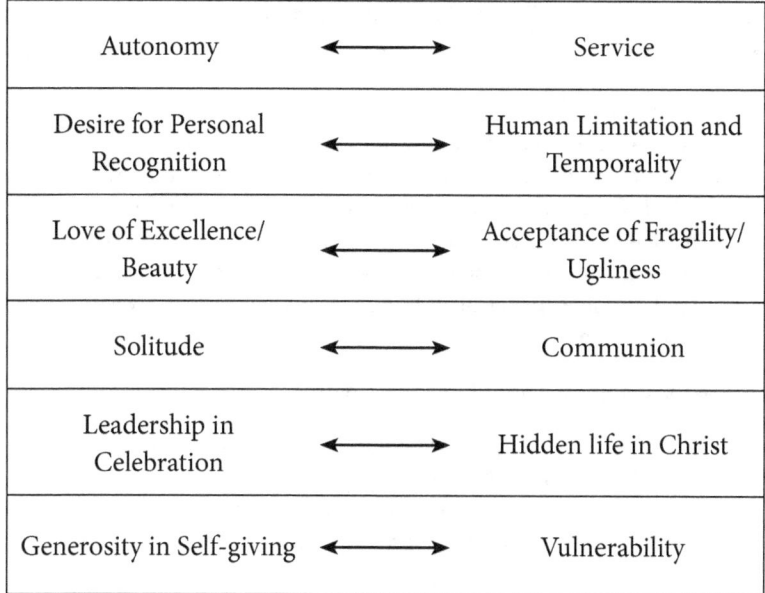

Figure 7.1

Steiner, when seeking to understand the phenomenon of art, asking why there is art at all, talks of the impulse behind its creation as a type of envy: "I believe that the making into being by the poet, artist and, in a way yet to be defined, by the composer, is *counter-creation*."[3] Picasso talks of the "other craftsman" who worked in six days! Something like: "Why was I not at the beginning, why is not mine the organizing deed of form coming into meaning?"[4] He qualifies this statement with an observation on the difference between men and women in this dynamic, which I would agree with in part, but as an intuition, I think it holds truth. Does genuine art not share some of God's own sense of creating? Surely to create implies a strong dynamic of self-appropriation and awareness of self. Rahner, in a short but inspiring piece on our need for creative writers, talks of those who "are engaged in constantly producing new expressions of their own nature

---

3. Steiner, *Real Presences*, 203.
4. Ibid., 205.

and spirit, [people] who are the architects of themselves."[5] Creating or composing implies a strong sense of self. However much one affirms that Christian life brings us to wholeness, following Another, and coming to the fullness of oneself in that journey implies dialectic tension. John Paul II talks about the *pathos* of the artist as a participation in God's own pathos:

> None can sense more deeply than you artists, ingenious creators of beauty that you are, something of the pathos with which God at the dawn of creation looked upon the work of his hands…you have admired the work of your inspiration, sensing in it some echo of the mystery of creation with which God, the sole creator of all things, has wished in some way to associate you.[6]

This pathos is not without tension or pain!

> *To be a poet and not to know the trade,*
> *To be a lover and repel all women;*
> *Twin ironies by which great saints are made,*
> *The agonising pincer-jaws of Heaven.*[7]

One is given the grace of sharing God's creative power and called to live in the awareness that it is a gift; one creates with all one's being, in such a way that what is born bears the mark of the artist, and yet one wants it to reflect only God; that which is born is meant for the world, yet for that to be so, one's heart seeks to live for God above and beyond all others; one must speak of the heights and depths of human experience, in all their pain and anguish,[8] without falling into the temptation of desperation. Beautiful as it may be, as an expression of the beauty God is, it is no easy calling to be a Christian artist. There is a dialectic dynamic, (cross and glory), intrinsic to the calling of a Christian to artistic creation.

In chapter 5 we have already spoken of the paradox in Christian spirituality of the beautiful and that which is perceived as ugly, or fragile. An aspect which is related to this is that of the quest for excel-

---

5. Rahner, "Prayer for Creative Thinkers," 130.
6. John Paul II, *Letter to Artists*, 1.
7. Patrick Kavanagh, "Sanctity," in his *Collected Poems*, 17.
8. "In words and in images, in their whole attitude and presentation they express what is in man because they proclaim what they themselves experience. And in expressing this let them express *everything*." Rahner "Prayer for Creative Thinkers," 130.

lence intrinsic to any artistic venture, and that of the call to inclusion and participation. In the name of inclusivity, at times the quality of Christian music has deteriorated. Both values need to be recognized and somehow defended, without one excluding the other. Christian artists, by their very calling, are at the very centre of attention when they offer their work as a means to somehow sense God's presence. Once again, the dialectic provoked is not an easy one. Contemporary culture tends to focus on musician and music, singer and song, as one. As a musician becomes popular, the composer or musician is thrown into the limelight. When the music shared is born of the experience of faith, and the person offering it is seeking to express *all* that Jesus is for them, in the hope of transmitting something of that faith, the openness required implies making oneself very vulnerable.[9] And the process of giving generously and retreating in order to write more is costly and purifying. Davies speaks of the human act as a place of radical and even disturbing freedom, for its openness and vulnerability.[10] The holding together of the call to follow Christ in and through music lives and moves in this realm.

Sedmak, when talking about the fundamental praxis of Jesus as a model for our own, states that "divine causality presents itself often in the mode of Damascus, it does not come 'cheap', without self-transformation, self-renewal, repentance and the commitment to new beginnings, however small."[11] He says it implies a process of kenosis. It would be helpful for Christian musicians to apprehend this truth: it is a costly vocation. Perhaps this is what is needed. Perhaps this form of pain is redemptive, and it births something of the "era's new heart," as sung by Cuban song-writer, Silvio Rodriguez, in a song that evokes much of what our truth of the Mystical Body, presented above all in chapter 6, seeks to present:

> *The era is birthing a heart.*
> *She's running out of strength, so great is the pain.*
> *So we must come running to help her,*
> *For it is the very future that is at stake.*[12]

9. I am indebted to Cristobal Fones, Chilean singer and songwriter, for the shared music making and conversations in which this realization came to light.

10. Cf., Davies, "Transforming Theology," 18.

11. Sedmak, "Wound of Knowledge," 155.

12. Rodriguez, "Era está pariendo un corazón." *Al final de este viaje*, 1997. "La era está pariendo un corazón/ no puede más—se muere de dolor / Y hay que acudir corriendo, pues se cae . . . / el porvenir." Translation mine.

These tensions are to be found both inside and outside the person of the artist. It has been said that the maturity of a Christian community, can be read in their capacity to assume and integrate their artists. If it is true that "Genius is the capacity for productive reaction against one's training,"[13] it is normal that there be some tension between belonging and creative expression. However, there are also tensions which are internal to the person creating. American composer, Aaron Copland eloquently describes the inner struggle a person sometimes faces in the moment of composing:

> The inspired moment may sometimes be described as a kind of hallucinatory state of mind: one half of the personality emotes and dictates while the other half listens and notates. The half that listens had better look the other way, had better simulate a half attention only, for the half that dictates is easily disgruntled and avenges itself for too close inspection by fading entirely away.[14]

Painful and demanding process, which, however is also a birthing place:

> *What happens next*
> *Is a music that you never would have known*
> *To listen for . . .*
> *You are like a rich man entering heaven*
> *Through the ear of a raindrop. Listen now again.*
>
> —Seamus Heaney[15]

---

13. Berenson, quoted in Storr, *Music and the Mind*, 115.
14. Copland, *Music and Imagination*, 43.
15. Heaney, "Rain Stick."

Bibliography

Principle Sources

Balthasar, Hans Urs von. "Celibate Existence Today." In *Explorations in Theology*, 4:383-97.

———. *Die Entwicklung der Musikalischen Idee: Versuch einer Synthese der Musik*. Braunschweig, 1925. Translated into Italian by Pierangelo Sequeri and published as *Lo sviluppo dell'idea musicale: Saggio di una sintesi della musica*. Milan: Glossa, 1995.

———. *Explorations in Theology*. Translated by A. V. Littledale et al. 4 vols. San Francisco: Ignatius, 1989-1995.

———. "Fides Christi: An Essay on the Consciousness of Christ." In *Explorations in Theology*, 2:43-79.

———. *The Glory of the Lord: A Theological Aesthetics*. Translated by Erasmo Leiva-Merikakis et al., edited by Joseph Fessio and John Riches. Edinburgh: T. & T. Clark, 1982-1989.

———. "God Speaks as Man." In *Explorations in Theology*, 1:69-93.

———. "Katholische Religion und Kunst." *Schweizeriche Rundschau* 27 (1927) 44-54.

———. *Love Alone Is Credible*. San Francisco: Ignatius, 2004.

———. *Prayer*. San Francisco: Ignatius, 1986.

———. "Religion and Kunst." *Volkswohl* (*Wien*) 18 (1928) 355-65.

———. "Revelation and the Beautiful." In *Explorations in Theology*, 1:95-126.

———. "Seeing, Believing, and Eating." In *Explorations in Theology*, 2:491-502.

———. "Seeing, Hearing, and Reading within the Church." In *Explorations in Theology*, 2:473-90.

———. "Theology and Sanctity." In *Explorations on Theology* 1:181-209.

———. "A Theology of the Secular Institute." In *Explorations in Theology*, 3:421-57.

———. "Tribute to Mozart." Translated by Maria Shrady. *Communio* 28 (2001) 398-99.

———. "Truth and Life." In *Explorations in Theology*, 3:269-77.

———. "La Verità è Sinfonica: Aspetti del Pluralismo Cristiano." Translated by Riccardo Rota Graziosi. In *Gesù e il Cristiano*, 253-304. Scritti minori 25. Milan: Jaca Book, 1998.

———. "What Is Distinctively Christian in the Experience of God." In *Explorations in Theology*, 2:29-40.

———. "Who Is the Church." In *Explorations in Theology*, 2:143-91.

Davies, Oliver. *Celtic Christianity in Early Medieval Wales: The Origins of the Welsh Spiritual Tradition*. Cardiff: University of Wales Press, 1996.

———. "Fundamental Theology and the Word." Given at the "Giornata di Studio" of the Department of Fundamental Theology, 2008. Online: http://www.unigre.it/Struttura_didattica/teologia/specifico/dipartimento_fondamentale_it.php.

———. "History and Tradition: Catholicism and the Challenge of Globalised Modernity." In *Edward Schillebeeckx and Contemporary Theology*, edited by Lieven Boeve, Frederiek Depoortere, and Stephen van Erp, 183–93. London: T. & T. Clark, 2010.

———. "The Interrupted Body." In Davies et al., *Transformation Theology: Church in the World*, 37–62.

———. "An Introduction to Celtic Spirituality." In *Celtic Spirituality*, edited by Oliver Davies and Thomas O'Loughlin, 3–25.

———. "Lost Heaven." In *Transformation Theology: Church in the World*, 11–36.

———. "Reading the Burning Bush: Voice, World, and Holiness." *Modern Theology* 22/3 (2006) 439–48.

———. "Soundings: Towards a Theological Poetics of Silence." In *Silence and the Word: Negative Theology and Incarnation*, edited by Oliver Davies and Denys Turner, 201–22. Cambridge: Cambridge University Press, 2002.

———. "The Theological Aesthetics." In *The Cambridge Companion to Hans Urs von Balthasar*, edited by Edward T. Oakes and David Moss. Cambridge: Cambridge University Press, 2004.

———. *A Theology of Compassion: Metaphysics of Difference and the Renewal of Tradition*. London: SCM, 2001.

———. *Touching God: Transforming Theology*. Oxford: Oxford University Press, forthcoming.

———. "Transforming Theology: A New Catholic Theology for Europe?" Conference given in Leuven, December 2008. Later published as "History and Tradition: Catholicism and the Challenge of Globalised Modernity." Referenced above.

Davies, Oliver, and Fiona Bowie. *Celtic Christian Spirituality: Medieval and Modern*. London: SPCK, 1995.

Davies, Oliver, Paul D. Janz, and Clemens Sedmak. *Transformation Theology: Church in the World*. Edinburgh: T. & T. Clark, 2007.

Davies, Oliver, and Thomas O'Loughlin. *Celtic Spirituality*. Classics of Western Spirituality. New York: Paulist, 1999.

Davies, Oliver, and Denys Turner, editors. *Silence and the Word: Negative Theology and Incarnation*. Cambridge: Cambridge University Press, 2002.

García-Rivera, Alejandro. *The Community of the Beautiful: A Theological Aesthetics*. Collegeville, MN: Liturgical, 1999.

———. "The Cosmic Frontier: Towards a Natural Anthropology." *CTNS Bulletin: The Center for Theology and the Natural Sciences* 15/4 (1995) 1–6.

———. "The Whole and the Love of Difference." In *From the Heart of Our People: Latino/a Explorations in Systematic Theology*, edited by Orlando Espín and Miguel S. Días, 54–83. Maryknoll, NY: Orbis, 1999.

———. "In Whom We Live and Move." In Alejandro García-Rivera and Thomas Scirghi, *Living Beauty: The Art of Liturgy*, 73–101.

———. *A Wounded Innocence: Sketches for a Theology of Art*. Collegeville, MN: Liturgical, 2003.

García-Rivera, Alejandro, and Thomas Scirghi. *Living Beauty: The Art of Liturgy*. Lanham, MD: Rowman & Littlefield, 2008.

Haughton, Rosemary. *Images for Change: The Transformation of Society*. New York: Paulist, 1997.

———. *The Passionate God*. London: Darton, Longman, and Todd, 1981.

———. *The Transformation of Man: A Study of Conversion and Community*. London: G. Chapman, 1967.

———. "Women and the Church." *Thought* 66/263 (1991) 398–412.

Janz, Paul D. "The Coming Righteousness." In Davies et al., *Transformation Theology: Church in the World*, 89–114.

———. *The Command of Grace: A New Theological Apologetics*. London: T. & T. Clark, 2009.

———. "Divine Causality and the Nature of Theological Questioning." *Modern Theology* 23/3 (2007) 317–48.

———. *God, the Mind's Desire: Reference, Reason, and Christian Thinking*. Cambridge: Cambridge University Press, 2004.

———. "Radical Orthodoxy and the New Culture of Obscurantism." *Modern Theology* 20/3 (2004) 363–405.

———. "Revelation as Divine Causality." In Davies et al., *Transformation Theology: Church in the World*, 63–88.

John Paul II, Pope. *Fides et Ratio*. September 14, 1998. Online: http://www.vatican.va/holy_father/john_paul_ii/encyclicals/documents/hf_jp-ii_enc_15101998_fides-et-ratio_en.html.

———. *Letter of His Holiness Pope John Paul II to Artists*. April 4, 1999. Online: http://www.vatican.va/holy_father/john_paul_ii/letters/documents/hf_jp-ii_let_23041999_artists_en.html.

Lonergan, Bernard, J. F. "Art." In *Collected Works of Bernard Lonergan*, vol. 10, *Topics in Education*, edited by Robert M. Doran and Frederick E. Crowe, 208–32. Toronto: University of Toronto Press, 1993.

———. "Belief: Today's Issue." In *A Second Collection: Papers by Bernard J. F. Lonergan, S. J.*, 87–99.

———. "Cognitional Structure." In *Collection: Papers by Bernard Lonergan, S. J.*, 221–39.

———. *Collection: Papers by Bernard Lonergan, S. J.* Edited by Frederick E. Crowe. New York: Herder, 1967.

———. "Dimensions of Meaning." In *Collection: Papers by Bernard Lonergan, S. J.*, 252–67.

———. "Existenz and Aggiornamento." In *Collection: Papers by Bernard Lonergan, S. J.*, 240–51.

———. "The Future of Christianity." In *A Second Collection: Papers by Bernard J. F. Lonergan, S. J.*, 149–63.

———. *Insight: A Study of Human Understanding*. 5th ed. Vol. 3 of *Collected Works of Bernard Lonergan*, edited by Frederick. E. Crowe and Robert M. Doran. Toronto: University of Toronto Press, 1992.

———. "The Mediation of Christ in Prayer." In *Collected Works of Lonergan*, vol. 6, *Philosophical and Theological Papers, 1958-1964*, edited by Robert C. Croken et al., 160–82. Toronto: University of Toronto Press, 1986.

———. *Method in Theology*. New York: Seabury, 1972.

———. "Mission and the Spirit." In *A Third Collection: Papers by Bernard F. J. Lonergan, S. J.*, 23–34.

———. "Natural Right and Historical Mindedness." In *A Third Collection: Papers by Bernard F. J. Lonergan, S. J.*, 169–83.

———. "Pope John's Intention." In *A Third Collection: Papers by Bernard F. J. Lonergan, S. J.*, 225–38.

———. "The Response of the Jesuit as Priest and Apostle in the Modern World." In *A Second Collection: Papers by Bernard J. F. Lonergan, S. J.*, 165–87.

———. *A Second Collection: Papers by Bernard J .F. Lonergan, S. J.* Edited by William F. J. Ryan and Bernard J. Tyrell. London: Darton, Longman, and Todd, 1974.

———. "Theology and Praxis." In *A Third Collection: Papers by Bernard F. J. Lonergan, S. J.*, 184–201.

———. "Theology in Its New Context." In *A Second Collection: Papers by Bernard J. F. Lonergan, S. J.*, 55–68.

———. *A Third Collection: Papers by Bernard F. J. Lonergan, S. J.* Edited by Frederick E. Crowe. New York: Paulist, 1985.

———. "Unity and Plurality: the Coherence of Christian Truth." In *A Third Collection: Papers by Bernard F. J. Lonergan, S. J.*, 239–50.

Nattiez, Jean-Jacques. *The Battle of Chronos and Orpheus: Essays in Applied Musical Semiology*. Translated by Jonathan Dunsby. Oxford: Oxford University Press, 2004.

———. "Fidelity, Authenticity, and Critical Judgment." In *The Battle of Chronos and Orpheus: Essays in Applied Musical Semiology*, 127–59.

———. *Fondements d'une Sémiologie de la Musique*. Paris: Unions Générale d'Editions, 1975.

———. *Music and Discourse: Toward a Semiology of Music*. Translated by Carolyn Abbate. Princeton, NJ: Princeton University Press, 1990.

———. "Musical Semiology: Beyond Structuralism, after Postmodernism." Translated by Jonathan Dunsby. In *The Battle of Chronos and Orpheus: Essays in Applied Musical Semiology*, 3–53.

———. "Reflections on the Development of Semiology in Music." *Music Analysis* 8/1–2 (1989) 21–75.

Second Vatican Council. *Dei Verbum*. In *The Sixteen Documents of Vatican II*, edited by Marianne L. Trouvé. Boston: Pauline, 1999.

———. *Gaudium et Spes*. In *The Sixteen Documents of Vatican II*.

Seeger, Charles. "Preface to All Linguistic Treatment of Music." In *Studies in Musicology II, 1929–1979*, 277–88.

———. "Prescriptive and Descriptive Music Writing." In *Studies in Musicology, 1935–1975*, 168–81.

———. *Primitive Culture*. Cambridge, MA: Harvard University Press, 1956.

———. "Speech, Music, and Speech about Music." In *Studies in Musicology, 1935–1975*, 16–30.

———. *Studies in Musicology, 1935–1975*. Berkeley: University of California Press, 1977.

———. *Studies in Musicology II, 1929–1979*. Berkeley: University of California Press, 1994.

———. "Toward a Unitary Field Theory for Musicology." In *Studies in Musicology, 1935–1975*, 102–38.

Sequeri, Pierangelo. "L'ascolto, la musica e il canto." In *L'estro di Dio: Saggi di estetica*, 219–72. Milano Glossa, 2000.

———. *Anti-prometeo: Il musicale nell'estetica teologica di Hans Urs von Balthasar.* Milano Glossa, 1995.

———. "Coscienza cristiana, ethos della fede e canone pubblico." In *"A misura di Vangelo": Fede, dottrina, chiesa*, edited by Marco Vergottini. Cinisello Balsamo (Milan): San Paolo, 2003.

———. *Il Dio affidabile: Saggio di teologia fondamentale.* Brescia: Queriniana, 1996.

———. "Dio in un'ottava: Il logos musicale, spazio per un nuovo umanesimo." *Il Regno* 2 (2007) 47–51.

———. *Eccetto Mozart: Una passione teologica.* Milan: Glossa, 2006.

———. *Estetica e teologia: L'indicibile emozione del sacro: R. Otto, A. Schönberg, M. Heidegger.* Milan: Glossa, 1993.

———. *L'estro di Dio: Saggi di estetica.* Milan: Glossa, 2000.

———. *L'idea della fede: Trattato di teologia fondamentale.* Milan: Glossa, 2002.

———. *Musica e mistica: Percorsi nella storia occidentale delle pratiche estetiche e religiose.* Vatican City: Libreria Editrice Vaticana, 2005.

———. *Non ultima è la morte: La libertà di credere nel Risorto.* Milan: Glossa, 2006.

———. *L'oro e la paglia.* Milan: Glossa, 2001.

———. *La qualità spirituale: Esperienza nella fede nel crocevia contemporaneo.* Casale Monferrato: Piemme, 2001.

———. *La risonanza del sublime: L'idea spirituale della musica in Occidente.* Rome: Studium, 2008.

———. *Sensibili allo spirito: Umanesimo religioso e ordine degli affetti.* Milan: Glossa, 2001.

———. *Senza volgersi indietro: Meditazioni per tempi forti.* Milan: Vita e Pensiero, 2000.

———. *Il Timore di Dio.* Milan: Vita e Pensiero, 1993.

———. *L'umano alla prova: Soggetto, identità, limite.* Milan: Vita e Pensiero, 2002.

Speelman, Willem Marie. *The Generation of Meaning in Liturgical Songs: A Semiotic Analysis of Five Liturgical Songs as Syncretic Discourses.* Liturgia Condenda 4. Kampen: Kok Pharos, 1995.

———. "Music and the Word: Two Pillars of the Liturgy." *GIA Quarterly* 19/4 (2008) 14–15, 44–45.

———. "Woorden kunnen worden verstaan, muziek moet worden gevolgd: Taal en muziek als fundamentale categorieën van de liturgie." In *Elke muziek heeft haar hemel: De religieuze betekenis van muziek*, edited by Martin Hoondert, 161–83. Budel: Damon, 2009.

———. "Words Can Be Understood, but Music Must Be Followed: Language and Music as Fundamental Categories of Liturgy." Delivered at the conference Singing God's Love Faithfully, Notre Dame, April 12–14, 2007.

Viladesau, Richard. *The Beauty of the Cross: The Passion of Christ in Theology and the Arts, from the Catacombs to the Eve of the Renaissance.* Oxford: Oxford University Press, 2006.

———. "Natural Theology and Aesthetics: An Approach to the Existence of God from the Beautiful?" *Philosophy and Theology* 3 (1988–1989) 145–60.

———. *Theological Aesthetics: God in Imagination, Beauty, and Art.* Oxford: Oxford University Press, 1999.

———. *Theology and the Arts: Encountering God through Music, Art, and Rhetoric.* New York: Paulist, 2000.

———. *The Triumph of the Cross: The Passion of Christ in Theology and the Arts, from the Renaissance to the Counter-Reformation*. Oxford: Oxford University Press, 2008.

Journals with Monographs on Music

Journal for the Scientific Study of Religion 45/4 (2006).
La Musique, Christus 223 (2009).
Philosophie de la Musique/Philosophy of Music, Revue Internationale de Philosophie 60/238 (2006).

Background sources

Ardui, Johan. "Truth, Rock Music, and Christianity: Can Truth Be Maintained in the Dialogue between Theology and Rock Music?" In *Theology and the Quest for Truth: Historical- and Systematical-Theological Studies*, edited by Mathijs Lamberigts et al., 199–212. Leuven: Peeters, 2006.
Arendt, Hannah. *The Human Condition*. Chicago: University of Chicago Press, 1958.
Armstrong, Hamilton Reed. "The Transmission of Faith Through Art." *Communio* 28 (2001) 386–97.
Artusi, Lorenzo. *Hans Urs von Balthasar: Un'anima per la bellezza: Origini dell'estetica teologica nell'Apocalisse dell'anima tedesca*. Panzano in Chianti: Comunità di San Leolino, 2006.
Astley, Jeff, and Mark Savage. "Music and Christian Learning." In *Creative Chords: Studies in Music, Theology, and Christian Formation*, edited by Jeff Astley et al., 219–38. Herefordshire: Gracewing, 2000.
Augustine. *The Confessions*. The works of St. Augustine: A Translation for the Twenty first Century. New York: New City, 1997.
———. "De Musica." In *Obras completas de San Agustín*, 39:49–361. Madrid: Biblioteca de autores Cristianos, 1988,.
Ayel, V. "Peut-on parler du ciel aux hommes d'aujourd'hui?" In Abbaye de St-André, *Fête de l'ascension*, 68–81. Assemblées du Seigneur 28. Paris: Cerf, 1969.
Balcomb, Anthony O. "Re-Enchanting a Disenchanted Universe—Post Modern Projects in Theologies of Space." *Religion and Theology* 16 (2009) 77–89.
Barbaglio, Giuseppe, et al. *Teologia: Dizionario San Paolo*. Cinisello Balsamo: San Paolo, 2002.
Barthes, Roland. *Elements of Semiology*. Translated by Annette Lavers and Colin Smith. New York: Hill and Wang, 1967.
Begbie, Jeremy, editor. *Beholding the Glory: Incarnation Through the Arts*. Grand Rapids: Baker, 2000.
———. *Music, Words, and the Future of Theology*. Oxford: Oxford University Press, forthcoming.
———. "Play It (Again): Music, Theology, and Divine Communication." In *Creative Chords: Studies in Music Theology and Christian Formation*, edited by Jeff Astley et al., 45–75. Herefordshire: Gracewing, 2000.

———. *Resounding Truth: Christian Wisdom in the World of Music*. Grand Rapids: Baker, 2008.

———, editor. *Sounding the Depths: Theology Through the Arts*. London: SCM, 2002.

———. *Theology, Music, and Time*. Cambridge: Cambridge University Press, 1997.

———. "Through Music: Sound Mix." In *Beholding the Glory: Incarnation Through the Arts*, edited by Jeremy Begbie, 138–54. Grand Rapids: Baker, 2000.

———. *Voicing Creation's Praise: Towards a Theology of the Arts*. Edinburgh: T. & T. Clark, 1991.

Bell, Ian. "An Elaboration of the Worshipful Pattern of Experience in the Work of Bernard Lonergan." *Worship* 81/6 (2007) 521–47.

Bellini, Paolo B. "Dio nella Musica di Ieri e Oggi." Delivered at the conference Dio Oggi, December 11, 2009. Online: http://www.cci.progettoculturale.it/questionedio/progetto_culturale_/iniziative_a_cura_del_progetto_culturale/00008605_Mediacenter.html.

Benedict XVI. "Address to Artists in the Sistine Chapel on November 21st, 2009." Online: http://www.zenit.org/article-27631?l=english.

———. *Deus Caritas Est*. Encyclical letter. Vatican City: Libreria Editrice Vaticana, 2006.

———. *La Musica: Un'arte familiare al Logos*. Vatican City: Libreria Editrice Vaticana, 2009.

Benjamin, William. "Music Through a Narrow Aperture: A Qualified Defense of Concatenationism." *Revue Internationale de Philosophie* 4 (2006) 515–22.

Berendt, Joachim-Ernst. *The Third Ear: On Listening to the World*. Translated by Tim Nevill. Shaftesbury: Element, 1985.

Best, Harold M. *Music Through the Eyes of Faith*. San Francisco: Harper, 1993.

Biancu, Stefano, and G. Pugliesi. *Il corpo: Teologia e saperi a confronto*. Assisi: Cittadella, 2009.

Blacking, John. "Expressing Human Experience through Music." In *Music, Culture, and Experience: Selected Papers of John Blacking*, edited by Reginald Byron, 31–53. Chicago Studies in Ethnomusicology. Chicago: University of Chicago Press, 1995.

———. *How Musical Is Man?* London: Faber & Faber, 1976.

———. "Music, Culture, and Experience." In *Music, Culture, and Experience: Selected Papers of John Blacking*, 223–42.

———. "The Problem of Musical Description." In *Music, Culture, and Experience: Selected Papers of John Blacking*, 54–72.

———. "Towards an Anthropology of the Body." In *The Anthropology of the Body*, edited by John Blacking. ASA Monograph 15. New York: Academic Press, 1977.

Boeve, Lieven. *God Interrupts History: Theology in a Time of Upheaval*. New York: Continuum, 2007.

———. *Interrupting Tradition: An Essay on Christian Faith in a Postmodern Context*. Louvain Theological and Pastoral Monographs 30. Leuven: Peeters, 2003.

———. "Resurrection—Interruption—Transformation: Incarnation as Hermeneutical Strategy." *Theological Studies* 67/4 (2006) 777–815.

———. "The Shortest Definition of Religion: Interruption." *Communio Viatorum* 46/3 (2004) 299–322.

———. "Theological Truth, Particularity, and Incarnation: Engaging Religious Plurality and Hermeneutics." In *Orthodoxy, Process and Product*, edited by Mathijs Lamberigts et al., 323–46. BETL 227. Leuven: Peeters, 2009.

Bono. *Bono on Bono: Conversations with Michka Assayas*. London: Hodder & Stoughton, 2005.

Bourke, Vernon J. *Augustine's View of Reality*. Villanova, PA: Villanova University Press, 1964.

Brown, Frank Burch. *Good Taste, Bad Taste, and Christian Taste: Aesthetics in Religious Life*. Oxford: Oxford University Press, 2000.

———. *Inclusive Yet Discerning: Navigating Worship Artfully*. Calvin Institute of Christian Worship Liturgical Studies Series. Grand Rapids: Eerdmans, 2009.

———. "On Not Giving Short Thrift to the Arts in Liturgy: The Testimony of Pope Benedict XVI (Cardinal Ratzinger)." *The Arts in Religious and Theological Studies* 17/1 (2005) 13–19.

———. *Religious Aesthetics: A Theological Study of Making and Meaning*. Studies in Literature and Religion. London: Macmillan, 1990.

Buckley, Michael J. *At the Origins of Modern Atheism*. New Haven, CT: Yale University Press, 1987.

———. "Atheism—Origins." In *Dictionary of Fundamental Theology*, edited by René Latourelle and Rino Fisichella, 49–55. New York: Crossroad, 1994.

———. *Denying and Disclosing God: The Ambiguous Progress of Modern Atheism*. New Haven, CT: Yale University Press, 2004.

Burgess, Andrew R. *The Ascension in Karl Barth*. Aldershot: Ashgate, 2004.

Byron, Reginald. "The Ethnomusicology of John Blacking." In *Music, Culture, and Experience: Selected Papers of John Blacking*, edited by Reginald Byron, 1–28.

Câmara, Hélder. *The Desert Is Fertile*. Translated by Dinah Livingstone. London: Sheed and Ward, 1974.

Campo, Cristina. *Gli imperdonabili*. Milan: Rusconi, 1975.

Casini, Claudio. *El arte de escuchar música*. Translated by M. M. Viudes. Paidós de Música 18. Barcelona: Paidós, 2006.

Casey, Tom. "Desire for the Spiritual in Popular Culture." *The Way Supplement* 90 (1997) 21–34.

Centro Aletti. *L'intelligenza spirituale del sentimento*. Rome: Lipa, 1994.

Chandler, Daniel. *Semiotics: The Basics*. London: Routledge, 2001.

———. *Semiotics for Beginners*. Online: http://users.aber.ac.uk/dgc/Documents/S4B/.

Chapungco, Anscar J. *Handbook for Liturgical Studies*. 5 vols. Collegeville, MN: Liturgical, 1997–2000.

Charru, Philippe. "L'écoute musicale, une voie spirituelle." *La Musique, Christus* 223 (2009) 294–302.

Charru, Philippe, and Christoph Theobald. *Le pensée musicale de Jean-Sébastian Bach*. Paris: Cerf, 1993.

Chesterton, Gilbert K. *Orthodoxy*. London: Hodder & Stoughton, 1999.

Christensen, Duane L. *A Song of Power and the Power of Song: Essays on the Book of Deuteronomy*. Sources for Biblical and Theological Study 3. Winona Lake, IN: Eisenbrauns, 1993.

Congregation for the Doctrine of Faith. *Donum Veritatis: On the Ecclesial Vocation of the Theologian*. Vatican City: Libreria Editrice Vaticana, 1990.

Cooper, Grosvenor, and Leonard B. Meyer. *The Rhythmic Structure of Music*. Chicago: University of Chicago Press, 1963.
Copland, Aaron. *Music and Imagination*. Cambridge, MA: Harvard University Press, 1961.
———. *What to Listen for in Music*. New York: Signet, 2002.
Corkery, James. *Joseph Ratzinger's Theological Ideas: Wise Cautions and Legitimate Hopes*. New York: Paulist, 2009.
Costa, Eugenio. "Una teologia della musica?" *Creddere Oggi* 19/6 (1999) 7–15.
Coupeau, Jose Carlos. "La espiritualidad del ocio: Elogio de María de Betania." *Estudios Eclesiásticos* 79 (2004) 73–96.
———. *From Inspiration to Invention: Rhetoric in the Constitutions of the Society of Jesus*. St. Louis: Institute of the Jesuit Sources, 2010.
Craig, Edward. *Routledge Encyclopaedia of Philosophy*. 10 vols. London: Routledge, 1998.
Crowe, Frederick E. "All My Work Has Been Introducing History into Catholic Theology." In *Developing the Lonergan Legacy: Historical, Theoretical, and Existential Themes*, edited by Martin Vertin, 78–104. Toronto: University of Toronto Press, 2004.
———. "Dialectic and the Ignatian Spiritual Exercises." *Science et Esprit* 30/72 (1978) 113–27.
———. "Linking the Splintered Disciplines: Ideas from Lonergan." In *Developing the Lonergan Legacy: Historical, Theoretical and Existential Themes*, 252–66.
———. *Method in Theology: An Organon for Our Time*. Milwaukee: Marquette University Press, 1980.
———. "Rethinking God-with-Us: Categories from Lonergan." *Science et Esprit* 41/2 (1989) 167–88.
———. "Son and Spirit: Tension in the Divine Missions?" In *Lonergan Workshop*, vol. 5, edited by F. Lawrence 1–19. Boston: Boston College, 1985.
———. "The Spectrum of Communication in Lonergan." In *Developing the Lonergan Legacy: Historical, Theoretical and Existential Themes*, 53–77.
———. "'The Spirit and I' at Prayer". In *Developing the Lonergan Legacy: Historical, Theoretical and Existential Themes*, 294–303.
———. *Theology of the Christian Word: A Study in History*. New York: Paulist, 1978.
Dasila, Fabio B., Anthony J. Blasi, and David Dees. *The Sociology of Music*. Notre Dame, IN: University of Notre Dame Press, 1984.
Davies, Oliver. "Fundamental Theology and The Word." Delivered at the Giornata di Studio of the Department of Fundamental Theology, 2008. Online: http://www.unigre.it/Struttura_didattica/teologia/specifico/dipartimento_fondamentale_it.php.
Davies, Stephen T., Daniel Kendall, and Gerald O'Collins, editors. *The Incarnation: An Interdisciplinary Syposium on the Incarnation of the Son of God*. Oxford: Oxford University Press, 2002.
Dawson, Gerard S. *Jesus Ascended: The Meaning of Christ's Continuing Incarnation*. London: T. & T. Clark, 2004.
De Monticelli, Roberta. *L'allegria della mente: Dialogando con Agostino*. Milan: B. Mondatori, 2004.

De Saussure, Ferdinand. *Course in General Linguistics*. Translated by Roy Harris. LaSalle, ILL: Open Court, 1986. Original French version edited by Charles Bally and Albert Sechehaye, *Cours de linguistique générale*. Paris: Payot, 1922.

Deledella, Gérard. *Charles S. Peirce's Philosophy of Signs: Essays in Comparative Semiotics*. Bloomington: Indiana University Press, 2000.

Dieuaide, Jean-Michel. "Du spirituelle en musique: Présentation de compositeurs contemporains." *La Musique, Christus* 223 (2009) 319–29.

Doran, Robert. "Ignatian Themes in the Thought of Bernard Lonergan." *Toronto Journal of Theology* 22/1 (2006) 39–54.

———. "Lonergan and Balthasar: Methodological Considerations." *Theological Studies* 58/1 (1997) 61–84.

———. *Psychic Conversion and Theological Foundations: Toward a Reorientation of the Human Sciences*. Chico, CA: Scholars, 1981.

———. "Systematic Theology Seeking Method: Reconciling System and History. In *Il Teologo e la Storia: Lonergan's Centenary (1904–2004)*, edited by Paul Gilbert and Nattalino Spaccapelo, 275–99. Rome: Editrice Pontificia Università Gregoriana, 2006.

———. *Theology and the Dialectics of History*. Toronto: University of Toronto Press, 1990.

Dryden, Donald. "Susanne K. Langer." In *Dictionary of Literary Biography*, vol. 270, *American Philosophers before 1950*, edited by Philip B. Dematteis and Leemon B. McHenry, 189–99. Detroit, MI: Gale, 2003.

Dufka, Peter. *L'arte musicale come espressione e stimolo della fede: La passione secondo Giovanni di J. S. Bach*. Rome: Editrice Pontificia Università Gregoriana, 2008.

Dulles, Avery Robert. *The Assurance of Things Hoped for: A Theology of Christian Faith*. Oxford: Oxford University Press, 1994.

———. *Models of Revelation*. Garden City, NY: Doubleday, 1983.

———. *Models of the Church*. Garden City, NY: Doubleday, 1974.

Dupré, Louis K. "Hans Urs von Balthasar's Theology of Aesthetic Form." *Theological Studies* 49/2 (1988) 299–318.

Ellis, Alexander J. "On the Musical Scales of Various Nations." *Journal of the Royal Society of Arts* 33 (1885) 485–527.

Endean, Phillip. "The Ignatian Prayer of the Senses." *Heythrop Journal* 31 (1990) 391–418.

Epperson, Gordon. *The Musical Symbol: A Study of the Philosophic Theory of Music*. Ames: Iowa State University Press, 1967.

Farrell, Thomas J., and Paul A. Soukup. *Communication and Lonergan: Common Ground for Forging the New Age*. Kansas City, MO: Sheed and Ward, 1993.

Farrow, Douglas. *Ascension and Ecclesia: On the Significance of the Doctrine of the Ascension for Ecclesiology and Christian Cosmology*. Edinburgh: T. & T. Clark, 1999.

Faure, Pierre. "La musique, un lieu spirituelle?" *La Musique, Christus* 223 (2009) 265–75.

Feehan, John. *The Singing Heart of the World: Creation, Evolution, and Faith*. Dublin: Colomba, 2010.

Foley, Edward. *From Age to Age: How Christians Have Celebrated the Eucharist*. Collegeville, MN: Liturgical, 2008.

———. *Foundations of Christian Music: The Music of Pre-Constantinian Christianity*. Collegeville, MN: Liturgical, 1996.

———. *Music in Ritual: A Pre-Theological Investigation*. Collegeville, MN: Liturgical, 1984.

———. "Toward a Sound Theology." *Studia Liturgica* 23/2 (1993) 121–39.

———. "Toward a Working Definition of Music in Ritual: A Pre-Theological Investigation." In *Music in Ritual: A Pre-Theological Investigation*, 9–13.

———, editor. *Worship Music: A Concise Dictionary*. Collegeville, MN: Liturgical, 2000.

Frazão de Jesus Correia, Jose M. "Penser la Dynamique Croyante de l'Humain. La foi comme nouveau parcours de théologie fondamentale chez Pierangelo Sequeri." STL diss., Centre Sèvres, Paris, Mémoire di Maîtrise en Théologie, 2005.

———. *Risonanza affettiva, appello etico, stile relazionale: Tratti di una fede vivibile e visibile*. Rome: Aracne, 2010.

Freud, Harry. "My Uncle Sigmund." In *Freud As We Knew Him*, edited by Hendrick M. Ruitenbeek. Detroit: Wayne State University Press, 1971.

Frith, Simon. *Performing Rights, Evaluating Popular Music*. Oxford: Oxford University Press, 2002.

Gaburro, Sergio. *La voce della rivelazione: Fenomenologia della voce per una teologia della rivelazione*. Cinisello Balsamo: San Paolo, 2005.

Gadamer, Hans Georg. *Truth and Method*. New York: Crossroad, 1992.

Gallagher, Michael Paul. *Clashing Symbols: An Introduction to Faith and Culture*. Rev. ed. London: Darton, Longman, and Todd, 2003.

———. *Dive Deeper*. London: Darton, Longman, and Todd, 2002.

———. *Faith Maps: Ten Religious Explorers from Newman to Benedict XVI*. New York: Paulist, 2010.

———. "Inculturation Debates: The Relevance of Lonergan." *Studia Missionalia* 52 (2003) 347–63.

———. "Inculturation: Some Theological Perspectives." *International Review of Mission* 85/337 (1996) 173–80.

———. "Lonergan's Newman: Appropriated Affinities." *Gregorianum* 85/4 (2004) 735–56.

———. "Newman on Imagination and Faith." *Milltown Studies* 49 (2002) 84–101.

———. "Post-Modernity: Friend or Foe?" In *Faith and Culture in the Irish Context*, edited by Eoin G. Cassidy, 71–82. Dublin: Veritas, 1996.

———. "Retrieving Imagination in Theology." In *The Critical Spirit: Theology at the Crossroads of Faith and Culture: Essays in Honour of Gabriel Daly*, edited by Andrew Pierce and Geraldine Smyth, 200–207. Dublin: Columba, 2003.

———. "Rifondazione metodologica della teologia fondamentale." In *Il Teologo e la Storia: Lonergan's Centenary (1904–2004)*, edited by Paul Gilbert and Nattalino Spaccapelo, 265–74. Rome: Editrice Pontificia Università Gregoriana, 2006.

———. "Theories of Faith Development." *Hekima Review* 25 (2001) 41–48.

———. "Truth and Trust: Pierangelo Sequeri's Theology of Faith." *Irish Theological Quarterly* 73 (2008) 3–31.

———. "University and Culture: Towards a Retrieval of Humanism." *Gregrianum* 85/1 (2004) 149–71.

———. *What Are They Saying about Unbelief?* New York: Paulist, 1995.

Gallo Isaza, Orlando. *Siendo en las cosas*. Colección autores Antioqueños, 1989.

Gelpi, Donald. *Encountering Jesus Christ. Rethinking Christological Faith and Commitment*. Milwaukee: Marquette University Press, 2009.

———. "Learning to Live with Lonergan." In *Finding God in All Things: Celebrating Bernard Lonergan, John Courtney Murray, and Karl Rahner*, edited by Mark Bosco and David Stagaman. New York: Fordham University Press, 2007.

Gentili, Antonio, *I nostri sensi ilumina: Saggio sui cinque sensi spirituali*. Milan: Ancora, 2000.

Gibran, Kahil. *The Prophet*. Middlesex: Echo Library, 2006.

Giles, Gordon. "Performing Theology Authentically." In *Creative Chords: Studies in Music, Theology, and Christian Formation*, edited by Jeff Astley et al., 76–88. Herefordshire: Gracewing, 2000.

Gilmour, Michael J. *God and Guitars: Seeking the Sacred in Post-1960s Popular Music*. Waco, TX: Baylor University Press, 2009.

Goettmann, Alphonse, and Karlfried Dürcheim. *Diálogo sul cammino iniziatico*. Rome: Appunti di Viaggio, 1996.

Gómez-Acebo, Isabel. *Pregare con i sensi: L'esperienze di cinque teologhe*. Milan: Pauline, 2000.

Gonzalez, A. *Teología de la praxis evangélica: Ensayo de una teología fundamental*. Santander: Sal Terrae, 1999.

Goujon, Patrick. "L'écoute e silence intérieur." *La Musique, Christus* 223 (2009) 335–42.

Greer, Taylor A. *A Question of Balance: Charles Seeger's Philosophy of Music*. Berkeley: University of California Press, 1998.

Greimas, Algirdas J. *Sémantique Structurale: Recherche de Méthode*. Paris: Larousse, 1966.

Greimas, Algirdas J., and Joseph Courtés. *Semiotics and Language: An Analytical Dictionary*. Bloomington: Indiana University Press, 1983.

Harré, Rom. "Is There a Semantics for Music?" In *The Interpretation of Music: Philosophical Essays*, edited by Michael Krausz, 203–13. Oxford: Oxford University Press, 1993.

Harwood, Dane. "Universals in Music: A Perspective from Cognitive Psychology." *Ethnomusicology* 20/3 (1997) 521–33.

Haselböck, Martin. "Creation and the Performer: An Interview with Martin Haselböck." In *Creative Chords: Studies in Music, Theology, and Christian Formation*, edited by Jeff Astley et al., 20–32. Herefordshire: Gracewing, 2000.

Higgins, Kathleen M. "The Cognitive and Appreciative Import of Musical Universals." *Revue Internationale de Philosophie* 4 (2006) 487–503.

Hoad, T. F., editor. *Concise Oxford Dictionary of English Etymology*. Oxford: Oxford University Press, 1996.

Hoover, Wilbur R. "Toward a Theology of the Christian and His Use of Leisure Time." *Brethren Life and Thought* 4/2 (1959) 60–68.

Hügel, Friedrich von. *The Mystical Element of Religion as Studied in Saint Catherine of Genoa and Her Friends*. London: Dent & Sons, 1923.

Huron, David. *Sweet Anticipation: Music and the Psychology of Expectation*. Cambridge, MA: MIT Press, 2006.

Jeanrond, Werner. G. *Theological Hermeneutics: Development and Significance*. New York: Crossroad, 1991.

Joncas, Michael J. "Liturgical Musicology and Liturgical Semiotics: Theoretical Foundations and Analytical Techniques." *Ecclesia Orans* 8/2 (1991) 181–206.

———. "Liturgy and Music." In *Handbook for Liturgical Studies*, edited by Anscar J. Chapungco, 2:281–321. Collegeville, MN: Liturgical, 1998.

———. "Semiotics and the Analysis of Liturgical Music." *Liturgical Ministry* 3 (1994) 144–54.

Jones, Tony. *Postmodern Youth Ministry: Exploring Cultural Shift, Cultivating Authentic Community, Creating Holisitic Connections*. Grand Rapids: Youth Specialties, 2001.

Kavanagh, Patrick. *Collected Poems*. London: Allen Lane, 1984.

Kearney, Richard. *Poetics of Imagining: Modern to Post-Modern*. 2nd ed. Edinburgh: Edinburgh University Press, 1998.

———. *The Wake of Imagination: Toward a Postmodern Culture*. London: Routledge, 1988.

Kelly, Anthony J. *The Resurrection Effect: Transforming Christian Life and Thought*. Maryknoll, NY: Orbis, 2008.

Kern, Walter, et al. *Corso di teologia fondamentale*. See vols. 2 and 4. Brescia: Queriniana, 1990.

Kivy, Peter. *Music, Language, and Cognition: And Other Essays in the Aesthetics of Music*. Oxford: Clarendon, 2007.

———. *New Essays on Musical Understanding*. Oxford: Clarendon, 2001.

Knasas, John F. X. "Why for Lonergan Knowing Cannot Consist in Taking a Look." *American Catholic Philosophical Quarterly* 78/1 (2004) 131–50.

Krausz, Michael, editor. *The Interpretation of Music: Philosophical Essays*. Oxford: Oxford University Press, 1993.

Kroecker, Charlotte. *Music in Christian Worship*. Collegeville, MN: Liturgical, 2005.

Kuhn, Thomas S. *The Structure of Scientific Revolutions*. Chicago: Chicago University Press, 1962.

Lane, Dermot. "Fifty Years of Theology." *The Furrow* 60, 7/8 (2009) 399–403.

Langer, Susanne K. *Feeling and Form: A Theory of Art Developed from Philosophy in a New Key*. New York: Scribner, 1953.

———. *An Introduction to Symbolic Logic*. 3rd. ed. New York: Dover, 1967.

———. *Mind: An Essay on Human Feeling*. 3 vols. Baltimore: Johns Hopkins Press, 1967.

———. *Philosophy in a New Key: A Study in the Symbolism of Reason, Rite, and Art*. 3rd. ed. Cambridge, MA: Harvard University Press, 1969.

———. *Problems of Art: Ten Philosophical Lectures*. New York: Scribner, 1953.

Lawrence, Fred G. "Grace and Friendship." *Gregorianum* 85/4 (2004) 795–820.

Leahy, Brendan. "Theological Aesthetics." In *The Beauty of Christ: An Introduction to the Theology of Hans Urs von Balthasar*, edited by Bede McGregor and Thomas Norris, 23–55. Edinburgh: T. & T. Clark, 1994.

Levertov, Denise. *Sands of the Well*. New York: New Directions, 1996.

Levinson, Jerrold. "Concatenationism, Architectonicism, and the Appreciation of Music." *Revue Internationale de Philosophie* 4 (2006) 505–14.

Lewis, C. S. *The Chronicles of Narnia*. New York: Harper Collins, 1980.

———. *The Screwtape Letters*. New York: MacMillan, 1961.

Lewis, Justin. *The Ideological Octopus: An Exploration of Television and Its Audience*. New York: Routledge, 1991.

Liddy, Richard. *Art and Feeling: An Analysis and Critique of the Philosophy of Art of Susanne K. Langer*. Rome: Facultate Philosophica Pontificia Università Gregoriana, 1970.

———. "Startling Strangeness: A Memoir." In *Lonergan Workshop*, vol. 20, edited by F. Lawrence, 233–51. Boston: Boston College, 2008.

———. *Startling Strangeness. Reading Lonergan's Insight*. Lanham, MD: University Press of America, 2007.

———. *Transforming Light: Intellectual Conversion in the Earlier Lonergan*. Collegeville, MN: Liturgical, 1993.

Lindbeck, George A. *The Nature of Doctrine*. Philadelphia: Westminster, 1984.

Lingerman, Hal A. *The Healing Energies of Music*. Wheaton, IL: Quest, 1995.

Lipsitz, George. *Dangerous Crossroads: Popular Music, Postmodernism, and the Poetics of Place*. London: Verso, 1994.

Louth, Andrew. *Discerning the Mystery: An Essay on the Nature of Theology*. Oxford: Clarendon, 1983.

Lovett, Sean Patrick. "An Interview with Artist Breda Catherine Ennis." *Logos* 12/4 (2009) 97–114.

Lynch, Gordon. "The Role of Popular Music in the Construction of Alternative Identities and Ideologies." *Journal for the Scientific Study of Religion* 45/4 (2006) 481–88.

MacMillan, James. "Creation and the Composer: An Interview with James Macmillan." In *Creative Chords: Studies in Music, Theology, and Christian Formation*, edited by Jeff Astley et al., 3–19. Herefordshire: Gracewing, 2000.

———. "Parthenogenesis." In *Sounding the Depths: Theology Through the Arts*, edited by Jeremy Begbie, 33–38. London: SCM, 2002.

Maillet, Gregory. "'A poem should not mean / but be': Lonergan and Literary Aesthetics." *Method: Journal of Lonergan Studies* 22 (2004) 57–91.

Mardones, José María. *¿Adónde va la Religión?: Cristianismo y Religiosidad en Nuestro tiempo*. Santander: Sal Terrae, 1996.

———. "La fe cristiana ante la modernidad, la post-modernidad y la cultura neo-conservadora." In *Pluralismo Socio-Cultural y Fe Cristiana: Congreso de Teología*, edited by Facultades de Teología de vitoria y Deusto. Bilbao: Ediciones Mensajero, 1990.

———. *Postmodernidad y Cristianismo: El Desafío del Fragmento*. Santander: Sal Terrae, 1988.

———. *La Vida del Símbolo: La Dimension Simbólica de la Religión*. Santander: Sal Terrae, 2003.

Martinelli, Paolo. *Testimonianza: Verità di Dio e libertà dell'uomo*. Diaconia alla verità 9. Milan: Paoline, 2002.

Martini, Carlo M. "L'ascension de Jésus." In *Fête de l'ascension*, edited by Abbaye de St-André, 6–12. Assemblées du Seigneur 28. Paris: Cerf, 1969.

———. "Bernard Lonergan al servizio della chiesa." In *Il Teologo e la Storia: Lonergan's Centenary (1904–2004)*, edited by Paul Gilbert and Nattalino Spaccapelo, 1–11. Rome: Editrice Pontificia Università Gregoriana, 2006.

———. *Saving Beauty: Cardinal Martini's Vision for the New Millennium*. Translated by A. Tulloch. London: St. Pauls, 2000.

McGann, Mary E. *Exploring Music as Worship and Theology: Research in Liturgical Practice*. Collegeville, MN: Liturgical, 2002

Merriam, Alan P. *The Anthropology of Music*. Evanston, IL: Northwestern University Press, 1964.

———. "Definitions of 'Comparative Musicology' and 'Ethnomusicology': An Historical-Theoretical Perspective." *Ethnomusicology* 21 (1977) 189–204.

Messenger, Troy. *Holy Leisure: Recreation and Religion in God's Square Mile*. Minneapolis: University of Minnesota Press, 1999.

Metz, Johann B. *Glaube in Geschichte und Gesellschaft: Studien zu einer praktischen Fundamentaltheologie*. Mainz: Matthias-Grünewald, 1977.

Meyer, Leonard B. *Emotion and Meaning in Music*. Chicago: University of Chicago Press, 1956.

———. *Explaining Music: Essays and Explorations*. Chicago: University of Chicago Press, 1973.

———. *Music, the Arts, and Ideas: Patterns and Predictions in Twentieth-Century Culture*. Chicag: University of Chicago Press, 1967.

———. *Style and Music: Theory, History, and Ideology*. Philadelphia: University of Pennsylvania Press, 1989.

Middleton, Richard J., and Brian J. Walsh. *Truth Is Stranger Than It Used to Be: Biblical Faith in a Postmodern Age*. Downers Grove, IL: InterVarsity, 1995.

Molino, Jean. "Pour une histoire de l'interprétation: Les étapes de l'herméneutique." *Philosophiques* 12/1 (1985) 73–103 and 12/2 (1985) 281–314.

Moloney, Ray. "The Person as Subject of Spirituality in the Writings of Bernard Lonergan." *Milltown Studies* 45 (2000) 66–80.

———. "The Spiritual Journey in the Writings of Bernard Lonergan." *Milltown Studies* 46 (2000) 112–27.

Mooney, Hilary A. *The Liberation of Consciousness: Bernard Lonergan's Theological Foundations in Dialogue with the Theological Aesthetics of Hans Urs von Balthasar*. Frankfurt: Knecht, 1992.

Moore, Sebastian. *The Contagion of Jesus: Doing Theology as If It Mattered*. London: Darton, Longman, and Todd, 2008.

———. *The Crucified Jesus Is No Stranger*. Mahwah, NJ: Paulist, 1977.

Morlans, Xavier. *El primer anuncio: El eslabón perdido*. Madrid: PPC, 2009.

Morris, Charles W. *Foundations of the Theory of Signs*. Chicago: Chicago University Press, 1970.

Moxó y Montoliú, Francisco de. "La Música Religiosa de Mozart." In *Dios es amor: Extensión universitaria*, edited by Javier Prades and Eduardo Torano, 163–77. Madrid: Facultad de Teología San Damaso, 2009.

Narmour, Eugene, and Ruth A. Solie. *Explorations in Music, the Arts, and Ideas: Essays in Honour of Leonard B. Meyer*. Stuyvesant: Pendragon, 1998.

Nettl, Bruno. *Blackfoot Musical Thought: Comparative Perspectives*. Kent OH: Kent State University Press, 1989.

———. *Folk and Traditional Music of the Western Continents*. Englewood Cliffs, NJ: Prentice-Hall, 1973.

———. *Music in Primitive Culture*. Cambridge, MA: Harvard University Press, 1956.

———. *The Study of Ethnomusicology: Twenty-Nine Issues and Concepts*. Urbana: University of Illinois Press, 1983.

———. *Theory and Method in Ethnomusicology*. New York: Free Press of Glencoe, 1964.

Newman, John Henry. *An Essay on the Development of Christian Doctrine.* London: Longmans, Green, 1890.

Ní Riain, Noirín. *Listen with the Ear of the Heart: An Autobiography.* Dublin: Veritas, 2009.

———. *Theosony: Towards a Theology of Listening.* Dublin: Columba Press. 2011.

Nichols, Aidan. *Scattering the Seed: A Guide through Balthasar's Early Writings on Philosophy and the Arts.* London: T. & T. Clark, 2006.

Nietzsche, Friedrich. *Thus Spoke Zarathustra.* Translated by R. J. Hollingdale. London: Penguin, 2003.

———. *The Will to Power.* Edited by Walter Haufmann, translated Walter Haufmann and R. J. Hollingdale, New York: Vintage, 1967.

Oakes, Edward, and David Moss, *The Cambridge Guide to Hans Urs von Balthasar.* Cambridge: Cambridge University Press, 2004.

O'Donnell, John. *Hans Urs von Balthasar.* London: Continuum, 1991.

O'Donoghue, John. "For the Senses." In *Benedictus: A Book of Blessings*, 57. London: Bantam, 2007.

Osto, Giulio. *Un pentagramma teologico: Music e teologia nella cantata Wachet auf, ruft uns die Stimmen BWV 140 die Johann Sebastian Bach.* Padova: Messaggero, 2010.

Paul VI, Pope. *Evangelii Nuntiandi.* Online: http://www.vatican.va/holy_father/paul_vi/apost_exhortations/documents/hf_p-vi_exh_19751208_evangelii-nuntiandi_en.html.

Piacenza, Maurizio. "Il patrimonio artistico della Chiesa: Mezzo di evangelizzazione, di catechesi e di dialogo." Report for the Plenary Assembly of the Pontifical Commission for the Cultural Heritage of the Church Cultura, March 28, 2006, Vatican. Online: http://www.vatican.va/roman_curia/pontifical_commissions/pcchc/documents/rc_com_pcchc_20060328_patrimonio-chiesa_it.html.

Pierron, J. "Le triomphe du Christ." In *Fête de l'ascension*, edited by Abbaye de St-André, 14–22. Assemblées du Seigneur 28, Paris: Cerf, 1969.

Piqué Collado, José. *Teología y música: Una contribución dialéctico-trascendental sobre la sacramentalidad de la percepción estética del misterio: Agustín, Balthasar, Sequeri; Victoria, Schöenberg, Messiaen.* Rome: Editrice Pontificia Università Gregoriana, 2006.

Pisarra, Pietro. *Il giardino delle delizie: Sensi e spiritualità.* Roma: AVE, 2009.

Pius XII, Pope. *Mystici Corporis Christi.* Online: http://www.vatican.va/holy_father/pius_xii/encyclicals/documents/hf_p-xii_enc_29061943_mystici-corporis-christi_en.html.

Pottie, Charles S. *A More Profound Alleluia!: Gelineau and Routley on Music in Christian Worship.* Portland, OR: Pastoral Press, 1984.

Pouthier, Jean Luc. "La musique au risque de l'histoire." *La Musique, Christus* 223 (2009) 303–9.

Prades, Javier, and Eduardo Torano. *Dios es amor: Extensión universitaria.* Madrid: Facultad de Teología San Damaso, 2009.

Pramuk, Chris. "'Strange Fruit': Black Suffering/White Revelation." *Theological Studies* 67/2 (2006) 345–77.

Predelli, Stefano. "Platonism in Music: A Kind of Refutation." *Revue Internationale de Philosophie* 4 (2006) 401–14.

Preminger, Alex, and Terry V. F. Brogan. *The New Princeton Encyclopedia of Poetry and Poetics*. Princeton, NJ: Princeton University Press, 1993.
Prinz, Julia D. E. *Endangering Hunger for God: Johann Baptist Metz and Dorothee Sölle at the Interface of Biblical Hermeneutic and Christian Spirituality*. Münster: Lit, 2007.
Quine, Willard Van Orman. "Two Dogmas of Empiricism."In *From a Logical Point of View: 9 Logico-Philosophical Essays*, 20–46. 2nd ed. Cambridge, MA: Harvard University Press, 1980.
Ratzinger, Joseph. *Un canto nuevo para el Señor la fe en Jesucristo y la ligurgia hoy*. Salamanca: Sígueme, 1999.
———. *The Feast of Faith: Approaches to a Theology of the Liturgy*. San Francisco: Ignatius, 1986.
———. "The Spirit of the Liturgy." In *The Essential Pope Benedict XVI: His Central Writings and Speeches*, edited by John F. Thornton and Susan B. Verenne. San Francisco: HarperSanFrancisco, 2007.
———. "Truth and Freedom." *Communio* 23 (1996) 16–33.
Rahner, Karl. "Anonymous Christianity and the Missionary Task of the Church." Translated by David Burke. In *Theological Investigations*, 12: 161–78. London: Darton, Longman, and Todd, 1961–.
———. "Art Against the Horizon of Theology and Piety." Translated by Joseph Donceel and Hugh M. Riley. In *Theological Investigations*, 23:162–68.
———. "Atheism and Implicit Christianity." Translated by Graham Harrison. In *Theological Investigations*, 9:145–64.
———. "The Body in the Order of Salvation." Translated by Margaret Kohl.In *Theological Investigations*, 17:71–89.
———. The Doctrine of the Spiritual Senses in the Middle Ages." Translated by David Morland. In *Theological Investigations*, 16:104–34.
———. *Encounters with Silence*. London: Burn and Oates, 1975.
———. "The Eternal Significance of the Humanity of Jesus for Our Relationship with God." Translated by Karl Kruger and Boniface Kruger. In *Theological Investigations*, 3:53–146.
———. "Experience of the Holy Spirit." Translated by Edward Quinn. In *Theological Investigations*, 28:189–210.
———. "Faith Between Rationality and Emotion." Translated by David Morland. In *Theological Investigations*, 16:60–78.
———. "He Will Come Again." Translated by David Burke. In *Theological Investigations*, 7:177–80.
———. *Hearers of the Word*. New York: Herder, 1969.
———. "The Historicity of Theology." Translated by Graham Harrison. In *Theological Investigations*, 9:64–82.
———. "Observations on the Problem of the Anonymous Christian." Translated by David Burke. In *Theological Investigations*, 14:280–94.
———. "On the Theology of the Incarnation." In Translated by Kevin Smith. *Theological Investigations*, 4:105–20.
———. "Poetry and the Christian." Translated by Kevin Smith. In *Theological Investigations*, 5:357–67.
———. "The Position the Woman in the New Situation in Which the Church Finds Herself." Translated by David Bourke. In *Theological Investigations*, 8:75–93.

———. "Prayer for Creative Thinkers." Translated by David Bourke. In *Theological Investigations*, 8:130–32.

———. "Priest and Poet." Translated by Karl M. Kruger and Boniface Kruger. In *Theological Investigations*, 3:294–317.

———. "Reflections on the Problem of the Gradual Ascent to Christian Perfection." Translated by Karl M. Kruger and Boniface Kruger. In *Theological Investigations*, 3:3–23.

———. *Spirit in the World*. New York: Herder, 1968.

———. "The Spiritual Senses According to Origen." In Translated by David Morland. In *Theological Investigations*, 16:81–103.

———. "The Task of the Writer in Relation to Christian Living." Translated by David Bourke. In *Theological Investigations*, 8:112–29.

———. "The Theology of the Religious Meaning of Image." Translated by Joseph Donceel and Hugh M. Riley. In *Theological Investigations*, 23:149–61.

———. "A Theology One Can Live With." Translated by Hugh M. Riley. In *Theological Investigations*, 21:99–112.

———. "Thoughts on the Possibility of Belief Today." Translated by Karl Kruger. In *Theological Investigations*, 5:3–22.

Rendina, Sergio. "La dottrina dei sensi spirituali negli Esercizi Spirituali." *Servitum* 29–30 (1983) 55–72.

Ricoeur, Paul. "Il contributo di una riflessione sul linguaggio a una teologia della Parola." In *Testimonianza, parola e rivelazione*, 51–71. Rome: Dehoniane, 1997.

———. "L'ermeneutica della testimonianza." In *Testimonianza, parola e rivelazione*, 73–108.

———. "Experience and Language in Religious Discourse." In *Phenomenology and the "Theological Turn": The French Debate*, edited by Dominique Janicaud et al., 127–46. Perspectives in Continental Philosophy 15. New York: Fordham University Press, 2000.

———. "Naming God." In *Figuring the Sacred: Religion, Narrative, and Imagination*, by Paul Ricoeur, translated by David Pellauer, edited by Mark I. Wallace, 217–36. Minneapolis: Fortress, 1995.

Rilke, Rainer Maria. *Duino Elegies and The Sonnet to Orpheus*. Translated by Alfred Poulin Jr. Boston: Houghon Mifflin, 2005.

———. *Letters to a Young Poet*. Translated by Joan M. Burnham. Novato, CA: New World Library, 2000.

Rixon, Gordon. "Transforming Mysticism: Adorning Pathways to Self-Transcendence." *Gregorianum* 85/4 (2004) 719–34.

Robert, P. "Theology and spiritual Life: Encounter with Bernard Lonergan." In *Lonergan Workshop*, vol. 10, 333–43. Boston: Boston College, 1994.

Robinson, John A. T. *The Body: A Study in Pauline Theology*. London: SCM, 1952.

Rousselot, Pierre. *The Eyes of Faith*. Translated by Joseph Donceel. New York: Fordham University Press, 1990.

Rupnik, Marco I. *Il discernimento*. 2 parts. Rome: Lipa, 2000, 2001.

———. "Il 'sentimento religioso' nel discernimento secondo San Ignazio di Loyola." In *L'intelligenza spirituale del sentimento: Con la traduzione Italiana del saggio di B. Vyšeslavcev "Il Cuore nella mistica Cristiana e Indiana,"* edited by Centro Aletti, 225–54. Rome: Lipa, 1994.

Ryan, Eilish. *Rosemary Haughton: Witness to Hope*. Kansas Cit, MO: Sheed and Ward, 1997.
Sacks, Oliver W. *Musicophilia: Tales of Music and the Brain*. New York: Knopf, 2008.
Saliers, Don E. "Integrity of Sung Prayer." *Worship* 55/4 (1981) 290–303.
———. *Music and Theology*. Nashville: Abingdon, 2007.
———. *Worship as Theology: Foretaste of Glory Divine*. Nashville: Abingdon, 1994.
Saliers, Don E., and Emily Saliers. *A Song to Sing, a Life to Live: Reflections on Music as Spiritual Practice*. San Francisco: Jossey-Bass, 2005.
Salmann, Elmar. "Mistica: Esperienza e teoria—storia e figure." In *Presenza di Spirito: Il Cristianesimo come gesto e pensiero*. Padova: Messagero, 2000.
Salmon, Wesley. *Scientific Explanation and the Causal Structure of the World*. Oxford: Oxford University Press, 1984.
Saussure, Ferdinand de. *Course in General Linguistics*. Translated by Roy Harris, edited by Charles Baly and Albert Sechehaye. LaSalle, IL: Open Court, 1959.
Savage, Mark. "Creation and the Listener: An Interview with Mark Savage." In *Creative Chords: Studies in Music, Theology, and Christian Formation*, edited by Jeff astley et al., 33–41. Herefordshire: Gracewing, 2000.
Sbatella, Licia. *La mente orchestra: Elaborazione della risonanza e autismo*. Milan: Vita e Pensiero, 2006.
Schenden, Greg. "Rock-n-Roll Saved My Soul." *New Wineskines* 1/2 (2006–2007) 2–15.
Schneiders, Sandra. *The Revelatory Text: Interpreting the New Testament as Sacred Scripture*. Collegeville, MN: Liturgical, 1999.
———. "Spirituality in the Academy." *Theological Studies* 50/4 (1989) 676–97.
Schopenhauer, Arthur. *The World as Will and Representation*. Translated by E. F. J. Payne. 2 vols. New York: Dover, 1996.
Scirghi, Thomas. "It Is Right to Give God Thanks and Praise." in *Living Beauty. The Art of Liturgy*, 105–15. Lanham, MD: Rowman & Littlefield, 2008.
Scruton, Roger. *An Intelligent Person's Guide to Modern Culture*. London: Duckworth, 1998.
———. "Notes on the Meaning of Music." In *The Interpretation of Music: Philosophical* Essays, edited by Michael Krausz, 193–202. Oxford: Oxford University Press, 1993.
Sebeok, Thomas A., editor. *Encyclopedic Dictionary of Semiotics*. Berlin: Mouton de Gruter, 1986.
Sedmak, C. "The Disruptive Power of World Hunger." In Oliver Davies et al., *Transformation Theology: Church in the World*, 115–41. Edinburgh: T. & T. Clark, 2007.
———. "The Wound of Knowledge: Epistemic Mercy and World Hunger." In Oliver Davies et al., *Transformation Theology: Church in the World*, 142–66.
Sequeri, Pierangelo. "Dio nella musica di ieri e oggi." Delivered at the conference Dio Oggi, December 11, 2009. Online: http://www.cci.progettoculturale.it/questionedio/progetto_culturale_/iniziative_a_cura_del_progetto_culturale/00008605_Mediacenter.html.
Sevez, Pascal. "Rock, Rap, Slam : Les jeunes e le mystère de la musique." *La Musique*, *Christus* 223 (2009) 276–82.
Shepherd, John, and Peter Wicke. *Music and Cultural Theory*. Cambridge: Polity, 1997.

Sirtori, Ivan. "La chiesa, ambiente di raccoglimento." *Vita Pastorale* 7 (2004) 104–11.
Sless, David. *In Search of Semiotics*. London: Croom Helm, 1986.
Sonnet, Jean-Pierre. *Le corps voisé: Petite suite Eucharistique*. Châtelineau: Taillis Pré, 2002.
―――. *Membra Jesu nostri : Ce que Dieu non dit que par le corps*. Châtelineau: Taillis Pré, 2010.
Spicer, Paul. "Easter Oratorio: The Composer's Perspective." In *Sounding the Depths: Theology Through the Arts*, edited by Jeremy Begbie, 179–92. London: SCM, 2002.
Špidlík, Tomàs. "I sentimenti spirituali nella tradizione patristica." In *L'intelligenza spirituale del sentimento*, edited by Centro Aletti, 81–100. Rome: Lipa, 1994.
Špidlík, Tomàs, and Marco I. Rupnik. *Una conoscenza integrale: La via del simbolo*. Rome: Lipa, 2010.
Steiner, George. *Real Presences*. Chicago: University of Chicago Press, 1989.
Storr, Anthony. *Music and the Mind*. New York: Ballantine, 2008.
Stravinsky, Igor. *Poetics of Music in the Form of Six Lessons*. Translated by Arthur Knodel and Ingolf Dahl. Cambridge, MA: Harvard University Press, 1947.
Streeter, C.M. "Glossary of Lonerganian Terminology." In *Communication and Lonergan: Common Ground for Forging the New Age*, edited by Thomas J. Farrell and Paul A. Soukup, 315–29. Kansas City, MO: Sheed and Ward, 1993.
―――. "Preaching as a Form of Theological Communication: An Instance of Lonergan's Evaluative Hermeneutics." In *Communication and Lonergan: Common Ground for Forging the New Age*, edited by Thomas J. Farrell and Paul A. Soukup, 48–66.
Stumpf, Carl. "Lieder der Bellakula-Indianer." *Vierteljahrschrift für Musikwissenschaft* 2 (1886) 405–26.
Sturrock, John. *Structuralism*. London: Paladin, 1986.
Subotnik, Rose R. "Toward a Deconstruction of Structural Listening: A Critique of Schoenberg, Adorno, and Stravinsky." In *Explorations in Music, the Arts and Ideas: Essays in Honour of Leonard B. Meyer*, edited by Eugene Narmour and Ruth A. Solie, 87–122. Stuyvesant: Pendragon, 1998.
Taruskin, Richard. *Text and Act: Essays on Music and Performance*. Oxford: Oxford University Press, 1995.
Tedoldi, Fabio M. *La dottrina dei sensi spirituali in San Bonaventura*. Rome: Antonianum, 1999.
Teresa de Jesús, Saint. *Obras de la gloriosa madre Santa Teresa de Jesús, fundadora de la Orden de Nuestra Señora del Carmen, de la Primitiva Observancia*. Madrid: J. Doblado, 1778.
Tertullian. *Treatise on the Resurrection*. Translated by Ernest Evans. London: SPCK, 1960.
Thom, Paul. "Towards a Broad Understanding of Musical Interpretation." *Revue Internationale de Philosophie* 4 (2006) 437–52.
Till, Howard J. Van. "Basil, Augustine, and the Doctrine of Creation's Functional Integrity." *Science and Christian Belief* 8/1 (1996) 21–38.
Tillich, Paul. *Systematic Theology*. 3 vols. Chicago: University of Chicago Press, 1951–1963.
Torno, Ormondo, and Pierangelo Sequeri. *Divertimento per Dio: Mozart e i teologi*. Casale Monferrato: Piemme, 1991.

Torrance, Thomas F. *Space, Time, and Incarnation*. Oxford: Oxford University Press, 1969.
Tracy, David. *The Analogical Imagination: Christian Theology and the Culture of Pluralism*. New York: Crossroad, 1981.
Trivedi, Saam. "Imagination, Music, and the Emotions." *Revue Internationale de Philosophie* 4 (2006) 415–35.
Turner, James. *Without God, without Creed: The Origins of Unbelief in America*. New Studies in American Intellectual and Cultural History. Baltimore: Johns Hopkins University Press, 1985.
Weakland, Rembert G. "Aesthetic and Religious Experience in Evangelisation." *Theology Digest* 44/4 (1997) 319–29.
———. "Music as Art in Liturgy." *Worship* 41/1 (1967) 5–15.
Weitzman, Steven. *Song and Story in Biblical Narrative: The History of a Literary Convention in Ancient Israel*. Bloomington: Indiana University Press, 1997.
Wells, Jo Bailey. "Why Do We Shrink from Joy?" In *Sounding the Depths: Theology Through the Arts*, edited by Jeremey Begbie, 213–17. London: SCM, 2002.
Wicks, Jared. "Loci Theologici." In *Dictionary of Fundamental Theology*, edited by René Ltourelle and Rino Fisichella, 605–7. Middlegreen: St. Pauls, 1994.
Williams, Rowan. "Making It Strange: Theology in Other('s) Words." In *Sounding the Depths: Theology Through the Arts*, edited by Jeremy Begbie, 19–32. London: SCM, 2002.
———. *On Christian Theology*. Oxford: Blackwell, 2000.
Winter, Miriam T. *Why Sing?: Toward a Theology of Catholic Music*. Washington, DC: Pastoral Press, 1984.
Woimbée, Gregory. *L'objectivité de la raison théologique: L'intellectualisme de Bernard Lonergan et la crise de la Vérité*. PhD diss., Pontificia Università Gregoriana, Rome, 2007.
Worrington, Wilhelm. *Abstraction and Empathy: A Contribution to the Psychology of Style*. Translated by Michael Bullock. London: Routledge and Keegan Paul, 1963.
Wright, Nicholas T. "Resurrection: From Theology to Music and Back Again." In *Sounding the Depths: Theology Through the Arts*, edited by Jeremy Begbie, 193–212. London: SCM, 2002.
Zabala-Lana, Félix. *Músicos Jesuitas a lo largo de la historia*. Bilbao: Mensajero, 2008.
Zuckerkandl, Victor. *The Sense of Music*. Princeton, NJ: Princeton University Press, 1959.
———. *Sound and Symbol*. Translated by Willard R. Trask (vol. 1) Norbert Guterman (vol. 2). Princeton, NJ: Princeton University Press, 1956, 1976.

Music: Songs Quoted and/or Music Accessed Online

Aguilera, Christina. "Beautiful." *Stripped*. RCA, 2002.
Black Eyed Peas. "Where Is the Love?" *Elephunk*. A&M/Interscope, 2003.
Blunt, James. "You're Beautiful." *Back to Bedlam*. Atlantic, 2004.
Cage, John. "4'33." Premiere performance by David Tudor, August 29, 1952, Woodstock, New York.
Coldplay. "Fix You." *X&Y*. Parlophone, 2005.

Eminem. "Beautiful." *Relapse*. Interscope, 2009.

Emmaus. "You're Beautiful." ©Tony Ryce Kelly, Rónán Johnston, Greg Fromholz, 1997. Emmausongs/IMRO.

Heaney, Maeve L. "Dancing in Our Minds" Online: http://www.fmverbumdei.com/main/maeveheaney/index.html.

Hillsong. "Carry Me." *Forever*. Hillsong Music Australia, 2003.

OCP Spirit and Song website. http://www.spiritandsong.com.

Rice, Damien. "Cold Water." *O*. Vector, 2002.

Rodríguez, Silvio. "La era está pariendo un corazón." *Al final de este viaje*. Sonoland, 1977.

Smith, Martin W. "Breathe." *Worship*. Reunion, 2001.

The Streets. "Never Went to Church." *The Hardest Way to Make an Easy Living*. Locked On Records, 2006.

Index of Authors

Ardui, J., 88, 326
Arendt, H., 260, 304, 326
Armstrong, H. R., 326
Astley, J., 249, 326, 332, 334, 339
Augustine, 159, 186, 221, 241, 246, 251, 252, 266, 268, 273, 275, 311, 326, 328, 340
Ayel, V., 258, 326

Balthasar, H. U. Von, 14, 19, 26, 84, 96, 109, 125, 139, 147, 161, 163, 170, 171, 188, 192–211, 217, 218, 220, 224, 227, 233, 234, 236, 240, 253, 255, 257, 258, 311, 316, 321, 322, 325, 326, 330, 333, 335, 336
Barbaglio, G., 12, 326
Barthes, R., 112, 249, 326
Begbie, J., x, 26, 27, 63, 125, 126, 139, 169, 192, 247–52, 299, 326, 327, 334, 340, 341,
Bellini, P. B., 97, 98, 327
Benedict XVI, 96, 193, 210, 241, 257, 283, 292, 327, 328, 331, 337
Benjamin, W., 63, 327
Berendt J. E., 140, 327
Best, H. M., 64, 327
Biancu, S., 144, 327
Black Eyed Peas, 7, 341
Blacking, J, 23, 29, 57–62, 100, 106, 142, 327, 328,
Blunt, J., 185, 341
Boeve, L., 4, 69, 154, 160, 307, 308, 311, 322, 327
Bono, 86, 328

Brown, F. B., ix, 26, 192, 230, 241–47, 328
Buckley, M. J., 137, 138, 155–57, 328
Burgess, A., 258, 328
Byron, R., 58, 59, 61, 327, 328

Cage, J., 104, 106, 341
Camara, H., 254, 256, 328
Campo, C., 273, 328
Chandler, D., 111–13, 328
Charru, P., 130, 328
Chesterton, G. K., 309, 328
Christensen, D. L., 6, 328
Coldplay, 6, 341
Cooper, G., 36, 329
Copland, A., 106–9, 118, 127, 320, 329
Corkery, J., xi, 329
Coupeau, J. C., xi, 75, 165, 329
Crowe, F., 16, 20, 71, 136, 147, 266, 267, 323, 324, 329

Davies, O., ix, 15, 61, 120, 131–33, 142, 145, 146, 152, 154, 160–62, 182, 193, 210, 211, 253, 256–62, 265–72, 274, 276–79, 285, 287, 293–97, 301–4, 309, 319, 321–23, 329, 339
De Monticelli, R., 291, 292, 329
De Saussure, F., $xiii$, 33, 67, 79–83, 112, 114, 120, 121, 236, 330
Dieuaide, J. M., 97, 330
Doran, R., 17, 18, 161, 171–76, 179, 323, 330
Dryden, D., 30–34, 330

Dufka, P., 106, 330
Dulles, A., 88, 330
Dupré, L., 197, 330
Dürcheim, K. G., 273, 332

Ellis, A. J., 49, 330
Eminem, 185, 341
Endean, P., 273, 330
Farrow, D., 258, 266, 330
Fisichella, R., 159, 184, 328, 341
Foley, E., 9, 28, 241, 330
Frazao De Jesus Correia, J. M., 215, 331
Freud, H., 143, 331
Frith, S., 33, 51, 65, 141, 142, 331

Gaburro, S., 107, 133, 331
Gadamer, H. G., 162, 331
Gallagher, M. P., *xi*, 137, 138, 141, 156, 193, 211, 237, 331
Gallo Isaza, O., 178, 332
Garcia-Rivera, A., *xi*, 10, 26, 84, 178, 192, 199, 233–41, 322
Gelpi, D., 175, 176, 234, 332
Gentili, A., 273, 332
Gilmour, M. L., 99, 332
Goettmann, A., 273, 332
Gómez-Acebo, I., 273, 332
Gonzalez, A., 14, 332
Goujon, P., 107, 332
Greer, T. A., 43, 332
Greimas, A. J., 114, 115, 120, 281, 332

Harwood, D., 100, 101, 332
Haughton, R. L., *x*, 2, 5, 13–16, 21, 22, 25, 61, 143, 145, 149, 158, 168, 171, 177, 179–81, 210, 214, 258, 260, 263, 272, 274, 291, 298, 299, 301, 302, 307, 309, 314, 323, 339
Higgins, K. M., 65, 332
Hoover, W. R., 164, 332
Huron, D., 39, 332

Janz, P. D., *ix*, 15, 25, 138, 144, 149, 152, 153, 154–63, 165, 180, 236, 260, 272, 322, 323
Jeanrond, W. G., 74, 75, 332
John Paul II, 145, 160, 318, 323
Joncas, M. J., 70, 241, 333

Kavanagh, P., *ix*, 192, 283, 318, 333
Kearney, R., 190, 333
Kelly, A. J., 258, 278, 304, 305, 333
Kivy, P., 63, 333
Kroecker, C., 9, 333
Kuhn, T. S., 230, 333

Lane, D., 290, 333
Langer, S. K., 23, 29–35, 38, 41, 165, 223, 231, 330, 333
Leahy, B., 193, 195, 333
Levertov, D., 135, 254, 286, 333
Levinson, J., 63, 333
Lewis, C. S., 103, 181, 273, 333
Lewis, J., 111, 333
Liddy, R., 35, 179, 334
Lindbeck, G. A., 287, 334
Lingerman, H. A., 98, 334
Lipsitz, G., 52, 290, 334
Lonergan, B. J. F., 10, 13, 16–18, 19, 21, 25, 27, 29, 34, 35, 43, 44, 50, 69, 71, 72, 101, 111, 112, 115, 124, 125, 128, 129, 136, 145, 146–53, 155, 158, 161, 162, 163–79, 181, 192, 199, 213, 224–27, 232, 236, 255, 256, 259–61, 267, 272, 284, 296, 297, 303, 307, 310, 311, 313, 323, 324, 327, 329, 330, 331, 333–35, 338, 340, 341
Louth, A., 21, 264, 334
Lynch, G., 65, 334

Macmillan, J., 249, 251, 334
Mardones, J. M., 156, 168, 172, 334
Martinelli, P., 171, 334

Martini, C. M., 186, 190, 334
Mcgann, M. E. 334
Merriam, A. P., 23, 29, 41–42, 49, 53, 58, 335
Messenger, T., 164, 335
Metz, J. B., 154, 336
Meyer, L. B., 23, 29, 35–41, 42, 223, 231, 249, 329, 335, 340
Molino, J., 24, 73, 76–77, 85, 89, 91, 335
Moloney, R., 150, 335
Mooney, H. A., 147, 199, 335
Moore, S., 308, 335
Morlans, X., xi, 144, 335
Morris, C. W., 112, 113, 335

Nattiez, J. J., 24, 44, 47, 52, 58, 60, 66, 68, 69–102, 103–6, 287, 313, 324
Nettl, B., 23, 29, 44, 46, 47, 48–57, 60, 64, 335
Newman, J. H., 159, 166, 169, 193, 197, 198, 276, 291, 331, 336
Ní Riain, N., 9, 336
Nichols, A., 203, 336
Nietzsche, F., 135, 186, 187, 218, 336

O'donnell, J., 193–98, 200, 209, 210, 336
O'donoghue, J., 276, 336
Osto, G., 221, 336

Paul VI, 137, 257, 336
Piacenza, M., 8, 336
Piqué Collado, J., 202, 203, 206, 207, 336
Pisarra, P., 273, 336
Pius XII, 285, 336
Pouthier, J.-L., 87, 336
Pramuk, C., 288, 336
Predelli, S., 65, 336
Pugliesi, G., 144, 237

Rahner, K., 31, 132, 167, 169, 177, 224, 225, 273, 308, 313, 314, 317, 318, 321, 337
Ratzinger, J., 6, 88, 96, 208, 220, 283, 328, 329, 337
Rendina, S., 273, 338
Rice, D., 7, 21, 342
Ricoeur, P., 73, 132, 133, 270, 338
Rilke, R. M., 177, 338
Robinson, J. A. T., 258, 308, 338
Rodríguez, S., 87, 319, 342
Rousselot, P., 197, 198, 338
Rupnik, M. I., 3, 273, 275, 338, 340

Sacks, O., 339
Saliers, D. E., 26, 192, 241, 252–53, 299, 338, 339
Salmann, E., 339
Savage, M., 326, 339
Sbatella, L., 35, 98, 223, 339
Schneiders, S., 5, 75, 273, 339
Schopenhauer, A., 143, 231, 241, 339
Scirghi, T., 233, 240, 241, 322, 339
Scruton, R., 97, 339
Sedmak, C., 15, 188, 189, 288–93, 296, 319, 322, 339
Seeger, C., 23, 29, 43–48, 51, 54, 55, 73, 128, 324, 332
Sequeri, P., x, xi, 4, 10, 11, 14, 15, 20, 21, 26, 35, 84, 96–98, 130, 133, 138, 139, 156, 159, 171, 183, 184, 186, 188, 192, 198–200, 202, 203, 206–8, 211–23, 236, 239, 259, 284, 286, 290, 299, 316, 321, 324, 331, 336, 339, 340
Sevez, P., 91, 339
Shepherd, J., 40, 42, 67, 339
Sless, D., 111, 340
Smith, M. W., 270, 342
Sonnet, J.-P., 1, 306, 307, 340
Speelman, W. M., xi, xiii, 25, 38, 39, 41, 42, 61, 68, 79–81, 85, 94, 110, 114–29, 130, 131,

148, 151, 163, 169, 220, 241,
249, 250, 261, 265, 266, 281,
287, 290, 295, 301, 310, 325
Špidlík, T., 3, 273, 340
St. Teresa De Jesús, 161, 274, 279, 340
Steiner, G., 3, 6, 10, 20, 22, 64, 166–68, 228, 259, 286, 300, 317, 340
Storr, A., 34, 39, 66, 140, 142, 143, 320, 340
Stravinsky, I., 59, 340
Streeter, C. M., 173, 340
Stumpf, C., 48, 49, 340
Sturrock, J., 113, 340

Taruskin, R., 87, 340
Tedoldi, F. M., 273, 340
Tertullian, 120, 340
The Streets, 7, 342

Thom, P., 65, 340
Tillich, P., 177, 247, 340
Torrance, T. F., 258, 341
Tracy, D., 74, 228, 230, 341
Trivedi, S., 63, 341
Turner, D., 155, 322
Turner, J., 138, 341

Viladesau, R., 26, 144, 147, 148, 175, 177, 192, 223–33, 325
Von Hügel, F., 138
Weakland, R. G., 18, 341
Weitzman, S., 6, 341
Wicke, P., 41, 42, 67, 339
Williams, R., 249, 341
Winter, M. T., 312, 341
Woimbee, G., 256, 341
Worrington, W., 140, 341

Zuckerkandl, V., 64, 341

www.ingramcontent.com/pod-product-compliance
Lightning Source LLC
Chambersburg PA
CBHW071151300426
44113CB00009B/1163